T0328136

'...a refreshing sweep of leadership genealogical history. Leave it to David Knights to delve into the undiscussable post-humanistic heritage of leadership meaning, especially its gendered identity, embodiment, ethics, and affect. If you ride along, your destination will be changed.'

Joseph Raelin, *Professor Emeritus, Management and Organizational Development, Northeastern University, Boston, MA, USA*

'Knights has written a timely and erudite rebuke to mainstream, or rather malestream, leadership scholars who have ignored or avoided many of the critical aspects of ethics, power and resistance in maintaining the status quo.'

Keith Grint, *Emeritus Professor, Warwick Business School, UK*

'David Knights brings his usual erudition and critical spirit to question some of the core assumptions on how we study and how we practice leadership. By focusing on its gendered, bodily and ethical dimensions, Knights rightly seeks to restore the missing heart to leadership and dispel many of the simplistic and wish-fulfilling assumptions that surround it. His book is a must for students, teachers and, especially, those who wish to lead in more enlightened ways.'

Yiannis Gabriel, *Professor at the School of Management at Bath University and Visiting Professor at the University of Lund, Sweden*

'This book is a refreshing and stimulating departure from well-trodden taken-for-granted conceptions of what leadership is and who leads. The book insightfully integrates thinking about gender, masculinity, the body and ethics to offer a novel perspective of leadership as ethically, embodied and involved engagement with self and others. Knights also draws upon his considerable practical experience to demonstrate the applicability of his ideas to leadership practice in different contexts.'

Stella M. Nkomo, *University of Pretoria, South Africa*

Leadership, Gender and Ethics

This book has a clear concern to offer a distinctive way of studying leadership so that it might be practiced differently. It is distinctive in focusing on contemporary concerns about gender and ethics. More precisely, it examines the masculinity of leadership and how, through an embodied form of reasoning, it might be challenged or disrupted. A central argument of the book is that masculine leadership elevates rationality in ways that marginalize the body and feelings and often have the effect of sanctioning unethical behavior.

In exploring this thesis, *Leadership, Gender and Ethics: Embodied Reason in Challenging Masculinities* provides an analysis of the comparatively neglected issues of identity/anxiety, power/resistance, diversity/gender, and the body/masculinities surrounding the concept and practice of leadership. It also illustrates the arguments of the book by examining leadership through an empirical examination of academic life, organization change and innovation, and the global financial crisis of 2008. In a postscript, it analyses some examples of masculine leadership in the global pandemic of 2020.

This book will be of interest generally to researchers, academics and students in the field of leadership and management and will be of special interest to those who seek to understand the intersections between leadership and gender, ethics and embodied approaches. It will also appeal to those who seek to develop new ways of thinking and theorizing about leadership in terms of identities and insecurities, power and masculinity, ethics and the body. Its insights might not only change studies but also practices of leadership.

David Knights is distinguished scholar in the Department of Organisation Work and Technology at Lancaster University Management School, and Professor at Oxford Brookes University Business School, UK.

Routledge Studies in Leadership Research

Leadership, Gender and Ethics
Embodied Reason in Challenging Masculinities

David Knights

Routledge
Taylor & Francis Group

NEW YORK AND LONDON

First published 2021
by Routledge
52 Vanderbilt Avenue, New York, NY 10017

and by Routledge
2 Park Square, Milton Park, Abingdon, Oxon, OX14 4RN

*Routledge is an imprint of the Taylor & Francis Group, an
informa business*

© 2021 Taylor & Francis

The right of David Knights to be identified as author of this work
has been asserted by him in accordance with sections 77 and 78
of the Copyright, Designs and Patents Act 1988.

Library of Congress Cataloging-in-Publication Data

Names: Knights, David, 1940- author.
Title: Leadership, gender and ethics : embodied reason in challenging
    masculinities / David Knights.
Description: New York, NY : Routledge, 2021. | Series: Routledge
    studies in leadership research ; 18 | Includes bibliographical
    references and index.
Identifiers: LCCN 2020039037 (print) | LCCN 2020039038 (ebook)
    | ISBN 9781138492509 (hardback) | ISBN 9781351030342
    (ebook)
Subjects: LCSH: Leadership--Moral and ethical aspects. |
    Leadership--Sex differences. | Masculinity.
Classification: LCC HD57.7 .K564 2021 (print) | LCC HD57.7
    (ebook) | DDC 174/.4--dc23
LC record available at https://lccn.loc.gov/2020039037
LC ebook record available at https://lccn.loc.gov/2020039038

ISBN: 978-1-138-49250-9 (hbk)
ISBN: 978-0-367-69893-5 (pbk)
ISBN: 978-1-351-03034-2 (ebk)

Typeset in Sabon
by MPS Limited, Dehradun

Contents

Acknowledgements

First, I must give a big thank you to Elaine Knights who has suffered my ill temper and periods of excessive work intensity but, more importantly, her helping me to redraft some of the chapters. While taking me to new places, this book has to acknowledge a long career as an academic in the field of leadership, management, organization and work. The book contains a few revised materials from a number of different publications some of my own but many involving colleagues with whom I have had the good fortune to work over the years. Special mention has also to be given to colleagues who have been especially important in my own development as an academic and as a human being. Since it is invidious to mention names, I simply say a big thank you to all those with whom I have collaborated over many years. The full references of those publications that have figured to some degree in this book are listed below, although others may have seeped subconsciously into the text.

Knights, D. (2002). Writing organization analysis into Foucault. *Organization*, 9(4), 575–593.

Knights, D. (2006). Authority at work: Reflections and recollections. *Organization Studies*: Vita Contemplativa Section, 27(5), 723–744.

Knights, D. (2015). Binaries need to shatter for bodies to matter: Do disembodied masculinities undermine organizational ethics? *Organization*, 22(2), 200–216.

Knights, D. (2016). The grand refusal: Struggling with alternative Foucauldian inspired approaches to resistance at work. In David Courpasson and Steven Vallas (Eds.), *The Sage handbook of resistance*. London: Sage, 98–120.

Knights, D. (2017). Leadership, masculinity and ethics in financial services. In John Storey, Jean Hartley, Jean-Louis Denis, Paul 'T Hart, & Dave Ulrich (Eds.), *The Routledge companion to leadership*. London: Routledge, 332–347.

Knights, D. (2019). Gender still at work. *Gender, Work and Organization*, 26, 18–30.

Knights, D., & Clarke, C. (2017). Pushing the boundaries of Amnesia and Myopia: A critical review of the literature on identity in management and organization atudies. *International Journal of Management Reviews*, Special Issue: Exploring the Registers of Identity Research, *19*(3), 337–356.

Knights, D., & O'Leary, M. (2006). Leadership, ethics and responsibility to the other. *Journal of Business Ethics*, *67*(2), 125–137.

Knights, D., & Omanović, V. (2016). (Mis)Managing diversity: exploring the dangers of diversity management orthodoxy equality diversity and inclusion. *An International Journal*, 35, 1, 5–16.

Knights, D., & Murray, F. (1994). *Managers divided: Organisational politics and information technology management*. London: Wiley.

Knights, D., & Tullberg, M. (2012). Managing masculinity/mismanaging the corporation. *Organization*, *19*(4), 385–404.

McCabe, D., & Knights, D. (2016). Learning to listen? Exploring discourses and images of masculine leadership through corporate videos. *Management Learning*, *47*(2), 179–198.

Introduction

What Is Distinctive About This Book?

In writing this book, I feel much like Foucault when he argued that if he had been asked to communicate what he already thought before he started writing, he would never have had the courage to begin. Writing, for Foucault, was about changing himself so as not to 'think the same thing as before' (Foucault, 1991). While not presuming any halo effect, I also was not sure what I was going to write before beginning, although I have certainly thought differently through writing this book. Why, you may ask, another book on leadership? Although many decades ago it was said that there were probably as many definitions of leadership as authors writing about it,[1] the equally apocryphal claim might be made that there are almost as many books on the subject as there are leaders. Of course, such a statement would depend precisely on which definition of leadership is selected. In this book, I prefer a very broad, or what one might say is a fully democratic, definition whereby, in some capacity, everyone is involved in leadership rather than an elite few. Consequently, there could never be more books on the topic than there are leaders unless we made the equally outlandish claim that all books are really about leadership.

This book has a clear concern to offer a distinctive way of studying leadership so that it might be practised differently. At the same time, I acknowledge that its practice often bears little resemblance to the way it is described in academic, or even popular, kinds of literature. In seeking to offer something new, I recognise that like all innovation, it builds on what has gone before and differs, therefore, only at the margins. One significant difference is its focus on the masculinity of leadership. Still, also, by considering bodily matters and ethics, the book explores comparatively neglected issues surrounding the concept and practice of leadership.

Given that I advocate the exploration of aspects of leadership relating to the body, masculinity and ethics, it is incumbent on me to provide some limitedly embodied narrative of the context of my concerns with these matters. This I do in Chapter 1, but first, I should explain my background in so far as it relates to leadership.[2] I did not follow a conventional academic career since I left school at 16 and spent several years working respectively in banking, textiles and insurance, both as an employee and then, in the latter industry, as a self-employed insurance broker. During all the years in self-employment, I also pursued educational activities largely as a hobby until eventually, I felt confident enough to apply for a full-time academic post. While studying full time for a degree, I continued to run my business and even when becoming a university lecturer, I maintained it on a part-time basis. I can honestly say that this practical experience did enhance my academic work and especially teaching. Eventually, also my engagement with business and corporations became a major source of funding as well as providing me with access to sites, partners and participants in research projects.

I also learned a lot about leadership as a practitioner and sought to put this to 'good' use in a practical sense through teaching, as well as theoretically in my research. I was also involved in leadership activities with the organisation studies staff grouping and, eventually, in two research centres and an academic-practitioner, collaborative research forum activity. The latter involved and was supported by funding of £1.5m from 20 major financial service companies for 17 years from 1994. Also, between 1990 and 1997, I was a Director of the £2.5m funded Financial Services Research Centre (FSRC) in the Manchester School of Management, UMIST. In the other research centre, I was the Deputy Director of the Economic and Social Research Centre Programme for Information and Communication Technology (PICT), between 1989 and 1995, managing the funding of approximately £1m. Later at another university, I had a short period as head of school.

At UMIST, I also managed a programme to give a formal degree status to the English Bankers examinations through my university. I was managing funds of over £6m and a staff of around 20 researchers and administrators, leading the bursar in the university to declare that the activity was much larger than many of the academic departments. Reflecting on this biographical history, I recognise that I was energised particularly by masculine norms of competition, conquest and control. Occasionally, my single-minded determination to succeed came up against resistant forces that disrupted the linear rationality of these projects, compelling me to rethink my career trajectory and reflect on my approach to leadership.

Meanwhile, through conducting empirical research in newspapers and financial services, my own practical experience of leadership as an emotional and bodily enterprise was confirmed. Yet, when consulting the vast literature, there was virtually no direct discussion of the emotional and bodily aspects of leadership. Partly because of the concentration on linear rational accounts of individual attributes, traits and characteristics that were deemed to have a causal relationship to effective leadership, this evidence of a highly masculine orientation to research was occluded or denied. While leadership has considerable emotional, bodily as well as rational content, research fails to examine the former partly because of the dominant, cerebral and disembodied energies of masculine reasoning. Just as we only notice the air we breathe when it becomes dangerously polluted, so masculine leadership is equally invisible except when, during wartime, it can be seen as deathly as air pollution. Of course, to detect these pollutants in processes of leadership is far more difficult than to measure air pollution, not least because they are camouflaged in a wide range of masculine political machinations.

The literature also seems to ignore the way that leadership is not exclusively about individuals but is a part of humanity's inheritance, involving all that we share in 'common [in] knowledges, languages, information, codes, affects'.[3] Leadership is not just constituted of character traits, styles, or propensities to be transactional, transformational or distributional. It also reflects access to 'common code and information resources as well as the ability to connect and interact with others in unrestricted networks'[4]) but these, and their implications for practice, are often ignored in the literature. One major implication of this focus is to understand leadership as an ethically embodied and involved engagement with a 'community of practice' shared by us all. Although I instinctively adopted this stance in practice, I did not realise this theoretically until writing critically about leadership. However, subconsciously I must have been aware of the many contradictions because after writing a couple of academic articles of leadership in 1992,[5] I abandoned the field. I felt that I had nothing more to say even though much of my writing continued to encompass, at least implicitly, what would be seen as leadership. I stopped using the term leadership or the discourse and networks of its genesis because it seemed too individualistic, psychologistic and reductionist. At this time, I saw no scope for a philosophically and gender-informed, ethical and embodied approach to leadership. A wealth of literature and this book contradicts the myopic view I once held.

In the late 20th century, building on gender analysis, deconstruction theory and psychoanalysis, there were signs of a critical approach to leadership studies.[6] It was not until the early 21st century, however, that this critical turn began to impact the mainstream.[7] Despite criticisms that this literature may not be particularly critical,[8] it has inspired me to return to engage with a critical discourse on leadership.[9] I have already claimed some distinctiveness for this book as far as it focuses on leadership concerning the body, ethics and masculinity. Yet, it also discusses identity and insecurity, power and resistance, and diversity and innovation that, while not entirely neglected in the mainstream literature, are concepts that remain severely under-theorised or marginalised.

The question remains as to what makes this text different from the several books that have developed critical approaches to leadership. Here I would argue that much of the literature in critical leadership studies (CLS) emerges out of a humanistic perspective that seeks to liberate leaders so that they can return to their authentic selves, and thereby release or emancipate followers, and society at large, from the toxic impact of their egotistic power.[10] Some go as far as to argue that we should not even study leaders, let alone seek to measure any behavioural content since it is most effective 'where leadership is not required'.[11] Few, however, have adopted a way of studying leadership that would be compatible with such a challenge. I argue, instead, that we must abandon humanism in favour of post or neo-humanism where the focus is on 'affect' as a way of understanding leadership as the 'invisible' space residing *in between* subject and object, mind and body, and leaders and followers.

This 'in-between' not only involves engaged bodies affecting other bodies and their (our) material and symbolic lives, it also energises these self–same bodies in ways that enhance their (our) capacity to be affective.[12] Besides, it energises us to explore the ambiguous in-between spaces that prevail on us to engage with, rather than seek to control, the other regardless of leadership relations. Fundamentally, affect reflects and reinforces ethics in which we identify with other bodies sufficiently 'for us to have [a real] ... concern'.[13] Leadership might then begin to resemble what has been described as the art of living an ethical existence, where true knowledge depends entirely on 'an essential position of otherness'.[14] There is massive bodily energy affecting leadership processes, and the outcome significantly affects us through a wide range of embodied experiences from anguish to euphoria, sadness to exhilaration, panic to passion, fear to courage, and pessimism to optimism, to mention only a few.[15] These processes, however, are open to endless capacities to affect and be affected[16] but also subject the body to a recognition of its own 'indeterminacy'.[17]

Of course, this approach violates scientific knowledge where there is an attempt to efface ephemeral phenomena that defy objectification. For science favours representations generated by sovereign subjects whose actions are deemed to generate knowledge of the world, including notions of leadership. Since academic studies of leadership have been dominated by psychology that subscribes to this scientific view, this book departs substantially from them.

What You Will Find in This Book

Despite the attention in everyday life and the volumes of literature given to its practice and theorisation, a major problem in the field is the tendency to take leadership for granted rather than to interrogate it fully.

This book seeks to correct this by exploring both the explicit and implicit assumptions underlying leadership discourses, theories and practices. The book is organised into 3 parts, the first reflecting generally on leadership studies, the second focusing on a range of concepts that are important but often neglected in the mainstream leadership literature, and the third, providing selected illustrations of these reflections and conceptual issues through some of my own research. The theme throughout is that leadership research is insufficiently conceptual and theoretical insofar as it fails to interrogate the assumptions that it brings to bear on its studies. Rather, it seeks to focus narrowly on the attributes of leaders, for example, personality or character traits, style, energy or drive, decision-making or negotiating competencies, technical or interactional skills, and transactional or transformative powers. These are seen as having positive effects on organisational efficiency, effectiveness, productivity and/ or profitability. A second theme is that empirical leadership research lacks integration with theory so that it fails to contextualise its findings and results, thus appearing to be empiricist.[18] There are exceptions, of course, where research adopts a contingency approach and seeks to identify the social and historical context as both a condition and consequence of events. A third theme is that research focuses too narrowly on the individual leader as if leadership were exclusively the property of individual persons who then attract followers. Again, there are exceptions where relational and practice perspectives understand leadership to be intrinsically collective, as an outcome of 'shared, symbolic or collective structures of knowledge' that derive from complex social interactions.[19] Fourthly and finally, there is an absence of substantial theorising and empirical research on the body and gender, and in particular, masculinities in leadership. This results in disembodied understandings and a neglect of other inequalities such as age, disability, ethnicity, race and sexualities, all of which lead to a dearth of ethics in leadership studies.

Organisation of the Book

While the book is divided into three parts, as with all attempts to distinguish or classify different themes or topics, these divisions are intended primarily to facilitate the reader's journey through the text. In this sense, they are heuristic rather than substantive for, broad-brush divisions, overviews, conceptualisations, and empirical materials are not separate but merge into one another in any sense-making enterprise.

Part I Leadership: An Overview

This part provides a broad overview of the field first, by discussing in Chapter 1 the ontological and epistemological foundations of leadership narratives, and in Chapter 2 articulating a genealogical type of history of the field of leadership studies.

The **opening of** Chapter 1 examines some of the false expectations that arise when leaders are celebrated and romanticised as heroes and heroines. This is concerned primarily with the tradition that attributes essential qualities to leaders who are then deemed to be charismatic, heroic, rational and perhaps even magical. This individualisation of the leadership as a property of persons was restrained a little in succeeding developments of the literature, especially where prescriptive ideals were abandoned in favour of an emphasis on contingent contexts, followers or practices. However, romanticising the individual continues to remain a legacy that is frequently rekindled, inadvertently implied, or simply taken for granted as proprietary conceptions of leadership are presumed. CLS reject objectivist epistemologies and positivist methodologies of the mainstream as well as its tendency to endorse rather than challenge how leadership legitimises the hierarchical political and social inequalities of contemporary organisational life. Nonetheless, CLS often continues to reflect and reinforce a humanistic ontology in which leadership is seen as protecting and enhancing the opportunities of followers to participate in organisational activities and thereby to realise their human potential. This is examined critically in the chapter, as also in the book as a whole.

Chapter 2 is concerned to provide a genealogical form of historical context for understanding the contemporary popularity of the theory and practice of leadership. There is no attempt to be comprehensive in this coverage for, such desires contradict the aims of this book in reflecting a masculine preoccupation with control by, exhaustively, leaving nothing to chance, instead, a brief overview is provided of pre-classical, classical, early modern, modern scientific and more recent challenges to the so-called scientific approaches to leadership. There is an attempt to be genealogical in focusing on the discursive and normative conditions that enabled leadership theories and practices to emerge, thrive and have a certain power and truth effect in different historical eras. Much of this analysis is speculative since, especially regarding the distant past in pre-classical, classical and the middle ages, leadership was not a topic of academic analysis. Rather it was subsidiary to narratives concerning forms of government, everyday life and wars.

However, since a well-documented genealogical study of the history of leadership[20] has already been published, there is no need to repeat the exercise rather than draw on such work where appropriate. This I do particularly when examining periods earlier than the 20th century, after which I provide a brief analysis of leadership theory from the Great Men (sic) through trait, behavioural, contingency, transactional and transformational theories to the more recent relational, practice and critical approaches. Modern theories before these more recent developments were conducted primarily by psychologists seeking to emulate natural scientists by reducing human attributes or behaviour to a set of quantified variables that were claimed to have a causal determination of leadership effectiveness. Leadership was seen as the property or possession of individuals but, by contrast, a majority of approaches since then have subscribed to critical, social constructionist, process, practice or post-structuralist perspectives that support relational and communal or collective understandings of leadership. These later studies have embraced a range of issues from a focus on followers through to collective and communal matters. Less frequently, there has been a focus on bodies and emotion, gender and ethnic diversity, power and resistance, as well as ethics and politics. Those sympathetic to genealogical approaches argue that the mainstream literature draws up a history of leadership as 'a teleological journey' that, after numerous blind alleys and false paths, culminates in a perfect nirvana of deep understanding that needs merely to be rigorously applied.[21] Each new theorist presumes to possess a panacea to treat the problems that their predecessors also claimed, but failed, to resolve. Of course, a genealogical history is aware that the problems are not independent, so much as defined in terms, of the solutions offered. Hence, the promises that leadership researchers often make have to be acknowledged predominantly as empty and vacuous rhetoric upon which history is likely to deliver its doom-laden verdict of despair.

Part II Conceptual Reflections on Leadership, Ethics, and Masculinity

In Part II, I explore many of the implicit or explicit assumptions or concepts underlying the various discourses, narratives, theories and practices of leadership. The selection is not exhaustive but directed toward the central themes of this book, which are identity and power, gender and diversity, the body and embodiment, and ethical discourses in leadership.

Chapter 3 discusses identity or subjectivity, anxiety and insecurity— topics that, despite a focus on individuals in the leadership literature, are widely neglected by the mainstream. Yet even without thinking about the close relationship between masculinity and leadership, which is a central concern of this book, identity is central to everything surrounding the notion of a leader. Anxiety and insecurity are also inseparable from questions of identity as they drive humans to seek some safe or secure place in identity, at the same time as they are often the unintended consequence of identity struggles. This is not only due to the heroic attributes often projected on to the leader but also simply because the literature has an overwhelming proclivity to locate leadership as a property of the individual. Yet leadership can be exercised either as a political and socially divisive weapon that poses a threat to the sense of identity. Or it can be seen as a means of solidifying community interests and practices that inspire a commitment to wider social norms and meaning. The chapter focuses on how identity, but more importantly attachments to a preferred or ideal identity on the part of both leaders and so-called followers, can damage social relations in ways that are counter-productive to organisational goals and developments. It also discusses the critical literature that gives considerable attention to the concept but still takes identity for granted. It, thereby, neglects to interrogate and challenge common sense preoccupations with, and attachments to, identity. Occasionally, preoccupations with identity result in creative, innovative and experimental ways of seeking to reduce or eliminate insecurity, although attachments to it can also render individuals paralysed or dumbfounded by the threats of its precariousness. This can stretch even to the point of a mental condition that is now seen to be one of the most rapidly growing problems of contemporary society.[22]

Apart from exploring some of the deep ontological and other philosophical routes of insecurity, the chapter also examines some ways of deflecting myopic activities that, in seeking to alleviate anxiety, can be a major source of its reproduction. Partly because of its association with psychology and psychoanalysis, notions of anxiety and insecurity are generally seen as the property of individuals. However, consistent with the theme of this book, I seek to elucidate how what may seem to be personal and individual is rarely exclusively so, since it invariably derives from broader social relations so that the anxiety and insecurity is a problem to be managed or resolved socially. The personalising of issues occurs as a result of the power of individualisation that constitutes subjects as the bearers of, and ultimately responsible for, what are social, not personal or individual, problems. It derives from what Foucault[23] describes as the constitution of subjects as an *effect of*, rather than an agential resource in, the exercise of power. C. Wright Mills[24] may not have seen the relationship between subjects and power in a Foucauldian manner, but he was concerned about the danger of focusing on 'private troubles' as if they were not also 'public issues' concerning 'matters that transcend these local environments of the individual and the limited range of his [sic] life'.[25] In this book, I seek to ensure that the personal and the social are not treated as separate entities when speaking about anxiety and insecurity. So, in this chapter, I argue that anxieties and insecurities are experienced at a personal level, but these are products of power and social relations, as well as of collective organisations and institutions.

In Chapter 4, I turn to the question of power and resistance. I argue that if power is neglected as many claim,[26] resistance is almost non-existent largely because the literature is largely concerned to promote the idea of leadership and show it in a positive light. There is much resistance, and this explains why many theorists have sought to encourage participative leadership as a means of its amelioration. Another way of countering authoritative or autocratic approaches to leadership is to focus on, and seek to give voice to, followers. However, power is not often interrogated in leadership studies and this tends to result in proprietary conceptions, whereby power is seen as something that individual leaders possess. Resistance is then seen in zero-sum terms of being the opposite of, rather than in relationship to, power.[27] The chapter draws on Foucault to show not only how power and resistance are inextricably intertwined but also the way that knowledge forms a part of the intricacy in so far as, in discourse and practice, none of these concepts can be extricated one from another.

The subject matter of Chapter 5 is diversity and gender, which has attracted the interest of students of leadership partly due to the dramatic impact of feminism and concerns about discrimination at work. Neo-humanists have argued that leadership and organisations are plagued by the domination of discourses of masculinity and their reproduction of binary epistemologies, ontologies and methodologies that render them linear rational and disembodied.[28] For example, it has been contended that there is a 'close connection between constructs of leadership, traditional assumptions of masculinity and a particular expression of male heterosexual identity'.[29] There is a denunciation of a 'macho' view of leadership, where the leader feels compelled to be 'hard' and 'controlling' and where respect is sought through fear and blind loyalty rather than a sense of mutual valuation and trust. A masculine controlling form of leadership is often counter-productive in terms of its ability to secure the full cooperation and commitment of participants in an enterprise. It is also damaging, emotionally and spiritually since discourses of masculinity compel the leader to repress or hide those impulses and aspects of social and bodily identity that appear incompatible with what is conventionally seen to be manly.[30] And, of course, this applies as much to women who feel pressured by the dominant cultural expectations that leaders should be tough and combative in their relationships with subordinates. Interestingly, leaders may often be gentle, subtle and even seductive; but it has been suggested that such features are rarely visible in the literature on leadership.[31] Acknowledging the presence of seduction, for example, can facilitate the development of innovation in leadership theory but we need to be cautious about the managerial appropriation of elements or trappings of this alternative conception of leadership for it can simply be a means to 'strengthen the status quo'. For people, especially men, who are captivated by the idea of '*life as a contest*', may mouth 'the language of care and consultation' to sound fashionable and/ or advance their careers.[32]

Chapter 6 is concerned to explore the potential for leadership research and practice to engage with embodied reason and emotion. The chapter begins by examining first, how the body has been marginalised in social science generally and second, the way that leadership studies have neglected the body at the same time as perpetuating particular disembodied masculinities. It analyses the conditions and consequences of this neglect and traces it to the domination of a cerebral, cognitive linear rationality that reflects and reproduces discourses and practices of masculinity. This rationality often generates disembodiment where researchers stand aloof as if unrelated either to their bodies or those of the participants in their research. For practitioners, this disembodiment precludes the very kinds of relationships with others that would lend impact to their leadership. I turn then to post-humanist feminism to explore the potential for an embodied framework to facilitate a challenge to the ethical limits of the prevailing theories and practices of leadership. Finally, the chapter theorises how the notion of affect can facilitate an integration of these concerns to offer a different way of thinking and feeling about leadership.

Focusing on Ethics, Chapter 7 begins by discussing how it is always tempting to trace contemporary ideas about leadership to a historical past, but this is dangerous insofar as history is reconstructed often in terms of our current cultural and political interests. Consequently, we have to resist popular views of leadership as deriving from the ancient Greek philosophers Aristotle and Plato, and perhaps also, the 15th Century Machiavelli whose book *The Prince*[33] seemingly justified some of the most ruthless and tyrannical tactics of many later leaders. In the case of the Greeks, the terms they used tended to correspond with excellence enabling others to pursue what they already knew, and our current translation of Machiavelli documents its incompatibility with contemporary democratic values. Still, it is necessary to draw on presently constructed interpretations of the past in the sense that whatever we write about in the present has already passed once we have put pen to paper. Leadership always attracts increased attention when moral and political conditions are seen to be in crisis or beyond human control, as has occurred frequently in very recent history. While crises extend across a wide range of conditions from climate warming, ethnic cleansing, pandemics, terrorism and wars, I focus primarily on those relating to social and economic organisation and concentrate specifically on the ethical scandals within contemporary corporations. To be more precise, the chapter examines critically how increased regulation is the routine response to these scandals and argues that this occurs largely because of a limited interrogation of ethics and its significance for our lives. It then explores other non-regulatory obstacles to the development of ethical leadership and, in particular, the domination of masculine discourses and practices within organisations. Finally, it explores whether leadership is not so much the solution, as part of the problem of, the crisis of ethics in organisations.

Part III Empirical Illustrations of Leadership, Ethics and Masculinity

In this Part, there is an attempt to apply some of the concepts and ideas of Part II to three selected fields of research: academia, innovation and change, and the financial sector. Finally, there is a Postscript in which I apply the ideas to what at the time of writing this book was the worst of global crises in the coronavirus pandemic. This third part of the book subscribes to what I see is a somewhat arbitrary distinction between theory and practice. However, for ease of presentation, the distinction is retained to provide some practical illustrations of the concepts and ideas discussed in the book. Still, it is important to recognise that the presentation of empirical research is not devoid of theory just as conceptualisations usually bear some relationship to everyday life and events, for they are irretrievably, mutually entangled. Actions reflect, reinforce and reproduce, as well as challenge, theoretical assumptions as much as theory is tested through practical experiences. Of course, theoretical deliberations and empirical research are expected to be a more reasoned, self-conscious and reflexive consideration of what occurs in everyday life, but we should never forget their inseparable heritage, nor indeed, as was discussed in the early part of Chapter 1, how theory is a form of practice.

The first Chapter 8 in Part III concerns academia where the empirical material and analysis for the chapter is drawn from research I conducted with my colleague Caroline Clarke. Some parts of it are drawn from my own life-time experience of working in universities and is, therefore, autoethnographic. However, most of the chapter draws on our joint research on academics—a project inspired by the belief that intellectuals *should* be 'inexhaustibly curious about the nature of their own activity'[34] as well as paying particular regard to the colonisation of university life by insidious neoliberal and managerialist practices.[35] Like many academics, and despite holding these convictions, we acknowledge that 'at times we are silent when we should speak/write our protest'.[36] We embarked on this project partly to understand why there has been a lack of protest/resistance in our own profession—which took the metaphorical form of travelling 'abroad to discover in distant lands something whose presence at home has become unrecognisable'.[37]

In recent years, university leaders have embraced a managerialist agenda where audit, accountability, and controls involve ranking, and competitive league tables based on 'rigorous' metrics of performance.[38] These have been criticised as gendered because they reflect and reinforce aggressive, competitive masculine demands on academic staff to meet a multiplicity of targets and standards.[39] Nonetheless, few parts of this literature challenge the dominance of aggressive forms of masculinity[40] and the complex embodied agents and material objects through which they are enacted in organisational practices.[41] By contrast, our research problematises the gendered organisation of academic life, first describing its impact on women and then anticipating a way in which the masculinity of leadership in universities can be challenged, potentially to become agendered. This is an alternative to the adversarial strategies of resistance that privilege precisely the same aggressive and instrumental tactics to secure change as prevailing dominant, masculine leadership regimes. For such strategies tend to close down spaces of ethically embodied relations that offer a different vision.

The second topic of research activity is Change, Innovation and Technology that is addressed in Chapter 9 and concerns how leadership has always been strongly associated with organisational change and innovation whether it be team-working, quality or knowledge management, the adoption of new technologies, processes and products or distributive arrangements. Although always contingent on the conditions of its genesis and application, innovation is what stimulates or reflects organisational change and the transformation of established practices. Leadership is usually involved at all levels of innovation from inception to accomplishment, although there is rarely ever finality. Since change is always in the process of completion, it is possible to identify key stages of achievement. Much of the research was conducted by my colleague Darren McCabe who was a research assistant on several Economic and Social Science (ESRC) research grants that I secured during an extensive period of leading the FSRC and the Financial Services Research Forum (FSRF) at Manchester University, and the latter subsequently at Nottingham University. However, several researchers and, in particular, Fergus Murray worked with me on technology in the financial sector that was funded by an 8-year ESRC Programme for Information and Communication Technology.

In Chapter 10, I focus on a broad range of research that colleagues and I conducted in the financial services around the turn of the 20th century. Around the time of the research, the sector passed through one of its most spectacularly horrific periods in its history, readily assuming the unwelcome crown of the 'unacceptable face of capitalism'. It continues to rail against a public that remains shocked as to how an industry can get things so wrong. Its impact was one of forcing everyone within the Western world to suffer an economic Armageddon. However, this now seems to pale into insignificance against the background of the COVID-19 pandemic of 2020. While the background of this chapter is the global financial crisis of 2008,[42] it also reports on research that was conducted on leadership, ethics and gender and innovation and organisational change, as reported in the previous chapter. In terms of leadership, ethics and gender, the global financial crisis provides us with the most dramatic material. As the governor of the UK Bank of England declared, it would seem there needs to be a concerted effort to ensure that ethical leadership is embedded in financial organisations.[43] However, the ethics that inform regulation is inadequate and the chapter suggests that there needs to be a reflection on whether a set of rules is sufficient to avoid such crises. Maybe these should be complemented, or replaced, by more ethical senses of leadership responsibility to, and embodied engagement with, others in organisational relations of common commitment. Ethical leadership has to escape from reliance merely on codes of compliance and ideals of utility or virtue and instead bear witness to a life that embeds relations in feelings, affects and responsibility to others rather than cognitive calculations of self-interest.

Chap 11 Postscript

While writing this book, the world witnessed perhaps the worst crisis since the Second World War or the economic depression that preceded it in the COVID-19 pandemic. Since leadership was quite crucial, it was impossible not to offer an analysis of how the pandemic was managed and the final chapter seeks to do this as a way of illustrating some of the arguments of the book. Drawing on many of the analytical concepts of Part II and their illustration in business or public sector organisations in Part III, I examine a range of masculine identities and insecurities, embodied and disembodied enactments of power as well as the ethical conditions and consequences of political leadership during the pandemic. Focusing primarily on the populist leaders of Brazil, the UK and the US, I describe how they engaged a range of masculinities in (mis)managing the crisis. Finally, it reflects on the implications of masculine leadership within democratic populism and demagogic totalitarianism for a post-COVID world.

Notes

1 Stogdill (1974).
2 This short autobiographical diversion draws partly from Knights (2019a, b).
3 Hardt and Negri (2009, p. viii).
4 ibid., p. x.
5 Knights and Morgan (1992), Knights and Willmott (1992).
6 Calás and Smircich (1991), Knights and Willmott (1992), Gemmil and Oakley (1992), Gabriel (1997); Sinclair (1998).
7 Collinson (2005, 2011), Alvesson and Spicer (2013), Tourish (2013), Bolden (2016).
8 Learmonth and Morrell (2016).
9 Knights (2017, 2018a, 2018b), Mabey and Knights (2018), Ciulla et al. (2018a, 2018b).
10 Sinclair (2007), Tourish (2016), Wilson (2016), Wilson, Cummings, Jackson, and Proctor-Thomson (2018).
11 Bolden (62016, p. 45).
12 Munro and Thanem (2018).

13 Gatens (2006, p. 39)
14 Foucault (2011, p. 7367).
15 Munro and Thanem (2018).
16 Clough (152009).
17 Clough (142007, p. 3).
18 Empiricism is the belief that all knowledge derives from sense experience rather than from ideas and reflective thinking.
19 Raelin (2016, p. 5).
20 Wilson (2016).
21 Harding and Learmonth (2008, p. 13).
22 Storr (2018).
23 Foucault (1997).
24 Mills (1959, p. 8).
25 Mills (1967, p. 396).
26 Collinson (2014), Fairhurst and Grant (2010).
27 Knights and Vurdubakis (1994).
28 Braidotti (2011, 2013), Knights (2015, 2018a), Pullen and Rhodes (2010, 2014), Pullen and Vachhani (2013).
29 Sinclair, (2005, p. 1; see also Knights and Tullberg, 2012).
30 Bederman (1995), Kerfoot and Knights (1993, 1996).
31 Calás and Smircich (1991).
32 Sinclair (2005, ch. 9).
33 Machiavelli (1961).
34 Scialabba (2009, p. 3).
35 Sparkes (2007, 2013).
36 Davies and Peterson (2005, p. 93).
37 de Certeau (1984, 50).
38 Willmott and Mingers (2012).
39 Thomas and Davies (2005), Bagilhole and White (2013).
40 Knights and Tullberg (2012).
41 Mol (2002).
42 Knights and McCabe (2015), Knights (2017).
43 Carney (2014).

Part I

Leadership: An Overview

In this part, I articulate an overview of the field of leadership studies. First, in Chapter 1, I examine the ontological and epistemological foundations of leadership narratives before showing how they reflect and reinforce a philosophy of humanism. In Chapter 2, I engage with a genealogical history of the field of leadership studies that culminates in contemplating a post- or neo-humanist alternative.

1 Reflecting on Leadership Studies

Introduction

At the point of writing between 2018 and 2020, the world has witnessed some of the most horrific events in its recent history concerning the wars in Iraq, Syria, Afghanistan, Yemen as well as at least another 18 military conflicts. For example, there was ethnic cleansing in Myanmar, resulting in more than 600,000 Rohingya people having to flee as refugees to Bangladesh. There was also terrorism throughout the western hemisphere, and mass shootings in France, the UK, the US and New Zealand, often perpetrated by lone men with the direct intention of harming civilians. Without intention, although often a result of human contributions to global warming, natural disasters have also hit many parts of the world, including bush fires in Australia; drought in North Korea, Southern Africa, and East Africa; earthquakes in Guatemala, Japan, Mexico and the Philippines; floods in Columbia, Guinea, Nigeria, South African Republic, Togo, South Sudan and the UK, and hurricane storms in the Caribbean and Japan. The Grenfell 24-storey tower block fire that killed over 70 residents in London can be more directly attributed to human failure to clad the building with fire-resistant materials. However, all these natural disasters pale into insignificance in the face of the Coronavirus global pandemic. For, at the beginning of 2020, there was the most dramatic lockdown and devastation of the world's social and economic life, perhaps matching that of the holocaust and the second world war. Despite a history of disappointment or failed expectations, there is still always an appeal to leadership to manage the fallout in almost all of these tragedies.

In the case of the Grenfell fire, the overwhelming outcry from the media, the public, and the surviving victims was an expectation that leadership could perform a shamanic ritual that would instantly heal the wounds. No matter who were the incumbents, the leaders were duly sacrificed at the altar of human expectation that far exceeded any potential endeavour in relieving the suffering. No better sign of this reversion to seeing leadership as salvation was when the UK Prime

Minister was admitted into a hospital, and then intensive care, with COVID-19 during the Coronavirus pandemic. At this point, the media displaced virtually all other news to discuss endlessly a potentially leaderless country, as if this was even more devastating than the pandemic itself.[1] Seemingly the numerous mistakes he and his government made were set aside in the frenzy of presuming the leader is of supreme importance. For shortly before announcing a lockdown of the whole nation, Boris Johnson had celebrated shaking hands with everyone and, more importantly, he constantly claimed that the Health Service was in perfect shape to manage the crisis when this was far from the case. Given the extent of these errors of judgement, should the media just have been wishing him well during his hospitalisation with a serious case of the virus but *not* displaying hysteria about his absence from the government? Moreover, on his recovery, he was then romanticised and heroized further as a great fighter who pulled through against all the odds. I return to this in the final chapter in discussing white masculine populist leaders in the context of the COVID pandemic.

While no one can blame the victims of tragedy for seeking solace from those in closest proximity who have adorned the trappings of power, this deification of leaders is also something of a tragedy that neither the media nor academic research seeks to alleviate. Indeed, for the large part, discourses surrounding leadership fuel false expectations by celebrating and romanticising leaders as heroes and heroines.

The social sciences are replete with concepts and phenomena that rise and fall with even greater regularity and timescales than that of great empires. Leadership in the business and management field can be seen as one such concept. Currently, it is seemingly on an upward trajectory for it has proliferated in the last few years as the pendulum has swung once again away from technology, toward human solutions to organisational problems. Dominated by psychology and prescriptive interventions in its early 20th century beginnings, the applied science of leadership went through numerous renewals, each believing it to represent 'progress' but none of which offered practitioners the golden bullet in terms of solutions to practical problems. Over recent time, a more critical approach has gained ground where there has been a challenge to the individualistic, often heroic, masculine and prescriptive approach of mainstream leadership studies.[2] This has partly taken the path, as here, of examining actual practices of, rather than imposing theoretical ideas, on leadership. However, it is acknowledged that theory and practice are difficult if not impossible to separate since a theory is itself a practice. Slightly paraphrasing what the philosophers Deleuze and Foucault have suggested, it may be argued that our theory is not a means of expressing, translating, or in search of an application to, practice: 'it is practice'.[3] Far from universalising or totalising what is theorised, it 'multiplies potentialities' (Hand, 1986: xlii). Inevitably, this is a statement with political intent because, despite experiencing the contrary, much theory seeks to place a specific closure around a field rather than 'open' it up to unknown multiple potentialities. Then, separating theory from practice is a political act of reproducing the status quo since wherever it challenges specific practices, it can be dismissed as mere theory (just academic) but when it is no more than (apparently) descriptive, it is self-validating.[4] Yet once we collapse the distinction between theory and practice, it is almost impossible to effect closures because we immediately see that all action is grounded in theoretical assumptions. What academics call theory is then only a more sophisticated or deeply thought out version of such theory/practice.

Alongside these concerns is a growing interest in ethics that has been stimulated by the multiplicity and magnitude of corporate and political scandals culminating in the global financial crisis (GFC) of 2008. As most advanced Western countries continue to struggle with the aftermath of the crisis through programmes of austerity, the political fallout has manifested itself in a growing far-right politics. This has been expressed in nationalism if not xenophobia, political isolation and economic protectionism, and a general rejection of the liberal established elite that is seen to have orchestrated the chaos. Although the global political turmoil cannot be wholly attributed to the proliferation of scandals, there has been a renewal of concerns about business ethics that now seemingly is extending beyond mere corporate social responsibility and/or the business case for ethics.[5] Also, it is clear that despite considerable rhetoric about the need for more ethical behaviour in business and politics,[6] routinely the response to misdemeanours is more regulation, *not* ethics.

While discourses of masculinity may not be quite as prolific as those on leadership, they can be seen as part of a wider literature on gender that also relates to issues of identity, diversity and inequality and these are topics of extensive concern throughout the social sciences.[7] However, much less of the literature links questions of masculinity and identity to matters of ethics and leadership that is a major focus of this book.[8]

The book draws upon a range of literature within leadership studies paying particular emphasis to ethics and gender where there has been a challenge to the various binaries that derive from the separation of mind from body and the domination of cognitive, linguistic and symbolic discourses over concerns with embodied and other material relations. Often described as a 'new spirituality', posthumanist researchers trace the neglect of the body to masculine modes of power and offer insights into the ambiguity, doubt and insecurity that befall us when the myth of certainty surrounding 'scientific' approaches to leadership is exposed. It also rejects prescriptive rule and norm-based approaches to focus on embodied engagement as part of what it means to practice ethical leadership. It is this recent concern with the body and gender identity that is endorsed here as part of an attempt to renew and revitalise leadership matters in the direction of serious concern with ethics.

This has resulted in a growing demand to focus more on the body and embodied ways of conducting research,[9] as well as to give attention to other material objects that are significant in human affairs. After several medical investigations, my attention to the body came about as the result of a very personal and painful experience of finding myself infertile. Despite writing about gender and masculinities at the time, my familiarity with the topic made me believe that I had managed the tragedy when I had only rationalised it at a cognitive rather than embodied level, and this eventually led to a brief nervous breakdown.[10] When our bodies are simultaneously subject and object of the same action, we are reflexive bodies for there is no living subject, reflexive or otherwise, without a body,[11] Consequently, there can be no human activity, and least of all any concerned with leadership practice, where the body is absent. Indeed, much of the mainstream literature, and especially that concerned with transformational, distributional and leaderly forms of leadership,[12] have seen charisma, inspiration and empathy as significantly embodied. For as humans, we relate not just verbally or cognitively but also with emotions and feelings expressed through our bodies. Indeed, our first encounter with anyone is embodied, and sexual attraction is experienced through the body usually before mental factors and reasoning come into play. Leadership is a corporeal activity in the sense of seeking to inspire and enthuse the corporate body as well as relating to bodies as individual subjects. Paradoxically it is only when leadership becomes a topic of analysis and investigation that disembodied conceptions of its everyday practice predominate. This is because of a subscription to cognitive and mentalist or linguistic and symbolic discourse that eschews the body and soul.

Despite the attention in everyday life and the volumes of literature given to its practice and theorisation, a major problem in the field is the tendency to take leadership for granted rather than to interrogate it fully. There are some exceptions[13] and one, in particular, entitled Revitalising Leadership[14] that provides a comprehensive challenge to the dominance of the mainstream scientistic paradigm[15] and, in that sense, provides an interesting platform from which to launch the present book as a sequel. I will, therefore, refer to it continually throughout this text by drawing on its organising framework for studying leadership. However, I will seek to develop its theoretical potential, while the contribution of Wilson et al. is a real inspiration for academics critical of the mainstream literature, they do not always deliver on their promise to revitalise leadership in both theory and practice.

What Is Leadership?

The concept of leadership has always carried with it a great deal of ambiguity, and some have argued that definitions are almost as numerous as the number of authors writing about it.[16] A couple of examples give us sufficient evidence to show that much of this definitional work is quite repetitive. It has been argued that leadership is 'central to the functioning of most societies' and simply 'involves at least two people in pursuit of a common goal'.[17] Similarly, drawing upon Northouse,[18] Silva defines leadership as 'the process of interactive influence that occurs when, in a given context, some people accept someone as their leader to achieve common goals.'[19] What these definitions have in common, and to which I examine critically in the next chapter, is that of assuming that leadership has already been accomplished rather than always in process of establishing itself as a performative effect of its practice.

Because of this problem of repetition, some authors dispense with providing definitions of leadership, arguing that there is a sufficient shared sense of its meaning not to labour further over adding to the numerous lists of more or less repetitive attempts to nail it down.[20] What is then suggested is that we should concentrate, instead, on ethical leadership manifest in the promotion of the fundamental values shared by members of our society.[21] Without a definition, however, Levine and Boaks argue that we cannot readily connect leadership to ethics if we do not know what it is. However, not until the end of their article do they present a definition based on the Aristotelian view of it as 'a master virtue that serves human flourishing'.[22] I will have more to say about this view of leadership in Chapter 2 not least because it just replaces one definitional problem with another in that what is "human flourishing" is even more difficult to agree upon than is leadership. However, its proprietary understanding of leadership as a property of persons is more problematic.

While I agree with Cuilla[23] that we do not need to ask the question as to what leadership is, my reasoning in reaching this conclusion is different from hers as far as I believe it is more important to interrogate what leadership *does* rather than what it is. Performative understandings of concepts escape the static and universalising implications of definitions and thereby direct our attention to the way that leadership, for example, changes dramatically depending on the context in which it is performed. This context is both historical and contemporary for it varies over time and space, is affected by cultural, economic, political and social conditions, and is different when leadership is exercised in one kind of an organisation in contrast to another. Also, by concentrating on how leadership is performed, we are immediately drawn to ethical matters, but in a way that does not require us to focus on the moral character of the so-called leader. Instead, we can examine the communal and collective sense in which leadership unfolds in different contexts and circumstances and this is entirely compatible with the critical and contextual approach adopted by Wilson and Wilson et al.[24]

Others have argued that over the last 50 years, the very term leadership has assumed a prevalence of actual dominance that is not justified and therefore should be abandoned in favour of earlier concepts such as management or even just administration.[25] They go even further by arguing that leadership has become sheer rhetoric through a misuse of phenomenological perspectives on the social construction of reality that obliterates any sense of truth based on evidence. The book's strength is to highlight how language obscures the power that underlies the proliferation of discourses and practices of leadership. This resonates dramatically with contemporary populist politics where truth becomes little more than the outcome of repetitive claims made by powerful leaders wherein any opposition is dismissed as fake news.[26] One limitation with the book's thesis, however, is the continued tendency to treat leadership as a property of persons even though occasionally acknowledging how it is applied to groups, organisations, and institutions. Another is to subscribe to a conventional conception of leadership in insisting that it is not just about occupying a powerful position in an organisational hierarchy but also one of unquestioned authority. In this sense, the term leader is seen as only applicable insofar as there are followers otherwise, what can it be seen to be leading? This results in the polemic against leadership perhaps, exceeding what, for the most part, is highly plausible. It also means that the book is short on recommendations of how to combat the deeply damaging language of leadership other than to suggest returning to the language of management. While this might remove the automatic assumption of a consensus to follow the leader, historical experience hardly supports their anticipation that a reversion to the language of management would undermine the social organisation of inequality or hegemonic control within corporations.

Revitalising Leadership

I have already suggested that Wilson et al.'s book is an inspiration for critics but falls a little short on its promise to deliver a revitalisation of leadership. First, it has to be said that the book's strengths overshadowed its weaknesses and, indeed, when I first read it, I wondered whether my contribution would be sufficiently different to justify publication. This is because Wilson et al. produced a comprehensive set of insights and criticisms of the mainstream literature and offered a fully contextualised alternative that is far in advance of many other texts on leadership. It is critical of many of the assumptions that pervade both the theory and practice of leadership and generates analyses of important spheres such as Supervision, Human Resource Management (HRM), Innovation,

Strategy and Governance to which they apply their theoretical framework to analyse them differently. The framework is a vast improvement on what else is available in the literature as it is broad-ranging and covers most of the issues that are important in examining the theory and practice of leadership. It is innovative and not just in the chapter on Innovation, where it promotes leadership that is neither top-down nor bottom-up but is generated through the middle ranks of the hierarchy. Here and in other chapters, it also demonstrates the importance of communication and how stories or dramatic narratives facilitate the reception of messages. These are further enhanced when their verbal or written texts are complemented by visual materials – cartoons, diagrams and pictures. The authors are also pragmatic in their concerns to encourage leadership to promote human well-being, but they are not unrealistic in expecting hierarchies of power and inequality to collapse. Another strength of the book is that it traverses fields of interest and research not often included in traditional texts so that the value of understanding leadership can be seen as important for an analysis of any sphere of business and organisation. The book draws on a diversity of discourses from practitioners to postmodern scholars, and from mainstream to critical theory narratives of supervision, HRM, strategy, and governance to provide a multi-dimensional analysis that departs from individualistic, heroic, or charismatic conceptions of leadership where it is often seen as a panacea for all ills.

However, this attempt to be inclusive if not exhaustive, even though an impossible task, could also be a weakness of the book. For their broad-ranging coverage sometimes sacrifices depth for a breadth of analysis. In one sense, this means remaining at the level of providing theoretical frameworks rather than *theorising* in the sense of generating concepts to advance a dynamic and embodied way of experiencing ourselves and the world differently. This is not an entirely fair criticism for the framework itself is drawing together a range of ideas that are not often integrated one with another—an especially valuable contribution in a field generally confined to describing narrow attributes of leaders in terms of the independent and dependent variables, that are seen to produce particular causal outcomes. Nonetheless, I feel that this is a mode of theorising, that while offering an improvement to a field that is little renowned for theoretical innovations, does not itself escape the positivism of constructing a quasi-deductive theoretical model and, in this sense, is an exemplification of precisely what it seeks to criticise. Moreover, given that the book claims certain theoretical originality, it has to be judged in these terms and examined critically as well as sympathetically. Many years ago, it was argued that a theory has to have a rationale and a mechanism[27]. Although the insistence on contextualisation may lay claim to the former, there is nothing to denote a mechanism such as the historical movements in Hegelian dialectics or the rhizomatic spread of disruptive concepts in Deleuze and Guattari.[28]

In effect, then, *Revitalising Leadership* generates a model or framework (see Fig. 1.1 below) with only a limited rationale and no mechanism, and this is imposed on, rather than emanates from, the empirical field.[29] However, this framework is not only limited theoretically, but also it does little more than describe different aspects of conventional notions of leadership that are categorised about challenges, purposes, activities and values and understood in terms of different contexts that condition their content. In their defence, however, Wilson et al. do make the qualification that their model is not a theory as such, but a metaphysical theoretical framework that forms the basis for the development of theory. Although the authors do not elucidate on what this means, I presume it to imply fundamental, essential assumptions that define reality before any precise theory or empirical observation. In their case, these assumptions revolve around insisting that any discussion of the challenges, purposes, values, and limitations of leader-follower relations be wholly contextualised.

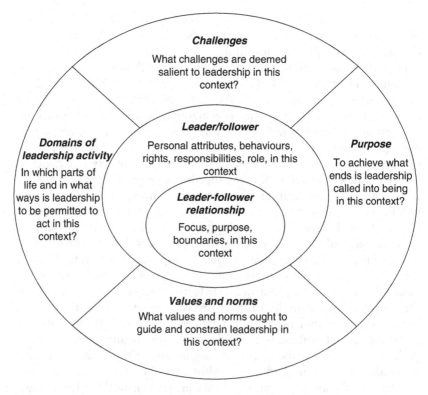

Figure 1.1 Framework for Studying Leadership Wilson et al. (2019, p. 47).

The authors describe this diagrammatic representation of their approach as a methodology rather than just a framework. While the framework certainly has some methodological implications, I would argue that its main value is heuristic and pedagogic, particularly in providing a way of systematically, if a little mechanistically, organising their book. Despite four authors, this enables there to be a considerable consistency between the chapters, although the critical perspective is not always maintained throughout the book. After the framework analysis, each of the chapters on five different substantive topics focuses on a contextual examination of respectively, Supervisors, HRM, Innovation, Strategy and Governance and a final one on Leadership Scholarship. The first two and last one utilises the framework by focusing on the challenges for leader-follower behaviours and responsibilities, as well as leader–followership relationships in terms of focus, purpose and boundaries. The other three chapters on Innovation, Strategy and Governance move across the different elements of the framework more fluidly.

There is no explanation either for the choice of topics or, other than claiming it provides a contrast, for choosing a mechanistic rather than a more fluid approach in applying the framework. I suspect that these seemingly arbitrary selections were based on the different interests or expertise of the 4 authors, but this is not revealed, so it remains a guess. However, if the diversity of issues were not sufficient, there is added another layer of complexity in elucidating 6 further issues surrounding the contextual landscape for leadership practice: globalisation, the financial, decline of 'authority', gender, knowledge/technology and climate change. I have taken some licence in shortening and perhaps, thereby, modifying their analysis, but once again, there is no rationale for selecting these aspects of the landscape. There is little doubt that these are all important contexts for leadership but, there are some strange omissions such as age, race, sexuality, famine, terrorism, types of political regime, and war, as well as epidemics[30] and/or pandemics.

Another problem is that while consistently following the framework introduced in Chapter 2, there seems to be a less than fully consistent approach between chapters in terms of whether they adopt a critical or a managerialist perspective. So, for example, in the opening chapter, the authors seek to revitalise leadership through rethinking 'what should constitute its purpose, focus and the role it plays in our organisations'. In doing this, they are committed to 'the constructive value of critical thinking' and, in particular, challenging the view that leadership can be seen as a panacea for solving 'every problem'.[31] Yet some of the chapters display a distinctly managerialist tone and share, with much of the mainstream, prescriptive and normative aims that lack the promise of theory promised in the first two chapters. So, for example, one chapter promotes the virtues of entrepreneurship and another focuses on the talent of individuals without seemingly recognising that these values contradict the attempts to discredit 'leadership science', where the 'effort to serve the interests of capitalism and managerialism is partisan, even ideological, in orientation'.[32] It is difficult to reconcile these conflicting tendencies in the book. Another example is that although eschewing prescription in the framework chapter, there are many prescriptions to the point of moralising elsewhere and this is partly because of an adherence to a humanist perspective that remains largely unacknowledged. Yet it is not just humanism that fuels these prescriptive inclinations; they seem to form part of a comparatively mainstream and managerialist aim to assist the business to be more economically successful. This is despite demanding, in the final chapter, that revitalising leadership should be applied not just to external organisations but also internally to the work of scholars who study it, as a dominant creed, is less visible when they offer a general prescription to extend leadership studies more widely across a range of sub-topics in an almost imperialist fashion—a trend that will only reinforce analyses that are superficial rather than deeply theoretical, and so this contradicts other messages in the book.

Some of the chapters do seek to develop the framework that was outlined above especially in showing how there are no universal HRM policies, innovations or strategies since they have to adapt to the particular context in which they are enacted. While in Chapter 1 there is a claim to 'question what is normally taken for granted',[33] the ontological and epistemological assumptions and the humanist ethos in which they reside are not questioned. So, for example, a clear enlightenment faith in humanism and the autonomous realisation of human potential or 'the process of "becoming" rather than "being"'[34] is present in many of the chapters. This often leads to an implicit pitting of the individual against the organisation where, for example, it is claimed that there is an impoverishment when practices 'enhance the organisational capability to the exclusion of the humans within the organisation'.[35]

By contrast, in this book, I want to break from this dualism between the individual and the organisation or society as it tends to direct us towards dialectical historicism. Such theory concentrates on 'becoming' rather than 'being' or future potential rather than existing power to affect self and others, to enhance our embodied actions and activities as well as our productive and collective imagination. In understanding Spinoza as a subversive critic of the convention, Negri has argued that the idea of transforming being (i.e. becoming) is a kind of destruction rooted in 'the effort at logical control of the world'.[36] By contrast, Spinoza and Negri explore the fullness of life as a means of enhancing our capacities to affect and be affected through a 'continuous proliferation of relations and conflicts that enrich being'.[37] While this is an attractive thesis, other theorists believe that the potential of affect is to transform us so that we become different.[38] If affect is always 'in transition',[39] it can never be stable enough to leave us always present in the moment, so perhaps we should remain neither for nor against 'becoming' so much as ever prescient to its dangers. One of these dangers is to embrace the humanistic myth of life holding the promise of realising one's potential in some future 'becoming' so that it is a treadmill of ever-receding ambitions or future senses of a secure identity. However, it is not necessarily a question of a state of 'being' in the present or 'becoming', as in some future, but residing in the space in between where we neither elevate 'what is', nor idealise 'what might be'. This means living in the present yet embracing change that may transpire in the future so as always to be in transition or within an in-between space.

Lest it is considered that these criticisms are dismissive of Wilson et al., this is not the case as their book reflects considerable advances in the study of leadership and overall, I am completely empathetic to its aims and scope. Indeed, it has inspired me to persevere with my contribution to the field, which is very much in the spirit of their work. While sharing the critical perspective of these authors, however, by contrast, this book favours a conceptual approach so that Part One critiques the domination of humanist ontologies, epistemologies and methodologies within most studies of leadership, whether mainstream or critical. I explore instead the possibility of post or neo-humanist,[40] sensibilities that focus on issues of gender and other discriminations and inequalities, as well as being concerned to demystify power/knowledge relations and to embrace embodied and ethical analyses of leadership. Following this, Part II seeks to theorise leadership by interrogating concepts of identity, insecurity, power and resistance, diversity and gender/masculinity, the body and embodiment, and finally, ethics. These concepts are selected because they have been central to much of the research and writing that I have pursued throughout my career. However, they are also concepts that mainstream leadership studies have tended to treat as peripheral to their focus on the individual or the personal attributes and skills of leaders, and the determinants of effective leadership. Nonetheless, I argue that they are fundamental to most forms of life, and leadership is no exception. They facilitate an understanding of leadership that goes beyond identifying personality characteristics, situational or contingent contexts. These concepts also assist us in exploring how leaders live their lives, how broad-ranging social and economic circumstances condition them, and how they affect activities and relations that stretch well beyond their organisation.

As would be seen from the contents page of their book, Wilson et al., (2019) draw on issues of change, ethics, gender, identity, innovation, and power that, although rarely given a central focus, are not so much ignored by the mainstream as simply under-theorised. So, for example, mainstream studies tend to speak in a social psychological manner whereby leaders are presumed to *possess* power rather than it to be a performative outcome of specific social and identity relations. Also, insofar as gender is a focus in the mainstream, it tends to be reduced to a discussion of the role of women rather than how leadership discourses and practices are gendered. Moreover, this under-theorising can even occur within the critical literature where these concepts are not marginalised but still treated sometimes in a proprietary fashion, so that leadership, power, identity and gender are presumed to be a property of individuals. An example is to be found in an article written by two of the principal exponents of critical leadership studies (CLS) where they argue that 'even the *possession* of a small amount of power increases people's willingness to engage in corrupt practices'.[41] While this is probably just an unconscious slip into proprietary conceptions of power that these authors elsewhere eschew, it is a reminder of how the mainstream on leadership has dominated thinking.

One other aspect of Wilson et al.'s, book, and of several other critical approaches, is the tendency to dismiss or even demonise the propensity for mainstream studies to quantify regardless of appropriateness. This is understandable particularly as the default in disciplines with scientific pretensions is only to value what can *be measured* even when what is measured is not valuable. However, this criticism can deflect attention from the inescapable qualitative aspects of such studies, and these require interrogation even though an excessive belief in measurement can blind both researcher and reader from identifying their underlying qualitative assumptions. Relatedly is another problem surrounding the tendency to challenge quantification without interrogating the epistemological, ontological, methodological and the political inclinations of such research. What grounds my departure from such critical perspectives, which otherwise I wholly endorse, is a recognition that the indiscriminate condemnation of quantification simply creates a binary between quantity and quality that is unconstructive, as are most dualisms.

However, this is not the only nor perhaps the most significant dualism to which these authors subscribe; despite claims to the contrary, they routinely reproduce the agency-structure and micro-macro binaries. I acknowledge that distinctions between 'this' and 'that' are inescapable since they are intrinsic to analysis, but the offence of dualistic thinking is to reify distinctions to create closure around them, often for purposes of securing the self of the perpetrator.[42] Such reifications, of course, are the basis of stereotyping the 'other' in ways that lead to horrific social practices of ageism, sexism, racism, xenophobia, and islamophobia—all seemingly gaining greater legitimacy within early 21st century democratic societies, currently experiencing political extremes of, mostly New Right but also Left, populism.[43] Wilson et al., as would be expected, draw well short of such stereotyping, but they seem not to reflect upon how any kind of binary thinking readily slips, almost unconsciously, into stereotyping. I now turn to more deeply philosophical issues of ontology, epistemology and methodology, only the latter of which the authors claim is one of their significant contributions to the field of leadership.

Table 1.1 Representational Methods

An Ontology and Epistemology That Understands Reality Through Representations and Disembodied Methods

Representations of:	Through	Objectification of:	Power/Truth Effects in Norms of:
1. Life	Biology	The body and its functions	Health
2. Language	Linguistics	Speech and writing	Communication
3. Labour	Economics	Production and exchange	Wealth
4. Leadership	Mainstream leadership studies	Leaders and followers	Effectiveness

Ontology, Epistemology and Methodology

Interestingly, while referring to their framework being metaphysical, there is little discussion of ontology, epistemology or methodology in Wilson et al. yet in an earlier single-authored book, Wilson gives them considerable attention.[44] Informed by Foucault's ontology,[45] she understands what it is to be and act like a human concerning discourse and, in particular, how we render 'things' intelligible through language. In this sense, words do not describe so much as constitute the reality to which they refer and are thereby gushing with power. This is perhaps a little more deterministic an interpretation of Foucault's ontology and epistemology than I would endorse for he always recognised the body and subjectivity as mediating discourse and the world of which it speaks. Nonetheless, it is an improvement on the general leadership literature that tends to leave unexamined fundamental assumptions underlying their accounts, despite these being crucial to knowledge production.

What informs my writing of this book is an ontology of embodiment, where the conventional binary between mind and body is eschewed on the basis that all human and animal life is necessarily embodied, insofar as the senses can never be detached from the mind whether or not affect, emotion, or reason is privileged. It also draws on a posthumanism or neo-humanism that is not anti-humanistic so much as sceptical of how humanism can too heavily elevate the human above all other species and materialities and result in confinement as great as any that it seeks to displace.[46] For humanist philosophies have tended to support universal values that are 'objectionable not only on epistemological but also on ethical and political grounds'.[47] This questioning of humanism and the universalism to which it subscribes is discussed a little later in this chapter, and in more detail in Chapter 2, but broadly it involves challenging decontextualised assertions, or what Foucault calls 'grand narratives', because they *impose* meaning, rather than *engage* with its emergence.

I have already raised ontological questions when asking what leadership is and arguing that this is a less important question than what leadership *does*, and how its practice affects a whole range of events, relations and subjectivities. Epistemologically, we never really know leadership or anything else for that matter, since all phenomena can be accessed only through their representations.[48] This has methodological implications, for whichever kinds of methods, tools and techniques we might utilise to investigate leadership, each will have its effect upon the representations that are produced even though we cannot precisely document the specific outcome. We do know, for example, how representations involve discourses that have the effect of constituting not only the objects under investigation but also the subjects who participate in such exercises, including ourselves as researchers.

The Table 1.1[49] draws on Foucault's archaeology and genealogy to summarise how the positive sciences have generated knowledge in ways that have resulted in certain power/truth effects.

Epistemological challenges to representational knowledge resist the objectification of what is studied, seeking instead to explore the conditions that make it possible for their power/truth effects to be undermined or transformed. So, in the case of leadership, we can see that when it is represented as a proprietorial right of the leader to define reality for those perceived to be followers, it is not only patronising concerning so-called followers but also raises unrealistic, if not wholly unrealisable, expectations concerning those designated as leaders. Several approaches have emerged over recent years—leaderless workgroups or team leadership, distributed or relational leadership, co-constituted or leadership-as-practice, ethical leadership and CLS that would seem to challenge the proprietorial ontology. These will be examined in more detail in the next chapter but, while offering numerous illuminating insights, many of them share some of the same limitations detected in the traditional mainstream literature. Not least is the problem of a thin line between encouraging communal and collective leadership and creativity and cultural grooming. The latter generates 'group think' where individuals are transformed into 'subjects that feel they can only secure their sense of meaning, identity and reality by committing themselves to the very practices that power invokes'.[50] While research around the concept was criticised as lacking empirical credibility because of considerable evidence of resistance, what was seen as the dangers of 'group think' remained as almost conventional wisdom among psychologists in the 1990s. So much so that critics have remarked on how it is 'incongruous that the concept warning us of the dangers of over-conformity itself becomes a victim of that conformity'.[51] This has not, however, prevented other academics, particularly economists, enforcing an orthodoxy that could be seen to have cost society dearly. For economists were lemming-like in their support for the securitisation and re-securitisation of debt as a panacea for sustaining perpetual economic growth, which almost inevitably imploded leaving us with the GFC and its austerity aftermath.[52] A similar orthodoxy has prevailed in leadership studies where psychology, as the dominant discipline, has sought to emulate the methods of the physical sciences.[53] Although the GFC of 2008 cannot be attributed to this attempt to claim scientific credibility, I will attempt to show in Chapters 9 and 10 that understanding leadership as a property of individuals leaves both theory and practice deprived of any means to challenge the then imminent financial Tsunami. Following a different trajectory, the chapter now turns to trace what can be seen as the historical conditions of neoliberal economics as one of the founding ideologies that generated the conditions leading to the GFC. This is the force of humanism in society at large, and more specifically in leadership theory and practice, whereupon in Chapter 2, I will develop a post-humanist critique followed by a neo-humanist enlightenment approach to its study.

Humanism and Leadership

Humanism has a long genesis that can be traced back to the classical Greece of Socrates and the ancient Rome discourses of Cicero. Socrates was a humanist insofar as his philosophy privileged human individuals and their development. Also, in believing that human freedom was contingent on knowledge and its production of truth, he devoted himself and ultimately his very life[54] to a dialogic, heuristic method of communicating with his students. This commitment to teaching centred on a belief in human potential, that to this day remains a mantra of humanistic thinking, but for Socrates was driven by an inner voice founded on spiritualism that was a legacy, it is claimed, of ancient Shamanistic practices.[55] Born more than 400 years after Socrates but in many ways following in his tradition, the Roman Cicero first established himself as a skilful political orator until he was sentenced to death by Claudius, the successor to the throne of Caligula.[56] This was the result of rumours of his affair with Caligula's sister, but then he was merely exiled because of ill health and presumed imminent mortality. At this point, he began to write and develop his political and moral philosophy that, given his practical participation in politics as a senior Senator and a close friend and adviser to the murderous Emperor Nero, seemed inconsistent if not oxymoronic. He was a pragmatist in maintaining his political standing with Nero even to the point of justifying the latter having his mother Agrippina the younger put to death, and some critics saw this as a contradiction of Cicero's humanistic belief in virtue. However, as a stoic, his focus was largely on the inner life—arguing that virtue and happiness cannot be gained through external events but only through the rational control of our reactions towards them. Consequently, accommodating to the political events of his time, including even the psychopathic Nero's self-indulgent, tyrannical reign, he was not wholly inconsistent. For, according to stoicism, ultimately what matters is to exercise our will through rationality since this is all that we can control. However, this also demonstrates how philosophies that emphasise the inner life, human potential and self-development, as does stoicism as well as humanism and Buddhism, may accommodate the most brutal of atrocities with impunity.

While humanism was embryonic in classical Greek and Roman literature, the axiom on which it built its edifice did not appear until the middle ages where, as all-powerful, humans at the centre of the universe, in the words of Pico Della Mirandola, 'we can become what we will'.[57] Under the auspices of the Renaissance, this human supremacy characterised a secular humanism that embraced individual will power, honour and infinite human potential as a new belief in humanity to dislodge and replace traditional faiths in an external deity. Only the ancient Greek and Roman commitment to reason and rationality are absent from this Renaissance version of humanism. Still, the loss of religious belief in salvation was operating to undermine humanism from within at the same time as it was subjected to a challenge by the Reformation from without. With no ultimate foundation, a precarious humanism began to be represented by the 'pale terror' of death and a 'culture reduced to the skull', where nihilism is all that remains.[58] Although free-will, reason and honour were to be the calling card for years to come, humanism would always be vulnerable given the lack of a foundational truth and a true foundation that transcended that which is human.

There was a great deal of self-doubt during the Renaissance and especially because of the challenge of the counter renaissance, protestant reformation, wherein there was a return to the metaphysics of Greek tragedy, as portrayed by Homer, where everything is predetermined rather than governed by free will. Despite this, the Enlightenment in the 18th century projected onto humanism the secular ideas of an autonomous, free rational subject whose potential had few, other than self-imposed, limits. It had already begun to bear fruit from the scientific discoveries of the 17th century, and the benefits of both science and technology, deriving from the application of free will and reason, were incontrovertible. This was reinforced by the industrial revolution for it dramatically transformed social and economic life to provide mass populations with an escape from destitution, poverty and illness. Rapid economic growth enabled large numbers of people to increase their standard of living beyond that of their parents and thus a humanist mantra of self-development and striving to realise one's potential was made increasingly plausible by the proliferation of opportunities for various forms of advancement. The philosophies of Kant and Descartes provided further sustenance for secular beliefs in rational autonomy and free will. Extended into the sphere of ethics through the utilitarianism of Bentham, it reduced any moral judgement to a metric for happiness and, in the economics of Adam Smith, to productivity and growth that could be generated through 'free' market relations and intensified trade. The Enlightenment enhanced the potential for humanist values to displace religious principles and leave the culture sailing without an anchor. This proves to be disastrous for the pursuit of the goals of human 'progress' when rough seas, created for example by the French Revolution, prevailed.

As a result of globalisation, whether formally Christian, Muslim or Hindu, civilization generally subscribes to an Enlightenment belief in autonomy, human rights and individual potential that extends back to the renaissance. There would be little dispute that individualism is dominant in the Christian, and even more so in the non-religious, West but it is argued that 'individual autonomy in community [also] is constitutive of an ethics of Muslim education'.[59] Not surprisingly, then, mainstream leadership discourse and practice has generally reflected and reproduced what can be seen as humanistic values of respect for, and expectations of, individuals to express and realise their human potential.

While contemporary CLS have abandoned objectivist epistemologies, they tend to retain this humanistic ontology. That is to say, a basic premise of their analyses is one of not only endorsing, but also promoting, the view that leadership should protect and enhance the opportunities of their followers to realise their human potential. Consequently, much of the critical literature reinforces notions of autonomy and competitive success and, by default, is complicit in reproducing the competitive individualism that otherwise it seeks to discredit.

Nowadays, however, we seem to be in a period of transition where the excesses of human supremacy are pitched against the intransigent forces of the natural world, all too ready to remind us of our folly. Notwithstanding the disaster of the Coronavirus pandemic, climate change is waiting in the wings of world history to wreak havoc on human and non-human life in an Armageddon of proportions never before visualised. But this is chasing ahead of myself for first I need to examine how leadership discourses develop 'as practices that systematically form the objects of which they speak'.[60] For accounts of leadership cannot avoid constructing the very activities they claim merely to describe.[61]

Notes

1 The country did not implode as also has been the case even when no government existed at all as in Belgium, Northern Ireland, Germany, Somalia, Iraq and others of recent time see Turner, https://www.bbc.co.uk/news/uk-politics-42570823, 2018.
2 Collinson (2014).
3 Foucault (1980, p. 208).
4 We say apparently because invariably theory constitutes the very practices it purports merely to describe (Latour, 2005).
5 Rhodes and Wray-Bliss (2013).
6 Carney (2012).
7 Knights (2015); Knights and Omanović (2016).
8 Pullen and Rhodes (2014); Pullen, Rhodes, and ten Bos (2015).
9 Thanem and Knights (2019).
10 Knights (2006).
11 Crossley (1995).
12 Raelin (2010).
13 e.g. Grint (2000); Ford, Harding and Learmonth (2008); Ladkin (2010); Raelin (2010); Wilson (2016).
14 Wilson et al. (2018).

15 Wilson et al. (2000) do not use the term scientism but it is perhaps more appropriate in referring to a form of knowledge where interpretation can be ignored since *meaning* is self-evident insofar as the social world is treated as identical with, or equivalent, to the natural world of objects.
16 Stogdill (1974); Yukl, (1989/2006).
17 Bishop (2009, p. 10).
18 Northouse (2004, p. 3).
19 Silva, (2018, p. 3).
20 Ciulla (1995) quoted in Levine and Boaks (2014, pp. 225–227).
21 Ciulla (1995, p. 17).
22 Ibid., p. 240.
23 Ciulla (1995).
24 Wilson (2016); Wilson et al. (2018).
25 Learmonth and Morrell (2019).
26 Knights and Thanem (2019).
27 Willer (1967).
28 Hegel (1807/1977); Deleuze and Guattari (1988).
29 This could partly explain the absence of the authors' fieldwork.
30 As discussed in the chapter on innovation but only metaphorically to illustrate how network relations accumulate like viruses spread geometrically rather than arithmetically and in 2020 the world is fully aware of this.
31 Wilson et al., (2018, pp. 1–5).
32 Ibid., pp. 12–13.
33 Ibid., p. 5.
34 Ibid., p. 75.
35 Ibid., p. 96.
36 Negri (2013, p. 4).
37 Ibid., p. 7.
38 These are discussed in Chapters 7 and 8.
39 Hynes (2013, p. 571).
40 Braidotti (2013).
41 Collinson and Tourish (2015, p. 587, my emphasis).
42 Knights (2015).
43 Roth (2017).
44 Wilson (2016).
45 Foucault (1972).
46 Foucault (1991).
47 Braidotti (2013, p. 24).
48 Kendall and Wickham (1999, p. 67).
49 This model is merely a heuristic device.
50 Clarke and Knights (2015, p. 1868).
51 Turner and Pratkanis (1998, p. 113).
52 Most commentators agree that few anticipated the GFC https://www.intheblack.com/articles/2015/07/07/6-economists-who-predicted-the-global-financial-crisis-and-why-we-should-listen-to-them-from-now-on.
53 Fairhurst and Connaughton (2014), Knights (2018a).
54 Falsely accused of corrupting young children, he was sentenced to death through drinking a mixture containing poison hemlock. See Plato (2007 [383BCE]).
55 Gray (2002, p. 25).
56 This summary of Cicero's life and work is largely drawn from Russell (2019) and also the Stanford Encyclopedia of Philosophy, https://plato.stanford.edu/entries/ancient-political/#CicRomRep, consulted 24.5.20.

57 Carroll (1993, p. 3).
58 Carroll (1993, p. 31).
59 Waghid and Davids (2017).
60 Foucault, (1972, p. 49) quoted in Dale (2001, p. 60).
61 Latour (2005).

2   Genealogies of Leadership in Practice and Theory

Introduction

It might seem like an oxymoron for a book that claims a divergence from the mainstream to be providing a linear historical synopsis of the literature on leadership. However, following a genealogical approach,[1] contemporary practices were visible in or could be traced to, certain events in the past. To make sense of how leadership is understood presently, it is necessary to understand the conditions that made them possible and not just their present manifestation. For a genealogical approach identifies features of the past that prefigure their prevalence in, and therefore illuminate, the present. It is important to see how leadership has evolved from excessively and explicitly totalitarian and elitist styles beginning with the ancient Greeks but continuing, through classical conceptions from early medievalism virtually until the industrial revolution and the enlightenment of the 18th century. In this latter phase of history, it can be argued that humanism prevailed to foster less autocratic or elitist styles of leadership although contemporary posthumanists perceive this as little more than the appearance, rather than the substance, of a liberating transformation.[2] For in many ways, humanism is simply camouflaging the autocratic legacies that remain within its practice; its repressive forces are just more subtle in generating self-discipline, performativity, and productivity through the mantra of realising one's potential.

Throughout this review, then, I will be looking to deconstruct the authoritarian and totalising strains within the perceptions of, and prescriptions for, leadership. I will also endeavour to show how the democratic and humanistic myths surrounding it effectively create 'smoke and mirrors' to conceal or disguise the autocratic elements within different theoretical or empirical accounts of organisational life. The chapter is organised through a division between the pre-classical period in ancient Greece, the classical Roman and modern eras followed by what can now be seen as post-structural and posthumanist periods through which the earlier eras have been constituted as distinct discursive formations. Finally, I assess critically the contribution of a recent genealogical study of leadership. However, the chapter begins with a brief overview of a genealogical history of leadership before turning to a more detailed examination of different approaches to the study of leadership.

A Brief Overview

Rather than slavishly trawl through the numerous different approaches to studying leadership in fine detail, I have chosen merely to provide a historical overview with a limited discussion of some typical and popular examples. Stretching back as far as ancient Egypt and Greece, polytheism was the underlying belief system and ontological force defining what is now described as a pre-classical era of leadership. Although ancient Greece had a mixture of monarchical and republican oligarchical city-states, Athens could claim to have founded the first quasi-democratic regime. Ancient Rome, by contrast, was republican but after the fall of the Roman Empire late in the 5th century CE, became monotheistic. This was the model for other European societies as they entered what is now called a classical age where monotheism largely in the form of Christianity became the dominant belief system to which leadership paid homage or at least lip service in the case of Machiavelli.[3] Of course, this was a period of sovereign rule where the monarch had absolute power, and disobedience was treated as tantamount to treason or apostasy since it was seen as a rejection of God's will.

As revolutions transformed some states into republics and others into constitutional monarchies, the absolute monarchical leader was replaced by the rule of law in Europe and, eventually in the New World as re-sistance to colonialisation proceeded. Yet, this was as much an outcome of enlightenment rationality and renaissance humanism as it was a de-mise of the sovereignty of the monarch. It challenged assumptions of 'divine, natural inequality'[4] that sustained hereditary monarchical power before the 17th century and this transformation of leadership and gov-ernmentality was the potential foundation for a more democratic and egalitarian order. However, the modern era displaced one monoculture of religious faith with another based on science or to be more precise scientism. Here an attempt was made in leadership studies to emulate the natural sciences by subordinating reason to rationality, meaning to measurement, quality to quantification and reality to reification.

Throughout much of the 20th century, leadership has sought to claim scientific respectability for its research and, in so doing, rendered itself increasingly obscure, if not irrelevant, to practitioners. However, the shortfall here has more than been compensated for by an army of management gurus converting the so-called science into soundbite chunks of wisdom and packages of leadership guidelines. These became readily marketable across the corporate landscape as well as providing hefty fees for the consultants. A displacement of the dominance of religion by science might have had the effect of undermining the 'natural order' of inequality but the ideas of superiority of existing leaders, or those destined for such a career, was reinforced by the concentration of this scientific approach on personality traits. For leadership studies simply reflected and reproduced the hierarchy of inequality either by claiming that leaders were inherently superior or by recommending recruitment strategies that ensured this was the case. Leadership was reduced to a series of traits that were seen to be inherited although, after some time, a behavioural approach rejected this idea of 'born to lead', opening up the idea that it could be learned through training.

This was a big change in the ontological position that for centuries had justified leadership as a part of the 'natural' order of inherited inequality, often ordained by God, to one where it might be seen as the result of learned abilities as well as genetic inheritances. A modern cynic might merely interpret this as a convenient way of expanding the field for management consultants to offer leadership development training. Still, to provide evidence of 'the one best way' of leadership, there had to be a form of measurement through scientific surveys of the effectiveness of various behaviours. This attempt by the science to discover the most effective kind of leadership graduated through a variety of approaches or theories each of which would claim superiority over what it sought to replace. These can be broadly categorised as focusing on the personality or characteristics of the leader, examining the situation or context, the relationship between leaders and followers, or conceptually associated with phenomena such as authenticity, process, practice, relationality or strategy. What is perhaps more important is to interrogate the conditions that make such discourses not only possible but also plausible. This has been accomplished to a high standard already in Suze Wilson's book that is one of the better treatments in providing a critically informed, genealogically researched and theoretically rich study of leadership.[5] I return to this at the end of this chapter to assess critically its value in studying leadership but now return to the pre-classical period.

Pre-classical: Leadership as Myths and Mystification

As a phenomenon, leadership has a long history extending as far back as 3035 years BCE and the 1st Dynasty of King Narmer, who unified the upper and lower Nile civilizations to create what has been described as the first civilized nation-state, subsequent Pharaohs in ancient Egypt,[6] the early Cretan civilization in Greece, the Indus valley which is now part of Pakistan and northwest India and to the 'Huang Ho walled settlements in China'.[7] While these examples were almost universally military in form, a little later in ancient Greece, we witnessed the mythical stories[8] of adventure and battle through Homer's Odysseus, who was imagined having performed miraculous feats of endurance and heroic leadership around 1000 BCE.

> The "Odyssey" starts by emphasizing that greedy, unrestrained, irresponsible leadership makes communal life intolerable for everyone. By contrast, a good leader respects his obligations to his people and ensures that they respect theirs to him and to one another.[9]

Much used as a resource for Foucault's posthuman embodied ethics, the pre-classical world of ancient Greece manifested many tensions and contradictions concerning leadership. By and large, in ancient Greece, leadership involved mutual respect and reciprocity, but this account is tending to read Greek leadership through contemporary Western eyes. On the one hand, this is lauding the sense of obligation and respect that is shown to others, yet on the other, denigrating its failure to condemn the revenge of mass murder committed against those who perpetrated disloyalty. However, if Foucault is to be believed, the figure of a 'man' or a leader in the sense of a responsible individual was not in evidence at this time and both obligation and revenge would simply be a reflection of societal normative, expectations and the honouring of tradition. To reinforce and reproduce these norms, of course, there had to be narratives, mythical or otherwise, recording their breach and then of the terrible fate of those committing such transgressions. Narratives, then, always have a rationale and a purpose which, in ancient Greece, seemingly was to secure order and stability by elevating the power of virtue and the disaster of vice. But, of course, this virtue was ordained by the Gods under whose tutelage mere mortals were in forced homage.

Few authors in the field have given as comprehensive a review of the classical Greek truth about leadership as has Wilson, who examines it in terms of the following four themes: the characteristics of leaders and followers; the responsibilities of leaders, the definition and purpose of leadership; and the scope of leader authority.[10] Seeking to provide a genealogical analysis, she sees leadership as offering a new solution to old problems of sustaining a 'totalitarian social order' of benefit to elites who claim that their rule serves 'the interests of all'.[11] From the middle of the 5th to the end of the 4th century BCE, Greek society suffered endless conflicts, disorder, troubles and wars culminating in the very damaging Peloponnesian War supported by Persia, lasting over 70 years and ending with the enslavement of Athens to Sparta. During this lengthy period, the society had been transformed from being governed purely by the aristocracy to an elite male democracy that nonetheless allowed no space for dissent and dealt with it either through exile or execution.[12] Yet even in its earliest evolution, some scholars questioned democracy not directly but through their philosophy. This began to focus on the reasoning that resulted in justifiable conclusions derived from a series of propositions where the argument did not commit the logical error of affirming the antecedent or denying the consequent. An example of the former would be to say that 1. This dog is an animal. 2 This is an animal. 3. Therefore, it is a dog; and of the latter, 1. All dogs are animals. 2. This is not a dog. 3. Therefore, it is not an animal. The absurdity of such false logic is obvious but when wrapped up in less familiar and more complex terms, it is not always so identifiable.

It was then the philosopher's duty to encourage reason that neither reflected false logic nor simply referred back to the Gods (as in ancient Egypt) or tradition and, through this reasoning, to uphold the social and moral order. The idea of 'perfect' leadership possessing absolute authority was deemed as an alternative to a flawed democracy for achieving this goal. Leaders are seen as distinct from everyone else in ancient Greek society because they possess the virtue of perfect knowledge derived from logical reasoning. We can see here the embryonic faith in reason but lacking the 'free will' that was much later to dominate the renaissance humanism of the Enlightenment.[13] However, determined by the Gods, there is a presumption that those already occupying leadership positions (e.g. state governors) and those possessing perfect knowledge are the same persons and they are also assumed to be rare individuals with an infinite capacity to devote themselves to the state and the wellbeing of its citizens. Conforming to what might be seen as masculine supremacy but also clearly paralleling the later beliefs in leadership as inherited, or what we would now call a genetic quality, the leader's superiority is unlimited and invulnerable. Nonetheless, it was tempered by a certain degree of humility and modesty, albeit often in a form that would today be seen as highly patronising. A superior leader was deemed necessary if only because of the already detected dangers of democracy in giving voice to followers, who might be lacking in both competence and confidence, and thus in need of constant assistance and guidance from the leader.

In the 6th century BCE, democratic principles of government were introduced to counter the aristocratic traditions of ancient Greece although only in Athens did any records remain to provide evidence of its forms. However, by the 4th century BCE, Thucydides was directly critical of democracy because he felt it consisted of few mechanisms for ensuring or developing 'good' leaders.[14] although he was seemingly abandoning the idea of leadership as an inherited quality. Plato also expressed his antagonism to democratic forms of leadership, partly due to the shock of seeing the masses put his teacher Socrates to death. Also, he felt it encouraged populist demagogues to promise the populace anything to secure their vote, often only then to create chaos by running their society into the ground.[15] Subscribing to an elitist philosophy, Plato was convinced that, despite only male adults with military service being qualified to participate in the decision-making procedures of the state, many were insufficiently educated and knowledgeable to do so. Through Socrates, he sought to demonstrate this in an allegory of the slaves in the cave who on release were unable to distinguish between illusions and reality because they lacked the clarity of abstractions and reasoning to overcome their reliance on bodily sensations. For in the dark of the cave, with a light shining through the opening, they saw the shadows of puppets against the walls of the cave as if they were real and when forced into the light were unable to shake off these images so continued to live an illusory life. To transcend the illusions of perception, we need abstract ideas that can identify what 'things' have in common independently of our sensual experiences and this requires knowledge only secured through long periods of education and training. He saw this illusory behaviour as responsible for the death of Socrates and Plato henceforth retreated from political action into pure contemplative philosophy.

While only those with knowledge acquired through education and learning were seen by Plato as fit to participate in developing the decisions that are crucial in governing society, Socrates devoted his whole life to developing this knowledge in all citizens to the point of his ultimate downfall. Might it then be argued that Plato's opposition to democracy was temporary, awaiting the kind of mass education available in contemporary Western democracies? For, the arguments he developed can be seen to have anticipated the enlightenment of the 18th century where faith in cognitive reasoning dislodged any other form of sensemaking so that only with the emergence of postmodern sensibilities in the late 20th century, were they subjected to some challenge. Other traces of the present to be discerned in Plato's deliberations reside in the almost universal rejection of direct democracy to be replaced by its representative form and the dangers of flirting with the former through referenda. As was seen in the UK in 2016, a referendum created great divisions in the country as the narrowly losing side generated a backlash against the democratic decision to leave the EU, claiming that it was based on inadequate or fake knowledge about the consequences of so doing.

In these senses, it is clear that although rule by an aristocratic elite is theoretically distinct from rule by the people, in historical practice, the lines between the two are blurred.[16] For elements of ruling through elites are inevitable when the population governs only indirectly under regimes of *representative* democracy, where a class of political leaders make the decisions of state. However, over a long historical period from ancient Greece to the 20th century, leadership has been religiously elitist where leaders have been seen as the representatives of God, rather than the people whether as citizens of the nation as a whole or as members of their organisations. This remained the case during what can be described as the classical era dominated by the form of government-generated in

Rome, which collapsed finally only after the fall of Constantinople in 1453CE.

From classical to modern conceptions of leadership

This classical era began in Ancient Rome with the dictator Julius Caesar in 31 BCE heading a small number of aristocratic families that monopolised the magistracies and dominated both senate and assemblies. Others suggest, however, that these elite politicians were more democratic in persuading assemblies of the people to accept particular laws.[17] Whichever version is selected, it seems clear that after winning a series of civil wars, Augustus was able to secure the support of Roman senators so that this was claimed as 'one of the most successful political settlement in history', and the basis of a republican rule for a further 3 centuries.[18] Only a century before the collapse of Rome and its empire (the causes still disputed), a significant change occurred in 312CE when Emperor Constantine converted to Christianity. This was several years after two emperors—Decius 249CE and Valerian 260CE—had attacked this minority religion and demanded a return to the traditional gods. When Decius was the first emperor to die in battle and Valerian the first to be captured by the barbarian enemy, Christianity was given a tremendous boost later to be restored, as a dominant creed, by Constantine.[19]

The classical era continued well into the middle ages through monarchical rule and what has been described as a 'mirrors for princes' discourse providing leaders with encyclopaedic guidance wherein prudence (the rudder) and virtue (the compass) were foundational.[20] However, because of the overwhelming belief in a totalising, interconnected reality designed by God that, while unknowable paradoxically must be obeyed, leadership was itself hegemonic and unquestionable. For any challenge to the sovereign was indeed a sacrilegious indictment and must be punished by torture through a public spectacle.[21]

Leadership as Sovereign and Absolute Power

It has been suggested that Scientific Management was an exemplification of how the earlier management theorists eschewed modern ideas of leadership.[22] Consequently, Frederic Taylor.[23] could be seen as the first architect of a modern approach to leadership since by separating conception from execution, he single-handedly sought to return the planning and organisation of work to a leader or manager, leaving the workforce simply to execute his/her decisions. In this sense, his thesis provides no better example of anticipation in the past that provides the conditions of possibility for a genealogical history of the present.[24] Had his thesis not been produced at a time when a democratic ethos was advancing with great momentum in the US, it might have gained more traction in his homeland, but its command and control character rendered it somewhat flawed in a liberal democracy. On the other hand, it was entirely compatible with the autocratic, totalitarian principles of the Soviet Union where it quickly began to thrive.[25]

The majority of studies of leadership develop a history of the subject that while paying some lip service to heroic leaders real or mythical from the ancient past, tend to outline the history as from the autobiographies of ex-senior executives. These usually support a 'Great Man' (sic) theory, where the qualities of leadership are seen to be a biological inheritance that reflects and reproduces common sense statements such as 'born to lead'. While displaying considerable egotism if not narcissism, these autobiographies only rarely offered any scholarly insights into leadership practice. Nonetheless, they were often the foundation for the development of trait theories that eventually were constructed by psychology, following a strict scientific model of hypothesis testing and analysis of causal variables. However, the essentialist nature of these theories was soon to invalidate them since if leadership is inherited from one's genes, there is no place for learning and education and this more or less undermines the basis for theorising, as opposed to simply describing the activity.

Consequently, behavioural theorists began to argue that the traits were social and not just genetic, so it was possible to teach people to develop the prized traits and to draw attention to what leaders were oriented towards. Still, there remained an attachment to arguments that saw traits, once identified, as universally applicable regardless of context or circumstances. Contingency and situational theorists eventually began to challenge this universality by identifying different leadership traits as applicable depending on specific conditions and contexts. These suggested that while traits were important, the context or situation would determine their appropriateness or usefulness. Later, traits were challenged all together when students began to focus on autocratic versus participatory or democratic approaches as well as the difference between transactional and transformational approaches to leadership. While transactional leadership was concerned with contractual obligations and responsibilities, transformational approaches focused on sweeping radical organisational changes inspired by leaders. More recent studies have embraced a range of issues from concentrating on followers, collective and communal matters, bodies and emotion and raising concerns about gender and ethnic diversity, power and resistance, and ethics and politics. A genealogical approach to studying leadership records critically the history as 'a teleological journey'[26] that, despite numerous blind alleys and false paths, may culminate in a deeper understanding of the discontinuity of events. Of course, each new theorist along the way would claim to have the panacea for the problems that their predecessors also anticipated resolving, but clearly failed. However, we see the exaggerated nature of these claims being exposed as one approach displaces another with as much speed as the fleeting fads of contemporary fashion,[27] thus giving the impression that the study and practice of leadership are about as ephemeral as the catwalks they resemble. Hence the rhetorical claims of leadership researchers have to be acknowledged as just that.

Critical Practices and Theories

Relational Theory

There are a number of adherents to a relational approach to leadership,[28] but I focus here on Dian Hosking's work as one of the earlier authors to develop an approach focused on dialogue 'free from selfish attempts to know and control other'. Such experiences can readily be observed 'in conversations that have no agenda', [and reflect an] 'ethics and local pragmatics' [that] 'open up "power to" rather than close down through "power over"'.[29] This 'relational constructionism makes no predictions, has no interest in control, does not offer explanations, and is not oriented towards producing objective knowledge of independently existing entities' …. 'It is a way of orienting to practice—to ongoing relational processes and the ways they (re)construct particular relational realities such as self as a knowing and powerful agent (scientist, leader, consultant) in relation to some "serviceable other"'.[30] The label of relational constructionism has not gained much traction perhaps partly because it freezes phenomena but also can be seen as a promotional strategy claiming superiority over other leadership theories in ways that her approach claims to abandon. Nonetheless, this is no reason to dismiss what is a vehicle for re-engagement that eschews 'dis-engaged (subject-object), dis-heartened (cognitive), dis-embodied and dis-enchanted (secularised and instrumental) ways of being in relation',[31] especially with regard to leadership. This approach coincides to a considerable degree with what I discuss later in this book in seeking to advance leadership as an embodied wisdom that is accepting of difference in its openness to 'otherness', both anthropologically and ecologically.[32]

Leadership, Gender and Diversity

Much of the leadership literature has been the focus of feminist and diversity critiques because of its focus principally on the values and preoccupations of establishment masculine elites and the dominant white middle class. Consequently, diverse groups whether minority ethnic, racial or disabled and/or gendered majorities are invariably ignored or denied their embodied existence within leadership studies. Since much of this book and especially chapter six is focused on gender and diversity, I need say no more here.

Sociomaterial Leadership

While a response to the material turn in social science that sought to acknowledge how social relations are part of a complex assemblage of material artefacts, bodies as well as human interpretations, sociomaterial leadership reflects how it is 'materialised through inter alia human bodily performances, architecture, clothing and other artefacts'.[33] Although often concealed both in theory and in practice, collectivities, bodily performances, material or non-human artefacts, and space and time are an inescapable part of the complexities of leadership practices. By focusing on these sociomaterial and embodied entanglements, this approach ensures that cognitive privilege does not override the passionate engagements of bodies and materials that constitute any practical accomplishments of leadership. Some theorists argue that material places and the embodied experiences of space have the effect not only of constructing but also of performing, leadership.[34] Insofar as sociomaterial approaches to leadership borrow from processual, relational, and leadership as practice perspectives, they also share with them an interest in aesthetic and ethical relations, as discussed in Chapter 7.

Leadership as Practice

This is another approach that is close to relational theory and resonates with sociomaterial approaches but seeks to emphasise and promote itself as superior to other approaches to the point of seeing itself as a social movement that seeks to mobilise political support for 'changing the conventional approach to leadership'.[35] Leadership-as-practice (L-A-P) avoids the frequent tendency in all, even critical, approaches that see leadership as a property of persons. It draws on posthumanist notions of intra-action[36] to understand leadership as an emergent and embodied process. This process is manifested in localised, experiential situations of inter and intra-active engagements that occur before they are represented cognitively in accounts, descriptions, theories or recorded events. Like other relational approaches, L-A-P encourages organisational members to reflect on their own activities, and through meaningful engagement with researchers, to be co-constituting partners in the practices in which they participate as well as in understanding, and providing accounts of, them.[37] Accordingly, a leadership-as-practice approach subscribes to a post-humanist framework that not only seeks to avoid reproducing the constructs inherited from the mainstream but also is concerned to incorporate other elements such as bodies, material objects and non-discursive aspects of leadership.[38]

Critical Leadership Studies (CLS)

Following the success of books and conferences around the theme of critical management studies (CMS) in the 1990s, a substantial number of authors claimed a parallel universe for critical leadership studies (CLS). Challenging the tendency of the literature to follow a mainstream focus of facilitating the practice of leadership largely for purposes of improving efficiency, effectiveness and, within the private sector, profitability, CLS examines critically it's underlying yet taken for granted assumptions.[39] Some criticise the presumption of organisational member consent with respect to leadership,[40] and question positive or Prozac views of leadership and, in particular, any notion that this is the polar opposite of toxic leadership.[41] Although there is rarely any acknowledgement of consensus within the mainstream literature, its existence can be discerned by the fact that insofar as any attention is focused on employee conflict, it is simply dismissed as a pathological 'resistance to change'. Of course, conflict within organisations is often simply suppressed for fear of its manifest expression encouraging those who resist the hierarchy. Many members of staff resent the unequal privileges and rewards surrounding hierarchical leadership, especially when witnessing what they see as leader incompetence. The mainstream literature, however, ignores the possibility of latent or underlying, endemic conflicts that can be traced to resentment regarding the inequalities of wealth, status and power, for it is more concerned either to facilitate competent leadership or at least, the appearance of it through various legitimising strategies.[42]

Critical analysis exposes the *appearance* of consensus as a function of leaders' ability to suppress conflict and claim that compliance or consent is in subordinates' own 'best' interests. In other words, the absence of *overt* conflict is often a consequence of relations of *dependence*. Subordinates are usually dependent on managers for a variety of workplace terms and conditions—for example, retaining their jobs, the allocation of tasks and responsibilities, increments in pay, overtime, promotion, future employment references, etc. Given this relative dependence, it is perhaps surprising that there is ever any conflict, especially of the kind that directly challenges management/ leadership.

Rather than apologising for, legitimising, or assisting leaders, critics are concerned to challenge their claims to automatic privilege and status and to pursue ways in which leadership might assume values of ethical standards, employee wellbeing and care for the environment. CLS, then, seeks to question the established order and mainstream leadership, where maximising returns to shareholders, productivity and/or minimising costs are the pre-eminent concerns. CLS also examine the dark sides, especially where leadership can readily be transformed into a cult that mesmerises believers and demonises those who challenge the message or its meaning.[43] Others are concerned with how leadership is treated in a dualistic manner in terms of 'individual/context; leaders/ followers; born/made leaders; task/people orientation; theory X/theory Y; one best way/contingent; organic/mechanistic, autocratic/participative, forceful/enabling; saviours/scapegoats; charismatic/quiet; and essentialist/constructionist'.[44] In addition, critical theorists argued that 'power processes and the politics of meaning', alongside questions of identity, had been almost entirely neglected by the mainstream,[45] or when power is considered, it is assumed to be possessed by leaders[46] and often is characterised by masculine and disembodied analyses.[47]

A Foucauldian Framework

Leader centric theories have tended to be criticised as individualistic, heroic and binary or dualistic in their elevation of leaders over followers[48]; and, as a consequence, attempts have been made to replace them with social constructivist perspectives that understand the image of the leader to be a construction of the followers.[49] However, this constructivism still displays all the characteristics of an 'entity' view where there are proprietary attributions projected on to, or claims on the part of, the individual whose leadership has been constructed. In a 'romantic',[50] follower-centric approach, the leader is seen as a socially constructivist outcome of follower commitment and dedication.[51] At one extreme, it is a little like the fan worship of celebrities and, at another, a patronising view of those who neither aspire to be nor are treated as, leaders. In constructivist perspectives, then, social relations are perceived merely to influence processes so that the primary source of the relationship is one or other side of the leader/follower binary. Consequently, action, agency and power remain the property of individuals rather than a reflection of their embodied relations as dynamically embedded in the social and material world.[52]

While deploying the same active verb, constructivists are contrasted with and seen as distinct from, *constructionists* who theorise leadership in a way that transcends the individual who is designated a leader. A social constructionist perspective is less offensive in describing leadership as a relationship of collective mutual stimulation between various members of an organisation, some of whom are perceived to be leaders.[53] While this perception of leadership as a relationship[54] has prevailed for some time, the caution that was raised more than ten years ago is still germane. For despite the rhetoric, there is still often a subscription to 'entity' and constructivist conceptions of leadership where 'relational processes are considered relative to individual characteristics that leaders and followers bring to their interpersonal exchanges'.[55] Termed 'entitative-soft', such a relational perspective focuses on the practices of leaders as individuals rather than 'foregrounding action and emergence', as does a practice approach that was discussed earlier.[56]

A constructionist approach recognises that leadership 'cannot be captured by the examination of individual attributes alone'[57] and this fully relational understanding theorises social relations as the very vehicles through which the embodied self, organisation and society are 'in ongoing construction'.[58] This embodied aspect of leadership cannot be ignored in the sense that all human encounters from our earliest experience of birth, through sexual attraction in puberty and to our eventual slow decay, as we become elderly, involve bodily awareness before mental and cognitive reasoning or rational reflection of our existence. This is precisely what Levinas meant by his conception of the face-to-face at birth that confirms ethics, in the form of responsibility to the Other, as prior to ontology or what it is to exist as a human being.[59]

To be fair, much of the mainstream and especially where it is concerned with transformational, distributional and leaderly forms of leadership does speak about the body and emotion in the form of charisma, inspiration and empathy. However, although we relate to each other not only verbally or cognitively but also with emotions and feelings expressed through our bodies[60], leadership studies focus primarily on rational decision-making activities. This is so even though leadership has to be seen as a corporeal activity in the sense of seeking to inspire and enthuse the corporate body as well as relating to bodies as individuals and groups. While in everyday practice the body is invariably centre stage, yet paradoxically when leadership becomes a topic of analysis and investigation in the discourse, disembodied conceptions predominate. Despite volumes of research, the bodies of leaders are often left on the doormat for people to fall over whenever they enter or leave the Royal Household of leadership studies. This is because of a subscription to cognitive and mentalist or linguistic and symbolic discourses that eschew the body and soul. Yet this disembodiment is difficult in the everyday practices of leadership insofar as it is no more possible to deny the body than the mind even though we are prone to describe our leaders as 'mindless' or devoid of emotional empathy. For our bodies are simultaneously subject and object of the same action and this not only facilitates but also obliges us to reflect about, our embodied being[61].

This renewal of leadership matters also demands an interrogation of the concept of autonomy and a reassessment of the humanist philosophy in which it is embedded. For there is little doubt that leadership trades on a laudatory elevation of autonomy as a medium and outcome of its theory and practice. An associated concern is to explore the concept of 'contingency' for how we respond to the 'contingent' is closely connected to our attachment to autonomy and our concern with self and identity. When we are deeply attached to human autonomy, as opposed to simply willing to use it against itself as a means of auto-critique, it seems that there is a preoccupation with order, harmony and stability or a concern to eradicate the contingent in both social theory and everyday life. By contrast, a Foucauldian approach, to which this book subscribes, is irretrievably contingent since Foucault's genealogy eschews all sense of causality and determinacy in favour of the precariousness of contingency.[62]

At the same time as refusing to support the idea of an autonomous self because of its failure to escape an individualistic sense of subjectivity that humanism seeks to sustain, it is nonetheless dangerous to be against autonomy per se. For some degree of autonomy (i.e. freethinking) is required to criticise the discursive practices of autonomy that have an individualistic effect on subjects. Paradoxically, then, autonomy is itself one of the necessary conditions of an auto-critique of the individualistic consequences of our humanistic preoccupation with the autonomous self. For, in order to critique an increasingly individualised society, there has to be a degree of critical self-reflection. Its absence would render us unable to stand apart from what we have become since the 18th century of humanistic discursive power that projects on to us an autonomy, which separates us from each other. This presumably is why Foucault retained an ambivalent relationship to Enlightenment reason, arguing that 'we must free ourselves from the intellectual blackmail of "being for or against the enlightenment"'[63]; equally, we should be neither for nor against autonomy, but retain a position that remains in between the extremes of individualism and collectivism or individualising and totalising. An ontology, epistemology and methodology of the in-between is what informs, inspires and integrates the analysis in this book, as elaborated in chapters six, seven and nine.

It has frequently been argued that our conventional understandings are fundamentally problematic not least because leadership is a contingent construction open to continuous change that our representations could never claim to accommodate.[64] Its problematic nature may also be attributed to the heroic status of the individual who is seen as a leader and this is a 'confusion that cloaks the modern definition of man himself'. For this 'figure of man' as a discrete individual that *only* emerged in the late 18th century 'is the major obstacle to an adequate thinking of contemporary experience'.[65] This is because it prevents us from thinking beyond the idea that individuals possess attributes such as personal traits, styles, transactional or transformational skills, charisma or power that are the medium and outcome of their leadership. Some contemporary studies seek to extend the idea of leadership beyond the individual to some kind of distribution that incorporates the followers, the community or simply practice but these radical conceptions struggle to secure a foothold in the absence of, but perhaps do anticipate, what Foucault describes as the 'death of man' in an aspiration that is 'beyond life and death'.[66]

One contemporary study that is outstanding in providing a Foucauldian inspired and genealogically informed approach to leadership is Suze Wilson's book[67] that is worth a critical review. This book seeks to question contemporary conceptions of leadership insofar as they fail to recognise its historically contingent, ontologically dualist and epistemologically representational groundings. As a consequence, there is no awareness of how the discourses of leadership construct what they claim merely to describe and, therefore, are unaware of their own political effects in producing and reproducing prevailing knowledge, subjectivities and power relations. Clearly, Wilson's work is congruent and compatible with my own but provides a more thorough genealogical analysis of the historical contexts in which discourses of leadership emerged as claims to resolve particular problematisation. These problematization are not independent of the solutions that are proposed and, therefore, a reflection of prevailing power-knowledge relations. However, they are contingent and, thereby, the unpredictable and underdetermined outcome of a range of conditions of possibility.

As can be seen, I think the strengths of this book far outweigh any weaknesses, but there are some limitations. While welcoming the author's declaration that, following Foucault, she avoids universals, there are a few that seem to creep back in and need to be addressed. For example, as is conventional in the mainstream literature but also among many critical theorists of leadership,[68] there seems to be an assumption that if we have leaders, we must have followers for if there were no followers the leader would have no one to lead.[69] Wilson tends to make this same assumption throughout the book, and the detailing of the subjectivity of the leader, the follower and their relationship is a dominant focus of the models that summarise its key findings.[70] Apart from treating this as a universal phenomenon, it has further implications. First, it naturalises, normalises and treats as neutral the phenomenon of leadership and followers and this is precisely what Wilson claims is problematic about much in the mainstream; second, it reinforces proprietary conceptions of leadership where it is seen as the property or possession of an individual; third, it can be condescending or patronising in relation to followers; and fourth, it presumes in advance what is to be investigated since if there are followers, then so-called leadership has already been accomplished rather than still in process, as Wilson otherwise argues.[71]

Process theory is clearly an improvement on the rational model since it recognises how meaning is an essential part of how leaders ensure that organizations change and are more effective in adapting to, but also transforming their environments. It focuses on organizational culture and how strategic leadership can shape the perceptions, values and norms of organisational members to secure efficiency and competitive success.[72] The limitation of a processual theory of strategic leadership, however, is that it relies almost entirely on leaders' own accounts of their practices and, thus treats strategy and leadership as neutral terms and as a resource, rather than a topic, of analysis. By so doing, it takes on the leader's interpretations as material, 'real' and 'objective' and organisational members as merely symbolic and subjective but capable of being transformed to render them compatible with what has been defined as strategic. This, of course, reflects the leader-follower dyad where knowledge flows down the hierarchy. One problem is that process approaches to strategic leadership rarely take into account how it has been made possible, and how its own discourse developed historically. Through the concept of strategy, for example, leadership was given credibility in the 1970s. Because of its deployment in the military as a response to economic declines in major western economies, it began to proliferate in business discourses. This was extensively reported in the media where particular strategic leaders were celebrated and eventually was extended to teaching leadership on MBAs in business schools. Consequently, and coinciding with Wilson's thesis, leadership discourses cannot be seen as independent of the practices that they describe and prescribe. Also, the emphasis on the organisational culture within processual approaches to strategic leadership has to be seen as a significant element of the power to 'take back control' of the organisation[73] through their effect in transforming individual members into subjects that secure their sense of meaning and purpose by engaging in the practices that are invoked by this discourse. Any critical analysis worthy of its name must continue to interrogate discourse and not merely seek to develop it for purposes of advancing its part in reproducing existing relations of corporate power and control and, informed by Foucault, my analysis is broadly within the same genealogical frame as Wilson.

However, when turning to the context, Wilson and also in her joint publication,[74] tends to treat it as material, 'real' and 'objective' rather than as a discursive effect of power. Of course, she is right to challenge the ways in which many discourses offer universal solutions to leadership problems independently of context. Nonetheless, the context cannot itself be taken for granted as if it is self-evident or interpreted in the same way by everyone. Of course, the 'sleight of hand' in the exercise of power is to do precisely this so that leaders will define situations as 'objective' and real so as to label any alternative understanding as irrational or misguided. Even, for example, when concerned with issues of climate change where there is a great deal of scientific consent, we cannot simply presume universal definitions or solutions. Although consensus emerges as an effect of the power of science to transform individuals into subjects that secure their sense of meaning and reality from the true effects of that knowledge, this transformation is never perfect or totalising. What ultimately is the problem of Wilson's analysis is a tendency to see the context as if it were independent of relations of power that come to constitute subjects in relation to it.

Because of the hyperbole and power effects of discourse, some critics go so far as to recommend abandoning the term leadership.[75] Learmonth and Morrell would want to replace it with the term management, but in terms of their concern to challenge existing social inequalities, I hardly think that it has any better record. Moreover, leadership is so embedded in our culture as to make its eradication from everyday life impossible, let alone from academic research, consultancy, organisational practice and, most importantly, politics. What is more important is to avoid treating leadership as the exclusive property of individuals as is common, so it has to be interrogated rather than taken-for-granted. To be fair, Wilson makes some attempt to do this in the last few pages of her book by challenging the leader-follower dyad and suggesting potential democratic developments. However, this is a little late as the rest of the book presumes the dyad. Even when speaking about taking a processual approach, she argues that leadership is concerned with 'the challenge of organizing a group of colleagues to achieve a common goal',[76] neglecting to ask the question as to how the so-called common goal came into being. This suggests that she is taking the view that leadership has already achieved a consensus on goals and thus is only concerned with the *means* of attaining them. While otherwise critical throughout the book, almost by default, she ends up here subscribing to a managerialist perspective in which espoused leaders pursue their goals irrespective of consent. A way out of this dilemma might be to explore a different approach to leadership.

A Neo-humanist Enlightenment Approach to Leadership and Its Development

While seeking to advance a posthumanist approach to studying leadership, it must be emphasised that this is not anti-humanist even though sometimes it may appear to be so. For this reason, as has already been argued, it is not appropriate to dismiss the enlightenment for that would be to throw out the embodied baby with the disembodied bathwater. Embodiment does not abandon reason any more than enlightenment rationality can dispense with the body. Clearly, the mentalist and rationalist metaphysics and methodology of Descartes did generate disembodied 'truths' that were rejected by posthuman philosophers such as Grosz, Foucault and Deleuze & Guattari as well as by posthumanist feminists such as Gatens, and Braidotti.[77] However, posthumanism is perhaps better designated as neo-humanism in the sense that it seeks not to deny or discount those humanistic values of respect for life and community that sustain civic culture, health and well-being. It is only about challenging individualising and totalising universals concerning human autonomy and the preoccupation with identity. So, for example, as already intimated, Foucault[78] argued that we should not be *against* the enlightenment insofar as its endorsement of humanism does provide us with the weapon of human rights with which to challenge its more oppressive tendencies to confine us to an autonomous individualised existence. At the same time, we should not be *for* humanism but alert to its dangers in assigning us to a lifetime of self-indulgence, struggling to realise an elusive and human potential as if this were the ultimate ideal of freedom.

Ordinarily, also, humanism extends its care and respect for humans to other sentient species, but the masculine and the human-centric pre-occupation with control tends 'to transform animals and nature into orderly, predictable and serviceable objects of human(istic) desire'[79]. Feminists have attempted to reverse this anthropocentric and speciesist tendency to treat humans as at the centre of the universe[80] by acknowledging the performative entanglement of humans, animals and material nature in complex mutual engagements of internally related, yet unbounded, elements whose form only unfolds through their intra-action[81].

In terms of leadership, however, it is the disembodied nature of most studies that a neo-humanist enlightenment approach abandons. Neo-humanists argue that embodiment is one of the necessary conditions of the kinds of engagement that is essential not only to ethical but also to creative, leadership. It renders leaders less preoccupied with themselves and their own identities, and thereby capable of being responsible to the other.[82] Consequently, we can re-imagine leaders as being effective not in spite of their bodies, but because they are more embodied and thus able to feel, as well as think, their way through problems. What can be seen as the 'absent presence' of the body[83] is precisely that which leaves studies of leadership bereft of some of the most important features of their reproduction. Often described as a 'new spirituality', neo-humanist research traces the neglect of the body to masculine modes of power and offers insights into the ambiguity, doubt and insecurity that befall us when the myth of certainty surrounding 'scientific' approaches to leadership is exposed.[84] It also rejects prescriptive rule and norm-based approaches so as to focus on embodied engagement as part of what it means to practice ethical leadership as a renewal of repressed leadership matters.

The message here, of course, is not to reject humanism but to turn it against itself since resistance is, then, cutting with the grain rather than against it.[85] Yet there is more to humanism than its preoccupation with autonomy, the self and human potential for it has also promoted charitable values and the treatment of one another humanely,[86] if often at the expense of other species and the planet. Still, the control mentality reflecting the domination of nature and the external world, often linked to prevailing anthropocentric masculinities within humanism, has sometimes spilt over from animal oppression into a parallel 'repression of other humans'.[87] During the pandemic of 2020, domestic violence gained the publicity it deserved, but human repression has a very long history and can be perpetrated by societies professing to endorse humanist values as much as by those swept away by totalitarian ideologies because, invariably, both reside in self-aggrandising attachments to masculine identities.

Unfortunately, human repression can also be as much self-inflicted as externally imposed, since when distant, the preoccupation with realising the self and identity is often lived vicariously through celebrity worship. So the *promise* of 'success' that inspires mass populations to continue participating in the seductive, 'realising our potential' merry-go-round will only be reversed through self-reflection regarding the myth of identity.[88] It is imperative then that we remain vigilant to the dangers of humanism as potentially oppressive in its self-disciplinary power to elevate ourselves, or those we celebrate, over anything that is different.[89]

Summary and Conclusion

This chapter has sought to provide a genealogical analysis of the discursive formations of leadership through its pre-classical, classical, modern and postmodern eras. Identifying autocracy and authoritarianism not to be too far beneath the surface of many forms of leadership in practice, even as in ancient Greece where democracy could be seen to have had its genesis, there has to be vigilance in every era. Until recently, scholarly work on leadership has had the misfortune of being almost completely dominated by the discipline of psychology or social psychology and thereby focused on the individual, albeit sometimes as a group member or follower and not exclusively as a leader. Most of the research attempted to emulate the natural sciences by relying on objectivist ontologies, where the discontinuity between the natural and the social world is denied. Here leadership is seen as an entity synonymous with any object in nature such as the existence of the earth's surface and its geological rock formations. This objectivism is supported by representational epistemologies, where knowledge is unproblematically captured in our cognitive and rational representations of leadership as if no process of interpretation serves to mediate the research subject and the object of investigation. Hand in hand with such ontologies and epistemologies are positivist methodologies that transform leadership into a set of causally related variables. The meaning of these variables is believed to be self-evident rather than contentious and, as a result, embodied humans are sacrificed to, or displaced by, 'scientific' rationality. Regardless of the diversity of perspectives prior to the development of critical approaches, leadership is seen to be the prerogative of individuals whose status can range from heroic to authentic and from coercive to participative.

Critical studies reject the mainstream on the basis that these ontological, epistemological and methodological restrictions obscure both the actual and the potential possibilities whereby leadership could be transformed. In addition, critical studies see that mainstream research on leadership typically neglects issues of power and resistance, identity and subjectivity, and gender and diversity—topics that are the lifeblood of critical theory. Following in this tradition, the following chapters reflect on these concerns but seek to embellish them by giving equal attention to affect the body, ethics, philosophy and politics.

It does this by contributing to both the theory and practice of leadership through offering a neo-humanist enlightenment approach to advancing embodied and ethical practices in ways that might be more effective in engaging people's commitment to its practice. It has drawn upon limited literature on philosophical and feminist theory to challenge normalising universals concerning human autonomy and the preoccupation with identity. It can be argued that Foucault's argument regarding the death of the subject led him into a cul de sac from which he did not escape until his later writings on ethics and care for the self.[90] However, in these later writings, he reflected on the self-formation process in order to generate a self that refuses to adhere to the individualising and totalising norms that have been imposed upon subjectivity through so many exercises of power.[91] In the next chapter, therefore, I interrogate the self so as to recognise how attachments to identity deflect subjects from confronting the full impact of its terror.[92]

Notes

1 Foucault (1980).
2 Braidotti (2013).
3 Wilson (2016, p. 89).
4 Ibid., p. 112.
5 Ibid.
6 Brier (1999, p. 20).
7 Grint (2011, p. 4).
8 There is a dispute as to whether Homer's narratives were based on actual historical events see https://www.dailymail.co.uk/news/article-1306042/The-legend-Homers-Odyssey-true-Archaeologists-palace-began.html.
9 Anhalt (2017).
10 For this reason, this section draws heavily on her scholarly work (see Wilson 2016, pp. 45–71).
11 Ibid., p. 68.
12 Cartledge (2006).
13 Carroll (1993).
14 Thucydides (2000).
15 Plato (2007 [383BCE]).
16 Wilson (2006).
17 Thiran (2019).
18 https://www.historyextra.com/period/roman/key-romans-dates-timeline-fall-rome-empire-when-founded-romulus-remus/ consulted 16.4.20.
19 Ibid.
20 Wilson, p. 76.

21 Foucault (1979).
22 Wilson et al. (2018).
23 Taylor (1911).
24 Foucault (1977).
25 Rose (1985).
26 Ford et al. (2008).
27 See Chapter 8 for more discussion of leadership as a fad and fashion.
28 Uhl-Bien (2006), Uhl-Bien and Ospina (2012), Cunliffe and Erikssen (2011).
29 Hosking (2011a, pp. 460–461).
30 Ibid., p. 463.
31 Hosking (2011b, p. 62).
32 Hosking (2011a, p. 465).
33 Hawkins (2015, p. 952).
34 Ropo, Sauer, and Salovaara (2019).
35 Raelin (2016, p. 1).
36 Barad (2007).
37 Raelin (2016, p. 8).
38 Crevani and Endrissat (2016, pp. 35–43).
39 Knights and Willmott (2017).
40 Collinson (2011).
41 Collinson (2012, p. 101).
42 Ford et al. (2008).
43 Tourish (2013).
44 Collinson (2014, p. 39).
45 Collinson (2014).
46 Tourish (2013, p. 8).
47 Knights (2017).
48 Collinson (2005).
49 Dachler and Hosking (1995).
50 While the term romantic is ordinarily deployed pejoratively to criticize traditional conservative views, Meindl (1995) sees it as a laudatory label for his preferred follower-centric theory of leadership.
51 Meindl (1995).
52 Knights (2015).
53 Burns (1978).
54 Cunliffe (2009), Fairhurst and Connaughton (2014).
55 Uhl-Bien (2006, p. 656).
56 Crevani and Endrissat (2016, p. 32).
57 Uhl-Bien (2006, p. 671).
58 Uhl-Bien (2006, p. 659).
59 Levinas (2002 [1989]). Other is capitalized since it refers not only to that which is beyond the human but also because other humans are a mystery that can never be wholly known.
60 Knights (2018b).
61 Merleau-Ponty (1962), Thanem and Knights (2019).
62 Kendall and Wickham (1999).
63 Foucault (1991 [1984], p. 45).
64 Wilson (2013, p. 10).
65 Bernauer (1993, pp. 64–65).
66 Ibid., p. 182.
67 Wilson (2016).
68 e.g. Collinson and Tourish (2015) who are criticized for this usage by Learmonth and Morrell (2019, p. 129).

69 Learmonth and Morrell (2019).
70 Wilson (2016, pp. 198–200).
71 Wilson (2016, p. 214).
72 Knights and Morgan (1992).
73 This was also one of the objectives behind Taylor's Scientific Management in separating management as organizers and planners from workers as merely executing their decisions.
74 Wilson et al. (2018).
75 Alvesson and Karreman (2016, p. 142), Learmonth and Morrell (2019).
76 Wilson (2016, pp. 215).
77 Foucault (2005, 2011), Deleuze and Guattari (1988), Gatens (1996), Grosz (1994, 2005), Braidotti (1991, 2011, 2013).
78 Foucault (1997).
79 Clarke and Knights (2019, p. 269).
80 Haraway (1991, 2008).
81 Intra-action is distinct insofar as it does not presume a prior separation of bounded entities in advance of their inter-action (Barad, 2007).
82 Ziarek (2001), Braidotti (2013).
83 Leder (1990).
84 Braidotti (2011, 2013), Thanem and Knights (2019).
85 Foucault (1997) see also note 386 in Chapter 5.
86 Braidotti (2013).
87 Wolfe (2011, p. 94).
88 Watts (1973).
89 beyond. Clarke and Knights (2015).
90 Foucault (1988b).
91 Foucault (1982).
92 Knights and Clarke (2017).

Part II

Conceptual Reflections on Leadership, Ethics, and Masculinity

In Part II, I explore many of the implicit or explicit assumptions or concepts underlying the various discourses, narratives, theories and practices of leadership. The selection is not exhaustive but directed towards the central themes of the book so that a chapter is focused on each of the following themes: identity and anxiety, power and resistance, gender and diversity, the body and embodiment, and ethical discourses in leadership.

3 Identity and Leadership

Introduction

Given that during the 1990s on average there were more than 3,500 books published on leadership every year,[1] it is surprising that with some important exceptions,[2] leadership studies are extremely limited in the attention they give to identity and subjectivity. Yet even without thinking about the close relationship between leadership and masculinity, where it is impossible to ignore the concept of identity, it can be seen as central to the idea of leadership. As soon as attributes of heroism, charisma, authenticity or a variety of skills are assigned to a leader, we are projecting on to that individual a distinctive identity that he or she will endeavour to solidify through gaining devoted followers. However, the fundamental link with identity is the proclivity to locate leadership in the individual. Of course, the focus cannot be wholly on the individual since the very notion of identity depends on a relationship with at least one 'other' and ordinarily several 'others'. As Mead argued, the 'self is a social process'[3] since it is formed through a multiplicity of interpretations of meaning in the numerous interactions that individuals have with others. Foucault goes further by arguing that identity is the normative ideal that transpires within the self-formation process whereby the subject is constituted through the very exercises of power that constrains her or him.[4] For power not only forms the subject but also 'provides the very conditions for its existence, and the trajectory of its desire'. ... 'The subject is initiated by a primary submission to power'.[5] This relationship between leadership and power will be explored much further in Chapter 5 where analysis of its inverse — resistance is also undertaken.

While the individual routinely strives towards a consistent sense of the self or identity, this must always remain illusory in the sense that it is dependent on multiple evaluations of others as well as one's own interpretations of their meaning. This renders identity precarious and transitory insofar as it is in constant need of social confirmation, reaffirmation and renewal from significant others who cannot be controlled, or in any way guaranteed, to conform to expectations.[6] As a consequence, anxiety and insecurity constantly rear their 'ugly' heads and our preoccupation with identity means that we are always a stone's throw from experiencing a mental health condition. In the US, it is estimated that throughout their lives almost half, and in the UK each year 25% of the population will experience a mental health condition.[7] No one would suggest that identity is the sole source of these conditions for there are numerous explanations from genetic or biological, neurochemical imbalances, brain damage, a traumatic experience in childhood, spiritual lacunae, nutritional inadequacies to simple problems of living. Nonetheless, the anxieties and insecurities surrounding our preoccupation with, and attachment to, our identities cannot be discounted in any study of mental health conditions. I know this from personal experience, as mentioned earlier since my masculine identity was existentially threatened on learning of my infertility when my wife was desperate to have children. Because of writing about masculinity, intellectually I had worked through this problem but only at the level of rationality rather than a fully affective and embodied engagement with the experience. Not surprisingly, I then experienced a dramatic mental breakdown of 7 weeks through which, according to the psychiatrist treating me, I was on the verge of being sectioned.[8]

Throughout life, there are few social constructions as ubiquitous as identity for it seems almost as sacrosanct as human life itself and even when it is not an explicit focus of concern, it is invariably an implicit aspect of events in both discourse and practice. Hardly a moment passes in the routines of everyday life where an occasion does not display the weight of identity claims by, for, or against, subjects. However, only when these are unsubtle, non-nuanced or seriously crude do people pick up on them — some of the best examples of the latter coming from the narcissistic, super-inflated yet insecure world of football managers such as Jose Mourino who never fails to claim responsibility for an individual's or the team's success yet manages always to attribute the reason for failure back to the players. Yet while in much of social life, egocentrism or narcissism is rife, it mostly manifests itself in an implicit, although not necessarily less destructive, manner. Academic management research also reflects the prevalence of concerns about identity for there has been over 202,000 peer-reviewed articles on the subject within the management field since 1990.[9]

This chapter is concerned to examine the attention given to identity and leadership within the critical literature as well as to unravel its neglect within the mainstream. It also provides a brief analysis of its associated links with anxiety and insecurity. This will involve brief forays into the historical past to highlight important contributions in analysing identity alongside associated terms such as self and subjectivity since these are simply convenient synonyms. Largely because of neglecting or displaying amnesia towards some of the earlier identity literature, contemporary critical authors tend to reflect and reproduce common-sense preoccupations *with*, rather than challenges *to*, identity. I question both the preoccupation with, but also the attachment to, identity and in so doing seek to generate more embodied and engaged understandings of social relations that displace contemporary thinking about the self and leadership. Finally, I summarise the arguments before examining the implications of the analysis for the remaining chapters concerning different aspects of leadership.

Rather than seeking to discover what's new in writing about identity, I would prefer to be more pedestrian by examining what has been forgotten in the rush for originality. Ultimately, this may be of much greater interest in understanding problems of leadership from the perspective of identity research. What then has fundamentally been forgotten in identity research, it may be asked? Surely such an extensive literature[10] has left no stones unturned, particularly given that identity is increasingly seen to be at 'the centre of intellectual debates',[11] and not least because it has become increasingly more important to individuals as fracture, fragility and fragmentation render it even more illusory. However, recent surveys of the literature on identity[12] show that ideas often overlap around a variety of concerns such as 'the extent to which identities are chosen or ascribed, stable or dynamic, coherent or fragmented, and motivated by desires for positive meaning and authenticity'.[13] This, as is the case with much of the literature, begs the question as to *what identity is* and instead rather presumes that it is so self-evident as to be unworthy of discussion except through the casual, lip service reference to such founding scholars of the idiom as Cooley, Freud and Mead. I am not seeking to promote some essentialist and unitary meaning around the concept, but simply to avoid taking identity for granted as if it is self-evident. Unless there is some discussion of what identity is and does, we simply reflect and reproduce common sense perceptions that readily treat it as an object to pursue, protect, manage or resist. In doing so, we limit the potential to interrogate our preoccupations with, and attachments to, an identity that often leads to its stranglehold over us. As was argued in Chapter 1, for a theory to have traction, it has to have a rationale and a mechanism,[14] and this will be referred to again in Chapter 4 in questioning the use of dialectics in critical leadership studies. While few authors speaking about identity articulate this, implicitly their rationale seems to be that of competition to ensure one's social significance and the mechanism of solidifying, stabilising and securing a sense of self. By contrast, I would support a very different rationale as that of contingency and so the absence of any certainty regarding socially lived experience and the mechanism as one of embodied engagement and responsibility to the other. This would result in less of an attachment to, and hence the preoccupation with, identity and its tendency towards a narcissism that invokes toxicity in social relations, organisations and institutions.

The chapter is organised as follows. First, it reflects on the failure to reflect on earlier discourses on identity and thereby a tendency to reinvent the wheel and this is followed by an analysis of the identity work literature. Despite its theoretical sophistication, this literature does not fully interrogate identity in the way that I argue is necessary if we are to develop a full understanding of identity in relation to leadership. The final section discusses leadership in relation to identity, anxiety and insecurity followed by a summary and conclusion that intimates how this analysis is fundamental to the succeeding chapters.

Drowning in the Presence of a Neglected Past

In contemporary literature, there is little concern to examine what identity is and what it does because of a fixation on the diversity of its different manifestations. The result of this fixation is that identity itself is not interrogated for attention is invariably drawn to describing and analysing the content of, for example, identity work, mind-sets or selective perception, and in-groups/out-groups or towards the various sites of its manifestation in gender, sexuality, race, age, disability and nationality. Further, avoiding any interrogation, identity is often linked to other topics with which it is associated such as power, politics, performativity and, of course, leadership that is the major focus here even though I do not intend to displace all attention onto the latter in this chapter. Interrogating identity is not difficult if we refuse to ignore some of the earliest authors who wrote about it and one such, at least within the social sciences, was George Herbert Mead whose insights are often neglected only to reproduce them in a version of reinventing the wheel.

While there seem to be few references to identity in Ancient Greece, although the conception of the self was well developed in the teachings of Socrates' (470–399 BCE) since much of his focus was concerned with improving and developing the reasoning and rationality of the self. Moreover, as Foucault[15] makes clear, a mastery of the self was prevalent in relation to a sexual desire among the Stoics in Ancient Greece (400BCE) as also in the Roman era, especially through the work of Seneca (4BCE–65CE). Nonetheless, identity itself can be traced as far back as Plato and for more than 3000 years, it has been central to systems of thought such as Buddhism.[16]

Plato's discourse on identity is entirely metaphysical. However, theoretically, it is possible to gain some insights through following his concern to clarify the relations between identity, sameness and difference and, in particular, his making a 'successful distinction of sameness and identity'.[17] He argues that for something to be the same as something else, it has to be identical with itself consequently, 'identity is conceptually prior to sameness' (ibid.). Thus, an object must have a coherent and self-contained identity for it to be the same as another object, but this contrasts with the human, who rarely is so internally consistent as to be identical with itself so, by definition, cannot be the same as someone else. From this kind of logic, identity for humans is then an oxymoron or a contradiction in terms and yet, in everyday life, it seems to prevail universally. Given also that social identity is dependent on another that is necessarily different, it can never be wholly self-contained and consequently, what generally distinguishes social identity is not sameness but *difference*. While aware that social, organisational, institutional or national identity trade on a notion of self-containment, coherence and sameness that sets it apart and often in enmity with that which is other, identity can only be an illusory fiction.

By contrast with this fiction, a Posthumanist feminist ethics is concerned to embrace and care for, and engage with, the lived experience of the other, however different.[18] In subscribing to these arguments concerning difference, we are led to understand how the preoccupation with identity and our attachments to it contradicts or at least renders problematic this ethics of engagement with difference. Paradoxically, while identity is contingent upon, it is often threatened by, 'the mere presence of the other',[19] and the more that we remain attached to our specific identity, the greater the threat.

This is not problematised in much of the leadership and organisation studies literature[20] because of its tendency to take identity for granted as a self-contained given; even when it is explored, the individualised preoccupation with identity is rarely challenged. To go further, it might be suggested that, at times, academics tend to treat identity in the same way as do laypersons, even though for the former it constitutes a topic for research while for the latter it ordinarily represents a mere resource in managing everyday life. Of course, academics are not only analysts and in their (our) practices, (we) may also behave in a commonsense way with respect to identity, thus treating it instrumentally as a way of overcoming insecurity. As a result, even though some authors raise the issue of identity as being fragile, precarious or temporal stability that 'appears to be either a momentary achievement or a resilient fiction',[21] they neglect to theorise why this might be the case.

Returning to this brief historical synopsis, outside of metaphysics, identity as a social phenomenon can be traced at least as far back as medieval times, although then it was mostly linked to ethnicity or ethnic consciousness.[22] Indeed, even as early as the 6th–10th century, the use of terms like 'populous, gens and natio' suggests 'the existence of something one can call, for lack of a better term, ethnic consciousness'[23] but one that was strongly 'connected to politics.'[24] And, of course, in the early 20th century, it was even more political when associated with nationalist and racist identities and the rise of the Nazi ideology of Aryan purity and superiority in Germany.

Outside of metaphysics, philosophically the concept can be traced back to Hegel, who developed a theory of the dialectics of recognition as the fundamental grounds of the formation of self. In his early work, Hegel's phenomenology develops a theory of consciousness, which concentrates on the self-subverting aspects of consciousness that are reflected in the master–slave relationship, where the identity of one negates the identity of the other and the negated seeks to destroy the relationship.[25] Later, Hegel turns his sceptical attitude regarding self-consciousness towards a more affirmative notion of the 'consciousness of *freedom* in mutual recognition', and this forms the basis of his ethics.[26] Here it is inter-subjective recognition, or what is essentially an identity, with its foundation in the family, but extending to other institutions and the state that is fundamental to freedom in society and ultimately to ethical life. The culmination of a succession of forms of consciousness was 'Absolute Spirit', a kind of perfection that for Hegel had already manifested itself in the Prussian State of his time, perhaps a dubious reconciliation of absolute spirit and absolute power.

Despite this long history, much of the contemporary literature that focuses on identity as a social or psychological phenomenon treats it as a modern concept of significance confined to a 40-year period around the turn of the 21st century. Let us, therefore, examine some of the earlier 20th century literature on identity to see if it gives any credence to different ideas than those that seem to have dominated the later analyses of identity within management and leadership or organisation studies.

Mead[27] developed a symbolic interactionist analysis of the formation of the self or what can equally be called identity by speaking about three concepts – the 'I' (the active), the 'Me' (conscious sense of oneself) and the 'Generalised Other' (social typifications derived from experience). Let us take an example that will be familiar to many reading this book of first entering university as a student where the 'I' or active self, will be anxious or at least uncertain about the experience and concerned about how others will perceive and relate to their 'me' or sense they have of themselves but through 'generalised other' understandings, knowing they are not alone and can presume that other students are experiencing the situation similarly. Also, when attending their early lectures, prior (generalised other) typifications of academics as clever and intellectual may quickly be eroded or confirmed as students experience their foibles or flairs and perhaps less, or more than, brilliant performances as teachers. We learn and develop such stereotypes partly to negotiate our way around the world. However, they may also be used selectively to perceive only those aspects of a person or situation which comply with particular expectations and, when negative, are extensively drawn upon in feeding prejudices (e.g. ableism, racism, sexism).

Symbolic interactionism went on to develop Mead's theory to show that human organisms do not just behave as a response to stimuli in accordance with previous patterns of reinforcement[28] but engage in interpretation through processes of self-indication.[29] In this sense, the world cannot be reduced to stimulus-response chains or a history of cause and effect. Still, actions arise out of processes of interpretation in which the individual 'I' creatively calls upon the symbols to define and assess situations in relation to its own sense of self (the 'me') or identity.

We shall return to these matters in Part III when discussing empirical research on different aspects of professional work for there is much vulnerability generated by the 'generalised other' expectations of competence and even perfection that the 'I' is inclined to invest in the 'me' not least because, whether real or imagined, these idealised demands and standards tend to exceed the capacity of those charged to deliver them. Insofar as there is so much invested in identities generally but in professional identities, in particular, they are precarious by virtue of a perpetual threat to their being undermined.

In sum, identity can be seen as individual self-consciousness inscribed in particular ideals of behaviour surrounding categories of persons, objects, practices or institutions. It is then constituted through 'generalised other', or more specific, exercises of power within which conceptions of identity come to be generated. This is far from being a determinate process since individuals actively exercise power in participating in the construction of, or of finding their own location amongst, competing discourses, rather than merely being 'positioned by' them.[30] In this sense, identity is never finished, or complete for it is an outcome of 'the unending and recursive perceptions of others' perceptions of the self',[31] a process that, while the same for everyone else, feel unique and threatening for the individual because it cannot be foreseen, predicted or controlled. These imprecise, temporary, uncertain and uncontrollable conditions, regardless of the appearance of confident performances, renders us as subjects forever anxious and self-doubting yet perpetually preoccupied with, more or less self-defeating attempts to solidify, stabilise and secure our identities. The ephemerality of identity, however, does not stop most people striving to bring it under control — to see it as a realisable panacea rather than a transient experience that can do no more than to provide us with a 'temporary respite' from otherwise intense 'anxieties and insecurities'.[32] The contemporary literature tends to focus on identity work that merely describes and analyses this kind of behaviour rather than interrogates its conditions of possibility.

Identity Work as Individualisation

Despite the limited interrogations of identity, 'identity work' remains a dominant force in the literature,[33] focusing primarily on individual agency and thereby reflecting and reinforcing excessive levels of individualism. Partly this occurs as a result of identity being treated as a property of individuals and narratives often legitimising individual material and symbolic success as a goal worth striving for through dedication and hard work. Because identity work is understood as an internal matter of working on the self, it is rarely fully self-conscious of how it is so closely tied to an ethic of success. Nonetheless, we so internalise and take for granted career, money, status and social media popularity, identity is as natural as the air we breathe. Consequently, identities are pursued with limited reflection as to their unattainability since because of its comparative nature, success is a constantly moving target that no one ever achieves. At the same time, it marginalises or displaces social and embodied bonds that are not simply part of the roller coaster of instrumentally using others as a means of securing the self. In failing to embrace an embodied engagement with others,[34] we readily feel isolated, anxious, and insecure and then even more preoccupied with chasing the elusive experience of a secure and stable identity. Failing to recognise that chasing achievement and success is the paradoxical source of our anxieties, we remain enraptured by promises of what might be achieved, in a future yet-to-come.[35] Even were success really attainable rather than an ever-receding illusory dream, because it is dependent on comparisons where there is invariably someone appearing superior, it can only be the prerogative of a minority of the population. By definition, then, the majority cannot escape a sense of comparative failure, inadequacy and even guilt at not realising their potential.[36] Yet, the identity at work literature continues to trade on ideas that we work at our identity to accomplish a favoured version of it. While empirically this is a reasonable description of what we are all inclined to do, there is very little hint that this might be an unrealisable, self-defeating aim.

It is in this sense that the identity work literature is not wrong so much as misleading for it encourages rather than disrupts the taken for granted sense of identity as an autonomously 'authored'[37] phenomenon. One of the more invidious aspects of identity work that the literature rarely speaks about is how it affects us all in its individualising of social relations. Yet, insofar as we are forever entangled within contingent relations that inevitably escape our ordering and control,[38] it is somewhat paradoxical for theorists to represent identity in this illusory manner, rather than perceiving it as the contested, fragmentary, contradictory and contingent phenomenon that it is *in practice*. Still, numerous articles merely describe, rather than interrogate the centrality of identity, and fall into the trap of conflating *attempts at,* with the *guarantee* of, securing particular identities.[39] For example, 'identity work' has been described as 'the range of activities individuals engage in to create, present and sustain personal identities that are congruent with and supportive of the self-concept'.[40] More recently, it has been argued that identities are 'regarded as temporary "fixes" concocted by individuals to impose a degree of coherence in the face of assorted vulnerabilities'.[41] Both of these descriptions seem to see nothing problematical in asserting that individuals 'create' and 'sustain' or 'concoct' their own identities as if they were in complete control rather than contingently dependent on the actions and interpretations of others. Moreover, they also project far more intentionality onto subjects than is ever evident since identities are much more often an unintended consequence of other actions that, we might argue, are 'only predictable in their precariousness'.[42]

I am not arguing that identity is a myth in itself so much as suggesting that seeking to render it secure, solid and stable is delusional since, by definition, it is ephemeral, indeterminable, precarious and transitory. Also, although a primary focus for individuals, our attachment to particular identities is rarely at the surface of our consciousness. For identity is much more likely to be an indirect consequence of pursuing other objectives such as, for example, climbing hierarchies, financial success, winning competitions, being popular within a social network, or having lots of friends or followings on Facebook. The consequences of these aspects of social relations are some sense of a valued identity to which we are then likely to become attached and it is this attachment, more or less ignored in everyday life and by the literature on identity work, that can be damaging to mental, as well as physical, health and wellbeing. For it involves what can be called an excessive 'productive narcissism' to 'maintain' an individual's 'idealised self-image', which can only serve to engender 'heightened insecurity, escalating personal demands, intensifying pressures on mind and body and acute competition'.[43]

As I have already argued, the literature on identity work reinforces individualistic, neo-liberal ideas regarding competitive success in careers, organisations and markets, together with a sense that any success or failure is wholly individual rather than social in its genesis and development.[44] In this regard, I want to highlight the self-defeating aspects of identity work, for it frequently encourages expectations for, or even an entitlement to, 'the somewhat narcissistic need for self-fulfilment'.[45] In subscribing to this mantra[46] we risk becoming ensnared in a self-perpetuating, vicious spiral of fixation with ourselves.

This individualisation is often legitimised by meritocratic values, even though its architect Michael Young was actually critical of the phenomenon. He believed that meritocracy concealed the fundamentals of inequality by blaming 'failure' on the individual's inability or effort and not as an inescapable feature of the social arrangements in which it resides.[47] Apart from deflecting any antagonism away from the source of the problem, this sense of personal responsibility for one's position in society can also generate anxiety and stress about falling short on social expectations that readily generate feelings of inadequacy potentially capable of arousing mental health conditions.[48] Displacing any organisational or societal responsibility for the pressures to realise particular standards of performativity, competitive targets and projected ambitions, this process ends up blaming the victims on the basis that they are insufficiently robust or resilient.[49] Paradoxically, then, these outcomes nurture a whole range of interventions by organisations and the state — counselling, mindfulness, coaching, stress management and other wellbeing initiatives — to seek to resolve problems of their own making. Focusing on symptoms, rather than their source, is like 'putting a sticking plaster on a cancerous wound'.[50] Moreover, insofar as these interventions fail to offer a cure, they may be far from progressing the wellbeing of those who are vulnerable in situations of unacceptable pressures in organisations.

So far, the focus has been on how organisations may (un)wittingly invoke potentially deadly practices at work, partly enabled by the desires of leaders and those they lead to mitigate anxieties and insecurities by confirming positive identities. In the remainder of this chapter, I explore how the literature on identity can be seen as reinforcing, rather than challenging, a preoccupation with identity, thereby contributing to its harmful effects on individuals and organisations.

Leadership: Identity and Insecurity

Even when identity is a consideration in studies of leadership, its self-defeating features are rarely a focus and indeed, the very concept of identity is mostly taken for granted as self-evident, rather than challenged.[51] This is not to argue that these studies are uncritical, but the focus of criticism is not identity itself. So, for example, there are some authors[52] critical from a deconstructionist position of demonstrating the heroic and gendered assumptions underlying studies and practices of leadership where there is a recognition of some connection with identity but little interrogation of it. Exceptionally in the literature, conventional essentialist conceptions of identity that understand it as 'fixed and objective' rather than 'multiple, open, negotiable, shifting, ambiguous, insecure and potentially contradictory' have been questioned by Collinson[53] although this view on identity and its implications for leadership is not developed[54] in the way that had been made possible by his own, and other earlier, contributions.[55] The limited space available to authors in writing for refereed journals could be an explanation here but there is a tendency more generally for identity *not* to be challenged and in this way presumed as an unproblematic feature of everyday life,[56] let alone leadership. Yet it is partly a leader's own attachment to an identity that is a condition and consequence of the prevalence of individualism, heroism, masculine machismo and various other ways of enhancing and celebrating the idea of leadership as the property of persons. Such 'themes of conquest and manly appetites' are frequently associated with the practice of leadership in Western and often non-Western culture.[57]

It may be asked what identity and insecurity have to do with leadership? Well, primarily identity is the link relating all social interactions for it is how we attribute meaning to a particular relationship. When it comes to leadership this is even more important because leading involves direction, guidance and support and few of us are prepared to accept advice let alone instruction unless the leader is credible and is respected. However, leaders often become so attached to their own identity and self-image as to damage relationships and nullify any positive impact that leadership might have. The problem is that seeking leadership is very often a claim to identity and securing the identity becomes the central preoccupation, which then undermines positive relationships with others and thus the productive power of leadership. While often a driving force both for leaders and those they lead, when leadership fails or is damaged, anxieties and insecurities are reinforced whereby identity work can become frenetic as a way of protecting self-image or limiting the erosion of credibility.

Also for many employees, the classical principles of leadership such as Scientific Management or Human Relations, let alone the proliferation of leadership innovations posing as science, were not necessarily experienced as a neutral and progressive technology. Often they were seen as a political and socially divisive weapon that felt like a threat to their sense of identity, solidarity and interests. To the extent that forms of scientific management encounter organised resistance, they provoke opposition to the aim of rationalising the workplace rather than operating to expose and remove irrational deviations from it. So, for example, 'humanistic' leaders are understood to possess a deep appreciation of individual and especially group psychology thus enabling an understanding of how the norms of workgroups can exert a stronger impact upon worker identity and behaviour than the rules and incentives imposed by leaders or managers. This is the central message of Human Relations thinking popularised by Elton Mayo, a Harvard academic. Mayo studied the influence of social factors, such as recognition of contribution and the operation of group norms (e.g., the socially acceptable level of effort and cooperation) upon the productivity of factory workers. According to him, 'Human collaboration in work... has always depended for its perpetuation upon the evolution of a non-logical social code that regulates the relations between persons and their attitudes to one another'.[58] Human relations thinking suggests that while economic incentives cannot be ignored, employees also seek to have their sense of identity developed and confirmed at work. By contrast, leaders are expected to focus exclusively upon the goals of the organisation and not upon their own personal interests in power and identity, or other concerns that might conflict with such objectives. However, as will be discussed in Chapter 4, although it is presented in the language of leadership and organisational goals, gaining the support of followers is often more an issue of power and identity than of commitment to the organisation. In a study of an engineering factory, it was shown how through a comprehensive system of 'normative control', highly educated employees became self-disciplining as they were symbolically entrapped within the reality defined by leaders in terms of the corporate interests.[59] Even so, employees remained fairly ambivalent and they related to corporate efforts to involve internalisation of company values with some irony and symbolic distance.[60]

Wherever identity is involved in leadership it can almost be guaranteed that anxiety and insecurity are lurking not far behind. For example, in my youth, one of the earliest jobs I undertook was in insurance sales that can be seen as a classic area of enterprise where anxiety and insecurity are driving forces. First, they are drivers in the sense that insurance is principally a product designed to render less unpalatable uncertain events in the future by providing financial compensation for their negative impact. In short, it offers some amelioration of anxiety that surrounds the risk of financial insecurity generated by future potential misfortunes. Yet where does leadership enter this set of events? It does so in the sense that the salesperson is engaged in leading people to do something that they would not otherwise do; that is to say, consume an abstract product the benefit of which is in the (often distant or indeterminable) future, and possibly after one's death. In our modern consumerist society, persuading people to sacrifice immediate gratification for some abstract and elusive future benefit demands leadership in the sense of leading them in a direction often contrary to their instincts. In this sense, sales skills are a form of leadership albeit a precarious one since failure is much more frequent than success and even the latter does not relieve the anxiety embedded in the task for a salesperson is only as 'good' as their last sale. Likewise, confirmation of one's preferred identity is similarly fragmentary and transient. In addition to the anxiety built into the work, remuneration in the form of commission or other rewards often directly linked to sales only serves to add pressure and insecurity into the mix. I realise that sales work would not conventionally be viewed as leadership largely because it does not necessarily generate a continuous following from the buyer although levels of loyalty are often generated, and it does not involve leading an internal workforce. However, salespeople are involved in persuading outsiders to trust, do business and trade with the organisation they represent, and this demands as much if not more leadership than when dealing with insiders who are already on side, as it were. Consequently, it is plausible to regard leading as an aspect of selling in the same way that selling is certainly an aspect of leadership. Hence, their association needs to be acknowledged, and we can just leave it at that.

What can be learned from this example is how anxiety and insecurity are inseparable from leadership practice even though much of the literature gives them little or no theoretical or empirical attention. These observations are not surprising for, as was argued earlier in this chapter, self-consciousness involves a sense of our separation as humans from that which is outside of ourselves. While this intensifies our actions intended to resolve the tension and bring about some reconciliation, it merely promises, rather than delivers, a reduction let alone an eradication of the anxiety and insecurity.

Clearly, self-consciousness is an asset in enabling humans to be creative, innovative and generally purposive, but it can also generate anxiety and insecurity because we can anticipate future scenarios, many of which may not be benign. One of those scenarios we often anticipate is a condition of material scarcity that poses a direct threat to life, and here the desire to survive directs human purposiveness towards the production or the appropriation of the means of remedying this scarcity. Precisely how this desire is fulfilled depends upon the cultural practices — customs, tradition, moral and religious beliefs that help us to make sense of, but also regulate, production and appropriation. Even in the most extreme of circumstances where life is endangered, a range of meanings frames our desires and their satisfaction. For it is impossible to separate material or biological survival from the concerns that human beings have with symbolic meaning and identity, as mediated through communication, consciousness and language, where cognitive and emotional reflections or rationalisations of our actions are enabled.

Anxiety and insecurity concerning our physical survival cannot be avoided especially when they are aroused by real or potential famine, natural disasters and human conflicts such as wars, and pandemics. Yet, in affluent societies of equal importance are anxieties aroused by threats to symbolic survival or identity. For every social encounter is capable of unsettling a stable or secure sense of self or identity, for example, any situation where we perceive ourselves to be vulnerable to social or interpersonal rejection or denial. Whereas (other) animals tend to react instinctively to stimuli in the environment, human beings interpret every situation through a self-conscious perception of what it means for symbolic, as well as material, security. The uncertainty and unpredictability of life are often then unbearable and hence, the attraction of leaders who offer or promise some sense of stability or remove the necessity to construct or interpret the meaning for oneself. The invention of God provided much of human civilization with relief from this responsibility to be in a continuous state of uncertainty in making sense of things, but in the 20th century, this crutch was partially removed from secular societies in the West. As Camus expressed it: 'One must choose a master, since God is out of style'.[61] Still, numerous false Gods and leaders have filled the vacuum as we seek to establish a solid sense of identity within social life and, clearly, leaders of various kinds readily become our salvation for good or for ill. Leadership, then, can be seen as both a medium and outcome of anxiety and insecurity.

Despite this, mainstream researchers are preoccupied with establishing the determinants of efficient and effective leadership so that a focus on anxiety, insecurity or even identity would seem like a distraction with no productive outcome. Might we see this as analogous to firefighters refusing to fire-proof buildings as this might diminish their indispensability? However, an analysis of anxiety might direct us towards showing how it can be alleviated, if not eradicated, by leadership that is not wholly preoccupied with work intensification and performativity.

One strand of the leadership literature has sought to do this by focusing on the way that leaders manage the emotions that are implicit, if not explicit, in the relationships between leaders and those they lead.[62] By resonating with people's experiences, leaders can connect with their 'unconscious wishes, desires and fantasies' and, thereby, release considerable 'emotional energy'.[63] However, this can easily backfire where there is any discrepancy between words and actions, resulting in the emotions turning negative against those who are seen to be deceptive or distrusted. A psychoanalytic contribution[64] traces the relationship between leaders and their followers to deeply felt emotions or primal fantasies regarding gendered stereotypical caring mothers and controlling fathers.[65] A psychoanalytic perspective suggests that leaders may help followers to contain their anxieties and toxic emotions, at the same time as arousing desires and fantasies in ways that may be inspiring and energising.[66] Psychoanalysis[67] seeks to challenge the idea of a discrete self, for this leads to an over-attachment to fantasies about individual achievement and notions of an idealised or perfect self[68] that is beyond reach because 'humans never reach the ego ideal'.[69] This challenge is also supported by posthumanist feminism both from within the physical sciences[70] and the social sciences.[71]

However, most leadership research neglects the psychic aspects of their subject matter as do leadership development and training courses where there is a parallel tendency to concentrate on leaders as heroic individuals who can transform organisations regardless of the context, whether psychoanalytic, cultural, economic or political. Paradoxically this neglect of context and anxiety is often counterproductive since it can actually generate what it refuses to confront, leaving practitioner participants anxious and insecure, not least because they sense that what is being taught is an unrealistic and unrealisable, empty rhetoric.[72] For the failure to treat seriously the insecurity, anxiety and ambiguity in the lives of those they teach, trainers expect leaders to be clear, confident, and in control in all situations when such security and stability is a mythical ideal and this can readily leave leaders feeling themselves to be failures when it is not achieved.[73]

Such high levels of anxiety are not healthy either for leaders or their so-called followers in that they focus the mind and the body on self-obsessive internalities or externalities such as popularity, fame and sycophantic validations that mistakenly are seen to relieve the symptoms whereas attention would be better directed at the egocentric disease itself. Organisations and institutions are full of leaders and followers that seem to exhibit symptoms of the narcissism surrounding this disease, the most publicly visible of which are our political leaders. So, for example, Donald Trump, Vladimir Putin, Silvio Berlusconi, Recep Tayyip Erdoğan, Kim Jong-un and Boris Johnson all appear egotistic[74] with a tendency towards autocracy regardless of any democratic constraints on their style of politics. Of course, these leaders will readily show certainty, confidence and conviction but this is a rhetorical flourish designed to conceal their fear of rejection and to compensate for their anxieties and insecurities.

But why would we attribute the same levels of anxiety to their followers? Well apart from believing that we all share some anxiety and insecurity as part of the human condition of self-consciousness, this is exacerbated among followers insofar as narcissistic leaders, like Trump, will 'feed' if not manufacture their bigoted prejudices and scapegoating tendencies. These are then perpetrated, by both leaders and followers who see in this a capacity to displace insecurities by demonising others as a means of elevating a falsely secure sense of self. On the part of leaders, this is a sense of self-aggrandisement. In contrast, for followers it is a form of hero(ine)-worship that has parallels with the mass consumption of celebrity status where followers or fans counter the mundanity of everyday life by living vicariously through the world ascribed to the subjects/objects of their fantasies.

If anxiety and insecurity are important conditions and consequences of leadership and the followers it seeks to cultivate, it hardly seems credible that it is ignored or marginalised by much of the literature. As has been argued, anxiety and insecurity have their roots in the self-consciousness that distinguishes humans from other sentient beings and material existence and that is a necessary if not sufficient condition for the development of language, culture, economics and politics in human society. Consequently, much of human behaviour is learned rather than instinctive. However, there is considerable controversy as to the relative importance of this distinction as between humans and other sentient and non-sentient species since organic survival and reproduction seem fundamental to all living matter. Also, the web of relations associated with ant, bee or dolphin survival and reproduction would seem no less complex than the human world although the fact that we humans study these other worlds to determine their complexity suggests, if it does not prove, an ontological discontinuity (i.e. a difference of species magnitude) between the two.

But this is not the only source since while the very organisational, cultural, economic, institutional and political outcomes of human development, at one level, may relieve anxiety and insecurity, at another, they simply intensify these peculiarities of the human condition. Almost all societies irrespective of political form seek to protect the survival and reproduction of those under their jurisdiction but a whole range of cultural, ethnic, national, racial, religious and political practices and ideologies can intervene to undermine and even violate the provision of basic securities for individuals. Hence, the genocide and ethnic cleansing of the holocaust in Hitler's Germany, the purges of Lenin and the Gulag of Stalin in the Soviet Union, apartheid in South Africa, the ethnic cleansing in the Balkans, the bombing of civilians in Syria and the recent apartheid against the Rohingya in Myanmar, South East Asia and many others equally as brutal if on a lesser scale.

A paradox is that while fundamental to any characterisation of leadership not least because of proprietary assumptions that see leadership as a property of the individual, identity itself is rarely theorised. Even in a book entitled *Leadership Paradoxes*, identity is only properly examined in the chapter on authenticity[75] where a multiplicity of identities is seen as rendering the idea of one authentic self as problematic, if not wholly paradoxical. These paradoxes were seen to concern breadth in relation to authenticity but by turning to a depth of self-awareness through mindfulness, it is argued we can become open not only to dissonances and incoherence in relations but also tensions with regard to consistencies and inconsistencies within the Self. One important inconsistency is where our attachment to being self-aware, for example, may, in fact, act as a barrier to self-awareness.[76] Without theorising this directly in terms of identity, this analysis is entirely compatible with my view that attachments to identity are an obstacle to leadership as a collective inspiration to action. Since authenticity is central to most theories of leadership that consider the issue of identity, I now turn to this literature.

Authentic Leadership

Discussions of identity in leadership studies seem to have been recently colonised by concerns with authenticity as if the legacy from existentialist philosophy were exhaustive of what is important about questions of identity in relationship to leadership. First introduced in 1983, the construct of leadership authenticity was seen to comprise responsibility both to oneself and the organisation in terms of actions, outcomes and mistakes, avoidance of manipulation in relation to subordinates and a privileging of the self as opposed to the requirements of one's role.[77] It has become an ever-more dominant focus since and especially in the years 2005-6[78] where the construct has involved four elements: (a) self-awareness; (b) relational transparency; (c) internalised moral perspective and (d) balanced processing of others' position,[79] although it has also been defined as simply a form of leadership that is effective as well as ethical.[80] In their different ways, these are all comprehensive understandings and later work has tended to focus more on the leader discovering a core sense of self and maintaining it through a diversity of temporal and spatial contexts[81]

Turning to existentialism from where the concept derives, we can see that some fundamental contradictions since, in the hands of leadership theorists, apolitical essentialism is imported that would have been anathema to the early popularisers of authenticity – Sartre and de Beauvoir for they recognised everything to be contingent. This is not to say that the absence of certainty and necessity was welcome since a viscous overflowing and excess of indeterminate reality was the source of meaningless nausea for Sartre. However, his resolution was to live an authentic life that rejected convention and, more importantly, constructed political projects to which he could be committed as a way of overcoming the absence of meaning.[82] While de Beauvoir shared the same political project of communism, she also had her own project and as a consequence is celebrated as the founding figure of the feminist movement. Insofar as the self is irretrievably a social construct that is perpetually in motion and escapes any reductionist attempt to render it orderly and stable, these existentialists were only able to allay rather than eradicate the meaningless void.

However, leadership theorists seeking authenticity seem unaware that their search for an essential 'true' self might have anything to do with the meaningless void, and so would be dismissed by existentialists as oblivious of their own bourgeois complacency and ignorance. While this is the most deep-rooted contradictory implication of having adopted an existentialist concept with little understanding of its significance, there are other inconsistencies since 'privileging the self rather than the role requirements' is not compatible with being fully 'responsible to the organisation for one's actions, outcomes and mistakes' or with 'balanced processing of others' position'. But all of this effort to be authentic is ultimately instrumental in that it is designed to secure better organisational performances.[83]

Authentic leadership stems from leaders being self-aware, aware of others and the context in which they interact as well as 'confident, hopeful, optimistic, resilient and of high moral character'.[84] In other words, it simply reflects that old American cliché of motherhood and apple pie – values that cannot be questioned but these are culturally specific to the US and, as has already been argued, fail to interrogate the notion of self or identity as outlined at the beginning of this chapter. They also contradict the original concept of authenticity, which is to refuse 'fitting' in with conventional views and acknowledging uncertainty and precarity rather than exuding confidence and optimism. Of course, fundamentally the weakness of this style coincides with most other theories in subscribing to what I described in Chapter 1 as a proprietary understanding whereby leadership is seen as the property of the individual leader rather than a collective and communal aspect of social relations. However, authenticity also reflects and reinforces a preoccupation with the self and could be seen as a disease that contradicts the social formation of the self and feeds a narcissism or its vicarious counterpart in living one's life through the celebrated status of others. In Buddhism, it is described as spiritual materialism[85] - a condition whereby the ego uses the symbolic sense of the spirit to seek to secure a solidity in the self when such stability is unrealisable because illusory. Authenticity is invariably such a pursuit rather than a means of creating and sustaining leadership that generates free and productive communal action.

Psychoanalytic approaches have sought to challenge how followers have tended to project paternalism onto their leaders and, in particular, the symbolic authority of the father that, while prohibitive, is deeply admired.[86] Authentic leaders seek to remove this association between their leadership and the primal father or master signifier by providing space for followers to decide for themselves. However, often what replaces the paternal authority is a leader who, while wholly engaging rather than distant and granting autonomy to followers, is an equally constraining authority that forces individuals back on their own self-conscience, and potential guilt, if they do not behave in the correct positive manner. Lacanian theorists have argued that this marginalising of any 'negative emotions is tantamount to occluding the dimension of lack necessary for desire and autonomy'.[87] What is necessary for authentic leadership is not the fostering of care or 'imaginary love' but an authority that acknowledges its contingency and historicity and can thereby facilitate the development of 'emancipation and autonomy'.[88] While contingency and historicity in leadership are to be welcomed, this analysis seems to reflect and reproduce a discourse of autonomy derived from enlightenment humanism which could well be just as repressive as either the paternal or the caring authority.

Summary and Conclusion

In this discussion of identity, it may seem that the focus has inclined toward the former rather than the subject matter of this book which is leadership. This has been intentional and will be repeated in other chapters for when books concentrate on leadership, they fail to interrogate the associated concepts that can illuminate its theory and practice. Consequently, in order to avoid this, it is necessary to give more attention to these concepts and only return to leadership once an exploration leaves us with sufficient analytical resources to expose the opacity as a means of rendering leadership intelligible.

My concern has not been to eradicate, but simply to encourage an interrogation of, identity for clearly it is an irremovable part of human interaction and social life even though it is often troublesome if not debilitating. These troubles primarily revolve around our self-obsessive attachment to particular identities that then preoccupy our time and energy in the illusory belief that we can secure, solidify and stabilise them and the world in which they reside. By treating identity as little more than a resource for security in everyday life, we forget that it is routinely dependent on unpredictable and often impetuous 'others' for confirmation of its claim to validity. I am therefore also not questioning how it is a central aspect of any theory or practice of leadership but what is at stake is the failure to challenge or interrogate the way in which individuals are subjectively attached to their identities. For these attachments often reproduce a narcissism with devastating consequences for organisations, their leaders and those they seek to lead, as well as for social relations in general. I agree with Foucault that 'self-attachment is the first sign of madness', where error is accepted 'as truth, lies as reality, violence and ugliness as beauty and justice'.[89] Nonetheless, this attachment to self or identity is something that many, if not all of us, share and certainly is vividly present and prevalent within discourses and practices of leadership.

Within the chapter, I also analysed anxiety and insecurity as a medium and outcome of the preoccupation with identity. Also, because the notion of authenticity relies on a conception of identity and is a very popular development in leadership studies, I devoted the final section to its analysis. Overall, I concluded that it lacks credibility in ignoring the existential roots of authenticity and in its psychoanalytic versions, uncritically subscribing to enlightenment, humanist legacies of autonomy and emancipation. While equally as neglected as identity itself, anxiety and insecurity are only of concern in leadership studies insofar ways of eradicating them can be found since they are seen to render leaders diminished or incapacitated. Identity, anxiety and insecurity are central to much of the analysis in the following chapters and especially the empirical studies in Part III of the book. For anxiety and insecurity are very often unconscious drivers of human behaviour including the pursuit of power, privilege, recognition, status, and wealth and in almost all societies a legitimate way of attaining these is through leadership. Consequently, every chapter in this book refer at least implicitly if not explicitly to identity, anxiety and insecurity as fundamental to organisational life and how leaders emerge, exercise their leadership, develop and often are displaced.

Notes

1 Grint (2000).
2 Collinson (2006, 2014), Collinson and Tourish (2015), Ford (2006, 2010), Lührmann and Eberl (2007), Ford et al. (2008), Crawford (2009), Sinclair (2011), Eubanks, Brown and Ybema (2012).
3 Mead (1934, p.178).
4 Foucault (2000)
5 Butler (1997, p. 2).
6 Knights and Clarke (2017).
7 https://www.mentalhealthfirstaid.org/2019/02/5-surprising-mental-health-statistics/;   https://www.mind.org.uk/information-support/types-of-mental-health-problems/statistics-and-facts-about-mental-health/how-common-are-mental-health-problems/
8 This may, of course, have been a strategy because, on several occasions, the psychiatrist insisted that I pull myself together since I had a nice wife, house and a good job! My eventual escape from the condition was an unwise choice to go 'cold turkey' on the drugs prescribed to me which, at least, gave me first-hand experience of the pain and suffering of drug addicts.
9 Clarke and Knights (2020) having consulted ABI/Inform indexes.
10 Brown (2015, p. 1).
11 Brown (2015, p. 22).
12 Brown (2015), Knights and Clarke (2015).
13 Brown (2015, p. 23).
14 Willer (1967).
15 Foucault (1990).
16 Brown (2015, p. 22).
17 Gerson (2004, pp. 310–311).
18 Diprose (1994, 2002), Ziarek (2001), Pullen and Rhodes (2013).
19 Ziarek (2001, p. 74).
20 E.g. Beech et al. (2102), Ybema et al. (2009), Gill (2015), Hoyer and Steyaert (2015).
21 Ybema et al. (2009, p. 301).
22 Geary (2012, p. 19–32).
23 Ibid., p. 20.
24 Ibid., p. 32.
25 Hegel (1807).
26 Williams (2000, p. 2, my emphasis).
27 Mead (1934); This brief exposition of symbolic interactionism reflects, but develops arguments made in Knights and Willmott (1999/2004).
28 Skinner (1953, 1971).
29 Blumer (1969, p. 14).
30 Knights and Kerfoot (2004).
31 Knights and Clarke (2017, p. 341).
32 Ibid., p. 344.
33 In a search through OUP in 2020, there were 17,952 articles and 45 books with some focus on identity work.
34 Elias (1978).
35 Grey (1994), Clarke and Knights (2015).
36 Knights and Clarke (2014), Costea, Amiridis and Crump (2012), Bauman (2008), Sennett and Cobb (1977).
37 Brown (2015).

38 Sartre (1938), Becker (1969, 1973).
39 Knights and Clarke (2015).
40 Snow and Anderson (1987, p. 1348).
41 Brown (2018, p. 4).
42 Clarke and Knights (2020, p. xxx).
43 Pullen and Rhodes (2008, p. 7).
44 Costea et al. (2012).
45 Lasch (1979, p. 102).
46 Costea et al. (2012).
47 Young (1958), Sennett and Cobb (1977).
48 Pilgrim (2017).
49 Newton (1995).
50 Clarke and Knights (2019, p. 273).
51 2017.
52 E.g. Ford (2006) and Ford et al. (2008).
53 Collinson (2005, p. 1428).
54 This is also the case in Knights and Willmott's (1992) empirical study of leadership although they had previously explored some of the ontological and social conditions of identity precariousness in earlier work (see Note below).
55 Collinson (2003), Knights and Willmott (1985, 1989, 1999/2004).
56 Knights and Clarke (2017).
57 Sinclair (2007, p. 7).
58 Mayo (1933, p. 120).
59 Kunda (1991, pp. 219–220).
60 Ibid.
61 Camus (1956, p. 40).
62 Burns (1978), Zaleznik (1989).
63 Gabriel (2011, p. 397).
64 Kohut (1971, 1976).
65 Gabriel (2011, p. 398).
66 Ibid., p. 402.
67 Lacan (1980), Laing (1990).
68 Clarke and Knights (2018).
69 Schwartz (1987, p. 332).
70 Barad (2007).
71 Grosz (1994), Braidotti (2011).
72 Cunliffe and Ford (2012).
73 Ford and Harding (2004), Ford (2006).
74 Egotism is a negative term that combines extreme self-preoccupation or conceit with a tendency to seek attention, and one of the primary characteristics of narcissists is their exaggerated sense of entitlement (see https://quantumbuddha.wordpress.com/2009/01/20/what's-wrong-with-politics-part-2-egoism-and-egotism/ and https://www.psychologytoday.com/gb/blog/evolution-the-self/201112/narcissism-why-its-so-rampant-in-politics).
75 Identity is mentioned in the Introduction but only in terms of being shaped by leadership. Bolden, Witzel and Linacre (2016, pp. 40–42).
76 Adarves-Yorno (2016, p. 125).
77 Henderson and Hoy (1983).
78 Gardner, Cogliser, Davis and Dickens (2011, p. 1123).
79 Alvesson and Einola (2019, p. 389).
80 Bhindi and Duignan (1997).

81 Kernis and Goldman (2006, quoted in Gardner et al. 2011).
82 Besides his treatment of these philosophically in Sartre (1956), they heavily informed all his novels from *Nausea* (1938) to his trilogy *The Roads to Freedom*, which included *The Age of Reason* (1947), *The Reprieve* (1949) and *Iron in the Soul* (1949).
83 Avolio and Gardner (2005, p. 334).
84 Avolio, Gardner, Walumbwa, Luthans and May (2004, pp. 803–804).
85 Trungpa (1973).
86 Gabriel (1997).
87 Costas and Taheri, (2012, p. 1209).
88 Ibid., p. 1211.
89 Foucault (2001[1961], p. 23).

4   Power/Resistance

It will come as no surprise for me to argue in this chapter that power and resistance are neglected in mainstream leadership studies[1] as are 'power processes and the politics of meaning'.[2] However, whereas resistance is conspicuous by its absence largely because the literature is predominantly concerned to *promote* the idea of leadership in a positive light, it is impossible to avoid speaking about power since it is necessarily exercised wherever leadership is practised. Still, the literature prefers to understate the sense in which power is integral to leadership and often uses the term influence as a seemingly less abrasive concept. This forms part of the literature's concern to distinguish leadership as a gentler persuasive mode of transforming their employees through energising them to perform in a committed and directed manner in contrast with management that more autocratically allocates tasks and expects them to be fulfilled. Thus, leadership is concerned with moving 'hearts and minds' towards a 'collective/communal sense of purpose',[3] so that resistance is displaced or deemed to be churlish.

There has always been resistance to leadership; otherwise, we would not have seen so many theorists encouraging participation to counteract the failure of authoritative or autocratic approaches to have their intended productive effects. In effect then, and despite their clear relevance to the study of leadership, power and resistance are rarely interrogated in the literature. Once again, to repeat what may seem like a mantra in this book, this is because of a common sense understanding of power as a property of individuals and, following the adage that 'a man's [sic] home is his castle', it seems to be treated as sacrosanct, and beyond the bounds of critical analysis. If power is not to be questioned, then resistance seems like an oxymoron—something never to be expected. Yet even when resistance is considered, it is often seen in zero-sum terms of being the opposite of, rather than in a relationship with, power.[4]

The chapter is organised as follows. Before discussing the paucity and limitations of the literature on power and resistance within leadership studies, I provide a limited review of discussions within the social sciences.

I then turn to leadership where apart from the recently developed critical leadership studies, discussions of power remain within a traditional framework of treating it as an object that can readily be measured but rarely understood and resistance is given little attention. This is followed by an examination of the critical literature that I argue still has a tendency to slide into proprietary conceptions of power and the understanding of its relationship to resistance in dialectical terms where resistance is always a struggle against power.

Power at Last!

Over a lifetime of teaching in business schools, I never fail to be amazed by how single-minded students are about pursuing a degree as a passport to career success, power and financial wealth. Given that life in contemporary society, whether in the home, in school, in the media or at work, seems in every way directed towards the individual achievement of power and status through career success, income and wealth, this is unsurprising. However, while not denouncing such tunnel-vision, it is possible to engage students in examining these values critically by deconstructing what is taken-for-granted, not least in asking them to reflect upon what they mean. Leadership is not a bad place to start for most students perceive of it is as a vehicle for advancing their cherished ambitions. Unfortunately, in most courses where this subject is on their curriculum, they are more likely to have their common sense reinforced rather than challenged. However, on the way they may develop some scepticism as to how numerous (although not exhaustive) lists of personality traits, behavioural skills and styles are meaningful ways of studying leadership.

It is noticeable how very few of the concepts (including power) that I have identified as important to the study of leadership are present in these lists. Indirectly, of course, the styles can be seen as aspects of power, but within the literature, power is the elephant in the room rather than interrogated as fundamental to any analysis of leadership.

Table 4.1 Typical Lists Characterising Leadership

Leadership Traits	Skills	Styles
Confidence	Adaptability	Autocratic/Authoritarian
Extraversion	Awareness	Charismatic
Honesty/Integrity	Communication	Democratic/Participative
Optimism	Decisive	Innovative
Tact	Empathy	Laissez-faire
Vision	Pedagogic	Paternalistic

What is Power? Luke's 3-dimensional Model

While it can be argued that theories of power have traditionally derived from political science, the most famous of which was written by the US academic Dahl,[5] the more comprehensive and analytically advanced analysis came from the British political sociologist, Steven Lukes[6] who found that the existing conceptualisations involving A's effect on B were too broad and non-specific. He argued that it was necessary to distinguish the overt from more subtle forms of power and to acknowledge the real or felt interests of the recipient. He conceptualised power relations in terms of three dimensions as follows:

1. Power to secure a decision in situations where there is some observable conflict of views;
2. Power to keep issues about which there are conflicting views on or off the decision-making agenda;
3. Institutionalised power to define reality in such a way as to ensure compliance because of the internalisation of norms even against people's so-called real interests.

The first dimension relates to the behaviour of individuals or groups that determine, or at least influence, the form and content of a decision or decisions. An example would be the Brexit campaign's Bus message[7] that claimed how, in leaving the EU, the UK would free up £350 m each week for the National HealthService. While a hugely exaggerated claim, and one that would never have been delivered but for the COVID-19 crisis, this exercise of power did have a considerable impact on the outcome of the Referendum in 2016.

The second dimension of power concerns highly controversial issues that are simply hidden from view by being left off the agenda. Here, where there is no, or limited, discussion of parts of the information that could enable a reasoned choice, then the power of certain groups is enhanced. Staying with the Brexit example, details of the complexities of the UK leaving the EU after 25 years were limited partly because they were either unknown or it was felt they would only confuse the electorate. However, after 3 years of failing to exit the EU, those in favour of a second referendum were convinced that if voters had known more about the problems, they would have voted differently.

Lukes's third and final dimension concerns how people in positions of power may so define reality as to secure a consensus and, by so doing, exclude controversial issues from the political agenda that might otherwise benefit the most disadvantaged. He contends that the 'real interests' and potential grievances of those subjected to power are obscured or distorted by powerful individuals and groups who can focus their minds on maintaining the prevailing structure of power relations. This third dimension of power is readily applied to many political events but one, in particular, stands out, for when the US and Britain went to war in Iraq in 2003, it was claimed that Saddam Hussein possessed weapons of mass destruction. After the war, however, these were never found. Consequently, despite flimsy evidence, President George Bush and Prime Minister Tony Blair defined the reality sufficiently convincingly to generate a majority public consensus in favour of war.

By focusing on the way that power is often exercised beyond specific points of conflict, Lukes' theory usefully draws attention to institutionalised relations. Here, behind-the-scenes, decisions are often made to exclude consideration of certain issues that may have a negative bearing on people who are already disadvantaged. Yet clearly, the first two observable and unobservable dimensions of power remain proprietary in that one or a group of persons possess the power to determine a decision or to deny it a platform. The third dimension is less immediately proprietary since it focuses on the institutionalised practices that are not directly related to the decision-making of individuals and groups about particular issues or their ways of excluding them from consideration. However, Lukes sees the norms that people internalise as having been defined as reality by those who have the power to control meaning. As a result, others are rendered powerless as they are not even able to recognise, let alone express, their own 'real interests'. This is not only proprietary but also a class-based conception of power where it is polarised between those who possess it and those who do not. Besides, it seems to assume that 'real interests' exist independently of relations of power and can be identified a priori. At best, this involves imposing interests on subjects in terms of class or some other category and at worst, a slide into essentialist notions of interests preceding one's entry into some form of sociality, as if an aspect of human nature. It fails to recognise how, while deeply entrenched, our interests are constituted through power relations.

Consequently, he does subscribe to a proprietary conception where power is presumed to be the property of persons grounded in class inequalities in which there is a polarization of those who possess power and those who do not. Class privilege then allows the powerful to define reality in such a way as to control meaning for others, especially those with little experience of middle-class cultural norms, dress and manners. As Amol Rajan argued, in a UK TV documentary about class barriers surrounding recruitment, qualifications are not enough as recruiters will discriminate against those who don't 'fit in', are deemed to lack 'polish' and confidence or have uncultivated or 'posh' accents, since employers still frequently conflate class and cleverness.[8] In research conducted on recruitment, it was also found that despite equal opportunity legislation since the 1970s, employers discriminate against women by adopting masculine norms that override any formal meritocratic requirements.[9]

In effect, but almost subconsciously, Lukes would argue that the 'real interests' of disadvantaged people are neglected by interpretations of merit being contaminated by class or gender norms that are hidden from view. Moreover, this institutionalisation of power whereby able-bodied, age, class, gender or racial norms, for example, effectively determine recruitment outcomes is frequently internalised as personal inadequacy on the part of its discriminated victims precisely because they have internalised the values of competition, meritocracy, individual talent and the success ethic that are the visible accompaniments to the procedures. Consequently, self-blame renders them powerless as, in Lukes's view, they are no longer capable of recognising, let alone expressing their own 'real interests'.

Unfortunately, Lukes's analysis is a little one-sided in focusing on the manipulations of the powerful because it neglects to consider how they might also be victims as well as perpetrators of their practices. It is, of course, a little difficult in a society that elevates the pursuit of material and symbolic success in the form of career, celebrity, fame, status and wealth to see these people suffering from their preoccupations with individual success and personal conquest, and clearly, this is relative since they do not experience hardship. However, in not questioning the benefits of their positions of power, Lukes simply reflects and reinforces a privileging of the very material and symbolic values that underlie the inequalities and discriminations of which he is critical. Also, he never thinks to ask whether the trappings of power offer their recipients a wholly positive experience rather than one that drives them to a life that can be full of despair because of its never-ending, competitive pressure to perform and succeed. Moreover, as it has been argued by those discussing the relevance of leadership to science fiction such as The Terminator films, leaders 'are powerful and powerless at the same time'.[10]

There are, also, some theoretical problems with the analysis because Lukes assumes a priori knowledge of the real, objective interests of particular individuals, groups or classes in society and, more importantly, that these exist before, or independently of, power relations. This has to be questioned for, following Foucault,[11] 'interests' are more a product or outcome of the exercise of power than its condition or underlying source. Foucault begins from the other side of this duality in recognising that as power is exercised, subjects along with their interests are constituted. Consequently, 'interests' can only be identified through the power relations that advance, yet simultaneously, conceal them. Because humans lack the biological self-survival instinct of other sentient species, even the latter is learned through parents exercising power over their children not to go too near to a fire, for example. If there can be no 'purity' free of power relations, Lukes' attribution of 'real' interests that were somehow lurking behind 'false' interests (or false consciousness) is fundamentally misplaced.

Lukes's reference to 'real interests' is little more than a discursive claim to privilege, individual autonomy and the self-interest that it reflects and reproduces. Lukes is a radical humanist who subscribes to a theory of human nature that treats the self as essentially autonomous and, therefore, potentially undermined or constrained by the forces of power. His identification of the three dimensions of power can be interpreted as a hierarchy of intensification of threats to this human autonomy, the most potent and insidious one of which is the third dimension. I agree with Lukes that power cannot be adequately conceptualised in terms of the first and second dimensions alone. However, the theory is fundamentally flawed by his radical humanist assumptions concerning power as a property of persons, autonomy and self-interest as preceding power, and identification of 'real' interests that can be reclaimed through challenging power.

In so far as Lukes's three-dimensional theory of power has been widely adopted, I have laboured over its content as well as its limitations but have provided no analysis of resistance. This also has a voluminous literature, but largely outside of the discourse on leadership since here it is neglected even more than the topic of power. It would be interesting to contemplate this neglect as linked to Foucault's[12] refusal to discuss resistance for fear of ideas about it being co-opted by power in ways that serve only to limit its disruptive effects, but this is not the case. I am dependent, therefore, on the more general literature within organisational and workplace studies to which I now turn to provide a brief history.

Resisting Leaders and Managers

Much of the earlier literature on resistance emerged from industrial relations and workplace sociology within the post-second world war period when there were endless discussions of labour conflicts and disputes surrounding management decision-making. In broad terms, research tended to subscribe either to a Marxist celebration of industrial conflict[13] or to a pluralist strategy of managing resistance through channelling it towards collectively bargained agreements, negotiated by trades unions as a means of sustaining social order.[14] It can readily be concluded that by the early part of the 21st century, the neo-liberal consensus had prevailed but not without the assistance of some fairly repressive legal constraints on labour and its trade union power base. The explanation for the collapse of struggles against the established order is too complex to provide a full account of here, but one major factor was that, despite fears of Bolshevik kinds of communist uprisings, *only* a minority of the labouring classes had concerns for the politics of socialist revolution or even socialism through democratic means.

Evidence for this is clear from the recent rise of populist governments of the right elected in the US and the UK and considerable support for the right of centre politics in Europe. The majority of Western populations sought simply to improve their economic situation largely through means legitimately supported by the existing state institutions. Labour process theorists, on the other hand, proceeded to develop theoretical and empirical studies of the workplace and employee relations but, as time proceeded, became more and more academic as they sought sophisticated explanations of the historical development of capitalism. Partly for this reason but also to distinguish themselves from a fast-developing interest in philosophically-informed post-structural analyses, they turned to a new neo-Marxist inspired critical realism.

Not least, these developments derived from their objection to a growing Foucauldian analysis of power and resistance that modified the traditional labour process view of class conflict. For Foucault, power was not exclusively negative and repressive but also positive and productive, particularly in its constitution of subjectivity or identity. Labour process theorists objected to any theory that diluted the Marxist historicist belief in a future revolution resulting from an intensified polarization of class interests and their conflicts. Consequently, they saw the introduction of Foucault into the debate as generating a diversion from the orthodoxy and therefore the clear symptom of a crisis on the left.[15] Concerning the analysis of the labour process, much of the value or otherwise of Foucault's work would appear to hinge on what one is to make of his account (or non-account) of resistance.[16] Foucault saw resistance as inseparable from, rather than denied by, power and certainly not its nemesis.

Power in Leadership Studies

While, as already indicated, students of leadership have tended to neglect any analysis of power and resistance, believing that leaders have legitimate power in the form of authority, making resistance unnecessary. From this perspective, resistance is only engaged in by a minority of troublemakers who are deemed 'abnormal or irrational'.[17] Part of this neglect could be attributed to the declaration by one of the most prominent figures in the field claiming that exercising power has nothing to do with leadership.[18] However, power is exercised by leaders in a variety of ways through, for example, the system of rewards and penalties, the hierarchical ordering of relations, recruitment and promotion, the allocation of tasks and responsibilities, creating and sustaining particular cultural values and norms, but also by defining situations in ways that are disproportionately beneficial to the advantaged.[19] Within the leadership literature, there is a paucity of studies examining these forms of exercising power. An exception is the literature on charisma, where there are critiques of how followers idealise, fantasise about, and can be seduced by leaders who are often damaging if not toxic in their effects on working relationships.[20] Throughout I provide numerous examples of these and particularly in Chapter 7 on ethics and in the final chapter where I discuss the response of populist, white masculine leaders to the Coronavirus pandemic.

Another form of power is manifest in what Collinson describes as Prozac[21] leadership where there are excessively optimistic, or even fake, claims about the conditions of a particular organisation, institution or society more generally and leaders use positive thinking as a way of 'enacting power, influence and identity'.[22] While there have been numerous examples of this in corporations that eventually were revealed to be unethical[23] and these are examined in Chapter 8, but this is also evident in politics, particularly among populist leaders such as Berlusconi, Bolsonaro, Johnson, Orbán and Trump and some of these are discussed in the final chapter, where I also provide a full definition of populism. Whatever is happening, such leaders put a positive spin on it to please their followers and over recent years we have seen how extremely risky this has been in the case of corporate scandals, the global financial crisis and the Coronavirus pandemic, but more of this later.

Within research, positive leanings are particularly evident in charismatic approaches to leadership, where it is claimed that the leader's positive enthusiasm and dynamism spread throughout an organisation resulting in deeper levels of commitment and performativity. A similarly positive attitude characterises authentic leadership, already discussed in Chapter 3, that alleges a deep self-awareness and reflexivity on the part of leaders who then inspire their followers through confident and optimistic visions designed to secure the trust and commitments of followers.[24] Both of these approaches have their critics, some accusing them of elevating positive thinking to spiritual or religious levels whereupon it can become oppressive or tyrannical,[25] and indeed the supporters of charismatic leadership have taken it in this direction in their promotion of emotional intelligence and spirituality in discourses of leadership.[26] They have a history to draw upon, especially in the US, of evangelical leaders such as Billy Graham that, through rhetorical skills, inspired mass populations searching for meaning but worryingly reminiscent of earlier demagogues.

A recent critique of charismatic and authentic leadership, as well as other theories that draw on positive conceptions of human life, has suggested that they lack rigour, are theoretically and empirically weak and are uncritical.[27] This critique goes on to argue that insofar as the concept of an authentic self is internal and unobservable, it cannot be studied empirically, and there is rarely much discussion of leadership perhaps because being true to the essential self is hardly compatible with the practical problems of mobilising others to get things done. Overall, 'the intellectual foundations they stand on are too shaky to warrant the popularity they have inspired within the scientific community'.[28] There is then a fundamental contradiction in the very idea of authentic leadership in that it is ultimately instrumental insofar as it can only be justified if it is seen 'to contribute to sustained performance',[29] whereas the only legitimate guide is one's deep self-reflection. Pursuing this line of thought, it is argued that genuine authenticity can have nothing to do with leadership. For leaders are expected to persuade others to follow a particular course of action, but if this involves simply enhancing organisational effectiveness, it becomes instrumental which contradicts any sense of authenticity.

Even if we disregard these internal incompatibilities and accept a managerial viewpoint, there are still contradictions since seeking an authentic self through self-knowledge and reflexivity may well generate too rigid a self-concept that is an obstacle to leadership where flexibility or 'playfulness' and 'openness' to a range of 'possibilities' is required.[30] She recognises that change or promotion move us out of 'our comfort zones' ... [whilst triggering] ... 'a strong countervailing impulse to protect our identities'.[31] However, there is no interrogation of identity or challenging what we have become through so many exercises of power even if these are self-inflicted in the false belief that it is possible to find the 'true', essential or authentic self through enacting power upon the self. This was attempted in Chapter 3, so I will not repeat the exercise here, other than to say that reflections on the self, although not to discover some essential or real self, maybe a crucial way in which to transform leadership into an aesthetic and ethical practice. It is also fundamental to resistance in leadership studies to which I now turn.

Resistance in Leadership Studies

Within the mainstream, there are few leadership studies of resistance. Therefore, it is necessary to look elsewhere, although, as we have seen in Chapter 2, critical leadership studies attempt to fill the vacuum. Outside of leadership studies, however, there is a wealth of material stemming back to the early industrial relations research on workplace conflict, industrial disputes and collective bargaining where strikes, working to rule, picketing and boycotts have prevailed as weapons of negotiation.[32] Later research revealed how resistance at work takes many diverse forms that cannot be reduced to the utilitarian calculation or the logic of economic instrumentalism that is represented by negotiations about conditions/wage–effort ratios as is reflected in both traditional industrial relations and labour process theory, both orthodox and neo-orthodox.

Beyond these perspectives, research on resistance that stands outside the formal institutions has taken a variety of forms. Roy, for example, studied how workers played numerous pranks, the most memorable of which was a routinely repeated theft of bananas out of one of their workmate's lunchboxes that thereby created amusing banter.[33] These rituals were understood only as indirect resistances to the subordination of shopfloor garment work in the sense that they were simply one way of relieving the boredom of the routines of their labour. In this case, the workers were so isolated from leaders that their resistance probably helped sustain the existing relations of power and subordination by channelling frustrations into 'harmless' fun, as was also the case in ac-counts of 'game-playing' on the shopfloor involving maximising bonuses in piece-rate work through what was described as 'making out'.[34] Although seeming like resistance to the official rules, this absorption in the game deflected workers from any direct resistance to their control and indeed by default played into the hands of leaders and managers in facilitating higher levels of productivity as a result of competing for bonuses.

What is significant in this study as in other research[35] is how resistance and consent are not necessarily discrete phenomena but often mutually embedded in workplace relations.[36] So, for example, resistance often takes the form of ridicule and humour such as 'taking the piss'[37] whereby in seeking to secure their masculine identities, shopfloor workers con-trast themselves with the 'effete' and effeminate human resource man-agers and others (e.g. the researcher) who are not involved in hard physical labour. They felt that human resource managers just delivered platitudes, including what they described as the US managing director's 'bullshit from Barney'.[38] However, there is a rationale in this ridicule or 'resistance through distance' in that they enjoy 'pulling the wool over the eyes' of leaders, for example, in ensuring that rates for a task are fixed at well below their capability always to have a 'bank' of output in reserve.[39]

This practice stretches back as far as the Hawthorne experi-ments[40] and many studies have given further examples of employees manipulating situations by withholding information from their leaders. The exact opposite strategy also occurs where, for example, a woman seeking promotion extracted as much information as possible from her leaders to build an effective discriminatory case against them, which the author described as 'resistance through persistence'.[41] Returning to the sub-culture of a masculine sense of toughness, it is interesting that when it counted to resist in a situation of redundancy, these self-same shop-floor workers found the 'hard' technical and mathematical financial accounts of the business plausible in a way that was not the case with those 'feminine' HR managers. They saw financial facts as grounded in the same way as physical labour, thus leaving the shop floor with no basis to resist their devastating impact on continued employment. Often then resistance in the form of humour may be enjoyable but only limitedly effective in challenging the power that subordinates shopfloor workers.

This would also often be the case for various kinds of resistance such as factory deviance or industrial sabotage[42] escape attempts,[43] fiddling,[44] organisational misbehaviour[45] and general treatment of the organisation like a cultural 'playground' in which joking rituals, 'ironic repartee', 'wilful rule-breaking' and other 'acts of rebellion' are prolific.[46] As with all rebellious behaviour, the outcome rarely extends beyond strategic replacements of personnel in what is no more than a circulation of elites. In this and other senses, while causing temporary disruptions, resistance simply facilitates the status quo within organisations. For as many have argued, without the imaginative breaches of conventions, norms and rules organisations would ossify.[47]

Although escaping from the tedium of the daily drudgery of routinised labour through fun may be a convenient distraction, it is far from a challenge to existing power relations. Nor is the cynical distancing that stems from workers feeling as though they are imprisoned in the corporation likely to stimulate change. While neglecting opportunities for playful and disruptive subversion of deviant activities, a third more optimistic alternative is explored of seeing work as more like the site of a parliament where there is a continuous cacophony of views and interests struggling for attention. Resistance then takes the form of a struggle or refusal to be drowned in a sea of conflicting voices.[48] Of course, our institutions and corporations have seen the potential in taking democracy to the people rather than monopolising it in a centralised body of governmental practice. Consequently, there is a continual encouragement, and even demand, to participate in all institutions in what might be seen as a pseudo-democracy that pervades every aspect of our lives. The media of websites, newspapers, magazines, radio and television bombard us with imperatives to be involved whether through letters, phone calls, emails, Facebook, Instagram, twitters or Internet sites in giving voice to our anxieties, opinions, experiences and votes. In the world of entertainment, the point has been reached at which programme production has become dependent on audience participation, which becomes the principal reason for their popularity and longevity. While the most extreme examples of these are Reality TV such as Big Brother, Dating Around and Love Island, TV talent shows such as X-Factor and Strictly Come Dancing, and hardly a single show, including even news programmes, is produced in the absence of consumers as an essential ingredient of the production process.

In the broader field of production and distribution, customer participation has been growing at an intense rate assisted by new technology that enables and imposes increasing levels of self-service in retail stores, online and especially through computer devices such as mobile phones and laptops. As unpaid functionaries, consumers become profit-making enterprises or sources of cost reduction for both private and public sector organisations. This is one part of a growing development whereby the laudatory symbols of democracy and participation are deployed as a means of transforming the whole population into collaborators in the expansion and intensification of labouring processes that sustain and advance corporate enterprise. But it does not stop there because employees are also pushed into engaging more and more as wholly embodied beings in the enterprise economy or enabling capitalism to draw upon bio-social resources beyond itself for its reproduction.[49] While leaders are clearly in the back office either at the point of retail or in the technology and media monoliths that enable these self-imposed yet nuanced controls to flourish, they are comparatively invisible and, therefore, difficult if not impossible to resist. In Chapter 9, I will focus on how not dissimilar processes are at work in academia whereby resistance to performative pressures from leaders would seem churlish and self-defeating because it contradicts the very cultural values of effective teaching, research and publishing that are the moral fibre of university life.

I turn now to an examination of Foucault's limited discussion of resistance which is somewhat different from CLS that tends to treat power and resistance, control and consent and other dualisms as a dialectical relation of interdependence[50] but, in not examining the rationale and mechanism of the theory, find it perfectly compatible with Foucault. Both of these have their origin in Hegel, as already discussed in Chapter 3, with the rationale behind dialectics reflecting a historicist belief in progress towards an ideal world. The mechanism revolves around the notions of a thesis, antithesis and synthesis in which conflicting, oppositional and polarised entities struggle to produce some synthetic compromise that may, of course, continue through numerous cycles before reaching the ultimate ideal, which for Hegel was the Prussian state of his day but for Marx, would have to await the collapse of capitalism through revolutionary socialism. Foucault rejected these kinds of 'grand narrative' and their universal claims and, in this sense, was unsympathetic to dialectics. This was also why he routinely refused to articulate his ideas on resistance because both in theory and practice, it is so readily co-opted by power and thereby emasculated.

Foucault

'there is no first or final point of resistance to political power other than the relationship one has to oneself'.[51]

The reluctant acknowledgement of the importance of subjectivity in theorising the labour process in neo-orthodoxy analysis combined with Fleming and Spicer's[52] idea that we focus on the struggle as the interface between resistance and power leads us to the later Foucault.[53] While understanding that capital is dependent on the consent and creative potential of labour, the neo-orthodoxy does not embrace this knowledge of the freedom of subjects to engage or disengage as a productive potential in resistance as well as in consent. The notion of struggle captures this but not fully in the sense that it is left under-explored in Fleming and Spicer.[54] The remainder of this chapter, therefore, seeks to fill this lacuna in the literature on resistance.

First, it should be acknowledged that this notion of struggle in which binaries between power and resistance are eschewed[55] emanates from Foucault's challenge to the neo-Marxist tradition of treating power as negative, coercive or repressive action upon subordinates and as the property of persons, groups and the state.[56] Because it demands the free cooperation, compliance or consent of those on whom it is exercised, power involves positive and productive as well as negative and coercive relations, and its capillary-like distribution means that it is rarely exhaustive of the space from which resistance emerges. Yet neither relations of power nor resistance are free of tensions and inconsistencies, not least because of how, in practice, they remain ambiguous and unpredictable slipping and sliding inside and outside of one another, and only the glimpse of a temporary solace within the transience of transition.

Several authors claiming to subscribe to a Foucauldian analysis speak about the micro-politics of resistance[57] but there are problems with this description. It would seem to have been hi-jacked from Foucault's objection to 'grand narrative' accounts that are more about exercising power than describing events and his consequent argument that all we can ever study or observe are localised situations of struggle where, for example, subjugated knowledge are deployed to challenge prevailing norms and power relations.[58] This is not to say that the 'global' is not already present in local events, but we cannot develop discourses of it independently from such events. Foucault refrained from using the notion of micro versus macro analysis as this establishes a false dualism, as it does in economics.

At first sight, the distinction between local and global might be seen simply to reproduce the dualism, albeit with different terms. However, this change in terminology breaks any association with dualistic thinking for global issues are always embedded in and affected by local events. Nonetheless, for Foucault who is more concerned with *being* non-dualistic rather than speaking about it,[59] given its grounding in struggles and resistance from situations of subjugation, this usage is a methodological rather than an epistemological prescription. So, for example, a local workplace struggle against the subjugated effects of sex discriminatory practices such as the example of 'resistance through persistence' described earlier, reflects global issues concerning universal human rights. But also, the global feminist movement generally informs this local struggle which, in its turn, contributes to claims regarding a more universal global campaign.

However, what is even more distinctive about Foucault's analysis is his argument that both the first and final point of the struggle against subjugation is the relationship with oneself or what one can say is the grand refusal to be what one has become through so many procedures, regulations and exercises of power.[60] This is ultimately the courage of truth as hyper and pessimistic activism involving a permanent critique of society through speaking the truth despite its risks whether merely to a person's career or to one's actual life.[61]

As CLS has argued, labour struggles can 'simultaneously resist and reproduce'[62] the power-knowledge relations that subjugate those in subordinate relations. Take again the example referred to earlier of 'resistance as persistence' where a woman challenged management's decision not to promote her through asserting her 'rights' for information and due process. Part of the reason for the decision was the gender insensitivity of masculine discourses within which management was steeped yet the successful challenge to the discrimination was made possible only by mobilising precisely such aspects of masculinity as assertiveness, aggressive determination and single-mindedness, linear rationality and restrained emotion. This is not to argue that these 'tough' aspects of behaviour are the prerogative of men for that would be to reinforce a masculine-feminine binary and, as has been argued, while it may not be clear exactly what is or are masculinity(ies), it cannot be seen merely to 'reduce down to the male body and its effects'.[63] However, it can be seen here that in challenging masculine decision-making, their (in) sensibilities are reproduced, as also is the case when women's (and minorities) concern with equal opportunity has the effect of reinforcing and intensifying the individualistic, competitive and masculine norms of business.[64] In short, when resistance seeks to challenge masculine domination and existing distributions of scarce resources, it often has the effect of reproducing the very values that it might otherwise seek to disrupt—namely, instrumental masculine and economic discourses through which power is exercised.

Because of this paradox, some critics have sought to redirect the focus of reflecting on resistance away from economic matters to those of ethics and embodied relations at work.[65] They have drawn on philosophical and posthumanist feminist ethics to draw attention to the absence of embodied relations in many management and organisational regimes. These are at least partly a function of the hyper-masculine ethos whereby disembodied linear rationality and aggressive instrumentalism combined with homosocial male bonding and often-homophobic sensibilities dominate relations and serve to advance and protect economic and political privilege.[66] Resistance to the relatively closed circle of masculine elitism that sustains the taken for granted privileges of leaders and managers is difficult and, as we have suggested, often ends up emulating precisely the masculine norms that it ostensibly denigrates. An alternative form of resistance could evolve from employees desire for 'an ethical engagement in the socio-political context of organisations'.[67]

Here we might see some questioning of the masculine disembodiment that sustains homosocial elitism and its preoccupation with competition for material and symbolic advantage. For these provide an impenetrable screen that removes subjects from the raw and unmediated embodied differences of the face-to-face relationships and allow for the displacement of any sense of an ethics of responsibility to the Other.[68] While eschewing intimacy and embodiment in social relations is not in itself instrumental, it has the effect of protecting individuals from even recognising let alone confronting the moral consequences of their actions. In particular, it leaves leaders cocooned in their self-contained sense of superiority and separation from those who do not, and by definition cannot, enjoy their material and symbolic privileges. The Enlightenment and its promotion of the rights of the autonomous self, combined with ideologies of equal opportunity, simply provides the rationale for a sense of self-satisfaction and justification for their advantages. In this sense, the Enlightenment reinforces individualistic responsibilities to the self in advance of any responsibility to the Other. When this preoccupation with the self is pre-eminent, morality is reduced to an exercise of power where the image of what it is to be ethical transcends any sense of responsibility. Of course, discourses and practices of corporate social responsibility and the domination of rule-based systems encourage this reduction of ethics to its mere appearance and image or minimal levels of compliance. Discrepancies will almost always occur between ethical being and its appearance in imagery, especially when ethics is reduced to mere compliance with rules. It is necessary once again to repeat the argument that obeying rules is not in itself an ethical act since the latter demands a moral dilemma or what is described as a situation of undecidability.[69] Compliance is essentially an instrumental act designed to avoid the shame or punishment that might result from a breach of rules and, in this sense, very far removed from ethics. It is only because of prevailing disembodied relations that compliance with rules can kindle claims to moral integrity and probity, as frequently occurs when corporate executives and politicians are caught up in national and international scandals.

While this is not resistance in the conventional sense, the appeal to ethical sensibilities has the potential to challenge and disrupt a whole range of oppressions. However, these seem to be readily deflected when corporate or political power subscribes to enlightenment values of human rights and respect for diversity. This is because, paradoxically, these values simultaneously reinforce both individualism and homogeneity. The individual has rights insofar as they do not undermine social order and stability. Levels of difference are acceptable, however, only as long as they can be managed through programmes that organise or eliminate the heterogeneity through its reduction to manageable classifications.[70]

Although resistance to enlightenment beliefs remains essentially subjugated, it can be contagious when it 'bears witness' to a form of ethical life and in this sense contributes to struggles that challenge and disrupt the prevailing social order.[71] Posthumanist feminist ethics is disruptive if only because it refuses to endorse the domination of disembodied masculine discourses that reduce materiality to economic performance and identity politics to preoccupations with securing the self through social confirmations.[72] By retrieving ethics from its deontological straitjacket in cognitively based rules or utilitarian predefined virtues, posthumanist feminists[73] dismantle the binary separations and hierarchies. They refuse to elevate the mind over the body or the self over other subjects in ways that reflect and reinforce dominant masculine discourses and practices. If ethics is about embodied engagements with the other, it 'precedes the intentionality of consciousness' that is concerned with the instrumental control of externalities. Consequently, the self becomes responsible for 'the other who is *different* from us but to whom we cannot be *indifferent*'.[74] Ethics is then a form of resistance that is characterised first and foremost by our refusing to be the self that we have become through so many exercises of power and subjugating demands.[75] Instead of resistance being characterised as negative and focused on dismantling existing relations, ethics of engagement involve a more positive and productive mode of self and potential social transformation.

Inspired by concern for the ancient Greek commitment to caring for the self, I subscribe to Foucault's[76] belief that 'there is no first or final point of resistance to political power other than in the relationship one has to oneself'.[77] While this may appear on the surface to be individualistic or even narcissistic, caring for oneself is 'not in order to escape from the world but in order to act properly in it'.[78] It reflects ethics of engagement embodying a 'position of otherness'[79] that is outside a preoccupation with the self as a socially sanctioned image or identity.[80] Identity is heavily gendered in so far as it reflects an instrumentally rational and teleological project with a specific goal that resembles, if not emulates, masculine (albeit self-defeating) attempts to produce an orderly and predictable world in which to secure a solidified sense of self.[81] Seeking to secure identity ordinarily involves a 'bounded, ego-indexed habit[s] of fixing and capitalising on one's own selfhood'[82] whereas the ethical and aesthetic self is a more open and ever-shifting subject positioning that embraces both a transformation of the relationship one has with oneself and others as well as a willingness to be truthful despite the risks.[83] To embrace this kind of subjectivity, our struggles of resistance have to involve a grand refusal to be what we have become through so many exercises of power[84] and this means disrupting representations and practices that reflect and reproduce ethics of narcissism in the pursuit of secure and solidified senses of the self.

Summary and Conclusion

This chapter has attempted to provide an overview of different approaches to power and resistance at work in organisations complemented by an analysis that draws on the later Foucault and certain posthumanist feminists. Accordingly, I turned first to examine the concept of power arguing that, while sophisticated and extensive, Luke's theory of power ultimately has some serious weaknesses that can only be resolved through an appeal to Foucault. The chapter then turned to the literature on leadership where it was seen that outside of CLS, power and resistance are either wholly neglected or marginalised in favour of focusing on legitimate authority and follower consent. While I drew on some of the critical literature to discuss power in leadership, I had to turn to literature outside the leadership field, as does CLS, to examine different forms of resistance from industrial relations to informal resistance and then the research on industrial sabotage. I then examined more contemporary forms of control through consumption and finally, an examination of the later Foucault as a means of understanding how resistance might take an ethical rather than a confrontational route.

Finally, it is important to indicate some of the implications of this analysis of resistance, and these can be viewed in terms of contributions of a theoretical, empirical and practical nature. Theoretically, it encourages research that refuses to treat resistance as a discrete phenomenon or as a binary separation from power. It breaks with dualistic forms of analysis, particularly those concerned with productive as opposed to repressive power, agency and structure, material and symbolic relations, and masculine and feminine discourses. Empirically it encourages research that is politically and philosophically aware and focused on ethics and difference. It seeks to inform social and political practice to support organisational and self-transformation that undermines economic rational self-interest and self-aggrandising narcissism. Practically, in the context of neo-liberal western economies that are ethically degenerate and have spawned numerous ethical scandals, culminating in the global financial crisis of 2011, there is some urgency for moral regeneration.[85]

For this reason, the chapter finished with a discussion of Foucauldian ethics and posthumanist feminism[86] since they offer an alternative form of resistance where ethics can be retrieved from its straitjacket in cognitive-based deontological or utilitarian rules. They break the binary separations and the hierarchical elevation of the mind and the self that reflect and reinforce dominant homosocial and heterosexual hegemony as encapsulated in heteronormative masculine discourses. This supports a view of resistance that refuses to restrict the analysis to confrontational, aggressive assertions of a masculine nature where there is only one winner. Instead and more positively, what is proposed is ethical engagements with both one's self and with others. These can be contagious when they 'bear witness' to a form of life that challenges and disrupts the prevailing social order regardless of the risks to one's own life. By returning ethics to a relation of bodily engagement 'that precedes the intentionality of consciousness', as argued earlier, concerns our responsibility to the other who is *different* from us but to whom we cannot be *indifferent*.[87] More generally, this literature challenges the dominance of cognition and language over experience and the body, not only in representational but also in social constructivist discourses.[88] By affirming the body and embodied relations,[89] the 'in-between' spaces of ambiguity and ambivalence, flux and flow, and fragility and fragmentation can be explored as a form of ethical agility that is discussed in greater detail in Chapter 7. Before that, I continue the theme of the domination of masculine discourses and practices through examining diversity and gender in leadership.

Notes

1 Collinson (2014), Fairhurst and Grant (2010).
2 Cunliffe (2009).
3 Knights and Willmott (2017, p. 297).
4 Knights and Vurdubakis (1994).
5 Dahl (1957) who defined power in terms of a relationship between people, but in his attempt to operationalise the concept reduced it to a set of equations represented by symbolic notations. While he believed that this enabled him to ascertain a comparative degree of power held by two or more persons, this mathematical reductionism was not ultimately persuasive.
6 Lukes (2005).
7 https://www.independent.co.uk/news/uk/politics/brexit-latest-news-vote-leave-director-dominic-cummings-leave-eu-error-nhs-350-million-lie-bus-a7822386.html consulted 22.7.20.
8 Break into the Elite, *BBC* 2, 29th July 2019.
9 Collinson, Knights and Collinson (1990).
10 Harding (2019).
11 Foucault (1980).
12 Foucault (1977, 1980).
13 Hyman (1972, 1975) in the UK and Gouldner in the US were advocates of this conflict model.
14 Clegg (1971), Flanders (1971) in the UK and Dunlop (1958) in the US adopted this position.
15 Thompson (1990, 1991), Fine (1979), Neimark (1990).
16 For example, Tanner, Davies and O'Grady (1992).
17 Collinson (2005, p. 1425).
18 Burns (1978).
19 Collinson (2011, p. 185).
20 Ibid., p. 186.
21 A drug designed to cure depression.
22 Collinson (2012, p. 89).

23 Knights and O'Leary (2005, 2006).
24 Collinson (2012, pp. 98–99).
25 Ehrenreich (2010, p. 74).
26 Collinson (2012, p. 99).
27 Alvesson and Einola (2019).
28 Ibid., p. 383.
29 Avolio and Gardner (2005, p. 334).
30 Ibarra (1999, pp. 55–58).
31 Ibid., p. 54.
32 Dunlop (1958), Eldridge (1968), Fox and Flanders (1969), Hyman (1975, 1978).
33 Roy (1952).
34 Burawoy (1979).
35 Collinson (1992, 1994).
36 Collinson (2011).
37 Knights and Collinson (1987), Collinson (1992).
38 Knights and Collinson (1987).
39 Collinson (1994, pp. 33–34).
40 Roethlisberger and Dickson (1939).
41 Collinson (1994, p. 47).
42 Taylor and Walton (1971).
43 Cohen and Taylor (1992).
44 Mars (1982).
45 Ackroyd and Thompson (1999).
46 Fleming and Spicer (2007, p. 3).
47 Bensman and Gerver (1963), Knights and McCabe (2003).
48 Fleming and Spicer (2007).
49 Fleming (2014).
50 Collinson (2005).
51 Foucault (2005, p. 252).
52 Fleming and Spicer (2007).
53 Foucault (1997, 2011).
54 Fleming and Spicer (2007).
55 Knights and Willmott (1999/2004, p. 113).
56 Foucault (1980).
57 Thomas and Davies (2002), Pacholok (2009).
58 Foucault (1977).
59 Knights and Vurdubakis (1994).
60 Foucault (1982, 1986, 1997).
61 Foucault (2011).
62 Kondo (1990, p. 221), Collinson (2011, p. 188).
63 Halberstam (1998, p. 1).
64 Knights and Tullberg (2012).
65 Kenny (2010), Painter Morland and Ten Bos (2011), Pullen and Simpson (2009), Pullen and Rhodes (2010, 2014).
66 Knights and Tullberg (2012).
67 Pullen and Rhodes (2014, p. 790).
68 Levinas (1985), Ziarek (2001), Pullen and Rhodes (2010).
69 Derrida (1982).
70 Noon (2007), Diedrich, Eriksson-Zetterquist and Styhre (2011).
71 Foucault (2011), Munro (2014).
72 Ziarek (2001), Braidotti (2011).
73 Barad (2003, 2007), Braidotti (2011, 2013).

74 Levinas (1985, p. 95, my emphasis).
75 Foucault (1982, 1997).
76 Foucault (1986).
77 Foucault (2005, pp. 251–252).
78 Gros (2005, p. 702).
79 Foucault (2011, Location 7589).
80 Ziarek (2001).
81 Clough (1992).
82 Braidotti (2011, Location 129).
83 Foucault (2011, Location 7384).
84 Foucault (1982).
85 Knights and McCabe (2015).
86 Barad (2003, 2007), Braidotti (2011, 2013).
87 Levinas (1985, p. 95; quoted in Barad (2007, p. 392) my emphasis).
88 Braidotti (2011).
89 Deleuze and Guattari (1988), Foucault (1997).

5 Diversity/Gender and Leadership

While this chapter has an initial focus on diversity encompassing a wide range of discriminatory issues, albeit often concerning minorities, I will concentrate my attention primarily on gender, which is hardly a minority matter. Partly, I take this focus because leadership is invariably gendered insofar as masculine discourses and practices have traditionally dominated it. Since the dramatic rise of feminism in the mid-20th century, gender has increasingly attracted the interests of students of leadership. As argued in Chapter 1, nations more broadly are plagued by the domination of discourses of masculinity and their reproduction of binary epistemologies, ontologies and methodologies together with their linear rational and disembodied analyses.[1] After discussing diversity more generally, the chapter focuses upon the 'close but obscured connection between constructs of leadership, traditional assumptions of masculinity and a particular expression of male heterosexual identity'[2] — a connection that readily can be forgotten when 'macho' beliefs about a 'hard' and 'controlling' leadership, based on fear or blind loyalty, are taken for granted.

The chapter begins with an examination of the dominant strategy of Diversity Management (DM), which has become popular because of its focus on how diversity practices can deliver financial benefits for the organisation. Its universal approach of treating discrimination homogeneously and intervening *only* if a business case can be proven is, however, problematic. There are various strands of equal opportunity and anti-discrimination theory that seek to challenge standardising the problem in this way. Not much headway seems to have been made, however, so the chapter turns to a more combined approach to see if a focus on intersectionality could increase the pressure for leaders to extend their horizons.[3] While DM has implications for our subject matter insofar as it 'opens up' a broader array of personnel to potential leadership positions, it is more of a management than a leadership strategy. Consequently, the chapter quickly moves on to discuss gender and particularly the domination of discourses and practices of masculinity in leadership where feminist posthumanism is examined as a discourse that has the potential to disrupt this heteronormative hegemony. Anticipating the subsequent chapter on the body, finally, there is a discussion of how leadership is often seductive in its persuasive intent even though this is denied or disparaged by practitioners as well as in the literature.[4]

Diversity Management

Interest in diversity concerning leadership has been growing since the turn of the 21st century not least because of anti-discrimination legislation that has been on the statute book of most Western democracies since the mid-20th century but also due to leaders recognising how discrimination involves mismanagement of human resources. As women occupy almost 50% of the US working population and in the UK 72% of women as contrasted with 80% of men between 16 and 65 are employed or seeking work,[5] it is not surprising that there is more concern to prevent them from being excluded from positions of leadership. Even so, as has been declared over and over again, sex and other diversity discriminations still occur not least on equal pay for equal work and promotion opportunities for women, disabled people and ethnic minorities. A common response especially promoted by management consultants is to develop programmes of DM.

For those seeking to transform organisations in the direction of greater equality and justice,[6] this new-found orthodoxy[7] was welcome but it is important to remain sceptical as far as it readily displaces all other alternatives,[8] as well as any concern with universal human rights. Also, its focus on the business case will often constrain any equality pursuits that might not have positive financial returns.[9] Moreover, DM discourse tends to decontextualise the problems of diversity as if they apply universally regardless of circumstance and the multiple bases of discrimination. One other major problem, reflecting but also reproducing this failure to problematise the narrow focus of DM, is its capture by a positivist tradition that generates a proliferation of technical studies. These seek to correlate quantitatively DM variables with organisational profitability[10] and, as one study found, how leader racial diversity impacted positively on firm performance.[11]

This reductionism of complex relations to two or more discrete independent and dependent variables is common within the mainstream of leadership and organisational studies. Although positive correlations may well inspire leaders to adopt DM, it is problematic in reproducing, rather than challenging, the stereotypes of diversity. This is because it subscribes to an objectivist epistemology that sees representations of different diversities, whether on the part of researchers or practitioners, as independent of politically energised social constructions. So, although it cannot be denied that marking out discriminated people arises because they are discriminated against, in freezing the label in objectivist representations that are then given scientific status through causal analysis, we simply reproduce the category. Only by acknowledging its socially constructed grounding can we hope to eradicate the discrimination surrounding it.

In addition to problematising the social construction of categories of people that have historically suffered discrimination, we can also counter DM's narrowing of the problem by broadening analysis along intersectional lines. This alerts us not only to a wider range of diversities and differences but also to their mutual interaction. For example, it highlights the exponential, discriminatory effects when a disadvantaged age, gender and ethnicity coincide. Consequently, it is necessary to reconcile the spectrum of different approaches to diversity relating to minority (e.g. age, ethnic, lesser abled, racial, religious and sexual preference) or majority. (e.g. women and class background) groups.[12] DM is highly ambiguous particularly in how it treats difference and sameness, within specific social/organisational-historical contexts. However, actors selectively prioritise particular sectional interests[13] although these tend to be marginalised by leaders unless they are seen as contributing directly to commercial or financial advantage. Managing diversity can then reproduce and sustain the very inequalities it ostensibly seeks to remove and can generate 'antagonism and resentment on the part of the "managed diverse"' not least because it 'depoliticises the gender conflicts and racial tensions that are endemic'[14] in organisations. Neither in theory or practice is this addressed so that there is a lack of development of the discourse and this is partly why it reinforces the discrimination that it purportedly is designed to eradicate.

These contradictions might suggest abandoning DM but, as Foucault has always argued, it is better to go with the grain and perform an autocritique that turns an idea that is popular against itself.[15] By drawing upon insights from other perspectives such as intersectional theory it is possible to see how contexts impact on both the problems and the solutions concerning diversity and disadvantage. This is not about producing compromises of liberal tolerance or accommodation nor one of constructing a universal representation to displace the multiplicity of localised voices. Rather, it is to see how DM might exceed itself when it is open to insights from intersectional theory, especially as 'a theoretical framework capable of recognising the multidimensionality of social life and the intersection of registers of power and knowledge'.[16]

By contrast with DM, intersectionality focuses on the multiplicity of identities surrounding different aspects of diversity that are in complex interaction with one another and often mutually constituting group-based disadvantages. Insofar as these identities are not just a product of simple accretion, by contrast with the singularity of DM's dimension, there is a qualitative difference like advantage or disadvantage. So, for example, an English white, middle class, heterosexual, protestant man may enjoy considerably more privileges than a gay, Muslim woman where, in the context of current Western culture, the multiplicity of stigmatised identities results in discriminations far greater than the sum of their parts. Because DM is focused so closely on the financial benefits of a diverse workforce, it tends to see the disadvantaged as homogenous groups independently of historical and socio-economic context. Differing with this view, intersectional perspectives perceive a great deal of variability, heterogeneity and complexity depending on the interlacing of different disadvantages concerning changing contexts.

Although the intersectionality perspective on diversity was introduced as a theoretical tool to demonstrate the exponential impact of multiple, interdependent discriminations, it has been adapted as a policy-making tool and methodology for generating social justice.[17] DM discourses and practices could benefit from developing an understanding of intersectionality since it illuminates several issues that are obscured by a narrow focus on the business case. What stands in the way of this potential development are the gendered masculine myopias within corporate leadership to which I now turn.

Gendered Masculinities in Leadership

It has been contended that there is a 'close connection between constructs of leadership, traditional assumptions of masculinity and a particular expression of male heterosexual identity'.[18] Despite laws, discourses and movements providing a platform for feminist challenges to the gendered nature of our institutions and organisations, there seems a reluctance to renounce a 'macho' or 'paternal' view of leadership. Such a leader feels compelled to treat subordinates either aggressively or manipulatively in the belief that their compliance can only be achieved based on fear or blind loyalty. Of course, there are more subtle or often subconscious modes of masculine leadership for it is recognised that a 'macho' or 'paternal' approach can be counter-productive in terms of securing the full cooperation of subordinates in conditions where this requires a sense of mutual valuation and trust.[19] Masculinities in leadership can be damaging, emotionally and spiritually as well as to the body of the leader who feels obliged to repress or conceal aspects of identity that are inconsistent with a tough, 'manly' or softer 'fatherly' image. Interestingly, leaders may often be gentle, subtle and even seductive but it has been suggested that such features are rarely visible in the literature on leadership.[20] However, acknowledging the presence of seduction can facilitate the development of innovation in leadership theory — something evident in certain theories of leadership and sexuality[21] although Sinclair cautions about the managerial appropriation of elements or trappings of this alternative conception of leadership to 'strengthen the status quo'.[22] While exploring the varied ways where sexual identities are brought to bear on leadership, Sinclair foresees how people, especially men, who are captivated by the idea of *'life as a contest'*, may mouth 'the language of care and consultation' to sound fashionable and/or advance their careers.[23]

The strong link between leadership and masculinities has been discussed and analysed from a diverse range of perspectives. At first, the focus was on the obvious demographic majority of men in the senior hierarchy and how that affected power relations and the consequences for women.[24] Although Moss Kanter was aware of the majority/minority problems, it was predicted that over time, the allocation of power in corporations would change to reflect more gender equality.[25] We now realise that her optimism was a little misguided, for the movement to a more equal allocation has been slower than expected and white men continue to dominate senior leadership and management positions in most Western corporations.[26] Moreover, although the numbers of women leaders have increased to some extent, they also often feel compelled to adhere to the dominant masculine culture surrounding leadership. Yet the conservative, consensual and individualistic character of assumptions around gender mask the domination and discrimination in social relations, including those along lines of class, race, ethnicity, sexual orientation, age, mental and physical ability, region, religion, as well as gender.[27]

My analysis sees gender as a condition and consequence of performative acts that are continually constituted, enacted and sustained through what has been called 'doing gender'.[28] Developing this perspective further, it has been shown how the allocation of labour, of wages and hierarchical positions, contribute to this social construction of gender.[29] As was discussed in Chapter 3, there is no essential identity lying behind performative acts that involve 'a process of iterability, a regularised and constrained repetition of norms'. These generate the conditions that enable subjects to be constituted so that this outcome can be seen as the 'materialisation of norms'.[30] Drawing on the theatrical metaphors of *performance* and *performativity*[31] enables us to identify mental and physical behaviours and attributes as instrumental in the production of 'the right kind of man (or woman)' according to the prevalent script. Relevant instances of these performative elements in producing and sustaining masculinity in leadership and business, for example, are: achieving a leadership position; being in receipt of high levels of remuneration; reflecting and reinforcing heterosexual norms and heteronormative values often through male bonding;"; 'thinking smart', presuming authoritative 'expertise'; and being prepared to take risks in pursuit of career success. No better example of this kind of gung-ho masculinity can be found than in the political leadership of Donald Trump and Boris Johnson, discussed in the final chapter. However, within business life, we find a variety of discourses where one element may be more important than another in different performative acts of masculinity.

There is a danger that in examining masculine performativity, we neglect the 'material, economic and physical foundations of identity and identity politics and indeed power itself'.[32] While not explicitly showing how these foundations can be explored other than through an extension of the sociology of the body to incorporate the analysis of masculinity,[33] Edwards own analysis of the body is restrained by his fear of it sliding into biological essentialism should any credence be given to the body as an agency. However, ascribing agency to bodies only involves biological essentialism or determinism if there is a Cartesian dualistic assumption of a separation between mind and body. This problem can be avoided by drawing on a Spinozian philosophy, where unitary ontology experiences and theorises the body and mind as the same.[34] Human agency cannot, then, be other than material and symbolic action that reflects and re-produces embodied cognition, which is a combined effect of deconstructing epistemological, and dissolving ontological, binaries.[35]

While it is still the case that the material and economic foundations of identity concerning masculinities remain under-researched, the contemporary global backlash against the neoliberal consensus intimates a realpolitik link between material and economic deprivation and an aggressive masculine, intolerance of difference. Moreover, this straddles the genders since women are as likely as men to embrace a 'hard-line' masculine aggression towards outsiders in the Far Right and White Supremacy politics of identity surrounding nationalism, economic isolationism and protectionism. So much so that it has been described as a viral disease that has spread exponentially, enrolling and mobilising large segments of the population in democratic societies as white, populist masculine leaders exploit and escalate specific grievances or deprivations.[36]

While these examinations of masculinities in terms of consumption, style and the body are important examples of masculine performances, they do not directly *interrogate* identity in ways that facilitate an analysis of what *drives* the performative desires. Even when books are devoted exclusively to the subject matter of identity,[37] they still tend to treat it as a resource rather than a topic to interrogate. So, for example, Fukuyama argues that the 'demand for recognition of one's identity is a master concept that unifies much of what is going on in world politics today'.[38] Included in this is the shift on the part of many white American, British and European populations to demand anti-immigration, nationalist and protectionist policies through supporting political leaders from the 'extreme right' who often appear to be authoritarian demagogues. Although sometimes almost as crude as the politics Fukuyama's analysis is seeking to explain, it is not without credibility since masculine identities are certainly threatened when their economic power is weakened as has happened for many workers in the post-second world war, free-market economies.

Whether or not open borders or European free movement of labour has been responsible for this rather than simple neo-liberal market economics is questionable, but the former has been scapegoated in so-called post-truth societies of the 21st century. However, there is little doubt that a politics of identity has begun to displace dominant 20th century views of Western electorates that in the past were captured by the phrase that 'it is the economy stupid'. Still, the analysis of identity in these accounts remains at the level of describing, rather than interrogating, identity and its performative foundations and, consequently, it adds little to developing an understanding of masculine discourses and practices.

Interrogating Masculine Identity

One particular value of performativity theory is that it escapes from the essentialism underlying a 'metaphysics of substance',[39] where the self is seen as a coherent entity that acts independently of the social relations through which it is formed, sustained and transformed. In modern western societies, and increasingly beyond them, this notion of the self as something substantial is commonplace and one result is that identity is often an overwhelming preoccupation. However, despite a rejection of the metaphysics of substance, the theory does not often interrogate how the preoccupation with identity is foundational to performativity, for it is significant to its cathexis drive to achieve competent performances, knowledge of which is important to an adequate understanding of masculine discourses and practices. All identities can be seen as driven by the pursuit of competent performances as the vehicle for gaining social recognition and as the means of attaining some stability and security for the self.

The demand for order and control seems even more intense for those seeking to secure their masculine identities but it has been argued that this 'avoidance of impermanence' and 'the tendency to conform, to normalise, to secure and control' is the pathway to a destructive technocratic 'nihilism'.[40] Yet this nihilism 'goes comparatively unchallenged in modern society' ... [for it is] 'transfixed by cognitively, masculine disembodied rationality'.[41] It reflects and reproduces self-defeating myths about securing identity when this is impossible given its dependence on others' evaluations and judgements that are by definition fragile, precarious and unpredictable. However, this does not deter masculine discourses and practices from embracing the pursuit of 'control, conquest, competitive success' and self-mastery through a 'compulsive preoccupation' with an identity that always remains beyond reach.[42]

For some men, the feminine 'other' is seen as a source of mystery and unknowability, and for that reason rather troublesome,[43] not least in so far as it intensifies an understanding of the world as precarious, uncertain and uncontrollable, thus exposing the masculine subject's autonomy and self-mastery as illusory. Yet autonomy is so central to ideas of masculinity, especially where this is reinforced by liberal enlightenment beliefs that cultivate humanistic ideologies of individualism and human potential.[44] However, this threat to autonomy reflects and reinforces an attachment to masculine identities that makes even more performative, if self-defeating, demands upon subjects to conform to strategies involving self-discipline as a means of securing meaning and reality.[45] Fears of the loss of autonomy are often displaced on to other 'objects' in the world and, in particular, machines, hierarchical subordinates, and animals that it would appear can be dominated and made controllable. But the precariousness of masculinity can result in the body becoming self-estranged in its all-encompassing desire for conquest as a response to threats that are as much self-induced as produced by others. In this sense, the drive to dominate the other reflects a fear of the internal contingency, which threatens masculine autonomy.[46]

Interestingly, feminists have for some time questioned autonomy and the Enlightenment philosophy to which it owes its allegiance[47] even to the point of rejecting it as a masculine concept premised on a mind-body, intellect-affect, will-nature dualism.[48] In a posthumanist development, feminists have criticised the enlightenment more generally as reflecting dualistic epistemologies, ontologies and methodologies that treat femininity as the emotional 'other' by contrast with the presumed cognitively rational masculinity that is in control of both the social and the natural world. It is not difficult to see this as part of a masculine preoccupation with securing the self through constructing an orderly and unfragmented world — a process that involves us seeing the world in our own image.[49] By providing 'grand' exhaustive accounts of reality, we fulfil this desire for order while simultaneously sustaining the security of our identities. Many feminists[50] see the humanistic belief in the pre-eminence of autonomy and rationality as the foundation of a masculine preoccupation with order and control.[51]

Leadership and Masculine Insecurity

It must be recognised that insecurity is not the prerogative of masculine subjects for Lacan's account shows it to be cross-gender. In the mirror image stage of ego development, a misrecognition occurs wherein the self identifies with a solid image of itself (the imaginary) as if this were solid, separate, discrete and independent of others,[52] another example of the metaphysics of substance. Insofar as everyday reality routinely contradicts this identification of self as autonomous, intense insecurity is generated that forever has to be denied, 'fixed' or managed. As was argued in Chapter 3, much discourse since the Enlightenment has given succour to imaginaries of the autonomous self, thus denying its fragility and precariousness in everyday life, and both masculinities and notions of leadership thrive on this valorisation.

The discourse of masculinity that involves homosocial bonding and hierarchical claims to superior wealth and status is closely connected with leadership. To attain a position of formal leadership, it is necessary to engage in conquest and control since these are the performative elements that mark out individuals from one another in the processes of competitive masculinity in organisational life.[53] In the past, leadership authority was relatively stable due partly to a more rigid organisation of class relations where positions were attained through a range of inherited privileges and, once secured, was virtually permanent. As reported in Chapter 4, there are still elements of this today where nebulous notions like 'polish' are detected and class and cleverness are conflated[54] but knowledge relevant for leadership has multiplied even though it is no more valid than when it was an arbitrary function of class privilege. The number of articles, conferences, books, seminars and workshops, consultancy and training programmes on leadership has grown exponentially resulting in leaders enjoying higher public profiles than historically has been the case. Yet this fame has come at a cost since leadership positions are shorter in length and more precarious than in the past for the average term of office of corporate CEOs is currently only 3–4 years. A common message from the Chairs of Boards is 'that our current leader has done a very good job but now the company needs another kind of competence'. Senior leadership positions in contemporary organisational life are socially risky if not always personally economically so[55] and thus the masculinity associated with them is quite fragile for, the spoils of conquest can readily be lost in the cut-throat, competitive world. One way of protecting the self from this potential symbolic violence is to develop strong (heterosexual) group norms, a standard dress code or uniform[56] and the homosocial male bonding.[57] These provide at least the appearance of security through leadership elites mutually confirming one another in their respectable middle-class masculine status.[58]

Despite the proliferation of discourses and hyperbole, there remains a paucity of knowledge about leadership that has practical significance not least because of the absence of a consensus concerning its validity. However, this neglects to consider how regardless of disagreements in the research field, knowledge is drawn upon in the exercise of power and this has an effect on the very production of such knowledge.[59] So, while leaders may not possess knowledge that can guarantee to generate predictable outcomes, its deployment in exercises of power often produces self-fulfilling prophecy effects that give it the appearance of certainty and predictability. This partly occurs through leaders exercising hierarchical and gendered power over subordinates, which in turn, often secures employee compliance, if only due to the unequal control over resources and rewards in organisations. Not that resistance is precluded by the exercise of this power, as was outlined in Chapter 4.

Of course, leaders are rarely naïve enough to believe that their knowledge has the status that is claimed for it in the pursuit of their legitimacy. They are also aware that what works at one point may not at another, and to legitimise their privileges they must forever be seeking new and exclusive knowledge. But the continuous necessity to be searching for and applying new knowledge is, in itself, anxiety-provoking and generative of insecurity.[60] There is, then, a double sense in which leaders are insecure: first, they are aware that knowledge does not have the certainty and stability of science even though their legitimacy is based upon a specialist 'expertise' that is dependent precisely on such [uncertain] knowledge. Second, these conditions make it necessary for leaders continuing to seek new knowledge that is capable of giving the appearance of exclusive expertise and masculine security. This, it may be argued, is one of the main reasons why those offering plausible prescriptions can very soon claim a guru status. From personality traits to transformative powers, the history of leadership is littered with prescriptive knowledge that claims to offer convincing responses to the demand for solutions to uncertainty. But these innovative solutions themselves promote continuous change that is threatening of routinised securities, especially given that the solutions often take the form of a fashion to be abandoned, almost as speedily as adopted, once a new solution emerges. In combination, these insecurities exacerbate the anxieties that we have already identified here and in Chapter 3 to be a feature of leadership and masculinity.

There is a link between this analysis of gender in leadership and the mind-body binary that is discussed in the next chapter for, it reflects and reproduces an image of men and masculinity as in control both physically and metaphorically and women assigned to their uncontrollable, unpredictable and overflowing bodies.[61] Few better exemplifications of how the gendered body is highly significant can be found than in TV and film media where physical appearance would seem to be much more significant for women than for men.

These discourses of masculinity are quite clearly embedded in leadership studies that embrace conceptions of heroism that stretch back as far as Homer's epic, mythic tale of Odysseus's 10-year voyage back home from his battle in Troy. Contemporary leaders have rarely struggled with the elements and war in the way that Odysseus is proclaimed to have done yet they often seek not dissimilar kinds of legitimacy. Their homosocial bonding and social exclusiveness support masculine claims to leadership that reflect and reproduce aggressive, technically rational, disembodied and competitively performance-oriented, instrumental pursuits of material and symbolic privilege.[62]

As so-called followers, women and their bodies are often disciplined to render them docile and productive, but when managing to attain leadership positions, their bodies leave them with a gender disadvantage since the grey elderly man is looked upon as wise and dignified in a way that is not the case for older women.[63] Feminists have sought to reverse this representation by re-imagining women leaders as effective not despite their bodies, but *because* they are more embodied.[64] This reversal disrupts the representation of leadership as being naturally masculine and devoid of eroticism and sensuality. However, it has been argued that leadership is and has always been embodied and steeped in seduction and sensuality. Yet, by devaluing the body or making it appear to be invisible, the dominant discourse can claim this is not so.[65]

I return to the seductive nature of leadership below but in refusing to accept these displacements, neo-humanists argue that embodiment is one of the necessary conditions of ethical engagement since it renders leaders and those exercising power responsible to the other and thereby less preoccupied with themselves and their own identities.[66] From this, it is reasonable to argue that the failure of ethical leadership both in theory and practice has an association with the dominance of white androcentric disembodiment, the dominance of individualism, preoccupations with the self, and heroism within leadership discourses and practices.[67] We can conclude then that what has sometimes been called the 'absent presence' of the body[68] leaves studies of leadership bereft of some of the most important features of its reproduction. Yet paradoxically it is often only when leadership becomes a topic of analysis and investigation that disembodied conceptions of its everyday practice predominate as disembodied masculine assumptions of cognitive control and proprietary power are privileged.

In addition to this gendered focus on the body in leadership studies, there is a growing interest in more philosophical approaches[69] where, in seeking to escape individualistic and dualistic approaches, this literature speaks about a leadership dynamic and notions of the ambiguous relational space in between leaders and followers that requires interrogation.[70] By linking this to Merleau-Ponty's[71] perspective on the flesh, Ladkin seeks to provide 'the material embodiment of an ontology of relationality'.[72] For it is through this sense of 'touching the flesh' metaphorically or physically that the various invisible aspects of leadership such as the embodied and felt experience of being in a leadership relation, the sense of community and vision, and the trust underlying these relations is conveyed. It is not just actual leadership dynamics that can be fleshed out in this way; it is also the research process itself since it is our bodies and 'embodied awareness'[73] that are intimately involved in producing 'insights or findings'.[74] Moreover, while the body and the senses are before any cognitive selection or interpretation, our own 'embodied responses' as researchers are crucial in sensing 'the interplay of the "visible" and the "invisible"'[75] within leadership encounters. It can even be argued that the invisible can itself have a 'material affect' ... 'on those who enter into leader-follower relations, as well as on those who study them',[76] and this conveniently *leads* us into our final section on seduction.

Leadership as Gendered Seduction

Again, as I argued in Chapter 4, leadership is closely linked to sales and, in this sense, to a form of seduction. However, the seductive nature of leadership is not restricted to sales for it has been argued that it is implicit in many of the classic studies of leadership and management. By processes of deconstruction, an etymological analysis and a close reading of classical texts, it can be shown how a mutual dependency of seemingly opposite concepts such as leadership and seduction exists at the same time while both culture and managerial rhetoric combine to conceal these dependencies.[77] More precisely, this analysis seeks to demonstrate the limits of conventional discourses on leadership in failing to acknowledge how 'leadership and seduction are alike and also to reveal the possible, concealed, gendered-ness (rather than neutrality) of both terms'.[78]

In re-reading some classic texts, these authors present Christian Barnard as identifying himself and leaders generally as God-like but who cannot help themselves from seducing their adoring flocks, something that the numerous exposures of sexual scandal in the Church vividly illustrate. Douglas McGregor is presented as democratic although reflecting a form of democracy where the privileged class create the conditions in which the people are seduced into believing in and following, their leaders. This way people gain a sense of identity 'in order to feel that they are somebody'... even though ... 'it is only a seductive joke!'.[79] Henry Mintzberg is understood to convey a promiscuous narcissism where an 'oversexed', ... egocentric 'leader is a permissible figure, under the illusion that others are equally empowered to counteract his advances'. ... But the acknowledgement that ... 'seduction may be happening out of fear is discounted'.[80] Described as compulsive masculinity, this kind of leadership reflects the prevailing desire to treat women as mere objects of sexual conquest and seduction as a means of sustaining homosocial, masculine superiority and adorning or embellishing the insatiable yet fragile ego. In this latter case, the question is why and how there is submission to this compulsion on the part of women and here it is argued that there is a quid pro quo of 'feminine narcissism'. This serves as a defence against the fear of masculine abuse taking the form of enhancing 'sexual attractiveness' ... thus ... 'avoiding mistreatment by getting to be among 'the chosen few' who are perhaps more used, but less abused'.[81] Finally, Peters and Waterman are considered as not only offering nothing new and therefore returning to the classics and, in particular, Burns's view of 'trans-forming leadership'. While involving the pursuit of the goals, values and motivations of leaders and followers, it 'builds on man's *(sic)* need for meaning, leadership that creates institutional purpose...'.[82] However, reflecting the postmodern turn, their leadership thesis is a pastiche defined by James[83] as a parody that lacks humour, but simply keeps on repeating Burns's copy of Barnard's argument without recognising its source in a 'homosocial libidinal economy of competitiveness and glory'.[84]

Before leaving this literature in favour of what they anticipate to be possibly a more positive alternative in utopian science fiction, the authors seek to turn their analysis on its head to demonstrate how seduction might be valorised over, rather than merely be in the service of, leadership. However, this proves impossible since all images of seduction derive from a male, homosocial and phallocentric culture. Their foray into utopian science fiction hardly fares any better but they conclude that this limitation of human agency is no reason to be pessimistic. Instead, they pursue what could be seen as a radical challenge to the current growth of identity politics that seeks to 'fix' the past, the present as well as the future in the image of the person fixing it. As they argue,

> Rather *than fixing* ourselves in the text (the typical imagery of 'universal truth-knowledge' in modern metaphysics) we prefer the imagery of a transient subject, never to be captured, always on the move, as so many points of pleasure on a woman's body. [...] this form of writing ourselves into the organizational text has provided us with the pleasures of resistance ... [while recognising] ... the limits of human agency.[85]

This summary of Calás and Smircich's article by no means does justice to their insightful yet complex, tongue-in-cheek parody of a selection of classical leadership studies. However, it is refreshing to read critics celebrating, rather than commiserating in, the limits of their interventions and it is nothing but a pleasure to share with them a realisation that we resist simply because we can, and not just to secure our identities in specific achievements or radical outcomes.

Summary and Conclusion

This chapter has been concerned to show how organisations and their leaders have recently adopted DM practices not ordinarily from any philanthropic concerns but because they make good business sense. Not least this is because discrimination of disabled, ethnic, racial and religious minorities or on grounds of age, gender or sexuality is illegal. This legal context, however, has emerged and is promoted culturally and politically by substantial groups of people who have had an impact on everyone including the leaders, particularly of the larger corporations. Consequently, these leaders have been anxious to claim the moral high ground for the benefit of public relations through introducing, advertising and giving publicity to their DM programmes.

While superficially this would seem a highly progressive development, analysis of these programmes presents rather a different set of conclusions, particularly given that in practice intervention in recruitment and career development usually only occurs when a clear business case can be proven. Furthermore, criticisms have been directed at their universal and standardised ways of treating difference so that many people fall through the cracks. The effect is one generally of normalising difference since unless an individual fits into a set pre-defined category, the DM programme passes them by. However, what is more of a problem is gender and particularly the domination of discourses and practices of masculinity in leadership. Through a discussion of feminist posthumanism, this heteronormative hegemony is challenged. In anticipating Chapter 6 on the body, the chapter ends with a discussion of how despite denying it, leaders are often seductive in their ways of relating to those they seek to persuade to follow them.

The issues of diversity and discrimination are clearly of significance for all the chapters of this book not least because it can be argued that the very concept of leadership is steeped in matters of discrimination and inequality. Of course, many of the discriminations surrounding leadership are legal because they are meritocratic even though others would argue this does not make them legitimate. However, these meritocratic discriminations and their claim to be legitimate are fundamental to hierarchically, unequal organisations, institutions and societies in which leadership resides.

Notes

1 Braidotti (2011, 2013), Knights (2015, 2018), Pullen and Rhodes (2010; 2014), Pullen and Vachhani (2013).
2 Sinclair (2005, p. 1, see also Knights and Tullberg 2012).
3 Styhre and Eriksson-Zetterquist (2008) and Holvino (2010).
4 Calás and Smircich (1991).
5 See https://www.dol.gov/wb/factsheets/qf-laborforce-10.htm and https://www.catalyst.org/research/women-in-the-workforce-uk/
6 Ashley (2010).
7 Özbilgin and Tatli (2008), Kirton and Greene (2009).
8 Knights D and Omanović, 2016.
9 Noon (2007, p. 778).

10 See, for example, Watson, Kumar and Michaelsen (1993), Robinson and Dechant (1997), Hambrick, Davison, Snell and Snow (1998).
11 Roberson and Park (2007).
12 see Chapter 3; also, Liff (1999).
13 Meriläinen, Tienari, Katila and Benschop (2009), Omanović (2011).
14 Lorbiecki and Jack (2000, pp. 27–29).
15 Foucault (1997).
16 Styhre and Eriksson-Zetterquist (2008, p. 578).
17 Bagilhole (2009).
18 Sinclair (2005, p. 1; see also Knights and Tullberg, 2012).
19 See Chapter 10.
20 Calás and Smircich (1991).
21 Ibid.
22 Sinclair (2005, especially Chapter 9).
23 Ibid.
24 Moss Kanter (1977), Collinson and Hearn (1996), Kerfoot and Knights (1996).
25 Moss Kanter (1977).
26 While more progressive than most economies, in 2015 women represented only 9.6% of UK executive board members but just 5.5% of FTSE 100 companies are led by women https://www.ft.com/content/5fc61080-ae2c-11e5-993b-c425a3d2b65a
27 Brod (1995).
28 West and Zimmerman (1987), Butler (1990, 2004).
29 Acker (1992), Gherardi (1994).
30 Butler (1993, pp. 94–95).
31 Schechner (2002).
32 Edwards (2006, p. 103).
33 Ibid., p. 151.
34 Deleuze/*Spinoza* (1988).
35 Deleuze and Guattari (1988), Knights (2015).
36 Ashcraft (2020).
37 Fukuyama (2018).
38 Ibid., p. iii.
39 Benhabib (1992). The term is generally deployed to indicate attributing universal essences to subjects and objects rather than seeing them as socially and performatively produced, See also Butler (1993, p. 12).
40 Levin (1985, p. 74).
41 Knights and Clarke (2017, p. 340).
42 Knights and Kerfoot (2004, p. 439).
43 Butler (1990).
44 Costea et al. (2012).
45 Knights and Clarke (2017).
46 Frank (1990).
47 Jagger (1983).
48 Fraser (1996).
49 Game (1990), Clough (1992).
50 Hekman (1990), Braidotti (2011).
51 Braidotti (2013).
52 Lacan (2001).
53 Kerfoot and Knights (1993).
54 Break into the Elite, *BBC* 2, 29th July 2019.
55 This is because parachute payouts for executives are very large indeed.

56 Mörck and Tullberg (2005).
57 Roper (1996).
58 I am aware that this could be analysed by drawing on psychoanalytic theory to show how guilt, concerning the desire for the mother and sacrifice in succumbing to the rule of the father, intensifies around transgression at the root of masculine insecurities. No doubt this is the case but, in this chapter, I seek to remain focused on the social processes that are a response to, but also serve to reproduce, this insecurity. For a less pessimistic analysis that challenges heterosexual normativity (as does Butler, 1990) see Walsh (2010).
59 Foucault (1980).
60 Watson (1994).
61 Grosz (1994).
62 Blomberg (2009), Knights and Tullberg (2012).
63 Trethewey (1999).
64 Bell and Sinclair (2016).
65 Calás and Smircich (1991).
66 Ziarek (2001), Braidotti (2013).
67 Knights (2015).
68 Leder (1990).
69 Cunliffe (2009), Case, French and Simpson (2011), Kupers (2013), Ladkin (2010, 2013), Tomkins and Simpson (2015), Ciulla, Knights, Mabey and Tomkins (2018a, 2018b).
70 Ladkin (2013), Uhl-Bien's (2006).
71 Merleau-Ponty (1962).
72 Ladkin (2013, p. 328).
73 Ibid., p. 325.
74 Kupers (2014, p. 336).
75 Ladkin (2013, p. 332).
76 Ibid.
77 Calás and Smircich (1991, p. 569).
78 Ibid., 570.
79 Ibid., 592. The notion of a seductive joke is Freudian in origin but in theory, it is understood as 'smut uttered by a man in order to seduce a woman - would only occur between males and females of the lower social classes. At the higher social level, the sexual joke would not take place between men and women. Rather, it will be a typical scene among *gentlemen* and will exclude the *ladies'* (Ibid., p. 580).
80 Ibid., pp. 592–593.
81 Ibid., p. 588.
82 Burns (1978, 1998, p. 82).
83 Jameson (1991).
84 Calás and Smircich (1991, pp. 593).
85 Ibid., p. 598.

6 Embodied Reason and Affective Leadership

As has been seen from previous chapters, there is a vast range of approaches within the field of leadership studies from 'Great Man' (sic) to classical/scientistic, from individualistic to relational and from critical to posthuman theories. In this chapter, I will largely be concerned with the latter end of this historical continuum but before turning to this, let me take stock by summarising where this book has taken us so far.

'Great Man' theories were often produced by hagiographic biographers or self-aggrandising auto-biographers who sought to advance universal principles with little attempt to research beyond their personal experiences. Scientistic theories have been primarily generated through psychology that seeks to emulate formal science and cerebrally divides the whole into its constituent parts in an attempt to identify what causes effective leadership. Furthermore, in their conflation of science with independent and dependent causal variables, they almost always seek to quantify what may or may not be quantifiable whether it be the personality traits, behavioural, transactional or the transformational skills of the leader. Relational studies, on the other hand, abhor the non-participative aspects of mainstream research and recognise the complexity of context and content in leadership. Practice approaches go a little further in acknowledging complexity and uncertainty and critique the serial, individual, control and dispassionate projections reflected in the mainstream studies of leadership. In their different ways, all are concerned with efficiency, effectiveness and enterprise either through hierarchical control or participative self-discipline.

Critical leadership studies challenge these managerialist aims and the positivist epistemology adopted by the mainstream. They also question leadership research for its neglect of power, inequalities and identity and for assuming that leaders are usually coherent, consistent and competent.[1] All of us who work in organisations are aware of the tendency for leadership to be incoherent, inconsistent and incompetent. Still, these problems have not always been *appropriately* attributed to the misuse of power, the reinforcement of inequalities and leaders' preoccupations with identity. This is because critics have not always succeeded fully in interrogating conceptions of power, inequality and identity and, more importantly, leadership itself.

What I also find limited or missing in many approaches is a gendered, embodied and ethical focus in studying leadership. While few mainstream theorists could object to this criticism, relational approaches would claim to be strongly ethical in promoting participation.[2] However, they rarely consider how this involvement of employees gives licence to self-discipline — a more sophisticated if subtle and effective mode of management control that sneaks in by the back door. This self-discipline could be seen as one of the 'greatest confinements' in that it forces us back on our own 'identity by a conscience or self-knowledge'.[3] As was argued in Chapter 1, most studies of leadership, whether mainstream or critical, converge insofar as they invariably subscribe to a humanistic philosophy in which there is an assumption in the mainstream that leadership facilitates individuals to realise their potential through the growth and success of the organisation. Critical approaches, on the other hand, understand this potential only being released when there is some emancipation from the power of leaders.

In this book, I depart from these humanist assumptions by drawing on the notion of affect. Here we can re-envisage leadership as not only more about a collectively shared experience but also concerned with making a difference through embodied energy. I draw on the notion of affect where this energy resides both in the bodies of individuals but also in their interactions that are part of the formation and transformation of the corporate body. While affect is never static enough to be captured in a concrete instance since it is forever in transition, it does enable the embodied subject to form habits that adapt 'to social context',[4] as well as to reframe or re-envisage externalities through its actions and relations. In making a difference, affective leadership enhances the capacity of others to act and in this way it is infectious, affecting not just other subjects but also the material and symbolic conditions of its practice. Post-humanist feminism criticises the gendered or masculine, disembodied aspects of leadership that, preclude or limit the development of affect.

The chapter begins by describing the neglect of the body, embodied reason and affectivity in leadership research and practice, exploring first, their marginalisation in social science, generally, and in leadership studies, in particular. Not only is the body substantively neglected in favour of cerebral accounts of, and prescriptions for, leadership but also debates and discussions are generally conducted in a disembodied manner. To illustrate disembodied research, I incorporate a few selected examples from my research where affect and the body were self-censored. Secondly, the chapter turns to an explanation of this marginalisation of the body and embodied narratives in terms of the Cartesian legacy – the body-mind binary that reduces the body to an anatomical abstraction and generates disembodied representations of reality. This is followed by an examination of the relationship between the Cartesian binary and discourses of masculinity where the body becomes a passive reflection of a higher rational order that governs its construction and functioning. A short excursion into existentialist responses to contingency and indeterminacy precedes the third section, where limited philosophical reflections on deconstructing and dissolving mind-body binaries and their disembodied representations are provided. For practitioners, this disembodiment precludes the very kinds of relationships with others that would lend impact to their leadership. I turn then to post-humanist feminism to explore the potential for an embodied framework to facilitate a greater challenge to the ethical limits of the prevailing theories and practices of leadership. I theorise how the notion of affect can facilitate the integration of these concerns to offer a different way of thinking and feeling about leadership. Finally, in a summary and conclusion, general arguments of the chapter are summarized before drawing out the implications of this analysis not only for other chapters in this book but also for future research. A fundamental question is how it might be possible for the study of leadership to free itself from the taboos on the body/emotion and, more importantly, conduct research in an embodied fashion.

Body Matters: Breaking Gender Binaries in Leadership

The body has always remained marginal in social science research and theory[5] including the subfield of leadership, despite heartfelt beliefs that 'bodies are restraints and resources but also media through which leadership is created, experienced and understood'.[6] Also, even though a growing literature over the last few decades, across a broad range of the social sciences and humanities, has focused on the body,[7] not much has changed in leadership studies.[8] Partly, the roots of this are epistemological insofar as science and rationality presume knowledge to reside exclusively in a relationship between the human mind and the world to which it refers. This leaves the knower's body out of the equation since it is seen as nothing more than a 'passive container for the mind'.[9] While the body cannot be discounted in this way, it reflects the 'anatomising urge' of dissecting the body into its constituent parts and re-organising it for scientific purposes through various anatomical classifications. Moreover, it has been argued that this urge cannot be dissociated from an earlier violence[10] albeit, one that generally remains only symbolic in contemporary knowledge production.

Taking the body and emotion as both a point of departure and of destination, the quotation at the beginning of this chapter reminds us that it is still necessary to recognise how embodiment remains a provisional condition of an ever-changing horizon of future possibilities.

However, in so many research reports and texts, the silencing of the body and emotion is the norm. It can be seen as one of the clearest indications of the gender binary that reflects and reproduces dominant masculine discourses in society. Popularised in absurdly wild, sexist self-help books such as *Men are from Venus, Women are from Mars*,[11] the gender binary is seen to separate men from women in terms respectively of rationality versus emotion, competition in contrast to collaboration, and material or instrumental action as against symbolic and intimate relations. Whereas Gray reifies the differences between the sexes and then offers guidance on how this knowledge can be used almost instrumentally in their relations with one another, more academic literature on masculinity seeks to theorise and transform relations.[12] Most of these books attribute the difficulties that men experience in their relations with themselves, each other and the opposite sex to be connected with repression or neglect of their emotions and the more vulnerable aspects of the body. Men's preoccupation with the achievement of goals through instrumental rational action leaves them devoid of self-awareness and embodied reasoning that might expose them to some of its contradictions. For example, its tunnel vision is often self-defeating insofar as it distances men not only from themselves but also from others in ways that disrupt collaborative activity.

Neglecting the body originates with the dominance of Cartesian metaphysics of separating the mind from the body, and then elevating the former over the latter – what has become known as a dualistic ontology. It has its sociological counterpart in the separation of fact and value to which Weber paid much attention.[13] He argued for a distinction between formal rationality, where the most rational means to a given end were chosen without much thought about the rationality of the end itself. By contrast, substantive rationality was more concerned with the values to which the end was directed than with the means to its attainment. While there are considerable overlap and fuzziness between these dimensions, a bureaucratic mode of organisation is closer to formal rationality wherein there are 'Specialists without spirit, sensualists without heart; this nullity imagines that it has attained a level of civilization never before achieved'.[14] Acknowledging the tunnel vision of bureaucrats, critics drew attention to some of the dysfunctions[15] of formal rationality because, by focusing on the means of achieving certain objectives, it displaced any concern with what ends it was meaningful to pursue. Criticisms, and even predictions of the imminent demise, of bureaucracy, continued to the end of the 20th century.[16] However, eventually, a backlash emerged that sought to defend bureaucracy against its critics who are often seen to neglect the diversity of forms, as well as the different contexts, in which it may or may not be an appropriate form of administration and organisation.[17] What can be concluded from the criticism and countercriticism is that the problem has been a reflection of the dualism between fact and value, means and ends, and rationality and emotion. Were one to start from a different place — perhaps a monistic rather than a dualistic ontology[18] — we may perhaps be less sanguine concerning the benefits of bureaucracy in allowing a reflection only on the means rather than the ends of any enterprise. Also, we may be less convinced of its inevitable decline because even though we might wish to debate goals and values, once agreed, no one wants ineffective or inefficient means of attaining them. The question is whether or not the technical rationality of this efficiency must preclude *embodied reasoning*?

This dominance of rationality is also a facet of existentialism with its fear and anxiety about the void that resides in a world of contingency and uncertainty, where any overriding authority such as God or the State is absent. Sartre expressed the 'horror of contingency' as a 'viscosity' that 'drags us down' and impedes our freedom.[19] Considering the contingent nature of all life, it is a little absurd for the philosopher of absurdity to have been so troubled by it but, as will be argued later, a certain masculine vision craves mathematical certainty to bring relief from the void and anxiety of a contingent, unpredictable and disorderly world.[20] Others have described this in terms of an anatomising urge wherein the objects of knowledge are dissected, fragmented and treated hierarchically often to render them abject and excluded, especially where the body and subjectivity are concerned.[21] Leadership is no exception to this characterisation of the production of knowledge and it is not difficult to see this as a reflection of a Cartesian, as well as an anatomical, legacy that is sustained through discourses and practices of masculinity.[22] It helps to understand how much social research, including studies of leadership and management, in particular, are dominated by cognitive rationality and often devoid of any sense of embodiment and emotional resonance.

Through reference to some of my empirical research and reflections on gender, work and organisation more generally, I now seek to develop an analysis of the academic self-censoring of the body and emotion in research where it reflects and reproduces masculine discourses. The main focus of this analysis is a discussion of identity and 'grand narrative' or universal theories that seek to provide an exhaustive representation of the world. These are representations that override contingency to present reality as orderly and stable as this renders identity, and more particularly the masculine self, more secure.[23]

Silencing the Body and Emotion

The silencing of emotion and references to the body in general leadership and management texts, research reports and, more particularly, those on methodology is the norm and can be seen as one of the clearest indications of the gender binary[24] that reflects and reproduces dominant masculine discourses in society.[25] For example, in a search of 7 major contemporary introductory textbooks on organisation behaviour and management, only one[26] has more than 2 sentences that might be seen as relating to the body or emotion and even here its 5 pages are focused on what they describe as non-verbal behaviour. For example, where pupil dilation and other bodily gestures contradict the actual words spoken may reveal whether the body is compliant with, or resistant to, cognitive speech. However, the marginality of the body is indicated more clearly when it is seen that less than 6 out of a total of more than 3,000 pages are concerned with anything remotely relating to the body and emotion.[27]

This is more or less the same when it comes to methodological texts where even when primarily qualitative in approach, virtually no reference is made to bodily or emotional issues. This despite the contingent, contextual and uncertain character of most research in leadership and management, which is at least partly a function of the obduracy yet the vulnerability of human bodies and emotions. However, the authority of masculine methodological conventions readily overrules the actual contingency, context and uncertainty encountered by researchers daily. As evidence of this, I draw here on a few examples from my past research where despite highly important contingent and disruptive, bodily and emotional features that affected the research, these were conveniently self-censored.

Personal Research and Self-censorship

I have selected out just three of many possible research projects where I experienced some emotional trauma but then self-censored it in any writing of reports or publications.

Newspaper Case Study

This project was conducted in the advertising sales department of a major regional newspaper as part of my doctoral research. I secured both management and union access to conduct participant observation research of the sales staff that had been considered less efficient than desirable. Just before beginning the research, senior management had called in a group of consultants who proceeded with a re-organisation of the department, which involved redundancies for one-third of the staff. The consultants were unaware of the staff's membership of the printing union so that they could supplement their income by working Saturday nights on the printing presses. To fight the redundancies, the staff formed their chapel and secured the support of the union for a strike that shut down the newspaper and this resulted in management immediately reinstating those whose jobs had been threatened.

A typical day would begin with all the sales staff reading the paper under the pretence that they were looking for sales opportunities which, on their admission, was patently not the case but was simply a 'skive'. After an hour and a half of this, a large group of the staff would meet up in the coffee bar for a very extended break or 'skive' when they would also plan what the social activities or 'super skive' would be for that day. Invariably this would involve just meeting in a pub at around 11:30 am and once the pubs closed at 3 pm, extending the drinking often at the Press Club until late afternoon when they would return to the office. Occasionally super-duper skives would take place whereby some of the staff would spend the day playing golf[28] or take a trip to major holiday resorts such as Blackpool, the Peak District or the Lake District in the UK.

It is clear that these salespeople undertook very little formal work and had the organisation not been a quasi-monopolistic supplier of advertising space, with a classified advertising department of telephone sales that sustained advertising revenues,[29] it probably would have collapsed commercially. Management sought to intervene at various points but whenever they tried to affect some control through closer supervision, such as accompanying sales staff on meetings with customers, generating sales targets and bonuses, or enforcing sales training, it came up against a union-backed outright refusal. Any attempt by management to try to manage the sales staff was seen as simply a vehicle for selecting out some of them for redundancy.

Eventually, the Father of the Chapel, who had quite strong intellectual interests and was thinking of returning to academic study, persuaded me to write down a summary of where I was up to in the research. I agreed partly because I thought it would be helpful to receive feedback from him as to the validity of my analysis but naïvely, in retrospect, because he passed it on to all the staff. My analysis generally took the form of suggesting that the impasse between management and staff could only be broken if both sides understood the relationship between power and responsibility. Immediately staff who felt most vulnerable to redundancy engineered a campaign to have me removed from the site for fear that I would start reporting to management about the skives. While the Father of the Chapel supported my staying, I had to present my case to a staff meeting organised by the union and the outcome was that 11 against 10 of the staff voted for me to be denied further research access.

Despite, but in retrospect probably because of, the emotional trauma of having been 'thrown out' of the field rather than leaving voluntarily, no mention of this was ever included in my PhD nor in any publications that I developed from the research. Several years after the event I am now able to express my upset, embarrassment if not humiliation at being forced to leave. I would argue that it was my masculine pride of being reluctant to acknowledge any personal failure that accounts for my leaving out such emotional traumas from these research accounts. Of course, this reluctance is supported by a whole range of rationales deriving from research methodology texts[30] where there is virtually no licence given for 'telling it like it is', or providing an account of the disruptions and divergences, the cul de sacs and false trails, or the numerous feelings of despair and helplessness as you struggle, often alone, to make sense of a project that seems to be going nowhere. Instead, these texts treat the research process as a unilinear, rational series of steps and stages culminating in an often anodyne and depersonalised account of various events.

Sex Discrimination in Recruitment

This research was funded by the Equal Opportunity Council (EOC) and involved two independent experiences of an emotional nature. The funding agency was concerned to demonstrate that the opportunities for women could improve immensely if only some of the subtle and indirect practices of discrimination could be exposed through research and then ultimately removed. While accepting this task, I wanted to incorporate into the research report the argument that while it is important to remove obstacles to equal opportunity, such ideals do in the end legitimise rather than challenge social inequality since they simply shift the basis of discrimination to merit and produce a meritocracy. In some senses, failure to succeed in a meritocracy leads to a loss of dignity and self-blame that can be more devastating than when the system can be blamed.[31] This involved not only conflict with the funding agency but also disagreement with my research assistant who was less concerned to challenge the EOCs position. Later this disagreement developed into a major emotional conflict between the two of us that for me, and perhaps also for him, was devastating. It would not be fair to detail this without permission but for me, it marked the dwindling of a very close friendship that would be difficult to retrieve, and this was extremely upsetting. It also disrupted the work in several ways yet when publications were eventually produced neither of us was sufficiently open to express these emotional tensions, let alone analyse them.

Death of the Subject

In a project of innovation funded by the UK University funding agency — the Economic and Social Research Council (ESRC) — one of the researchers seemed to take Foucault's claim regarding the death of the subject rather too literally and died, after falling over a balcony whilst on holiday in Mexico. Whether this death was in any way suicidal will never be known but the researcher had struggled to develop reports on his research. A second researcher, also under pressure to produce his research findings, absconded taking all his data with him after having been pressed to provide a report of his findings. From a relative of his, I learned that he had gone to Germany, but he left no address and was impossible to trace. These events were extremely upsetting emotionally since it is impossible not to feel responsible for such unfortunate outcomes. However, they also had severe implications for the research since much of the data was either stored on numerous tapes or non-existent. While, as research supervisors, we cobbled together what we could, none of these emotional traumas was given attention, other than in the section on extenuating circumstances, in the final report to the funding agency. Such is the level of disembodiment that devastating experiences of the death or derailment of research subjects are swept under the carpet as unfortunate contingencies. Their disavowal can only be a reflection of deeply embedded masculinities that dismiss or rationalise experiences because of their threat to the linear-rational programme of completing a research project.

Masculine Disembodiment and Emotional Impoverishment

In partial defence of my disembodiment in these accounts of the research process, I could argue that the events took place before I had become fully aware of the all-too-frequent displacement of the body and feelings because of a masculine dominated, cognitive myopia. However, given the development of our ideas about masculinity within the research on sex discrimination in recruitment,[32] this should not have been the case. It demonstrates how even when research is focused on the body and masculinities, we can remain locked in a cognitive paradigm. So, while writing about the masculinities of our research participants, we failed to reflect on our masculinities. This neglect is even worse because it has been argued that these comparatively detached interpretations of research participants is a form of authoritative denial of their voice and, in that sense, instrumental use of others for our benefit as researchers.[33] This is quite bizarre since many of us writing in the field of critical leadership pride ourselves in our self-reflexivity and capacity to learn about ourselves through our engagement with research participants.

Cognitive awareness of a phenomenon, even when concerned with the body and emotion, does not guarantee embodied reasoning and behaviour. This is because our everyday practices are informed by heavily internalised norms and beliefs whose transcendence depends precisely on transformations that such transcendence anticipates. It is not, then, surprising to find disembodied research even when focused on the body and emotions for these can become just another object to capture and control, to organise and order, or to manage and manipulate. Examining the proliferating literature on emotional labour, authors have criticised its tendency to provide a merely cognitive and disembodied view of research participants.[34] This reflects and reinforces the dualistic trap of perceiving the body as separate from the mind as well as an inclination to bring the irascible, uncertainty of the former under the control of cognition. For example, Hochschild argued that 'to become an emotional labourer is no easy, ephemeral accomplishment'.[35] However, she falls into the trap here of associating emotion with the ephemeral rather than the somatic but then drawing the inference that the mind or cognition has to take control to make such emotional labour (commercially) effective. She provides no sense of bodies, emotions and cognition as a coherent whole, indivisible from one another and the sense of what is the lived experience of acting and thinking. Instead, Hochschild's discourse represents the body as 'a hollowed-out sense of the somatic and corporeal as an ephemeral and *false* surface'.[36] Yet, it is bizarre to separate the emotions (feelings) from the body:

> as though there were a bodily state housed in the basement with feelings dwelling upstairs. Feeling, as feeling oneself to be, is precisely the way we are bodily. Bodily being does not mean that the soul is burdened by a hulk we call the body. ... We do not "have" a body; rather, we "are" bodily.[37]

Nietzsche also celebrated the body and its senses and sought to free them from the torment of a puritanical conscience.[38] Later, existentialism also described the tormented experience of nausea as we are confronted with the viscous sense of excess and overflowing that is the lived experience of bodily existence.[39] Philosophers such as Nietzsche have been seen as dissidents and subversives residing very much in the underground of intellectual life and in the shadow of mainstream Cartesian thinking that has dominated Western thought since the Enlightenment. Only occasionally does the body resurface as, for example, in the work of post-structuralists such as Judith Butler, Michel Foucault, Gilles Deleuze and Felix Guattari, Luce Irigaray, Julia Kristeva, Toril Moi,[40] more broadly in feminist cultural and political studies in the writings of Susan Bordo, Elizabeth Grosz, Rosemary Hennessy, Dalia Judovitz, Ladine McWhorter and Iris Marion Young,[41] and in organisation studies, in the work of Joan Acker, Karen Dale; Marta Calás and Linda Smircich, and Torkild Thanem and David Knights.[42]

The Cartesian Legacy

It is commonplace to recognise that silencing the body and emotion beneath a blanket of cognitive comfort is traceable to the mind-body dualism of Descartes, who reduced the body to an anatomical and disembodied abstraction. Here there can be an effect without any substantive presence so that the mind is engaged in a ritualised attempt to dispose of its bodily 'other'. Regarded as superfluous, and even unpleasant or disgusting, the body is marginalised, and closure of meaning is constructed around such reason.[43] In short, by valorising the mind in this way the cognitive aspect of the body is seen to displace that which it is not — the amorphous, diffuse, unpredictable and ever-changing organic form that is its lived experience. In such models, human agency is an expression of thought alone so that ... 'the body is disenfranchised from action'. This is ... 'not just metaphysical but also technological since objectification and instrumentalisation of the body' ... is achieved ... 'through its reduction to a mechanical device — a machine'. ... 'The Cartesian body is no longer defined by custom, experience or habit. Reason is its sole guide and defining principle'.[44] An even common-sense phrase such as it is 'just a matter of mind over matter' prevails on us to control our bodies rather than allow them to interfere with the orderly, cognitive certainty and purposive intent of rational action. Certitude founded on mathematical principles is what lies behind the binary, as was clear in the angst and anomie prevalent in the existentialist discourses of Sartre and others.

As remarked upon earlier, existentialists were overwhelmed by the contingency of nature and its disorder, excess, viscosity and tendency to overflow or leak to violate representations that have sought to eradicate its uncontrollable 'impurities'.[45] Sartre, in particular, longed for the certainty that only mathematical rationality could bring about,[46] although later he settled for an alternative in the rigid politics of the Soviet communist regime.[47] Sartre's existential anxiety concerning the uncontrollability of the world and desire for it to resemble the certainty of a mathematical model is, arguably, closely linked to his attachment to deeply masculine discourses. This might be seen as ironical given that his lifetime partner — Simone de Beauvoir — has been claimed as the greatest post-Pankhurst 20th-century feminist.[48] A further irony is that de Beauvoir collaborated with Sartre in his 'unhealthy' masculine sexual pursuits and his fascination with celebrity.[49] Of course, forms of masculinity and their earlier discursive construction as manliness were deeply taken for granted until the late 1970s,[50] after which they began to be deconstructed by pro-feminist men and feminist women.

The philosophical basis for Sartre's existentialism, and his preoccupation with personal projects to overcome meaninglessness, was phenomenology and its focus on the notion of intentionality as that which makes a subject assert itself, or at least its significance, concerning the object and ultimately to another subject. Phenomenology would then seem to provide a philosophical justification for the intentional ego, instrumentally transforming the world into a resource for its stability, security and 'success'. This may well account for the popularity of phenomenology especially in western social science where it seems to encompass few enemies.[51] If the social world were one where collective virtues and values thrived, this legitimisation of instrumentalism would probably not have much significance. However, as both a medium and outcome of an individualised society, it supports a continued belief in the 'hidden hand' of self-interest in 'free markets' as benefiting everyone through the trickle-down effect of wealth production.[52] On the other hand, the individualistic grounding of existentialist philosophies perhaps accounts for their demise. In many senses, they are a continuation of the Cartesian binary where ego-centric individuals seek to secure meaning for the self through ordering the world in their image according to personal projects or suffer emasculation in the face of a meaningless void.

This privileging of one side of a binary — the so-called objective over the subjective, individual over society, reason over emotion, linear rationality over other forms of rationality is all part of elevating masculine above feminine discourses and subjectivities. Since the body and emotion are always associated with females, the subordination of women to men is natural to the logic of Cartesian rationality.

Women are seen like nature itself to be a passive or inert frame upon which culture or sex is inscribed through the constructions of men and masculine institutions. There is a denial of embodiment from the framework of male subjectivity that leads to its 'sexless' and impersonal appearance.[53] By contrast, nature and the female body are seen simply to submit to the discourses that govern and discipline their organisation and regulation through specific power /knowledge relations. While the Cartesian binary was tacitly underpinned by non-explicated masculine rationality, it is only in the late 20th and early 21st century that a displacement of the body and emotion has been explicitly deconstructed as reflecting discourses of masculinity.[54]

Masculine Discourses

A preoccupation with masculine identity can be seen to have had its genesis in a range of effects stemming from the growth of civilization. As far back as the French revolution, civilization had laid the ground for the rise of feminist demands for equal rights but left men emasculated as they struggled to live up to images of the gentleman steeped in moral rectitude and social reputation as the measure of manhood.[55] This same idea of civilization was eventually drawn upon to re-establish male power and authority. But it had to be tempered by a return to more primitive notions of male sexuality and virility as part of the shift whereby masculinity was seen less as social reputation and more as a claim to personal identity.[56] While this claim to personal identity has continued to hold sway throughout the whole of the 20th century, it was not until the early 1970s that masculine identity began once again to be the focus of attention as insecurities and anxieties surrounding it proliferated largely in response to threats from a more virulent feminism.

The politically radical 1960s spawned a massive revival of feminist politics and one that, in contrast to its earlier demands for the franchise, turned its attention more directly to everyday gender relations. In both institutional and organisational life, male power became a target for critique in the new rapidly expanding feminist discourse, and there is no question that many men felt weakened and vulnerable as a result. More recently, discourses on masculinity focused on nature/nurture binaries where sex is seen as purely biological and gender derived from cultural and social learning. This kind of analysis drew on role theory where there was perceived to be a radical separation of the person from their behaviour so that gender was seen as separate from the self.[57]

Role theory was, of course, an aspect of functionalism with its assumptions that the two genders were in harmony with one another and therefore, functioned to maintain the social system. Critiqued generally for its conservative, consensual and individualistic character, feminists in the 1970s objected to its universal treatment of the genders. Besides, it was seen as masking domination and discrimination in social relations, including along lines of class, race, ethnicity, sexual orientation, age, mental and physical ability, region, religion, as well as gender.[58] The focus gradually moved to a notion of gender identity, which was seen as much more unstable and precarious than that depicted by role theory. Gender identity began to be understood as something that was accomplished or achieved by meeting certain performative standards in social interactions. To accomplish a masculine identity, for example, it was necessary to demonstrate high levels of strategic rationality, competitiveness and conquest, especially of a sexual nature.[59] Personal or emotional matters were considered taboo even among intimate friends, if that is not an oxymoron, and men were generally driven by a no-nonsense practical pursuit of material and symbolic success. Gradually, as evidence rendered this model of phallic masculinity too heavy a stereotype, the literature demonstrated that there was a multiplicity of masculinities. However, many authors began a trend in confessional narratives as it became 'de rigueur' for men to express their so-called repressed emotions and anxieties stemming from that repression.[60]

Much of this literature displayed remorse and regret concerning the pressure that masculinity had placed on men to be sturdy and stalwart and never to give in to their emotions. A wide variety of responses resulted, some accepting the challenge to change to accommodate feminist demands for more sensitivity ('New Man'), others attempting self-indulgent assertions of a new 'tough' yet emotional positive narrative of the masculine self in returning men to the past in what was believed to be their manly battle with nature.[61] As more and more mothers chose to advance their careers outside the home, some 'new men' embraced the idea of becoming househusbands or house-partners looking after children and keeping house. By contrast, the 'Iron John' fraternity sought to engage in collective hand ringing rituals of expressing themselves and reversing a history of so-called repressed emotions. Simultaneously they sought to re-assert their masculinity with increased vigour, through developing survival skills such as logging, hunting and fishing and living in the wild. This kind of programme seemed necessary for middle-class city dwellers while affluent men in the countryside had never abandoned the expression of tough masculinity and male bonding through such activities as shooting, hunting and fishing. This return to a preoccupation with masculinity coincided with the rapid advance of the gay movement, which constructed a new 'softer' and stylish masculine image for homosexuals but one that also strongly impacted images of the 'new man' in the 'straight' community.

While taking a proliferation of forms, these shifts in what it was to be a man could be seen, at least in part, as a reflection of the postmodern desire to render the masculine/feminine and mind/body binary problematic and to deconstruct it, not only in theory but also in practice. However, at the same time as the binary is deconstructed, it is also reproduced since whether the distinction between men and women or masculinity and femininity is being exaggerated or diminished, the terms of the binary remain in place. So, despite a voluminous literature on masculinity, only a limited number of authors have focused on challenging the binary polarisations that are also reproduced by concerns to *reverse* the historical privileging of the mind and its silencing of the body and emotion.

Dissolving the Mind/Body Binary

Deconstruction theory challenges the binary at the level of epistemology in, for example, exposing the concealed assumptions about the self and identity that condition the possibility of our disembodied representations of life. It also allows us to identify the dominance of linear progressive, masculine rationalities that marginalise the body and emotion. As we shall see in Chapter 7, these disembodied masculine rationalities direct us all but, more importantly, leaders who can impact greatly our ways of life. They do so in such a way as to displace ethics from thinking and feeling. While this has to involve some reflexive assessment and reformulation of ourselves, this is not a smooth path to an ethical way of life. Even for Foucault where the 'the telos of his ethics' was a 'curiosity' to 'get free of ... [him] ... oneself',[62] he declared a view of 'friendship [as] reciprocity' as distinct from sexual relations that are not.[63] By contrast with friendship, he asked whether, concerning sex, we might become more reciprocal by taking into 'account the pleasure of the other?'.[64] However, reciprocity and the idea of taking the other into account reflect masculine discourses of separation between self and other — a separation that can only be bridged by the recognition and attempted fulfilment of each other's (instrumental) self-interests. In this sense, Foucault is unable 'to get free from' himself, particularly his internalised masculine subjectivity. For this continues to reside in instrumental pursuits that are, at best reciprocal, rather than embedded in an embodied ethics of engagement and relationality.[65]

We then remain locked in a cognitive deconstruction, rather than an embodied dissolution, of the domination of mind over matter. What may be necessary is to break away from the mere epistemological deconstruction of mind-body and other binaries where we only show them as reified polarities that can be challenged. Deleuze and Guattari seek an ontological dissolution of 'the body as a discontinuous, non-totalisable series of processes, organs, flows, energies, corporeal substances and incorporated events, speeds and durations'.[66] Their bodies-without-organised-organs[67] can be seen as a reconceptualisation that displaces the teleology or intentionality of consciousness or what, throughout this book, I have been describing as the preoccupation with identity. This is to reject the normalised life that reflects and reinforces a rule-based morality rather than one where ethics is a project of refusing the subjectivity that has been imposed upon us as subjects.[68] In speaking about becoming-woman,[69] their dissolution of the body might be seen as simply dissipating masculine identities but, in effect, it is about the deterritorialisation that disavows identity per se.

While there is a substantial debate both for and against Deleuze and Guattari's thesis where some see it as a masculine appropriation of feminism,[70] Grosz is inspired by it to re-theorise the body and self as neither a psychical or corporeal substantive entity but more as an effect of 'the pure difference that constitutes all modes of materiality', and especially the sexed body.[71] This sexed body, she claims, has to be theorised in non-patriarchal terms if women's autonomous self-representation is to be developed. Otherwise, the tendency for male philosophers to reproduce phallocentric representations[72] that do violence to women and minorities is left unchallenged.[73] Grosz opts, then, for a different way of *dissolving* traditional binary polarities between mind and body. Through an inversion, the mind and body are understood as in a process of continually becoming one another such that the inside or psychic aspects drift into the outside corporeal self and vice versa.[74] In this way, she has sought to rethink the self and subjectivity through re-theorising the body to depart from both Cartesian mind-body, and Freudian conscious-unconscious mind, binaries.

That said, the theories of Deleuze and Guattari do allow us to 'acknowledge the normative operations of sex and gender without prioritising either'.[75] They also provide us with a potential way of thinking about leadership and organisation that would facilitate a diminishing of the dominant masculine ethos, where power and control eviscerate relations of ethical engagement. If a non-binary and embodied form of thought is to be established, there is a need to criticise not just representationalism but also realism since they both subscribe to a separation of words and things.[76] In the former, too much power is acceded to language whereas in the latter, too much power is given to an unknowable reality that has determinate effects on the structure of relations. A way of doing this is through 'agential realism' where matter and meaning, nature and culture, body and mind, and emotion and cognition are seen as performatively entangled as agents and products of one another.[77] Despite productive power reflecting this performative entanglement, masculine discursive practices within leadership often deny the entanglement through an anthropocentric and individualistic elevation of cognition. This may have several contradictory consequences, the more vivid of which has been the corporate moral scandals culminating in the global financial crisis discussed in Chapters 7 and 10.

Perhaps, even more important are the health pandemics and global warming that are at least partly an outcome of the exploitation of animals and the environment for human self-interest. Agential realism makes it clear that material and symbolic, body and mind, and nature and culture are not 'in a relationship of externality to each other for they are 'mutually implicated in the dynamics of intra-activity'.[78] The term intra-action, as opposed to interaction, is crucial because the latter presumes a prior separation of bounded entities in advance of their interaction. In contrast, the former captures an engagement of, internally related yet unbounded elements that are emergent through their entanglement. Rather than a separation of the world and knowledge, the merging of ontology and epistemology generates practices of knowing in being, or what is termed 'onto-epistem-ology'.[79] Having developed both the epistemological deconstruction and the ontological dissolution of binaries, the discourse of agential realism generates not only the conditions that make possible but also the moral imperative for, embodied reason and ethical engagement that is now discussed through the notion of affect.

Affect and its Affects in Leadership

How contemporary studies of leadership have challenged the reductionism within 'scientific' attempts to 'capture' the elements that render it effective has opened up space to examine affect and affections by returning to the medieval philosopher Spinoza.[80] For Spinoza, affect relates to how 'the body's power of acting is increased or diminished, aided or restrained'.[81] While affective research approaches are still embryonic,[82] occasionally authors suggest that leadership should not be studied at all as, paradoxically, it is most effective 'where leadership is not required'.[83] As yet, few offer an alternative way of studying leadership that is compatible with this challenge to the mainstream. However, it may be argued that affect provides precisely such an alternative embodied approach to understanding the 'invisible' as residing *in-between* subject and object, mind and body, and leaders and followers. Science has always sought to efface such ephemeral phenomena that defy objectification; instead, it favours representations generated by sovereign subjects whose actions are deemed to generate precise knowledge of the world, including notions of leadership. But this in-between not only involves affectively engaged bodies affecting other bodies and their (our) material and symbolic lives, it also energises these self-same bodies in ways that enhance their (our) capacity to be affective. It also energises us to explore the ambiguous in-between spaces that prevail on us to engage with, rather than seek masculine control over, the Other regardless of leadership relations. Fundamentally, affect reflects and reinforces ethics whereby we identify with other bodies sufficiently 'for us to have ...[a real] ... concern'.[84] Perhaps leadership might begin to resemble what Foucault describes as the art of living an aesthetic existence, where true knowledge depends entirely on 'an essential position of otherness'.[85] For, there is massive bodily energy affecting leadership processes and the outcome significantly affects us through a wide range of embodied experiences from anguish to euphoria, sadness to exhilaration, panic to passion, fear to courage and pessimism to optimism, to mention only a few. These processes, however, are open to endless capacities to affect and be affected, but also subject the body to a recognition of its own 'indeterminacy'.[86]

Yet why refer to *affect* as opposed to feelings or emotions? While affect incorporates feelings and emotions, the latter are more static, concrete and individualised, referring almost always to individual sentient, and usually human, beings. By contrast, affect is dynamic and inter-corporeal as well as referring to material objects and not exclusively, humans. It should be defined, therefore, 'in terms of its autonomy from conscious perception and language, as well as emotion'.[87] So, for example, a feeling or emotion is a state of being, or the property, of a sentient subject at a singular moment in time. By contrast, an affect is always in transition moving from source(s) to destination(s) often in reciprocal fashion and can just as readily be virtual as real.[88] We affect a vast range of material, animal and human phenomena, as they affect us. Consequently, affect cannot be seen as the property of a person so much as reflecting a complex web of relations or networks. Although 'affect is subjectively felt as a sense of freedom or potential that adds intensity to action and events', ... [it] ... 'can not be *reduced* to a property of the subject'.[89]

By focusing on affect, I am not inventing something new so much as acknowledging the body as simultaneously the subject and object of its action. How it affects and is affected by other bodies in ways that may enhance or destroy the capacity for reasoned action is an important focus. As has been argued, traditional thinking about leadership has often been constrained by proprietary understandings that attribute essential qualities to leaders that render them charismatic, heroic, rational and perhaps even magical. Limitedly, this individualisation of the notion of leadership as a property of persons has been restrained in succeeding developments that emphasise the context, the followers and practice. Nonetheless, romanticising or idealising the individual leader remains a legacy that is frequently rekindled, sneaked in by the back door, or simply presumed in the form of proprietary views of power, as was discussed in Chapter 4.

Summary and Conclusion

This chapter has examined the way that researchers tend to be self-censoring regarding the body and emotions when reporting or publishing their work. To illustrate this, I took three separate examples from many that I could have drawn upon from my research career where I had avoided reporting on major emotional traumas that affected myself, possibly colleagues and the research. I sought to account for this self-censorship in terms of my attachment to a masculine identity and its legislative denial of disaster, disruption or disturbance of cognitive and rational research pursuits. This was then examined through a broader understanding of mind-body and gender binary thinking and the literature on masculinity. This was followed by a discussion of the Cartesian legacy and existentialist ways of responding to contingency, indeterminacy and uncertainty.

I then proceeded to examine discourses of masculinity that reflect and reproduce the mind-body binary of Descartes along with several other binaries. Here I concluded that while the body and emotions have been comparatively taboo topics in social science, and particularly leadership research, addressing this lacuna often serves to reproduce rather than deconstruct or dissolve the gender binary. In examining philosophical and feminist literature that seeks to dissolve rather than merely deconstruct the binary, I followed two approaches that have a more satisfactory outcome than most deliberations in this field. The first focused on disrupting the binaries through theorising how the mind and body flow into one another in processes of becoming that challenge the domination of masculine sensibilities. The second was concerned to build on the deconstruction of representational epistemologies to develop an integration of epistemology and ontology through embracing the entanglement of matter and meaning, body and emotion, and masculinity and femininity. This provided the basis for an analysis of affect as an embodied approach to understanding leadership that resides *in-*

*between*subject and object, mind and body, and leaders and followers. This further confirms the importance of eschewing proprietary conceptions of, and masculine behaviours in, leadership.

This concern for a more embodied and less masculine theory and practice of leadership is inspired by pro-feminist research that seeks to free itself from the body/emotion taboo to generate the acceptance and respect for difference as a way of reversing sex and other inequalities and discriminations. One implication of this analysis is that research on leadership might in the future avoid its ignorance of the body, in all its manifestations of age, disability, ethnicity, gender, race and sexuality. Also, this means that the body has significance for the subject matter of most of the other chapters in this book on identity, insecurity, power and resistance, and diversity and gender and, especially, the next chapter on ethics for, as it is often claimed, business ethics is often informed by masculine discourses that preclude a feminine voice.[90]

Notes

1 Learmonth and Morrell (2019).
2 Uhl-Bien (2006), Raelin (2014).
3 Foucault (1982, p. 212).
4 Hynes (2013, p. 571).
5 Levin (1985), Turner (1992), Shilling (1993), Williams and Bendelow (1998), Dale (2001), Thanem and Wallenberg (2015).
6 Falkman (2016, p. 85).
7 For example, a trans-disciplinary journal Body and Society was launched in March 1995 and has pioneered and shaped the field of body studies. However, feminist and literary studies, gender and ethnicity research, and sociology more generally have all given more attention to the body.
8 cf. Munro and Thanem (2018).
9 Dale (2001, p, 58).
10 Ibid., p. 25; Sawday (1995, p. 15).
11 Gray (2008).
12 Tolson (1977); Connell, (1987); Brittan, (1989), Seidler (1989); Cohen (1990); Hearn and Morgan (1990); Rutherford, (1992); Brod (1995).
13 Weber (1949).
14 Weber (1930/2001, p. 168).
15 Merton et al. (1961).
16 Castells (2000).
17 du Gay (2000).
18 Spinoza (1677/1883).
19 Bakewell (2017, p. 105).
20 Philosophers were not alone in their search for certainty in the world, and in some cases, driving them to suicide. For example, 'Ludwig Boltzmann's struggle to prove the existence of atoms and probability eventually drove him to suicide. Kurt Gödel, the introverted confidant of Einstein, proved that there would always be problems, which were outside human logic. His life ended in a sanatorium where he starved himself to death. Finally, Alan Turing, the great Bletchley Park code breaker ... died trying to prove that some things are fundamentally unprovable (*BBC 2*, 2008).

21 Dale (2001).
22 Judovitz (2001).
23 Clough (1992).
24 Linstead and Brewis (2004).
25 Knights and Kerfoot (2004).
26 Huczynski and Buchanan (2001).
27 The books consulted are as follows: Fincham and Rhodes (1999); Huczynski and Buchanan (2001); Jackson and Carter (2007); Knights and Willmott (2007); Martin (2001); McAuley, Duberley and Johnson (2007). All these books incorporate a critical edge so may have been expected to include more references to the body and emotion.
28 The staff seemed to like the danger of possibly being caught by management since they were renowned to take time out to play golf and occasionally to drink at the Press Club. Both sides could, of course, claim that these events were simply about entertaining business clients.
29 This department was also a part of my research and that of one of my doctoral students and is reported in Knights and Roberts (1982).
30 Increasingly there have been exceptions to this, but I discovered few of them at the time of my fieldwork.
31 Sennett and Cobb (1977).
32 Collinson et al. (1990).
33 Wray-Bliss (2002); see also Wray-Bliss (2003).
34 Dale (2001) and Witz, Warhurst and Nickson (2003).
35 Hochschild (1983, quoted in Witz et al., 2003, p. 37).
36 ibid., 36.
37 Heidegger (1979, pp. 98–99; quoted in Levin, 1985, p. 49).
38 Nietzsche (1968, p. 434).
39 Sartre (1938).
40 The following are mere examples and not intended to be exhaustive of authors that have contributed significantly to theorizing the body and embodied theory in the tradition of the philosophers of subversion: Butler (1990, 1993, 2004); Foucault (1979); Deleuze and Guattari (1988); Irigaray (1980); Kristeva (1991); Moi (1985, 2001).
41 Bordo (2004); Grosz (1994); Hennessy (1993); Judovitz (2001); McWhorter (1999); and Young (2005).
42 Acker (1990, 1998); Calás and Smircich (1991); Dale (2001); Thanem and Knights (2019).
43 Derrida (1982).
44 Judovitz (2001, p. 68).
45 Sartre (1938/1949).
46 Murdoch (1953).
47 Sartre (1991).
48 Several writers, however, now interpret her philosophical framework as closer to Merleau-Ponty's than to Jean-Paul Sartre's see McWeeny (2017).
49 Seymour-Jones (2008).
50 Tolson (1977).
51 One highly significant opponent of phenomenology is Michel Foucault who, according to Danaher et al. (2000, p. 11), regarded it as an essentialising theory 'which relied on an absolute and ahistorical quality or "truth"'. This is seen to derive from the 'ability of human beings to understand the world and their involvement in the world' (ibid.). This total rejection of phenomenology could also be seen as having its downside in Foucault not being able

to elaborate the vulnerability of subjects to discipline and power as having its condition in insecurity (Knights, 1990; see also McNay, 1994).

52 Smith (1793/1976).
53 Judovitz (2001, p. 9).
54 Linstead and Brewis (2004).
55 Bederman (1995).
56 Tosh (1999, p. 219).
57 Brod (1995).
58 Ibid.
59 Kerfoot and Knights (2002).
60 Seidler (1989); Cohen (1990); Rutherford (1992).
61 Bly (1990).
62 Foucault (1985, p. x, quoted in Foucault, 1997, p. xxx).
63 Foucault (1985, p. 257–258, quoted in Foucault, 1997, p. xxviii).
64 Ibid.
65 Haraway (1991); Barad (2007); Braidotti (2013).
66 Deleuze and Guattari (1988, p. 145).
67 Gatens (1997).
68 Foucault (1982).
69 Deleuze and Guattari (1988, p. 276).
70 Sotirin (2011, pp. 116–130).
71 Grosz (1994, p. 208).
72 Ibid., pp. 154–155. This is a reference to Deleuze and Guattari's (1988, p. 145) focus on reducing the body to ever-smaller fragments that culminate in an indiscernible imperceptibility — or dissolving the body, as we know it.
73 Ibid., p. 188.
74 Grosz (1994, p. xii).
75 Gatens, (1997, p. 164).
76 Foucault (1973); Bardon and Josserland (2010).
77 Barad (2007).
78 Ibid., p. 184.
79 ibid., p. 185.
80 Spinoza (1883 [1677]).
81 Spinoza (1883 [1677] III quoted in Deleuze, 1988, p. 49).
82 Knights (2018a); Munro and Thanem (2018).
83 Bolden (2016, p. 45).
84 Gatens (2006, p. 39).
85 Foucault (2011, Loc. 7367).
86 Clough (2007, p. 3); Clough (2009).
87 Massumi (2002, quoted in Clough, 2007, p. 3).
88 Massumi (2002).
89 Hynes (2013, p. 561 Orig. emphasis).
90 Calás and Smircich (1997, p. 53).

7 Ethics and Leadership

In this chapter, attention is drawn to the importance of ethics as fundamental to leadership even though historically, there have been numerous violations of what would be seen as acceptable moral behaviour. We cannot detach leadership from what it means for those subjected either directly or indirectly to its demands and expectations. On the other hand, meaning is itself historically contingent even though leadership is almost always viewed from a position of contemporary concerns or a 'history of the present'.[1] It is then always dangerous to contextualise any contemporary conception of leadership merely by tracing its history for this has already been reconstructed in terms of our current interests.[2] Consequently, we have to resist popular views of leadership as if they can be derived directly from the Pharaohs of ancient Egypt or the Greek philosophers Aristotle and Plato, and perhaps even more so, the 15th century Machiavelli whose thesis seemingly justified some of the most ruthless and tyrannical tactics of many later leaders.[3] For, in the case of the Egyptian Pharaohs, their leadership was claimed to be a gift from the Gods; for the Greeks, the terms had more of correspondence with excellence and facilitating others to pursue what they already knew; and our current translation of Machiavelli relates to its inconsistency with contemporary democratic values. We can see, then, that what binds followers to a leader is most often some mediating force such as the Gods in ancient Egypt and Greece, warrior success in ancient Rome, superstition and myth in Medieval societies, religious fear in Catholic Europe, Calvinist conceptions of predestination in 18th century Protestant Britain, democracy in the 20th century and the perpetual construction of demons and enemies in contemporary Trumpian populism.

In seeking the 'best constitution', the Ancient Greeks were not searching for a new morality but seeking to insert a 'principle of ethical differentiation within the problem of the government of men'.[4] Foucault describes this as a truth that is brought to bear in how the political leader relates to him or herself—a difference in thought from convention and what are seen to be taken-for-granted certainties. Their elite democracy was exceedingly fragile because there could never be an organisational or institutional framework to guarantee that truth was at the heart of the self-formation process of leaders.[5] While rule by aristocrats was displaced in 6th century BCE Greece, its democratic alternative was criticised just 200 years later as it did not guarantee 'good' leaders[6] and was in danger of encouraging populist demagogues that promise the populace anything to secure their vote and then have a tendency to run society into the ground.[7] It is difficult not to draw parallels here with what seems to be happening in contemporary western democracies, especially where populist leaders have secured power through feeding prejudice, nationalism and sometimes xenophobia, as voters seek scapegoats for their feelings of relative deprivation. Whether their isolationism and populism would have run their economies into the ground is impossible to determine now that the pandemic has intervened to create a global recession. Of course, Keynesian economics has become de rigueur so may allow us to escape the worst effects of what cannot avoid being too different from the 1930s world depression.

The chapter begins by focusing on the numerous corporate scandals, including the global financial crisis (GFC), at the turn of the 21st century and examining how these are depicted as either a crisis in leadership, in ethics or both. While accepting that ethics is fundamental, there is often a lack of interrogation of its diversity and differential effects, which takes up the second part of the chapter. Instead, ethical failures are simply treated as matters for regulation, whereby codes of behaviour and rules are established. Policed with hefty fines for their breach, normative standards are sustained by setting an example through the naming and shaming of deviants. However, the regulation solution to financial mismanagement is highly problematic not least because insofar as it works as a constraint, it tends to stifle creativity and innovation. Moreover, given the number of scandals, it tends not to work, not least because the practitioners are usually one step ahead of the regulators. Hence, it resembles the farmer closing the barn door after the horse has bolted. More importantly, it fails to generate ethical behaviour as opposed to mere compliance or quite often, deviance where creative leadership is diverted towards finding loopholes in the rules. In these deliberations, it will be questioned whether there is not something of an oxymoron in thinking of ethics and capitalism in the same breath since the engine driving capitalism is individual, economic self-interest, not a responsibility to the other. So rather than presuming that a good dose of ethics will cure capitalism of all its ills and protect it from its tendencies to self-destruct, the chapter considers alternatives to subscribing to the readily available rationale of regulation. The third section explores other non-regulatory obstacles to the development of ethical leadership and, in particular, the preoccupation with identity. A further question is raised here as to whether leadership is not so much the solution as part of the problem of practical ethics in that, as Wray-Bliss argues, it serves to simplify and contain opposition to its power, sustains fragmented and individualised employee responses to its effects, and provides legitimacy for the privileges of those occupying its hierarchical ranks.[8] Finally, there is a summary and conclusion where the implications of this analysis for the other chapters are discussed as well as an exploration of areas for further research.

Scandals and the Response

There is a general view in the literature that the ethical quality of an organisation is dependent on its leadership, establishing appropriate norms and principles.[9] From a brief traverse through the multiplicity of ethical scandals throughout history, it is clear that numerous leaders either fail to accomplish this task or had no intention of doing so.

For ever since the insolvency of the Medici Bank in 1494, the South Sea bubble of 1720 and the eventual closure of the Dutch East India Company in 1799, corporate scandals have become commonplace in capitalist economies. However, the turn of the 21st century seemed to have more than its fair share of business catastrophes. In 2001, Enron was the biggest file for bankruptcy of all time, but less than 2 years later, it was exceeded by Parmalat, and a further record was broken when Lehman Bros went bankrupt in 2008, leading to a GFC from which even in 2020, much of the western world is still suffering the after-effects. Other less dramatic scandals such as WorldCom, Allied Irish Bank, National Irish Bank, Freddie Mac and Bernard Madoff's Ponzi Scheme also occurred around this time and the majority involved false accounting and financial fraud, with several criminal prosecutions. Even though the scale of the GFC far exceeded the other scandals, and although 334 persons were prosecuted, none of these was a CEO or a Wall Street official.[10] While this largely involved fraud of an accounting or financial nature, scandals have extended and proliferated beyond finance to include environmental pollution (BP, Volkswagen), electronic data breaches (Yahoo, Facebook, Cambridge Analytica, Equifax, Kobe Steel, TSB) and technology more generally (Apple, Samsung).

Some critics attribute these scandals to the pre-eminence of a focus on increasing shareholder value and how this has been stimulated and legitimised by Western business schools. 'We - as business school faculty - need to own up to our role in creating Enron's', ... for the excesses of contemporary corporations have ... 'their roots in ideas developed in business schools over the past 30 years' [for] 'it is our theories and ideas that have done much to strengthen the management practices we are all so loudly condemning'.[11] More specifically, it is claimed that diverse, and often deviant, ways through which corporate leaders seek to boost share prices and pay themselves extortionately high salaries and bonuses can be traced to business-school courses on strategy, transaction cost economics and agency theory.[12] But the mantra of shareholder value is not the only problem for it is also argued that students taking Master of Business Administration courses (MBAs) are not 'trained to manage', partly because they have been fast-tracked to senior positions without ever properly learning their own business from the inside. Nonetheless, 'they are determined to lead. So, a trajectory has been developed to take them around management into leadership. The trouble ... is that many of these people make dreadful leaders, precisely because their hands are off the business'.[13] Others simply blame business schools for failing to incorporate ethical standards and values in their courses, while tending to inculcate students with amoral economic self-interests that are then self-legitimising.[14]

Apart from the last point which is difficult to challenge in so far as where ethics is taught, it is usually as an option on the margins rather than an integral element within all the courses, I am sceptical of these explanations for corporate scandals. First, while these authors[15] are critical of the scientist or linear causal approaches of those teaching in most business schools, these explanations rely precisely on such causal analysis. As a consequence, they elevate the power of business school education well beyond its likely effects. Furthermore, evidence to support their case for the domination of shareholder value either in corporations or in business school education is either absent, or it is highly selective and inconclusive. Moreover, the opposite view is conveyed by The *Portable MBA* series published since 1970[16] and enjoying sales exceeding 600,000 copies to date and bound, therefore, to have been adopted by numerous MBA faculty[17] and also by other programmes in the US.[18]

However, there is a problem with the thesis of the MBA creating a corporate world in which ethics is either non-existent or sufficiently marginalised to prevent it from acting as a constraint on corruption. Not least this is because it failed to produce strong evidence to support the claim. Left unquestioned in any argument is the view that it is possible to demonstrate the presence or absence of a direct linear causal relation between the content of MBA syllabi and the behaviour of managers; both supporters and critics of the thesis differ only as to what form the content, and hence the behaviour, takes. That is to say, Goshal and Mintzberg assume that business education results in a preoccupation with shareholder value and thereby ethical paucity whereas the critique of this thesis argues that the evidence is not adequate to make such a claim. Neither question the causal epistemology that lies behind their opposing positions; if they did, it would be realised that the direct effects of business education or knowledge on management and leadership practice cannot be readily identified or denied. Both rely on a diffusion model of dissemination that presumes knowledge to be formed independently of practice. Accordingly, linear development from genesis and invention through to innovation and application is perceived to occur smoothly and without much dissent. This view of knowledge generation and application has been much contested because it fails to acknowledge the complex actor-networks that surround how theory and practice are mutually embedded in their enactments.[19]

Although business schools and their faculty may love to think that they make a difference in the world, significantly influencing their students about the work they perform after the university experience, insofar as there are effects they are much more likely to be diffuse and unamenable to traditional conceptions of causal analysis. Some have questioned the value of the MBA for its failure as a vehicle for career success or managerial performance[20] whereas others have dismissed it and the business schools since they do little more than cultivate the unethical, neoliberal values of managerial self-interest.[21] Once again, however, the assumption is that a direct causal relationship between the educational achievements of MBA students and their career success is to be expected or that they end up as ethically vacuous puppets of a morally corrupt education. Instead of challenging the causal model, these authors prefer to cast aspersions on the MBA for not delivering what approvingly is expected of it or disapprovingly how it leaves students devoid of morality. The career benefits of MBAs are implicitly assumed, but business schools rarely make direct promises or causal claims for this would subject them to an ethical dilemma when the inevitable disparity manifested itself. They would then have to challenge the causal model presumed in research and begin to recognise how relationships between knowledge, education and practical outcomes are more elusive, mutually interdependent and complex than is portrayed by a simple linear chain of causation.[22]

Challenging the causal accounts in this way, however, is not to deny entirely any relationship between MBA education and business practice. Indirectly, the effect of education in leadership or management and business may be more sustaining where the values in MBAs reflect and therefore reinforce those that the students held before their educational experience and that are then found in business practice. So, for example, many students see the MBA as a passport to career success. In the private sector, this means contributing to corporate success as measured by profit and returns on investments to shareholders or in the public sector, providing the most efficient service. Ethics teaching, even if integrated into all courses, is unlikely to diminish the careerism of students for it is 'clear that most business and management students pursue their studies to facilitate self-advancement. Their approach, in other words, is instrumental'.[23]

Conversely, few demonstrate the kind of 'subject loyalty' that traditionally exists in, for example, the humanities. Consequently, it can be seen that the values of personal success exhibited by MBA students are virtually a carbon copy of, or isomorphic with, corporate thinking and therefore it is to be expected that they will support and sustain the kinds of behaviour that lead to a preoccupation with shareholder, at the expense of other, values. Interestingly, a colleague recently discussed with Irish MBA students of the participation of National Irish Bank (NIB) in assisting their clients in evading tax. Many students in the class felt that the bank had done nothing immoral, arguing that the tax evasion was customer-driven and that the banks were simply providing a service. Moreover, taking a customer viewpoint, the students argued that the fraud was justified because, for so many years in Ireland, the government charged extremely high rates of tax. Here the values of MBA students reflect those of an economically individualistic instrumental society that elevates private over public goods, even to the point of breaking the law to ensure that individual accumulated wealth is protected against tax liabilities. These students were in the first week of their studies, and it is hardly likely that their MBA programme directly inculcated them with the kind of values that sustained a justification of the NIB tax scandal, albeit not necessarily advancing a set of values that would directly contradict it.[24]

In effect, then, my argument suggests a weak case of the thesis promulgated by Goshal and Mintzberg, not the *strong* one that they present. That is to say, insofar as MBA education involves a concentration on shareholder value, this does not directly determine managerial behaviour; it simply reflects and reinforces what is already an overwhelming aspect of corporate consciousness, and this is the result or measure of individual career success—a preoccupation of those students who decide on an MBA education. There is then a direct coincidence between the values of students, the content of MBA programmes, and corporate consciousness. Consequently, it cannot be presumed that the MBA is a major impetus for corporate corruption of the kind witnessed in recent scandals. But nor is it reasonable to think that teaching ethics within leadership and management courses would militate massively against corporate corruption.[25] This is not an argument *against* introducing ethics courses in business schools but simply an acknowledgement that their effect is likely to be marginal, partly because of the countervailing power effects on managerial and leadership subjectivity of other discourses and practices before, within and after, being educated in business schools. In the debate on MBA education, both claim and counterclaim would seem to be premised on a wholly exaggerated view of the power of the MBA to affect leadership in corporate life.

If this is the case, it is necessary to direct attention not particularly at Business Schools but to society in general and business corporations in particular. Perhaps a more important contribution would be to explore conceptions of leadership and ethics in social and business life more generally. Here we could assess whether ethical leadership secures not only a sufficiently central focus but also the extent to which it challenges individualistic preoccupations with the self and identity that generate the pursuit of material and symbolic success, thus fueling the shortcuts culminating in the ethical failures surrounding the modern corporation.

If recent corporate scandals cannot be attributed principally to the pre-eminence of a model of shareholder value and the marginality of ethics in MBA education, is there an alternative account? One possible candidate is to focus on the failure in ethical leadership that more generally can be traced to the dominance of individualism within post-enlightenment discourse and practice. This individualism manifests itself in a pre-occupation with the self—that is, an overwhelming, although often self-defeating, concern to have one's self-image confirmed by others. Traditional ethical discourses, including those specific to the business, as well as most modern approaches to leadership, do not divest individuals of their preoccupation with, and attachments to, the self.

Reflections on Ethics and Leadership

Leadership

Keith Grint well articulates my concerns about relationship studies in his claim that the trait, contingency and situational approaches are constrained by some form of essentialism and determinism (see Fig. 7.1), whereby leadership is seen to be determined by personality (trait), the environment (situational) or by matching the appropriate traits to different environments (contingency).[26]

The problem with the *trait*, or heroic personality, approach is that it concentrates on the qualities of the individual as essential and universal aspects of leadership regardless of diverse contexts. Leadership is seen as almost equivalent to genetic inheritance and cannot, therefore, be taught or improved upon. It often elevates the leader to heroic status through myth or hyperbolic expectations. These are rarely met although occasionally can be as a result of what is seen as the Pygmalion effect, where there is a general encouragement of exceptional behaviour. Leaders are always in search of this effect and use a variety of techniques such as targets, teams and threats to achieve it. This is noticeable where sports supporters can stimulate the very best from their heroes and be seen almost as an invisible extra player when especially rapturous. When leadership is seen in this way, it is closer to the behavioural and to some extent, the situational approach since followers are actively helping to transform the leader. Not much modification is required to see leadership not in terms of genetics but as a process of learning through social relations, and this is endorsed by behavioural, charismatic, transactional and transformational theories. Although remaining broadly individualistic,

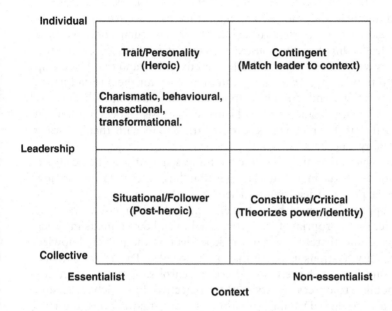

Figure 7.1 Essentialist and non-essentialist leadership (Elaborated from Grint, 2000, p. 2).

these approaches subscribe to a less essentialist view by acknowledging that leaders can develop through experience and training. By contrast, the *situational* approach perceives the context as essential but the qualities of the individual leader of less relevance so that there are no universal styles of leadership for it will change depending on the circumstances or situation. This approach encompasses followership theories where the leader is seen to be an interactional outcome of or conditioned by, those deemed to be led. Once the situation is defined, leaders can be taught the appropriate skills necessary to lead in particular contexts that it is presumed are readily captured through their essential features. Particular leaders could grow into the job, assuming a competent analysis that discloses the essence of the situation. The exact opposite of this is the *contingency* approach where you have to match the right leader for each circumstance or contingency rather than secure his or her adaptation to the environment.

In addition to their essentialism and determinism, mainstream leadership theories tend to reflect and reproduce the autonomous subject of Enlightenment thinking since leadership is invariably seen to be the property of individuals, not that of social groups or institutions. Such individualistic and often psychologistic theories of leadership are opposed by constructionist approaches, where the argument is that leadership is about neither an essential individual nor an essential context but an outcome of interpretation.[27] Within such frameworks, leadership would simply be the embodied manifestation of collective and communal interpretations of appropriate behaviour in particular contexts. In this sense, leadership and the context in which it is practised are mutually constitutive of one another. If leaders fail to understand that leadership is about interpretation, there is a greater tendency for them to fall back on the conventional individualistic approaches to leadership, which is likely to make ethical leadership problematic because leaders become pre-occupied with their image as leaders rather than with their ethical responsibility to others.

The constitutive approach eschews any sense of essential characteristics or contexts in favour of understanding interpretation as at the centre of practical leadership. There is no 'one best way' as with the other approaches since both leaders and led are precisely those who interpret the appropriate forms of leadership and the contexts in which it is located and therefore are not independent of the power, knowledge and identity relations in which they are embedded. Part of the activity of leadership is that of exercising power to enrol supporters or followers and mobilise resources in pursuit of the objectives for which leadership is deemed necessary. Defining situations in ways that capture the imaginations, identities and interests of those that are to be led may then be seen as leadership, but it can just as well be manifest in the whole group, team, organisation or institution as in any one individual designated as the leader. A contemporary political example of the individualistic form of this kind of leadership is Donald Trump.

Ethics

In moral philosophy, the literature variously emphasises consequences, actions and character. *Consequentialist* theories involve two main strains - Egoism and Utilitarianism. Egoism attributes morality to action that is freely pursued as no more than individual self-interest. In the late 18th century, Adam Smith was a major exponent of this form of consequentialism because he believed that in a market economy, the aggregate effect of individuals acting in their self-interest was beneficial for all.[28] A modification of this form of consequentialism is Utilitarianism that calls for the maximisation of goodness in society by measuring the probable outcome or consequences of an action that will be seen as ethical insofar as it produces the greatest benefits for the most people.

Two central principles underlie these consequentialist theories: first is that the rightness or wrongness of an act is determined by the results that flow from it, either for the interests of the individual (egoism) or for a majority in society (utilitarianism) and second, is the hedonistic principle, which argues that pleasure is the only good and pain the only evil and that human beings are pleasure-seeking individuals. The first results-based principle is problematic in relying on a simple linear causal relationship between a moral act and its consequences, a characteristic of the theses on the good or bad effects of the MBA that I critiqued above. By contrast, the hedonistic (behaviourist) theory is not linear but tautological insofar as the pleasurable or painful consequences (responses) are *not* independent of the ethical act (stimulus) that is deemed to be their cause.[29] Moreover, there is the problem that de Tocqueville identified concerning majority rule - of minorities being disenfranchised or suffering for the sake of the pleasure of the largest group.[30]

While consequentialism and especially its utilitarian branch is to be found in leadership studies, the more favoured approach is that of deontology and virtue ethics. *Deontology* focuses strongly on the ethical act, and most have concentrated on universal rules that provide standards of right and wrong behaviour such as lying and deceit is wrong, whereas honesty and trustworthiness are right. Deontology assumes universalisability and appeals to universal principles (e.g. promise-keeping and truth-telling). A simple example suffices to show how universal rules even regarding telling the truth are absurd since during the Hitler regime disclosing the whereabouts of Jews was tantamount to passing a death sentence on them so lying had to be the more ethical stance if interrogated by the Gestapo.

Deontology's most famous exponent was Kant[31] who emphasised the use of reason to work out a consistent set of moral principles that cannot be overridden. Kant's Categorical Imperative suggests that we should act only on that maxim whereby thou canst at the same time will that it would become a universal law'. This is, of course, consistent with the Christian principle that you should not do to others what you would not have done unto yourself. According to deontology, to be autonomous is to be a lawgiver to oneself, or self-governing. It perceives humans as rational beings and, in contrast to Utilitarianism, values rationality and reason over pleasure. Deontology, in contrast to consequentialism, protects the individual more than society. Deontology emphasises universal rights such as freedom of speech, freedom of consent, the right to privacy or freedom of conscience.

However, conflicting rights, such as freedom of speech and the right to privacy make rights-based ethics rather complex. There are further difficulties associated with deontology and, in particular, it is difficult to see how rules and obligations can ever account for, or dispense with the need for continuous deliberations about, the complexity of moral life. In producing un-reflexive compliance to rules, deontology removes the moral dilemma[32] and results in de-sensitising us to our moral judgment.

Finally, we have *virtue*-based ethics.[33] Here, morality is internal and is not based on rules or rights, but in the classic notion of character (honesty, fairness, compassion and generosity). It extends as far back as Aristotle and Plato and centres on the agent, the character and dispositions of persons rather than viewing ethics to be in actions or duties. Thus, morality should be expressed in the form 'be this', not in the form 'do this'.[34] The central question here then is 'what sort of person should I become?' Nonetheless, to avoid an over-reliance on a relatively arbitrary and almost inexhaustive list of character traits, virtue-based ethics does depend on excellent persons acting well (out of spontaneous goodness) and thereby serving as exemplars of ethical behaviour that can inspire others. This practice of 'bearing witness' through one's way of life has its roots in pre-Aristotelian Cynicism and often involves breaking with 'the conventions, habits and values of society'.[35] However, by contrast with deontology, virtue ethics focuses exclusively on the agent rather than the act and, in this sense, is highly or wholly decontextualised in a way that is inconsistent with the practice of 'bearing witness' as a transformational exemplar. Having provided a summary of the different approaches to moral philosophy, I now turn to the literature on leadership and its underlying ethics.

Ethical Leadership

There is a growing body of research which positions leadership as having a central role and responsibility in constituting organisational or business ethics. For example, it has been argued that the crises that business and society face today are the crises of leadership and ethics,[36] that conformity to ethical requirements is a responsibility and depends on leadership in the organisation,[37] and proposes that leadership approaches should be more collaborative than controlling and more values-based than outcome-focused.[38] Drawing on the case of the Salomon Brothers, researchers traced the source of unethical behaviour to the character of its leader John Gutfreund who was always willing to cover-up illegal behaviour and moulded the organisational culture to focus on short-term business goals regardless of moral or legal propriety.[39]

Given the individualistic and psychologistic approach taken in the study of leadership generally, it is not surprising that the literature on ethical leadership has a strong focus on character and, therefore, is often driven by virtue ethics. Many researchers focus on the development of a specific virtue essential in leadership, for example, the emphasis upon 'meekness' that is seen to be a fundamental personal quality for the highest-level leadership: 'meekness' is not about 'powers foregone' but 'powers controlled and exercised with discernment'.[40] Similarly, there has been a focus on 'integrity' which, it has been argued, forms the foundation of character and is essential to sustainable global leadership since, without integrity, leaders will never generate goodwill or trust.[41] Drawing on Plato's work, Takala[42] emphasises the virtues of 'prudence, courage, temperance and justice', in his investigation of ethical leadership. By contrast, Whetstone suggests that virtue ethics can act as a complement to deontology and consequentialism in a tripartite ethic because one can have more than one reason for doing something: 'moral reasons can include both the duty to act *and* the consequences expected from the act *as well as* the belief that so acting is characteristic of the kind of person one wants to be'.[43]

While virtue ethics can be seen to share similar essentialist tendencies that have been heavily criticised concerning all but constructionist approaches to leadership (see Fig. 7.1), there are merits in those versions of virtue that draw on the work of Aristotle and MacIntyre. Takala, for example, argues that our virtues are not essential properties of individuals since they are a product of complex relationships with the wider community[44] and Arjoon stresses individual and collective responsibilities as well as character development. He dismisses deontology because it focuses on the minimalist or negative aspect of ethics, rights and duties and suggests that virtue ethics is more fundamental than the other moral philosophies: 'the virtue of responsibility or justice ... allows us to recognise and respect the rights of others, which is the source of our obligation and a sense of duty for the welfare and happiness of others'.[45] This reflects the view of Thomas Aquinas, who regarded virtue ethics as being more vital than other ethical theories and who suggested that every moral question could be reduced to an assessment of virtue. In the following section, I explore further the idea of virtue presented in the work of Aristotle and MacIntyre and consider how a Levinasian ethic of responsibility can complement it.

Ethics, Subjectivity and Responsibility

So far, I have outlined how the ethical leadership literature has begun to draw primarily on the concept of virtue and particularly the post-Enlightenment virtue ethics of MacIntyre. In a not dissimilar fashion to Nietzsche, Macintyre rejects the enlightenment view of ethics as rational action based on duty or rules (deontological) or the greatest happiness for the largest number (utilitarianism). Drawing on Nietzsche's demystification of enlightenment morality on the basis that its rational foundation is no more than a mask for the expression or assertion of subjective will (the will to power), he argues that 'there can be no place for such fictions as natural rights, utility, the greatest happiness of the greatest number'.[46] We have then to abandon reason in favour of the will—a will that relentlessly seeks to reinvent itself in pursuit of morality that is wholly original to the self and not simply compliant with some tradition. It is much less concerned with what rules an individual ought to obey and why s(he) should obey them than with what kind of a person should I become, and how I should live my life—an inescapably practical question, which Enlightenment morality fails to address directly.[47]

Macintyre acknowledges that Nietzsche's genius has been to identify the problem rather than the solution,[48] but this is perhaps because the

Ubermensch (Superman) feeds the megalomania of despotic and tyrannical leaders as well as reinforcing, rather than challenging, the individualism of the age. The failure to contest Nietzsche's claim that morality was little more than a disguise of the will to power, was due to Enlightenment philosophers rejecting the 'Aristotelian tradition'. This has meant that rules have displaced moral character or the good life to the extent that 'qualities of character then generally come to be prized only because they lead us to follow the right set of rules'.[49] In a post-Nietzschean world, all rational groundings of morality fail, but a return to Aristotle's virtues might just save us from moral nihilism.[50]

The virtues of concern here are those that promote community values and solidarity rather than those that express heroism in the liberal individualistic sense of the term. For Aristotle, a hero is not one who merely gains the approval of others because of her or his achievements; heroism and the honour associated with it is attributed to those who exercise virtues that sustain social life, perhaps through excellence in a certain endeavour. These virtues return us to a pre-modern mode of civilization where the legacy of the Enlightenment in possessive or competitive individualism and a preoccupation with the self, image or identity are unknown. There is no sense of a separation of individual and society since human behaviour is never simply an individual acting in his or her self-interests but rather a reflection of what it means to be a member of that society. Of course, contemporary economic self-interest and the pursuit of fame and glory are equally reflections of what it is to be a member of our society. It is just that this society has become amoral because the competitive pursuit of individual success transcends any moral obligation to live the 'good life' and seek excellence for its own sake, rather than for personal material and symbolic reward. Resistance to the desire for social approval, above all else, involves challenging the subjectivity that has been imposed upon us through routine exercises of power and that constitutes us as subjects turned back in on ourselves and tied to our own 'identity by a conscience or self-knowledge'.[51] The neoliberal ideology even more than the enlightenment generates the kind of individualisation that renders us frantic for others to confirm our sense of being real. For it encourages a preoccupation with the self that secures itself principally through social confirmations reliant on the acquisition of material goods and symbolic images. This acquisitiveness can easily transfer to internal non-material images when identity is secured through an attachment to some spiritual faith—a state of ego that has been described as spiritual materialism.[52]

Aristotelian virtue ethics is concerned less with a list of character traits so much as a capacity for judgment that enables people to move towards the attainment of their goals (telos) that lends intelligibility and meaning to life. Telos and excellence are not fixed and determined for all time and is not an individualistic dimension of life but socially embedded for choosing what to do as individuals is about discovering who we are in a relationship with others and our membership of organisations, communities and societies.[53] Virtue is integral to telos but is a never-ending, developmental pursuit and always a process of learning for self and others.[54]

By drawing on Levinas' ethics,[55] it may be possible to understand the responsibility to the Other as precisely the teleological project that could reconcile the Aristotelian virtues and Nietzsche's concern for individuals to remake or re-create themselves. Ethics can only serve as a guide on how to behave in particular localised contexts for the self is not the autonomous entity that is valorised in enlightenment thinking. Rather, it is simply the medium and outcome of social relations, so there is no incompatibility between a continual reformation of the self in pursuit of ethical life and the responsibility to the Other demanded by Levinas' ethics. For ethical leadership cannot exist without overcoming the pre-occupation with self that is the legacy of the Enlightenment thinking on autonomy. Through his emphasis on responsibility as prior to processes of self-formation, Levinas provides a means to overcome this pre-occupation although, as Foucault makes clear, it does mean refusing to be what we have become through so many exercises of power.[56]

He rejects the autonomous self of the Enlightenment and suggests that self-interestedness has no part to play in ethics, and this demands a radical questioning of its taken for granted presence in contemporary neoliberalism.[57] The problem with Enlightenment thinking is that it encourages responsibility to the self in advance of responsibility to the Other. When a pre-occupation with the self is pre-eminent, morality is reduced to an exercise of power where the *image* of what it is to be ethical transcends any sense of responsibility.[58] Levinas seeks to challenge philosophies of liberal individualism with an alternative ethic of responsibility. He suggests that moral thinking involves addressing ontology as well as ethics for it is the moral act which brings about, rather than follows, social existence. Ethics, therefore, is before being: responsibility for another is not an accident that happens to a subject but precedes essence in it, it has not awaited freedom, in which a commitment to another would have been made'.[59]

The self is not autonomous for it is constituted through face-to-face relationships and always in line with the expectations of the Other. Our encounter with the Other is an interruption 'a risky uncovering of oneself, insincerity, the breaking up of inwardness and the abandonment of all shelters, exposure to traumas, vulnerability'.[60] Through this interruption, subjectivity is constituted - that is, through the passivity of an exposed self rather than the activity of an autonomous self. The Other is a source of both our freedom and responsibility, for 'it is this creation of the meaning of the Other, and thus also of myself, that my freedom, my *ethical* freedom, comes to be'.[61]

The moral project is one of responsibility and the heart of ethics rests in the face-to-face interaction with the Other. The Other may call upon us through words or actions, but it is sufficient for the Other merely to come in contact with us for us to be compelled to respond: 'The face opens the primordial discourse whose first word is obligation'.[62] This cannot be denied, not because of any human rights, but simply because the Other exists and this very existence makes us morally responsible, a limitless responsibility. We never completely understand the demands of the Other for the Other who is 'higher than me and yet poorer than me' is unique, different from all other persons and objects yet such responsibility does not demand reciprocity; it is a non-symmetrical relation.[63] The Relationship with the Other is non-instrumental and not based on an imperative outside the self; it is about inexhaustive care for the Other. Responsibility to the Other cannot be passed on for the ethic of responsibility is absolute. It must be noted that we are not only responsible to the Other, we are also responsible for ourselves to the Other, and we must defend ourselves to the Other for the Other challenges the self's right to exist.

Having considered the ethical relationship between the self and the Other, it is also necessary to consider what happens when there are multiple and competing others. We can only be fully responsible in relationships of intimacy since in everyday social relations the form of responsibility is ordinarily limited to social and legal conventions. From the moment the third party enters, according to Levinas,[64] we must compare. In the face-to-face with the Other, there is no judgment, but from the moment the Third Party makes an entrance, judgment and justice are required and rationality takes the place of passion. Levinas acknowledges the unavoidability of falling into law once there is an encounter with the multiplicity so that while critical of deontology, he nonetheless accepts its necessity. For, obviously rules and constraints are necessary to maintain social order.[65] In the case of many crimes, human life itself is at stake so to ensure respect for the law, it is necessary to expose or make an example of those that violate the ethical code. Yet this does illustrate its limits in that without a basic ethic of responsibility to the other, the law only serves to expose rather than prevent unethical behaviour, at best revealing an enemy such as a murderer or a terrorist that must be deprived of liberty either through incarceration or even death.[66] An example of this occurred recently when large financial corporations were named and shamed by the regulator for failing to comply with regulations concerning money laundering and tax fraud.[67] However, Levinas is insistent that the fundamental pre-social responsibility inform ethics to the other for justice emerges not from the rational calculation of different entitlements but a face-to-face responsibility to the other.[68] In terms of leadership, this is about engaging in and taking responsibility for, the heated ethical dilemmas that justice entails.[69] Of course, the exposure serves as an example to others and thereby indirectly prevents unethical practices but since such compliance is purely instrumental in avoiding sanctions, it is questionably ethical.

The critique of deontology, therefore, is not an attempt to displace it entirely for third party conflict requires judgment and such judgment involves an assessment of both conduct and character. However, sympathy towards virtue ethics resides in view of the telos or moral project outlined by MacIntyre as a perfect accompaniment to Levinas's responsibility to the Other. An ethic of responsibility moves us away from a pre-occupation with the self towards an indeclinable and unlimited responsibility to the Other, experienced in the face-to-face interaction and driven by inexhaustive care.

I desist from proposing an ethical model or programme since that is to impose ethical rules or principles, which is to rely too heavily on the very deontological rules or utilitarian principles that can only be seen as a *complement* to, not a substitute for, an ethic of responsibility to the other. Also, on the basis that one size does not fit all, it is more appropriate for institutions to develop ethical policies that suit their distinctive circumstances. Ethical discourse is not about providing universal blueprints or models of correct behaviour and rules that are deemed to realise them. Rather, what is necessary are ways of thinking that may enable people or institutions to behave ethically concerning their circumstances and contexts. However, a good practice is not so newsworthy as ethical scandal and in recent history, there have been no shortages of these to the point at which many speak about a crisis of leadership although literature outlining effective resolutions is much less prolific.[70]

Whose Crisis?

Since the corporate scandals of the late 20th century culminating in the GFC of 2008, there have been multiple claims that leadership is in some ethical crisis[71.] Yet, it has also been argued that 'the more ethically debilitating crisis is that we (are exhorted to) defer to leadership to solve organisational ethical ills in the first place'.[72] Such deference privileges leaders in the senior hierarchies of corporations to preside over ethical questions and assume the moral high ground for their organisations.[73] Is this a clear example of how, because of the foundational status of ethics in society, it cannot be separated from politics? For ordinarily, power is exercised within an ethical frame since this is the way that it is justified or legitimised, enabling its untroubled enactment or pursuit. In situations of absolutism where sovereign authority, coercive force or enslavement prevail, moral consent is unnecessary because legal right or naked power can ensure obedience. Discourses that claim a leadership crisis are simply reverting to a period of history where power resided exclusively in the sovereign who was expected to maintain the social order by whatever means. Yet, by contrast with the classical tradition of sovereignty, power in the modern era is no longer the preserve of a single authority but is dispersed, distributed and devolved into every niche in society; it traverses institutions, organisations, every day and, in doing so, deploys as well as determines and discerns as well as differentiates knowledge. Power/knowledge is neither a property of, nor possessed by, persons for it only exists in its exercise and hence is a strategic, tactical and often ephemeral aspect of social relations rather than a discrete entity to be protected under all circumstances.

Leadership Ethics as Embodied Engagement

These ethical scandals can be seen as a reflection of how organisations are paradigmatically grounded in technical rationality that denies or ignores the social embeddedness of their programmatic routines and, consequently, becomes wholly detached from the bodily, material and tangible aspects of lived experience. No better illustration of this dematerialisation of relations can be found than in the financial sector, for example, in the trading of mortgage and other credit securities created by complex derivatives and the (re)bundling of a diverse range of loans into tradable commodities. Conventional explanations for the crisis that followed the proliferation of innovative intangible products vary from, at one extreme, blaming the engineering, mathematics or science graduates that created them to the other, of attributing the cause to the excesses of those seeking to buy property beyond their means of servicing the loan. In between these extremes, however, greedy bankers and intermediaries or sales staffs are blamed for their failure to assess risk properly in pursuit of their financial interests either in the form of the growth in value of their stock options or their bonuses and commissions. While these explanations may appear to revolve around attributing some failure to real live human beings, this is something of an illusion insofar as we can see that it is their particular cognitive, instrumental and technical pursuit of economic interests that underlies the decision-making in almost all these cases. This instrumental rationality is, of course, not ordinarily directly a topic for reflection since it is just taken for granted as normal and unremarkable behaviour and celebrated since wealth is given heroic status or rationalised in mythical claims that there is a trickle-down effect of wealth accumulation from the top to the bottom.

Unfortunately, the literature on leadership in general and ethical leadership, in particular, does little to shake the foundations of this paradigm, not least because instrumental rationality reflects and reproduces the masculine sense of self where mastery of oneself, as a means to control that which is other, is fundamental. The closest such a rationale can get to responsibility is a reciprocity of exchange where each gains some instrumental benefit from the relationship. This, of course, is the foundation of market exchange and capitalist economics but is far removed from Levinas's ethics that is located in 'pre-rational and affectual relations with "the other"'[74] where 'the other counts more than myself'[75]. What is needed is an ethics that is not subjugated to masculine, rational organisational self-interest but is prefaced on an infinite responsibility to the other.

However, there is a different set of literature that focuses on the possibility of developing an embodied and engaged mode of ethical leadership. This involves challenging the faith in disembodied, instrumental rationality and attributing a major condition of the possibility of financial failure precisely to this ideology.[76] Through an embodied engagement with one another in our organisations, we would avoid seeking solutions to ethical crises in the very technical and instrumental rational pursuits that were important conditions of their possibility. As many commentators have pointed out, those largely regulatory strategies attempt to salvage economic growth out of the embers of the 'burn out' but simply store up problems for tomorrow and/or for future generations. Maybe it is time to restore materiality to corporate business and the body to those leaders responsible for its development. Of course, concerning finance, the intangible nature of products and services can never be eradicated since money as a medium of exchange, a unit of account and store of value is abstract and at some distance from the materiality which is its condition and consequence[77]. However, we should never forget that its continuity is inseparable from the trust that real embodied human beings have in one another to accept money as a substitute for the goods and services concerning which it is a mere proxy. As many commentators have remarked, the very term credit has its origins in the Latin term *credo* meaning belief, faith and trust. Yet, this is precisely what now is in short supply given the risks with other people's money that our banking leaders took to advance their careers and finances, albeit legitimated by an equally disreputable ideology of corporate greed dressed up as corporate growth.

If there is an ethical leadership question to answer here, given the apparent inadequacy of current discourses, what is to be done? A first step has to be the resuscitation of ethical leadership and organisation, but we must begin by turning away from the 'preconceived ideas and institutionalised norms' or established ways of speaking about ethics[78] that are reflected in deontological, consequential and virtue approaches. For when there is an appeal to morality through notions of rule compliance, a 'hidden hand' or the unintended consequence of everyone pursuing their material (economic) or symbolic (identity) self-interests, ethics becomes precarious as it is always a poor second that readily falls down the cracks in the pavements of everyday life. Instead, we can look to promote an ethics of active bodily engagement with others whereby leadership could then bear witness to an organisational life beyond passive compliance and subordination or the preoccupation with an identity that only reflects and reproduces (often masculine) ideologies of individualism and individual self-interest. Ethical leadership can only advance through discourses and practices of embodied engagement where members of organisations are actively involved in their relations to the point at which individuals' preoccupations with their own identities is radically diminished. An analogy to ethical leadership might well be the idea of rhythm that has been described as that which is imposed and yet we consent to in our very 'participation' for we are 'carried away by a song to the point of dancing involuntarily to it ... [I]t entails a loss of one's identity, "a passage of oneself to anonymity"'.[79]

Of course, talking about ethical and embodied engagement does not necessarily bring it about but a good part of the conditions that might make it possible is to reflect more critically on why, despite a forlorn and failed history, organisations and institutions keep returning to traditional conceptions of ethics. As has been argued, these involve deontological systems of rules and regulations that stifle innovation or direct it towards finding legal loopholes; speculative yet nonetheless quantitative utilitarian calculations of the ethical consequences of behaviour; or resort to a notion of good character in the virtuous leader. This analysis implies that in the first instance education in business schools including leadership development and executive education programmes need first to ensure that ethics is not only embedded in the curriculum but that it reflects, as here, on the practical failure of its applications when drawing exclusively on traditional discourses of deontological, consequential and virtue ethics. Embracing the ethics of embodied engagement would have practical benefits well beyond recent leadership developments, whether of mainstream or critical inclination.

Summary and Conclusion

This chapter has focused on the numerous ethical scandals culminating in the GFC that corporate businesses have recently exhibited and has sought to explore critically the response, which has been primarily to expand regulation. Invariably treated as a crisis of ethics, leadership or both in the form of a crisis of ethical leadership, there is little interrogation of the diversity of ethics and their differential effects—a lacuna that the chapter has sought to seal. After exploring a range of ethical traditions, I conclude that deontology, consequentialism and even virtue ethics have some fundamental flaws. I turn, therefore, to the ethics of responsibility subscribed to by Levinas and although it is beyond reproach in many senses, there are difficulties in reconciling the different and conflicting demands, when outside the intimacy of a 2-person relationship, to the point at which it is virtually impossible to reach a compromise considered fair by all.[80] Justice, then, is not a simple task of applying rules to adjudicate moral dilemmas but always a reminder of one's vulnerability to reverting to achieving a face-saving outcome or in one's interest rather than that of others. Nonetheless, this is what ethical leadership is about—'navigating the ethical quandaries and dilemmas that leading other people, and being responsible for them, inevitably raise'.[81] Just because there is little possibility of perfection, nor indeed any concern to secure such an image, leaders can still be rational about a range of substantive values but also recognise that rationality is ultimately grounded in a pre-rational responsibility to the other.

The chapter ended by discussing complementary posthuman ethics that involves embodied engagement with one another in organisations in ways that retain a responsibility to the other as its central rationale. As embodied engagement, ethical leadership could be seen at least partly to reflect the philosophy of Spinoza[82] whose valorisation of 'the joyful passage from passivity to activity' is seen as a necessary condition of ethical behaviour.[83] I return to this below, but one of the greatest obstacles to the development of this kind of ethical leadership is the presumption that the leader has exclusive responsibility for ethics and the associated preoccupation with protecting our own identity that maintains the myth for us all. In this sense, it is appropriate to argue that leadership is as much a part of the problem as the solution to a crisis of ethical leadership.[84] This is not to say that we should throw the baby out with the bathwater and be rid of leadership, or at least its nomenclature, altogether and revert to a discourse on good old reliable management, as some critics propose.[85] Leadership is never going to go away and we are reminded of this vividly whenever there is some kind of crisis whether it be terrorism, global financial meltdown, a pandemic or ethics. Nonetheless, the critics are introducing a healthy scepticism into the debate by demonstrating that leaders are only as 'good' as those they profess to lead, are not superhuman as they are often expected to be, and are embodied humans not the detached, impersonal and distanced arbitrators of conflicts, as they sometimes appear.[86] Most importantly, we cannot abandon our responsibility to others by passing it onto a single leader and, consequently, leadership like power has to be seen as widely distributed, dispersed and the responsibility of us all. This, of course, has been recognised in a range of literature from servant to authentic transformational leadership and from relational to practice theory approaches but the limitation of these, not lightly to be dismissed, theories is that they tend to presume harmony and thereby neglect the 'complex, politically charged relationships in which leaders are embroiled in practice'.[87]

This takes us to another set of arguments that are complementary to the earlier discussion of posthumanist ethics, for what is called 'affective leadership' focuses on 'how people relate to each other regardless of hierarchical status'.[88] Inspired by the philosophy of Spinoza, Munro and Thanem conclude that affective leadership can be summed up in terms of five components, paraphrased as follows:

1. Only obedience to reason, not to individual leaders is ethical;
2. People are capable of collective action without interference from leaders;
3. Joyful affects increase our collective powers of action, but sad passions should be avoided because they decrease them;
4. Joyful encounters that accord with our reason enhance our capacity to affect and be affected;
5. These facilitate the cultivation of friendships, but good encounters must be organised beyond the constraints of the capitalist political economy and the co-optation of ethics by leadership appeals to care and empowerment.[89]

While I am wholly supportive of scepticism toward leaders, there is some danger here of dismissing leaders altogether. That is unless they emerge as 'free members of the multitude'[90] as some self-governing group cultivated through 'reason and friendship which stems from active joyful affects such as love and kindness, devotion, and daring'.[91] Their examples come from social protest movements that are radical partly because, in contrast to those involving charismatic leaders like Gandhi or Martin Luther King, they are anarchic and leaderless. Consequently, they do not restrict 'people's freedom and collective power to exercise our capacities to act and be acted upon'.[92] We know that a complex society would struggle to survive without some form of organisation that is likely to involve leaders. So while demystifying leaders is one way of generating scepticism about their providing a solution to the problem of ethics, it is less healthy to abandon them altogether. For, social movements and their participants can just as easily be romanticised as are charismatic leaders. Consequently, although this analysis provides numerous insights for examining ethics and leadership, I think it needs to be complemented by Levinas's understanding of ethics as prior to ontology, the social, and most importantly, a preoccupation with self and identity.

These questions of ethics and responsibility to others are as inseparable from leadership as are many of the other concepts discussed in this second part of the book and they figure in most of the chapters that follow. In the context of the 2020 pandemic, it will be interesting to see how the sense of responsibility to others has transformed the collective consciousness of peoples globally. Narratives that examine the immediate problems of Covid-19 are numerous, and I add to them in the final chapter of this book. However, until the pandemic is no longer a threat to human life, it will be impossible to assess its full ethical impact on community relations.

Notes

1 Foucault (1979), Case, French and Simpson (2011, p. 246).
2 Foucault (2011, Loc. 7420).
3 Machiavelli (1961).
4 Foucault (2011, Loc. 7420).
5 Ibid.
6 Thucydides (2000 [411BCE]).
7 Plato (2007 [383BCE]). Is this reminiscent of some contemporary political leaders?
8 Wray-Bliss (2013, p. 87); see also Learmonth and Morrell (2019).
9 Painter-Morland (2008).
10 https://www.ft.com/content/de173cc67c79-11e7-ab01-a13271d1ee9c consulted 18.2.20.
11 Goshal (2005, p. 75).
12 Caulkin (2005), Mintzberg, Simons and Basu (2002, p. 69).
13 Mintzberg (2004, p. 1).
14 Anteby (2013).
15 Goshal (2005), Mintzberg (2004).
16 Collins and Devanna (1990).
17 Tiratsoo (2004a), Starkey and Tiratsoo (2007). Mintzberg's thesis relies on evidence from the Business Roundtable, a 'group of chief executives of America's largest corporations' who have changed their emphasis in recent time. Whereas in 1981, statements were made that suggested some 'balance' of the legitimate interests of different 'stakeholders' by 1997, '"the paramount duty of management and boards is to the corporation's stockholders"' (Mintzberg quoted in Tiratsoo, 2004a). Yet in the 1997 statement, Mintzberg chooses to ignore a paragraph that reflects precisely the same concern that the 1981 statement had in a more pluralistic stakeholder view of corporate interests as necessary to the long-term interests of shareholders (The Business Roundtable, 1997, p. 3 quoted in ibid., p. 2).
18 Boyle (2004).
19 Latour (1987, 2005).
20 Pfeffer and Fong (2002, 2004).
21 Parker (2018).
22 Grey (2004, p. 178).
23 Tiratsoo (2004b, p. 4).
24 Majella O'Leary provided this data and it was directly referenced in Knights and O'Leary (2006).
25 After all, while there is more clamour now for business ethics courses, they have been taught in some form or other for over 20 years (see ABS, 2004 quoted in Tiratsoo, 2004b).
26 Grint (2000).
27 Grint (2000, p. 2).
28 Crane, Matten, Glozer and, Spence (2019).
29 Chomsky (1970).
30 de Tocqueville (1998).
31 Kant (1949 [1879]).
32 Derrida (1992).
33 that is is the natural extension of the Greek definition of 'ethos', or character.
34 Stephens (1882, p. 1).
35 Foucault (2011, p. 184 quoted in Munro, 2014, p. 1133).
36 Arjoon (2000).
37 Minkes, Small and Chatterjee (1999, p. 328).

38　Maier (2002).
39　Sims and Brinkmann (2002, p. 327).
40　Molyneaux (2003, p. 347).
41　Morrison (2001).
42　Takala (1998).
43　Whetstone (2001, p. 102).
44　Takala (1998).
45　Arjoon (2000, p. 162).
46　MacIntyre (1981, p. 114).
47　Ibid., p. 118. In this articulation of virtue ethics, Macintyre was preceding Derrida (1992) who demonstrated how compliance with a rule or norm was obedience to authority whereas ethics involved an issue of troubling undecidability and Foucault (1982) who insisted on us 'bearing witness' as a transformational exemplar through refusing the conventions and norms that made us what we are.
48　MacIntyre (1981, p. 118).
49　Ibid., p. 119.
50　Ibid., p. 117.
51　Foucault (1982, p. 212; 2009 [2007], p. xxx).
52　Trungpa (1973).
53　MacIntyre (1981, p. 223).
54　Ibid., p. 219.
55　Levinas (1969, 1981, 1985, 2002 [1989]).
56　Foucault (1982).
57　Rhodes (2020, p. 11).
58　Levinas (1969).
59　Levinas (1981, p. 114, quoted in Chalier, 1993).
60　Levinas (1981, p. 48).
61　Bauman (1993, p. 86).
62　Plato (2007, p. 327).
63　Levinas (1998, p. 202).
64　Ibid.
65　Durkheim (1887, quoted in Giddens, 1971, p. 70).
66　Knights, Noble, Vurdubakis, and Willmott (2002).
67　https://www.informanagement.co.uk/2019/06/28/name-and-shame/ consulted 25.2.20.
68　Rhodes (2020, p. 11).
69　Ibid., p. 59.
70　Anhalt (2017), Gill (2011), Krantz (1990), Smith and Peters (1997).
71　Ciulla (1995), Minkes et al. (1999), Tourish (2013).
72　Wray-Bliss (2013, p. 98).
73　I am broadly sympathetic to rejecting the exclusive appropriation of ethics by, or its attribution, to leaders. However, I shall return to this in the conclusion to argue that likewise, we cannot exclude leaders from the realm of ethics.
74　Rhodes (2012, p. 1319).
75　Levinas (1969, 47 quoted in ibid).
76　Knights and McCabe (2015).
77　There is not space here to examine the complexities of conceptions of money but for a detailed and radical analysis see Ingham (2004).
78　Pullen and Rhodes (2013, p. 4).
79　Levinas (1987, p. 4), Sparrow (2013, Location 467).
80　Rhodes (2012).

81 Ibid., p. 322.
82 Spinoza (1677/1883).
83 Gatens and Lloyd (1999, p, 7).
84 Wray-Bliss (2013, p. 98).
85 Learmonth and Morrell (2019).
86 Wray-Bliss (2013, p. 91).
87 Rhodes (2012, pp. 1320–1321).
88 Munro and Thanem (2018, p. 52).
89 Ibid., p. 64.
90 Ibid.
91 Ibid., p. 63.
92 Ibid., p. 62.

Part III

Empirical Illustrations of Leadership, Ethics and Masculinity

In this Part, many of the issues discussed in Part II of the book will be re-examined concerning three selected areas of research in which I have been engaged during my career. These are academia, innovation and change, and the financial sector and each of them involved certain periods of ethnographic engagement, interviews as well as a documentary investigation of organisations and the broader sector in which they are embedded. A major concern of this kind of research is 'to get inside the defining process of the actor to understand his [sic] action'.[1] However, there is also a recognition that while research participants affect the researcher, this is not a one-way process and there needs to be an ethic of responsibility for 'power relations abound in the interview context [such that ... academic research] 'can textually reproduce its superiority over, and distance from, those whom it purports to represent'.[2] I have been guilty of this even though I have tried to engage with my research participants and not just treat them as a resource for producing academic texts. Evidence of this is in a short vignette of the advertising department in Chapter 7 in Part II, where my engagement with participants backfired on me when they prevented the research from continuing. I had gained an intimate sense of friendship with many of the staff. However, their experience of compulsory redundancies on the advice of management consultants deployed before my research resulted in some strong suspicions that I was a managerial spy. As a consequence, when given the opportunity, they resisted the continuation of my research. While this was upsetting for me at the time, it made more sense once I became familiar with Foucault's distinctive analysis of power and resistance, for it was a vivid illustration of how they are integral to one another and relational rather than a property of persons.[3]

8 Academia and Education

Introduction

In recent years, university leaders have embraced a managerialist agenda involving the adoption of discourses and practices, 'originating in the private sector'[4] incorporating audit, accountability, and management controls.[5] Based on 'rigorous' metrics of performance, universities and academics are competitively ranked against one another in league tables that are, then, selectively deployed in recruitment marketing. These practices have been criticised as gendered, reflecting and reinforcing aggressive, competitive masculine demands on staff to meet a multiplicity of targets and standards.[6] However, the literature[7] tends not to challenge the dominance of aggressive forms of masculine leadership,[8] and often disregards the way that organisational practices are enacted through complex relations of subjects (agents) and objects (materials and bodies).[9] Our research problematises these representations of academic life, together with those narrow conceptions of resistance that focus exclusively on traditional challenges to leadership. By privileging instrumental values and closing down spaces of embodied affects that offer an alternative vision of resistance,[10] workplace conflict discourses remain locked in an adversarial agenda. This involves simply emulating the mainstream focus on advancing the goals of leaders with a concern to promote the equally instrumental interests of those they lead.

Drawing on posthumanist perspectives,[11] I pose the question as to whether leadership within masculine managerial regimes is difficult if not impossible to resist in universities? One of my concerns is to provide a novel and powerful alternative to current formulations of the gendered organisation of academia and academic resistance. The data sections report on how academics tend to struggle with dominant masculine discourses and practices of managerialism, sometimes saying that they are almost impossible to resist and, at other times, claiming subtle and diverse ways of disrupting these masculine norms. Some feelings of impotence in the face of audit, accountability and performativity were misplaced because while often reified as binaries, power and resistance are far from polarised mutually exclusive categories or events. The chapter also seeks to explore the 'in-between' spaces of ambiguity and ambivalence by departing from the polarised binaries of power and resistance, and gender identity and material bodies. Overall, its contribution is to address the lacunas within leadership studies concerning resistance and ethics, particularly concerning 'the absence of the body, the negation of the feminine and the need for a theorisation of subjectivity that is not solely based on [masculine] domination'.[12]

One question that needs continually to be asked throughout this brief excerpt from an empirical study is the extent to which managerialism in university leadership reflects and reproduces the dominance of masculine discourses and practices. Insofar as this is the case, the resulting competitive individualism, work intensification, targets and league tables encourage the displacement of the ethics of responsibility to students for whom academics have a duty of care and to colleagues with whom collaborative and communal relations are vital elements of intellectual development.

Also, as participants in the very field of exploration, it is impossible to stand outside of our implicit ethnographic knowledge of academe, and so must 'adopt a dual stance ... of being both immersed [in] and estranged [from]' what we are studying.[13] Such immersion does, of course, bring benefits as well as disadvantages, particularly as this inclusivity should render us less subject to 'impression management'[14] from our participants. Some of the disadvantages of becoming a 'strange insider' were that we experienced feelings of discomfort, disruption, and at times disillusionment with a community with which we held membership. Such notions of detachment have their limits, however, for in conducting this research we must 'dispel any notion of' independence or dispassion[15] for inevitably some aspects of our research have been privileged over others to achieve particular effects.[16]

The chapter begins by providing a selective discussion of masculine managerialist leadership and posthumanism in pursuit of a more embodied and engaged approach that can be applied to analysing the empirical data on resistance in academia. First, the data confirm some existing arguments around the experiences of (gendered) academia and the apparent impossibility of resisting; second, this impossibility is challenged as a more embodied *a*gendered engagement with academic life is considered. In a discussion section, I explore feminist ethics and the turn to affect. Here, I challenge the cerebral and instrumental discourses of masculinity that prevail in leadership regimes where managerialist practices prevail and resistance to them often takes an adversarial form. In a summary and conclusion, I argue that embodied and ethically engaged affective relations reflect an alternative kind of resistance with a potential to disrupt masculine managerialism by rendering academic work more open and innovative.

Masculine Managerialism and the Possibilities of Posthumanism

In universities, as in other institutions, gender 'is a fundamental organising principle ... that cuts through other social identities'[17] and many researchers have found high levels of sexual inequality, and a culture that remains deeply masculine,[18] which renders 'inexplicable' the limited 'research on women's positions in academia'.[19]

Two clarifications are needed before proceeding. First, it is important not to treat gender as simply equivalent to those 'natural properties of biological men and women, but as the socially produced pattern of meanings that distinguish the masculine from the feminine'.[20] Equally, even though a dominant masculine discourse revolves around logocentric[21] or phallogocentric[22] linear rationality, there are a multiplicity of masculinities or femininities, with fragile and fragmented, as well as porous and permeable, boundaries. Second, resistance has been very commonly defined in terms of action or behaviour that is intentionally opposed to something and is readily recognised by others as resistance.[23] While this is analytically helpful in describing explicit and adversarial forms of resistance such as industrial disputes, it deflects attention from more latent, localised and informal enactments such as difference and deviance or ethical engagement that can have equally disruptive affects.

For my purpose, the focus on struggles as refusal, voice, escape or creation[24] lends itself to the more subtle, fluid, ambiguous and dynamic conceptions of resistance. There is considerable ambiguity around what 'counts as resistance and when resistance counts'[25] so that the conventional polarities between consent/compliance and resistance/struggle have to be abandoned in favour of acknowledging a multiplicity of fragile and unpredictable aspects to processes of contestation.[26] It is also important to depart from discourses and practices that are disembodied since the body as well as the mind is inextricably implicated in all human agency, including acts of resistance.[27] These approaches offer the potential to develop ethical agility to enrol and mobilise the ambiguous and in-between spaces that enable the enactment of practices and new imaginaries extending beyond, and resistant to, pre-established authoritative knowledge.[28]

New managerialism has established itself in universities under a variety of different guises: student satisfaction surveys (NSS), quality assessment audits (QAA) and the research excellence framework (REF), which competitively determines the amount of research funding that universities receive.[29] These mechanisms are deemed to be 'highly gendered'[30] and bound up with masculine 'narratives, forms and values'[31] that reflect and reproduce masculine phallogocentric linear rationalities,[32] where calculable results displace any sense of content, quality and process. Sometimes described as 'entrepreneurial masculinity', the elevation of performative (target-driven) instrumental individualism and competitive ranking prioritises organisational commitments, thus suppressing domestic or home-life narratives.[33] However, insofar as there has been discussion of resistance to managerialist leadership, it has been driven primarily by a humanist ontology and a masculine representational epistemology,[34] which posthumanist feminists have challenged. Paradoxically, however, it can be argued that managerialism itself, and not just resistance to it, has emerged out of humanist essentialism that 'affirmed the conclusive triumph of self-assertive and self-expressive subjectivity as sole primordial authority'.[35] This humanist construction of subjectivity was fundamental to human existence and generated (or contaminated) leadership thinking to generate and sustain a managerial practice as one means of accomplishing the dream of realising human potential.

Within the literature, posthumanism is defined and deployed in a variety of ways, and like most perspectives, it has a diverse range of meanings. On the one hand, it can refer to the death or decentring of the subject focusing on the discursive practices of power as constituting human life.[36] On the other hand, with feminism, it has been argued that posthumanism simply 'takes as its object of study networks of relations rather than discrete people, groups, and texts'.[37] In another version, it draws attention to notions of affect as a 'capacity for activation',[38] which can be seen as 'in-between' consciousness and the body, rationality and emotion, and the individual and society.[39] More generally, posthumanism seeks to counter the human-centric emphasis of humanism by attending to the material and technical artefacts, or other non-human agents such as animals and plants.[40] Thus there is a rejection of anthropocentricism and the presumption that humans have sovereign rights over all they survey, and opposition to 'the fantasies of disembodiment and autonomy, inherited from humanism'.[41]

While some of these differences can divide posthumanists into factions, the common denominator seems to be their criticism of the privileging of the subject in ways that elevate human autonomy, rationality and teleology. Many feminists have been opposed to Humanism because of its liberal individualism, 'which defined perfectibility in terms of autonomy and self-determination'.[42] Others have also been critical of liberal or neo-liberal positions that involve a disembodied instrumental, careerist individualism – highly reflective of the subjectivity of contemporary academics who have been subjected to the performative demands of new managerialism.[43]

However, some are of the view that the 'dismissal of humanist feminism' by posthumanists 'is not only philosophically suspect but also politically short-sighted'[44] since the humanist position is much more complex and diverse than any of its critics acknowledge. We are inclined, therefore, to follow a description of posthumanism as marking 'the end of the opposition between Humanism and anti-humanism' to go beyond these 'lethal binaries' in search of more affirmative alternatives.[45] In this way, we can be opposed to individualism without abandoning or dismissing all humanistic values, such as the respect for life and community.

Given this qualification, the post or neo-humanistic ontology and epistemology enables us to refocus the study of resistance beyond equal opportunity, or those adversarial contests often perpetrated in a heavily masculine manner. Its potential is a break from convention in refusing to reduce ethics 'to universalist principles dictated by' masculine 'reason', towards being fully 'concerned with the specificity of human embodiment'.[46] By focusing on the small informal and often incremental disruptions of taken for granted masculine norms and practices, the chapter seeks to expose the phallogocentric conditions and consequences of the gendered organisation, and the implicit, if not explicit, sexism among ostensibly liberated men in academia.[47]

If complemented by theories that identify affect as an unrealised potential or virtuality we can 'reconfigure the very meaning' of resistance,[48] since this enables a departure from the established idea of resistance predicated on a deliberate and observable reaction to that which it contests. In this way embodied affect accesses spaces 'in-between' matter and consciousness, instrumental rationality and emotional irrationality, the macroscopic and the microscopic, and the individual and the collective, so that we can resist supporting one or other side of a positive-negative dualism. Rather, it generates community or the multitude that is 'neither directed by some central point of command or intelligence nor is the result of a spontaneous harmony among individuals, but rather emerges in the space between, in the social space of communication'.[49] It is not a product of the individual or the collective totality but of the space where bodies affect and are affected by one another in perseverance to enhance their capacities for life.[50] This promises a kind of ethical agility whereby it is possible to explore the ambiguous in-between spaces, or what is described as the supplements[51] that replace some shortfall in, or enrich, prevailing relations. Eschewing the disembodiment of the 'phallic figure of pleasure through domination',[52] these spaces prevail on us to engage with, rather than seek to control, the Other[53] in ways that energise the imaginary. Fundamentally this is an embodied ethics 'depending upon the recognition of another body that we take to be sufficiently similar to our own' ... [or possibly different] ... 'for us to have concern for it'.[54]

This is an ethics of primordial responsibility in the sense that it coincides with every face-to-face encounter where our very identity/ subjectivity is constituted. It is not as an active outcome of autonomy and rationality so much as a passive exposure to the Other, which involves 'a risky uncovering of oneself'.[55] In Derridean terms, it is the notion of *undecidability* that underpins these ethical concerns, encouraging us to refrain from making distinctions between Others; for *tout autre est tout autre*.[56] This means that we cannot make decisions based on some basic rule, convention or stereotypical belief that we know what is good for the other. Still, we have to remain other-oriented for the art of living an aesthetic existence depends entirely on 'an essential position of otherness'.[57] Only by discarding the human-centric pursuit of identity handed down to us by humanism can we begin to abandon the preoccupation with self that precludes a position of otherness.

Masculinities and Academic Performance

In the study Caroline Clarke and I conducted, we found considerable evidence of masculine preoccupations with identity, as academics seek to comply with, rather than resist, intensified managerial pressures of accountability, audit, rankings, quality evaluations and other performative pressures that are imposed on university staff by their leaders. Our research also confirms the view that masculine discourses and practices remain dominant within academic leadership[58] despite claims that universities are 'gender-neutral',[59] so it remains the case that women academics are rarely on a level playing field with their male counterparts. Partly, this can be accounted for because they assume or are allocated a disproportionate share of administration, teaching and student-related tasks[60] and partly due to a culture of sexism in a masculine dominated universe.[61] This sexism often is sustained by men who, like myself, are supportive of feminist challenges to the gendered order. For we can readily be 'wolves in sheep's clothing', complicit by our inaction or failing to intervene in the reproduction of inequalities. Besides, this can extend to a range of other intersectional inequalities around ableist, ageist, class, gender, sexuality, race, and nationalist identities. As academics, we are always in danger of advancing critiques of phenomena 'while failing to acknowledge our location and complicity in' their reproduction.[62] This is facilitated by our distance from the relations that we can easily objectify through our 'academic gaze', thereby 'erasing the subjectivity' of our research participants whilst treating ourselves as 'irrelevant to the knowledge' we produce.[63] So as men, we may appear pro-feminist and genuinely convinced of our support for gender equality, whilst at the same time consciously or subconsciously reinforcing masculine privileges. This occurs at all levels but has its greatest damaging effect on gender relations when enacted at the higher levels of leadership where masculine discourses and practices predominate.

One strategy of resistance is for women to emulate the dominant masculine norms of competitive instrumental individualism, even though this simply legitimises and reproduces managerialist regimes.[64] Another is to claim for women some kind of superiority such as sensitivity in managing detail, staff or relations with students, for example, but this reinforces the prevailing tendency for them to be assigned administrative, teaching and student-related tasks that advantages men in a way not dissimilar to the gender inequality effects of the domestic division of labour. Both these strategies, however, subscribe to what in earlier chapters was described as a conception of truth that sustains instrumental, disembodied and identity-seeking masculine identities.[65] Might it be possible to refuse the masculinised linear-rational subjectivity that managerialist leadership imposes on academics? Doing so, we could reconstruct our morality to re-affirm a set of values that are antagonistic to prejudices and discrimination not only relating to gender but also ableism, ageism, homophobia, homosociality and racism.

Although constructed as sites of presumed Enlightenment and knowledge, there has been little sign of transformation in universities, for a 'competitive and manipulative masculinity ... continues to haunt the academic world'.[66] For example, despite representing half of UK non-professorial academic staff, only 20.8% of professors are women.[67] Therefore, in common with many other professions, academia is increasingly populated by women, and thus feminised numerically, while a masculine 'gendered substructure'[68] is upheld and exacerbated by new managerialist practices surrounding university leadership.

Despite legal and cultural interventions to promote gender neutrality and equality in academia, masculine practices and privileges have ensured that they are ineffective for 'both gender inequality practices and gender practices are manifold in today's universities'.[69]

The research findings are now presented under several different discursive headings relating to the topic of gender, beginning with inequalities within the academic institution itself, then work intensification and finally, the central theme of this chapter which is resistance.

Gender at Work in Academia

Even though women are increasingly populating academia, masculine gendered hierarchies remain predominant,[70]

We do now have a lot more female staff, although not so many are at professorial levels. (Senior Lecturer, Female)

It was male-dominated – most definitely – when I first came here ... for a long time, we had no female professors [out of 52] and then we only had one (Lecturer, Female)

Although there has been some improvement for women in terms of securing lecturer grade appointments, promotions at higher levels have been less frequent. An explanation for the under-representation of women in professorial posts is their 'less developed research profile'. However, this is often a reflection of domestic demands and/or because females often take up a disproportionate burden of administration and teaching. For example, it has been found that on average, associate male professors spend an extra 7.5 hours per week on research, while females spend 8 hours more on teaching.[72] Our study shows how these normalised and naturalised demands on women are reproduced through their assuming a disproportionate responsibility for administration and teaching.

Our research indicates that masculine norms, discourses and practices are all-pervasive in Universities,

It's a masculine environment and I think the academic identity is masculine ... maybe because it's a Business School? (Lecturer, Male)

It's all men on the management team – needless to say, ... and you think "God, no, it hasn't changed has it?" (Professor, Female)

Despite the pervasiveness of these descriptions in our study, 'there are virtually no studies on how women live within the supposedly universal masculine symbolic order of academia.'[74] Symbolism, however, was a topic commented on by several of our participants,

So, if you are expressing your femininity, clearly you're less of a scholar. (Senior Lecturer, Female)

Expressing imagery in this way (i.e. resisting masculine symbolism and objectifying the female body) or presenting the self as feminine appears to undermine and disturb any claim to competence, intellectualism and professionalism. It can closely resemble the kind of abject sense of self that is experienced by women as a loss of dignity[75] or insofar as knowledge production is embodied by maleness, the 'imaginary body' is always contradicted or disrupted by symbols of femininity,[76] which are often concealed in the workplace precisely to avoid these disruptions. However, stereotypical assumptions of femininity were all too common,

While this reflects a gendered stereotype for, she assumes that women have 'natural' communication skills, all the quotes (and many not been drawn upon here) suggest that universities are masculine institutions. For females, resisting this gender identity may mean adopting the strategies, criticised above, that sustain and reproduce the very masculine order their feminism would seek to disrupt. For the pressure of masculinity prevails upon women to behave like men whereupon they gain inclusion and are routinely referred to as 'just like one of the boys'. Men remain comfortable with this since rather than threatening, it reinforces the legitimacy of their masculine discourses and practices.

Here is another example of one of our women participants pursuing this kind of emulation by adopting, rather than questioning, masculine career strategies,

I can remember saying to him that I'm determined to be a Professor before I'm 45 and I think back and think "crikey, did I say that?" It sounds incredibly instrumental and arrogant, I suppose. But I don't think it was that I think it was just a case of I'm not going to be categorized as being just a 'good egg'. Someone's who's a nice colleague but is just part of the wallpaper. So, sort of quite determined. (Female lecturer)

On the basis of 'if you can't beat them, join them', it is not appropriate for me to criticise this behaviour especially as I climbed up the greasy pole, albeit at nothing like the speed that was proposed here. However, as argued earlier, it does legitimise and reproduce the masculine managerialism that privileges men by contrast to women, as well as many other deprived minorities. Here is another example of a woman following this strategy,

Resisting work that is less valued by the institution or transferring such tasks onto colleagues is arguably both a condition and consequence of the increasingly masculine practices of managerialism, which have tended to exacerbate the already gendered nature of universities. Moreover, these strategies often lead to peer exploitation[77] and displays of aggressive and competitive behaviour,

There's much more trying to outdo people [now], I think there's a lot of out-doing going on ... shipping work onto other people which creates masses more on their workload (Senior Lecturer, Female)

... some people haven't met my expectations about what collegiate means ... how I interpret their understanding of being in an academic environment is that it has to be competitive and challenging through combat, rather than supportive discussion (Lecturer, Female)

Arguably, the masculine ethos within universities can bring problems for all academics as, by definition, not everybody can meet the 'elite' demands of success. For, it is difficult to balance the competing demands of publishing in the highest-ranked journals, producing impact case studies, and fulfilling all the quality teaching targets, not to mention increasing administrative tasks. During the coronavirus pandemic, academics had the further burden of developing new skills to provide online teaching facilities. However, there are a variety of reasons, why this competitive elitism is more problematic for female academics, not least of which is that 'while work-life pressures affect all faculty', ... women frequently experience additional pressures ... 'because both universities and families are gendered'.[78]

Identity at Work in Academia

I suppose I don't feel I'm an academic in the proper sense (Male Lecturer).

Under leadership regimes in which new masculine managerialism prevails, the growing demands to perform to a high level in all spheres has intensified. Meeting these hierarchical expectations in delivering output advantages the men significantly for the reasons we have given,

the formal bureaucracy says I need to publish four good articles by 2012 and, if I do that, de facto, I become a good academic, because I get a promotion ... if I do it again, in another four years, I'll be a Professor and it's as simple as that. (Male lecturer)

'Some of it comes from the university ... some of it comes from your own desire to do well and improve yourself ... to climb the greasy pole (Male Senior Lecturer).

'Every time I do a piece of fieldwork I'm looking at trying to get another publication out, [thinking] "where will it take me when I leave here?" (Male Lecturer)
there's almost a Fordist element to publishing and once one paper's finished then you are thinking about the next paper ... increasingly, it's beginning to feel like a production line' (Male Professor)

Work Intensification and its Gendered Impact

While the intensification of work is experienced in all spheres, the importance of publications has resulted in the process becoming more like the Fordist conveyor belt in manufacturing. Increasing managerialism and its performative demands to achieve targets, secure rankings and manage the self in heavily instrumental and productive ways, are intensifying the pressures to prioritise work above other aspects of life. There is a struggle to juggle these pressures that are particularly taxing for women because the 'competing commitments of paid work, home and family remain stubbornly persistent and highly gendered'.[80] Our research also demonstrates the connection between gender and the infinite potential for academic work to encroach on other aspects of life,

I don't feel that academia is a job that you can switch off from ... when I've got a bit of spare time at home, I will be checking email or doing something. (Senior Lecturer, Female)

I probably do work ridiculously long hours and I'm not saying I want that. I would prefer a more balanced life (Lecturer, Female)

Because of the gendered nature of non-work life, women also suffer disadvantages due to the unbounded nature of academic work in universities. Men with families often rely on their partners to do the bulk of the childcare, as well as other domestic duties, so they are freer to do academic work, especially at home, where demands from students are limited. By contrast, women with caring responsibilities do not have this free space and, consequently, their research profiles usually suffer in comparison with those of their male colleagues.[81] This simply reinforces the gender disadvantages of masculine models of practice that 'alienate many women',[82]

So I'm constantly feeling that my day is being encroached on with all of the family things that I'm involved in and then I'm carrying this angst about, "oh my God, I haven't done my quota of work today, so I'll have to do some when the boys go to bed" or whatever. I'm just in a constant whirl of, you-know, not playing the part properly ... not being a proper mother; not being a proper academic; not being a proper researcher; not being a proper teacher and just winging it between all of them. (Senior Lecturer, Female)

Here the participant constructs ways in which she is falling short of certain idealised images: the ideal mother, and the expectations relating to what constitutes a 'proper' academic.[83] Inevitably the academic self becomes highly exposed 'because the real or imagined demands of others invariably exceed the capacity of ordinary human beings to meet them'.[84]

Clearly, much gender disadvantage occurs because of familial and other social norms and the unequal gender sharing of caring responsibilities experienced by women, but there are other 'complex considerations affecting women's position in academia ... [that] ... extend beyond marital status and the presence or absence of children'.[85] Of significance here is the self-policing, self-discipline and guilt from which women find it hard to escape given their comparatively invisible history. When combined with 'the cultural legacy of subordinate status and an imbalance between care for others and care for the self',[86] the pressure is immense. For many it has meant that a 'woman's decision to advance her career within or outside academia is influenced by the apparent trade-off between family responsibilities and career orientation',[87] and much of our data confirmed this,

I'm struck by the fact that the successful female colleagues here don't have children and ... I mean there are a few successful female colleagues but [name] doesn't have any children – she's a Professor ... I think that having a family is prejudicial to success without a doubt (Lecturer, Female)

This can be seen as a classic exemplification of the strategy of women emulating men in order to succeed but, as has been argued, this further legitimises and reproduces the masculine managerialism that is oppressive to all.

While the gendered division of labour is prominent in the domestic sphere, it is replicated in the business school,

I was asked to do the MSc in HRM; my colleague was asked to be the Chair of one of the big committees; another colleague was asked to be the Chair of the entire undergraduate scheme and we said to him (HoD), "have you noticed that what you're actually doing here is giving us all the jobs?" Male colleagues coming in years after us were getting none of this (Lecturer Female)

This is unsurprising and resonates with studies indicating that men are more likely to indulge in macho distancing or 'tactical resistance'[88]; so either they are not asked to take on these jobs, or they refuse them.

Agendered Alternatives?

My concern here is to convey the possibility of transcending or transforming the gendered agendas of organisational life in universities, which has to involve some resistance to prevalent masculine managerialist leadership, norms and procedures. While our research witnessed no collective or confrontational resistance,[89] some staff refused to adhere to the masculine managerialist performative demands for research output, often at the cost of their formal careers.[90] Resistance need not be wholly adversarial or understood exclusively as the polar opposite of control, otherwise it is in danger of emulating the very masculine assertiveness and autocracy that feminists or pro-feminists would seek to undermine. Rather, it can be the refusal to comply with specific instructions, for these often-informal struggles when aggregated may be disruptive. A 'quiet' or 'velvet' resistance'[91] where academics sought to engage ethically in teaching, rather than just comply minimally with technical procedures is illustrated here,

I teach to ensure that everybody's involved so I work my hardest to ensure that every person in the room is actually appearing engaged. I will work my socks off to make sure everybody's there and gaining something from it (Senior Lecturer, Female)

Another participant was upset that many academics were not taking their responsibilities towards students seriously,

[we should be] passionately concerned with students coming out with a fantastic education, having learned loads, having open minds, having developed people .... (Reader, Male)

Such an *aporia* of infinite responsibility[92] concerning the problems of caring/making room for the other (student) expressed by the lecturer, versus the singular other (institution, or self), expressed by his manager is very much a question of ethics, as discussed in Chapter 8 Considerable friction arises from discursively constructing teaching and research as irresolvable binaries that demand an inevitable 'division of focus and attention'.[93] It is between these extremes where tensions lie but we can always act differently, refusing the self we have become,[94] as an enactment of 'embodied intellectual subject[s] who must find a way to act within and between the contradictions'.[95] Even Foucault felt some discomfort in teaching in the sense that it involves 'exercising a relationship of power with respect to an audience'.[96] Davidson[97] continues by summarising Foucault's thinking which I paraphrase: the traditional teacher first makes his audience feel guilty for their lack of knowledge; then obliges them to learn what the teacher knows; and finally, seeks verification that they have indeed learned what they have been taught. Here, Foucault inadvertently seems to have transgressed his thesis on the positive and productive aspects of power. For, surely, care for the self is consonant with care and responsibility for others, as the self or identity is the mirror image of the other and vice versa. Consequently, the power reflected in teaching need not present us with irresolvable contradictions since learning occurs for both academic and student in a two-way process. The same goes for researcher and participants in research for, in both cases, the interaction between the two activities is a condition and consequence of mutual learning.

Of course, one of the effects of a more dominant form of power is to individualise subjects and separate them off from one another through dividing practices[98] that separates the 'good' from the 'bad'. This only serves to demonise those that refuse or fail to comply with the prevailing performative demands. When the university is only really concerned with throughput and output, whether it is students through the door, publications or research grants, then a desire for engagement can be seen as a mode of resistance to the managerialist norms of the organization. Such engagement was far from scarce, as many of our participants were passionately involved with their work and in particular, their teaching,

It is just the joy of working and thinking really, to have an influence on a bunch of students who 'got it', who begun to understand and got enthused about something, I get really enthused, when they're involved, engaged (Senior Lecturer, Male)

I don't like the word 'educator' too pompous and arrogant – teacher has a more interactive connotation. I never assume the role of dominance ... it's always created *with* my students. (Senior Lecturer, Male)

This is a departure from disembodied hierarchical notions of 'knowledge transfer' from the brain of the omniscient lecturer into the passive 'empty vessel' of students, who suffer from a 'lack' that needs to be filled. Rather, it is reminiscent of the notion of 'giving birth to ideas'[99] in an emergent and mutually constituted fashion. Here, everyone learns something, for it comes 'from an encounter with that which is wholly other ... and brings more than I can contain'.[100] Teaching was seen as such an embodied experience that it could profoundly affect the body, even to the point where the anticipation was sufficient to alter physical routines,

You-know, I have different bowel movements on the days that I'm teaching because the anxiety just gets into me and it's because of the performance, fantasizing about what can go wrong – it's agonizing (Reader, Male)

Teaching; it's a very demanding job I find, and tiring, and it drains me. It's nerve-wracking to stay in front of students on a constant basis (Senior Lecturer, Male)

Staying explicitly with the body, despite the pressure for research output, some academics managed to engage with their students, but often subordinating their physical health, personal life and wellbeing in the process,

'I did nearly get ill because I was just so exhausted' (Lecturer, Female)

'I wake to do writing between three and nine am. Borrowing from my personal life is ultimately damaging beyond all possible belief ... that's a job killing the person.' (Senior Lecturer, Female).

This is another illustration of how compliance and resistance are not necessarily mutually exclusive but overlap. There is a recognition that the body itself is resisting being treated so instrumentally, a result largely of having 'been taught to neglect, despise, and violate our bodies, and to put all faith in our brains'.[101] These unintended consequences overlap, for contradictions and separations between the body and mind were ubiquitous in our study,

I suppose my image of an academic is somebody who is always in their head, but too much time in my head and I'm itching to do something else ... but the practical bit runs out after a time, the academic bit runs out as well, so I feel I am two halves (Senior Lecturer, Male)

For others, this separation of mind and body was irrelevant, and academic life was even said to be a form of love,[102]

I love my students who spark in me an interest (Lecturer, Female)

I love teaching, I love writing and I love ideas (Professor, Male).

Relatedly, academics can be affected by emotional engagement to the point at which it can be seen as an enactment of resistance in enhancing their own and others' capacities for life,[103] while simultaneously undermining a target and performance culture where instrumental achievements of end results are all that count. A number of our participants were convinced that the pursuit of narrow purpose-driven results by both staff and students was a hollow endeavour and extremely threatening to those values associated with the 'expressed traditional culture' of academia.[104] To clarify, this is so because 'work is tied to ethics itself ... [meaning] I expend myself, give myself up',[105]

I have proof that we've inspired people, but I think the mechanisms both dull the people who are delivering, and the people who are qon the receiving end (Senior Lecturer, Female)

These mechanisms of continuous evaluation and ranking of both staff and students produce or reinforce instrumental behaviour that precludes learning as an end in itself,

people don't respond about the kind of ideas they're engaged in, instead, its which journals they are writing them for. What it means to do research has ... narrowed (Professor, Male)

The performative culture and hegemonic economic indicators[106] were reported to be part of the reason why some academics had become less engaged in their teaching and research and more preoccupied with output, changing 'focus from what they are doing to the fascination of being the one doing it'.[107] Arguably such a self-conscious preoccupation with the performative self and future results is at the expense of embodied engagement with, or is a means of escaping from, the present.[108] However, such instrumental practices were utterly rejected by some,

I think the job, by necessity, ends up being something you are, rather than something you do ... I think being an academic - it has to be part of you. (Lecturer, Male)

Others also refused to be compliant with the performative demands because they thought independence and engagement was precisely what universities were about, everybody comes to work at the university because they value that they don't have to comply as much with a pre-defined idea of what you should think, how you should think, what you should do, how you should do it. (Senior Lecturer, Female)

So whilst managerialist leadership imposes demands on academics to be highly productive in terms of research and publications, this can only have massive implications for their other work and especially the ethics of responsibility to the student for whom they have a duty of care. However, some academics refuse to comply with such performative demands because their sense of themselves or identity is related to other values and especially a responsibility to students,

I'm not the most strategic person, that's probably my big downfall. I take research and teaching equally as seriously, which is why I'm probably still a lecturer. I do think that we owe that duty to students ... this is where the belligerent side of me kicks-in; I used to get told by my HoD ... "you're your own worst enemy" (Lecturer, Female)

In attempting to reconcile these seemingly opposed demands, women can experience a tension where they simultaneously 'collude with and resist their own marginalisation in academia',[109] generating what can be seen as a dynamic dance between resistance and compliance. For, by resisting informal norms of meeting publication targets and spending more time with the students (and administration) the participant complies with her job description, but although val*ued*, teaching and administration are not valu*able* in terms of career progression. The ultimate twist in the tale is for the Head of Department in a typically masculine fashion, to deflect responsibility for the failure to be promoted back onto the employee,[110] so her very compliance is constructed as deviance.

Such acts of 'velvet' resistance in response to managerialist demands were not just restricted to those at the bottom of the academic hierarchy, for even Deans can resist,

There is the missive, or a directive from the centre saying "in the next three days, do a report on x and send it back". And you don't do it. I would never do this to a student, but I would do this to various 'high-standing' individuals. (Dean, Male)

Refusing to disengage in relations with students, and not complying from a position of comparative seniority could prove to be quite disruptive, especially if emulated by others who saw similar opportunities for quiet resistance. Some did of course,

... That would be resistance. To take on some of these very dangerous procedural expectations from Government and bureaucracy to say, "look, no, we're not doing this". (Professor, Male)

Beyond potential obstructions to mechanisms of control, there was also talk of explicit individual resistance to the disembodied 'publish or perish' mantra that has been reinforced in academia,

A significant number of people didn't conform to the new regimes - not publishing, still placing significance on teaching and other activities, ... making a choice. [The penalty was] just no promotion.(Professor, Male)

Some academics continued to adopt this engaged course of action, even at the risk of non-survival[111] purely because they wanted to engage more ethically with their work,

There's just a lot of contradictions between real scholarly commitment and this willingness to play that instrumental game and I think, at my own peril, I don't really do that enough. You need to do what *you* think is important. (Senior Lecturer, Female)

So, my passion is whatever I'm doing, to do it really well and by my own judgement. I'm not really that interested in other people's judgements of me (Reader, Male)

Sometimes it was the subject matter of the work itself that constituted engagement and resistance simultaneously,

Room for resistance? I think the very work I'm interested in, that I pursue is a form of resistance because you talk about the ethical-political or embodiment, or sexualization at work, or gender, and yes, you can count that as a form of resistance (Lecturer, Female)

In what might be seen as a combination of adversarial and informal resistance, this participant positioned it as an act that required collective action to maximise impact and safeguard individuals from punitive retaliation,

The only way is to withdraw and say, "we are not doing this. Are you going to sack us all?" ... It's like "just say no" (Male, Professor)

Discussion

Despite leadership claims to be 'gender-neutral',[112] our research confirms that university life is dominantly masculine[113] and, largely by default, prevents women academics from enjoying a level playing field. However, it is not just at the level of discourse that inequality prevails, for the body is also presumed neutral while being implicitly masculine:

'Man is the model and it is his body that is taken for the human body; his reason which is taken for Reason; his morality that is formulated into a system of ethics'.[114]

And, of course, this gendered construction is so institutionalised that women are just as likely to subscribe to it as men, for 'academics are *gendered* embodied subjects, and as such are not only subject to forms of gender domination and subordination; they also may (often unwittingly) reproduce those forms'.[115] So, these days, 'the idea of 'organisational activism seems confrontational and perhaps even impossible'.[116] This may be part of the explanation for limited resistance, but another obstacle is the appeal of leadership regimes to laudatory concepts such as accountability, quality, flexibility and transparency[117] that it would seem churlish, if not wholly contradictory, to resist. However, the managerialist adaptations of these concepts distort their laudatory intent by focussing on a narrow technical interpretation, where the primary concern is merely to provide external regulatory bodies enforcing written documentary evidence of accomplishments. Consequently, it is more about the appearance of 'good' work rather than any substantive outcome, and this precludes 'legitimate criticism', and can result in 'cynicism'.[118] Indeed, not only are academics *not* resisting these demands but they (we) 'are fully implicated in their enactment'.[119] This is the case, despite managerialist leaders continually eroding many of the values, traditionally associated with academic work[120] and, as we have seen from our data, this is particularly problematic where 'individual members of the academic community depend upon, and exploit, the gendered labour of others'.[121]

I have already argued that women assume a disproportionate share of caring responsibilities both domestically and at work and this disadvantages them in research. Even when relatively unencumbered by dependent others, 'the abjected maternal body is displaced onto all women (whether they are mothers or not)' and is frequently 'conflated with the feminine'.[122] That is to say, being a woman is problematic because 'women's identities as individual agents are often subsumed by their collective identities as reproductive and sexualised bodies, in a manner which does not apply to men'.[123] Despite the difficulties of challenging both the gendered and performative aspects of managerial leadership, we found indications of 'in-between' spaces in which less adversarial, but more informal and embodied localised, resistances were in evidence. Others have also theorised these more subtle and embodied forms of resistance where 'a path of "active engagement"' is followed with opponents, in contrast to passive resignation or adversarial confrontation.[124] This 'middle ground' strategy was adopted by US religious institutes of women who were subjected to an Apostolic Visitation of sisters from the Catholic Church that was organised to assess and correct their presumed transgressions. Through their embodied and emotional engagement, these women managed to subvert the original objectives of the audit and were able to justify and normalise 'the heterogeneity of beliefs, values, and practices' that previously had been seen as seditious.[125] This could be seen as an inversion of the co-optation of resistance by powerful organisations since these women engaged with the values and norms of the institution to render their own 'transgressions' less threatening and legitimate.

The 'affective turn'[126] that has been discussed in earlier chapters[127] provides a way of broadening the notion of resistance to accommodate such diversity, for it has drawn attention to the virtual and potentially transformative 'forces not yet captured in subjective forms'.[128] In the past, the notion of affect has tended to be conflated with emotion but recent theory[129] has suggested that it is a virtual force lying behind the production of concrete human action. For the capacity to affect and be affected precedes the individualised subject that we have become through so many exercises of power. Not that affect is some pre-social essence, for it is only social in an open-ended way, and 'in a manner "prior to" the separating out of individuals',[130] who are competing with one another to secure status and identity. Although affect is not erased, it is overridden often where individuals are 'transformed into subjects that secure a sense of meaning, identity and reality' through engaging in the practices that power invokes.[131] Affect, then, is not so much a dimension of the subject but that the subject is a dimension of affect and indeed is 'in excess of conscious perception'.[132] Whereas the subject is constituted through exercises of power that it takes considerable reflexive energy to transcend, affect is a part of that energy with a potential to resist the subjugation. For, affect is an unrealised immanent potential or virtual reality that becomes manifest in action. However, it is because this bodily charge or potency 'is only vaguely felt and rarely recognised as such that contemporary power, and indeed resistance, can exploit affect so effectively'.[133] Subjects tend to be unaware of their capacities to affect people and things partly because unlike emotion that is a state of being, affect is always in 'transition', and open to endless opportunities for creative and productive action.[134]

When affect is understood in terms of virtual capacities, the body can serve as a 'barometer' in recording transitions and these reflect and reproduce the 'freedom that is always more than what is left after power has had its way'.[135] It resides in the space between rationality and emotion, the collective and the individual, and a state of being (past/present) and one of becoming (present/future). Affect can, then, be imagined as freedom that makes it possible to refuse to live *only* through the norms and subjectivities that have been imposed on us through so many exercises of power.[136] It can also generate fresh light on how the body is also a part of the process of giving birth to ideas whereas, when the mind is in the ascendency, it tends simply to impose meaning rather than face a space that threatens identity. In teaching, this imposition of meaning is acceptable to students who are 'passively waiting' for material that they see as enabling their successful 'progress' through the course and providing security for their identity.[137] Despite this, and the disruption it may generate, creativity is a relational process occurring in the space that resides in between minds or their ideas, and bodies or their affects.

It is claimed that 'space is the relationship between bodies' because it is always in 'between things, inside things, or outside things'.[138] Drawing an analogy with music, Watts argues that the melody is the space or the 'interval between the tones' ... because these are 'not periods of silence but "steps" of varying lengths between points on the musical scale'.[139]

When disembodied, we simply deny these ambiguous and in-between spaces in our attempts to impose meaning and authority on the world to render it stable and orderly for this is how subjects feel they can secure identity. Nonetheless, these spaces remain despite our desire to deny them, and the growing post or neo-humanist literature confronts us with the contradictions, thus forcing us to reflect on, if not theorise their ambiguities and fragilities. We have already seen how theories of affect facilitate a reformulation of our notions of resistance. They alert us to the ambiguity and ambivalence surrounding the in-between spaces of bodily transitions that work 'largely below the level of conscious perception',[140] but always accompany our actions.

Of course, seeking ethical agility in the in-between spaces cannot guarantee to disrupt the masculine edifice that fuels disembodied practices of managerial leadership in organisations such as universities. That is why several organisational scholars have turned to philosophy and posthumanist feminist ethics as a way of challenging the absence of embodied relations within regimes of leadership.[141] So, for example, it has been argued that while focusing directly on acts or micro discourses of resistance is important, there is a need for some elaboration through an examination of resistance that derives from 'the desire of an ethical engagement in the socio-political context of organisations'.[142] This challenges the competitive individualism that reflects and reproduces masculine disembodiment in organisations where subjects are removed from the raw and unmediated embodied differences of the face-to-face relation in which an ethics of responsibility to the other would be difficult to displace.[143]

One problem is that the comparative success of feminism to demand social change has been built to some extent on the resources of human rights and Enlightenment humanism, the latter of which has also been embraced by managerialist and leadership norms. Yet, while many feminists reject humanism because it endorses the individualised and autonomous subject, no other mechanisms exist through which to challenge the powers that subjugate so we have to appeal to human rights, which means we can be neither for nor against the enlightenment but must simply retain a scepticism about its dangers.[144] Levinas is more concerned with its dangers because the autonomous self encourages responsibility to the self in advance of responsibility to the Other,[145] or *tout autres*.[146] When a pre-occupation with the self is pre-eminent, morality can be reduced to an exercise of power where the image of what it is to be ethical transcends any sense of responsibility. This is broadly the approach of posthumanist feminists who seek to retrieve ethics from its straitjacket in cognitive-based deontological or utilitarian rules where binary separations between, and an elevation of, mind over body, and self over Other reflects and reinforces dominant masculine discourses. By returning ethics to a relation of bodily engagement 'that precedes the intentionality of consciousness', we necessarily privilege 'our responsibility to the other who is *different* from us but to whom we cannot be *indifferent'*.[147] More generally, this literature challenges the dominance of cognition and language over experience and the body not only in representational but also in social constructivist, discourses. For although the latter was seen as a refreshing and radical departure from micro psychological or macrosystems analysis, it remained highly cognitive, linguistic and disembodied in its focus, concentrating on the conditions and consequences of construction rather than the processes of its accomplishment.

By contrast, an affirmation of affect, the body and embodied relations allows us to explore the 'in-between' spaces of ambiguity and ambivalence, flux and flow, and fragility and fragmentation as a form of ethical agility. Moreover, while a necessary condition for the possibility of ethics, embodied engagement with both human and material artefacts is more compatible with the intra-actions within which the natural and social world are mutually embedded.[148] While this may not be resistance in the conventional sense, the appeal to ethical sensibilities has a greater potential to reverse gendered disadvantages in organisations. These would also challenge myopia where masculine, managerialist leaders demand more of everyone and everything, and where perpetually 'the meaning of life is projected into the future',[149] which of course can never be realised. It also places some ambivalence around identity politics[150] and its preoccupation with securing the self through social confirmations.

Summary and Conclusion

Drawing on primary empirical data, this chapter has sought to illustrate some problematic issues concerned with managerialist reform in business schools, its differential effects on gender relations and the extent of resistance to its coercive demands. Although our research found little evidence of collective co-ordinated resistance to managerialism, there were many instances of individuals seeking to divert or disrupt some of the more oppressive features of academic life. Building on these glimmers of an often-gendered refusal to be dominated by these productivist and performative regimes, it has sought to examine posthumanist feminist calls for a rejection of identity politics in a celebration of difference and embodied, ethical engagement with the other. Such a refusal to be preoccupied with identity to render the self 'open' both in mind and body to alterity is wholly in the spirit of intellectual and scholarly endeavour. Here, different ideas and ways of being in the world, perhaps, can be seen as more important than seeking fame and fortune in academic celebrity. Since masculine managerialist leadership either intentionally or unintentionally promotes the latter, we need to find new ways of resisting whilst preserving the values of academia as an embodied, communal and ethical way of life. If this limited resistance were to be mobilised in the direction of building embodied, ethically engaged academic communities, future generations might see an effective challenge to leadership in our universities to render current dominant masculine preoccupations merely a historical blip.

The chapter has addressed the way that it is not just the masculine demands of university leaders for productivity and performance that reflect and reproduce gender disadvantages. They occur also because of familial and other social norms and the unequal share of caring responsibilities experienced by women. However, there are further 'complex considerations affecting women's position in academia ... [that] ... extend beyond marital status and the presence or absence of children'.[151] As indicated earlier, of significance is the self-policing, self-discipline and guilt that women experience whereby they often end up caring more for others than for themselves.[152] Moreover, gender disadvantage is cross-discipline and cross-national since few universities world-wide practice family-friendly policies even when they ostensibly have adopted them.[153] Many of our respondents commented on how they felt torn between the conflicting demands of work and home and how each was always compromising the other leaving them rarely free of guilt. This is a classic example of the aporia of undecidability where it can't be otherwise, since when we talk of one thing we must necessarily neglect another, and we can never wholly justify any decision made.[154]

Maybe this can serve as a springboard to reinforce the pockets of localised resistance that we found; this may then subvert the smooth flow of managerial controls as individuals refuse to comply fully with the demands of the regime, even though this explicitly disadvantages them in terms of career. While managerialism is not gender-neutral, neither is this form of resistance, for more women than men adopted an attitude of refusal. Also, it should be acknowledged that this form of resistance could easily be accommodated as a marginal irritation. rather than confronted as a disturbing and disruptive force. Consequently, it may never develop in the embodied and engaging way that is its potential. Nonetheless, academics (not exclusively women) can subscribe to a growing posthumanist feminist challenge to discourses and practices of masculinity. First, however, it needs to be acknowledged that they elevate hierarchical material and symbolic success, both in terms of the individual and the organisation, and its pursuit wholly through instrumental rational and disembodied strategies of competition, conquest and control.

Caroline Clarke and I embarked on this project partly to explore the apparent lack of protest in our profession, and yet we are not able to escape from these issues ourselves. So, for example, in writing this chapter there is a little irony in publishing about, yet reproducing, the very performative demands in universities that I have been criticising. In part, this criticism can be ameliorated because writing and publishing on this topic is a form of resistance in itself, particularly when the academic audience is both the subject and object of the research. Perhaps more important, however, is an acknowledgement that, as critics, we can never be outside of the cultural and political practices we critique. For, as critical or intellectual activists argue, as academics we are in a privileged position in terms of co-constituting the world with our students, other academics and the public. The question is are we merely 'consolidating norms, or are we contesting their hegemony'?,[155] and if so, for what reasons? While on the surface this may seem straightforward, it is far from the case because while the 'knowledge we produce and the work we do as academics "matter"',[156] we have no way of knowing, let alone controlling, whether this is interpreted and enacted upon or not. As Foucault puts it, 'People know what they do; frequently they know why they do what they do, but what they don't know is what what they do does'.[157]

Some humility is necessary if we are to avoid adopting the moral high ground where, as critics, we readily accuse others of hypocrisy because their behaviour can be seen to exemplify precisely what they claim to critique. So, no matter how convinced we are of our political position, we need to take care not to be too assertive for 'autocriticism never divides the object from the negating subject' ... as it is 'as much about self-analysis as challenging the neoliberal orthodoxy'.[158] Consequently, we do have to be conscious of what we are doing when we proliferate discourses that are critical of doing precisely this. Is it merely a form of identity construction and maintenance - not 'a truth but a desire to *be a particular way*.'[159] Clearly, it can be seen as complying with taken for granted senses of the self that were challenged in Chapter 3 insofar as, I am '*still* doing'[160] my writing and publishing my work. However, not to do so because of a fear of this criticism achieves very little other than an implicit questioning of the 'publish or perish' mantra that leadership can readily disavow or ignore.

Of course, we can leave academia rather than just 'drop-out' from some of the pressures that managerial leadership imposes but unless we have some independent means of survival to spend our lives as 'agent provocateurs' of our political beliefs, this is not a practical solution. Also, from the outside, this would have little impact on the masculine, competitive chasing of rankings for self and one's university. Consequently, we perhaps have no choice but to criticise from within for it is not writing and publishing, per se, that is a problem so much as doing it principally for the rankings. Writing will always remain a radical medium alongside direct action, as has been made evident within feminism and civil rights movements, even though backlashes frequently disrupt any sense of linear continuity. Similarly, through our actions, we embody the intimate, dynamic and entangled nature of the 'tango dance' of struggle, at the intersection between power and knowledge, and resistance and compliance. Is this then, possibly, an exemplification in practice of the very theoretical deliberations about the (im)possibility of resistance with which this chapter has been concerned?

Notes

1 Blumer (1969, p. 16).
2 Wray-Bliss (2003, p. 321, Orig. emphasis).
3 Knights and Vurdubakis (1994).
4 Kolsaker (2008, p. 514).
5 Willmott and Mingers (2012).
6 Thomas and Davies (2005), Bagilhole and White (2011, 2013).
7 Kolsaker (2008), Winter (2009).
8 Knights and Tullberg (2012).
9 Mol (2002).
10 Hynes (2013).
11 Braidotti (2011, 2013).
12 Kenny and Fotaki (2015, p. 189).
13 Ybema and Kamsteeg (2009, p. 103).
14 Goffman (1959).
15 Humphreys (2005 843).
16 Watson (1995).
17 Van den Brink and Benschop (2014, p. 461).
18 Thomas and Davies (2002, 2005), Bagilhole and White (2013), Savigny (2014).
19 Fotaki (2013, p. 1255).
20 Pullen and Rhodes (2008, p. 7).
21 Derrida (1997).
22 Cixous (2010).
23 Hollander and Einwohner (2004).
24 Fleming and Spicer (2007).
25 Thomas and Davies (2005, p. 732).
26 Kondo (1990), Fleming and Spicer (2007).
27 Hynes (2013).
28 Fotaki, Metcalfe and Harding (2014).
29 Knights and Clarke (2014), Clarke and Knights (2015).
30 Fisher (2007, p. 506), Acker (1990).
31 Deem (1998, p. 66).
32 Derrida (1982), Cixous (2010).
33 Thomas and Linstead (2002, p. 88).
34 Knights and McCabe (2015).
35 Costea and Amiridis (2016, p. 66).
36 Foucault (1980, 1982).
37 Hallenbeck (2012, p. 25).
38 Massumi (2002, p. 25), Clough (2007, 2009).
39 Hynes (2013).
40 Harraway (1991), Latour (2005).
41 Wolfe (2010, p. xv).
42 Braidotti (2013, p. 23).
43 Clarke and Knights (2015).

44 Stavro-Pearce, Barratt and Cunningham (1994, pp. 218–220).
45 Braidotti (2013, 37–39).
46 Gatens (2006, p. 26).
47 Armato (2013, p. 589), Fotaki et al. (2014).
48 Hynes (2013, p. 563).
49 Hardt and Negri (2004, p. 222).
50 Spinoza (1677/1883), Thanem (2011, p. 121).
51 Derrida (1997/1967).
52 Fotaki et al. (2014, p. 1253).
53 As previously, the term is capitalised to convey that we can never know the other in their infinite differences, see note 158.
54 Gatens (2006, p. 39).
55 Levinas (1985, p. 48).
56 Derrida (1994).
57 Foucault (2011, Loc. 7367).
58 Harley (2003); Harding, Ford and Gough (2010).
59 Harris, Thiele and Currie (1998, p. 259).
60 Bagilhole and White (2013).
61 Savigny (2014).
62 Armato (2013, p, 589).
63 Ibid., pp. 587–588.
64 Archer (2008).
65 Hekman (1999).
66 Learmonth and Humphreys (2011, p. 3).
67 THES (2013).
68 Acker (1990, p. 197).
69 Van den Brink and Benschop (2012, p. 74); see also Demos, Berheide and Segal (2014).
70 Acker (1990), Savigny (2014).
71 Doherty and Manfredi (2006, p. 558).
72 Misra, Lundquist, Holmes and Agiomavritis (2012).
73 Davies and Thomas (2002).
74 Fotaki (2013, p. 1253).
75 Butler (2011).
76 Irigaray (1985).
77 Worthington and Hodgson (2005).
78 Misra, Lundquist and Templer (2012, p. 302).
79 Knights and Clarke (2014).
80 James (2014, p. 273).
81 Doherty and Manfredi (2006).
82 Harris et al. (1998, p. 145). Although in the UK and the US, women represent almost 50% of academics, only between 25% and 30% of professors are women. https://www.timeshighereducation.com/news/proportion-of-female-professors-up-but-still-below-a-quarter/2018824.article.
83 Gabriel (2010).
84 Knights and Willmott (2004 [1999], 72).
85 Fotaki (2013, p. 1254).
86 O'Grady (2004, p. 91).
87 Joecks, Pull and Backes-Gellner (2014, p. 518).
88 Worthington and Hodgson (2005, p. 103).
89 This is not to say it is absent but usually, it is in response to direct threats of redundancy in universities (see Knights and McCabe, 2016 for a case study in the UK).

90 Clarke and Knights (2015).
91 Shirazi (2009); Shirazi uses the term 'velvet Jihad' to explore the quiet resistance of Muslim women. The word 'velvet' is borrowed from the non-violent revolution that took place in 1989, which led to the collapse of totalitarian communism in Czechoslovakia.
92 Derrida (1999).
93 Evink (2009, p. 471).
94 Foucault (1982; 1986).
95 Davies and Peterson (2005, p. 93).
96 Foucault (1994, p. 786).
97 Davidson, ibid., pp. xv–xvi.
98 Foucault (1982).
99 Irigaray (1985).
100 Levinas (1969, p. 51).
101 Watts (1951, p. 58).
102 Clarke, Knights and Jarvis (2012).
103 Spinoza (1677/1883).
104 Keenoy (2003, p. 152).
105 Standish (2001, p. 513).
106 Lorenz (2012).
107 Ekman (2013, p. 18).
108 Watts (1951).
109 Fotaki (2013, p. 1251).
110 Ekman (2012).
111 Davies and Peterson (2005).
112 Harris, Thiele and Currie (1998, p. 259).
113 Harley (2003), Harding, Ford and Gough (2010).
114 Gatens (1996, p. 24).
115 Fotaki et al. (2014, p. 1240)
116 Holtzhausen and Voto (2002, p. 77).
117 Lorenz (2012).
118 Lorenz (2012, p. 620).
119 Burrows (2012, p. 368).
120 cf. Davies and Peterson (2005), Sparkes (2007).
121 Worthington and Hodgson (2005, p. 8).
122 Fotaki (2013, p. 1257).
123 Gatrell (2008, p. 14).
124 Giorgi, Guider and Bartunek (2014, p. 287).
125 Ibid., p. 290.
126 Clough (2007), Wetherell (2015).
127 More specifically, Chapters 1, 6 and 7.
128 Hynes (2013, p. 565).
129 Massumi (2002), Clough (2009).
130 Hynes (2013, p. 564).
131 Knights (2006).
132 Adkins and Lury (2009, p. 9).
133 Hynes (2013, p. 565).
134 Ibid., p. 573.
135 Ibid., 572.
136 Foucault (2011).
137 Fotaki et al. (2014, p. 1251).
138 Watts (1989, p. 28).
139 Watts (1989, 27).

140 Hynes (2013, p. 567).
141 Kenny (2010), Painter Morland and Ten Bos (2011), Pullen and Simpson (2009), Pullen nd Rhodes (2010, 2014).
142 Pullen and Rhodes (2014, p. 790).
143 Levinas (1985), Ziarek (2001), Pullen and Rhodes (2010, p. 234).
144 Foucault (1984, 32–50).
145 Levinas (1985).
146 Derrida (1994).
147 Levinas (1985, 95, my emphasis).
148 Barad (2007).
149 Gray (2013, Kindle Location 740).
150 Braidotti (2011, Kindle location, 122).
151 Fotaki (2013, p. 1254).
152 O'Grady (2004, p. 91).
153 Forster (2001), Demos et al. (2014).
154 Derrida (1995).
155 Contu (2020, p. 740).
156 Ibid., p. 753; see also Cabantous, Gond, Harding and Learmonth (2016).
157 [1961] 274.
158 Fleming (2015, p. 189).
159 Coetzee (1992, p. 280, cited in Learmonth & Humphreys, 2011).
160 Zizek (1989, p. 32).

9 Change, Innovation and Technology

Leadership has always been strongly associated with organisational change and innovation, whether it be quality management, business process re-engineering, team working or the adoption of new technologies, processes and products. Although always contingent on the conditions of its genesis and application, innovation is what stimulates or simply reflects organisational change or the transformation of established practices. All levels of innovation usually involve leadership of some kind although, in our research, we often found more persistence from lower down the hierarchy than from the top, as leaders were often subject to the nefarious impact of fads and fashions. Consequently, innovations are often an outcome of less senior staff activity even though formal leaders invariably appropriate the credit when these are successful.[1] This provides us with some evidence for the idea of opening up traditional hierarchical conceptions of leadership to the possibilities that can be realised through its collective and distributed form. Of course, in their claim for credit, formal leaders frequently draw attention to their contribution in establishing the social and cultural context that is conducive to communal and collective innovation. This reflects the view of leadership as a dynamic process enabling a culture of challenging and imaginative creativity that inspires everyone involved.[2] However, as we shall see, espousing collective and distributed leadership is different from its enactment. In their enthusiasm to drive employees along predetermined linear tracks, leaders often lose the plot in nurturing their own masculine images more than engaging with their staff. Presenting their masculine credentials, for example, through metaphorical images of sport or war can disengage or distance many of those they seek as followers. This failure does not necessarily arrest the determination of leaders to persevere for leadership discourse lives by the vacuous cliché of 'if at first you don't succeed, try, try again'. Rarely does this self-promotion embrace a collective or communal, as opposed to an individualistic, sense of leadership.

Much of the leadership literature of recent time has taken a discursive approach, whether focusing on local, or more global analyses. In doing so, the literature has shifted attention away from the persona of the leader whether as the hero with super-human powers typical of the myths and legends of classical Greece, or as possessing 'essential' traits and characteristics such as 'charisma', 'drive', 'initiative', 'intelligence', and 'integrity'. Consequently, it draws more on context and the contingency of situations and sees leadership as distributed among everyone in an organisation rather than simply restricted to those in formal leadership positions.[3] Also building on but rejecting either an essential individual or an essential context, constructionists see leadership as an embodied outcome of collective interpretations of specific contexts.[4] In this sense, rather than being treated as discrete entities, leadership and the context in which it is practised are mutually constitutive of one another.

In this chapter, I seek to examine not only the leadership of innovation but also the innovation of leadership, the latter of which is an underlying theme of this book more generally. The chapter begins with an analysis of what innovation is but, in failing to establish much consensus, turns to the more sensible question of what it does. In exercising power, leaders are involved in constituting the subjects who are the recipients of its decisions,[5] but this does not necessarily mean those they lead are simply passive, especially concerning innovation. We observed numerous examples of subordinates taking the initiative in proposing or developing, as well as just executing, innovations. In this sense, power is almost as much 'bottom up' as 'top down', although this is not recognised in the formal hierarchy. Secondly, the chapter examines some of the research that colleagues and myself have conducted on leadership involving innovation particularly in the financial sector and in information technology. Finally, I summarise the chapter before concluding that it provides some empirical support for the earlier arguments of this book concerning the prevalence of different masculinities, the domination of disembodied rationality and their implications for ethics in contemporary leadership and organisation.

What is Innovation?

According to leading consultants on innovation, there would seem to be even more definitions of innovation than there are of leadership but as a result of asking the question to 14 leading consultants, it was summarised as follows: 'Executing an idea which addresses a specific challenge and achieves value for both the company and customer'.[6] Having gone through this painstaking exercise, which has to be seen as a promotion for his consultancy services, it is not clear that the result is much of an improvement on *The Oxford Dictionary* definition of innovation, which is to 'make changes in something established, especially by introducing new methods, ideas, or products'. Furthermore, this definition is more inclusive in refusing to limit innovation to the private sector. It is also more neutral as far as it does not presume innovation to produce change that is positive for organisations and their clients. Clearly, innovations cannot predict their future value otherwise they would not be new and, therefore, the definition provided by this eminent consultant is actually self-contradictory. Nonetheless, it is not only consultants but also academics who concentrate only on the positive sides of innovation. This is manifest in their descriptions of Americans as 'great business innovators' ... [in expressing their] ... individualism, self-reliance, a willingness to accept risk and a propensity for change'.[7] In addition, the assumptions within this literature are that autonomy, individualism, risk-taking and change are inherently 'good' even though there are probably as many examples of negative, as of positive, consequences resulting from innovation, although failure is often quickly deleted from the history books. This is an example of how people, including academics, *construct* what they claim merely to *describe*,[8] and is one reason why we should concentrate attention on what innovation *does* rather than what it is, as was done in Chapter 1 in relation definitions of leadership.

When writing about innovation several years ago, Darren McCabe and I argued that one tendency, especially in the US, is to associate it with an ideology of the 'American Dream'. This is a vision of everyone having access to 'unimaginable individual success and prosperity',[9] and thus believing in the Horatio Alger myth of 'rags to riches' and meritocracy[10] that sustains a social order of individualism and social inequality. Of course, numerous success stories tell of people entering the 'pearly gates' of celebrity from humble beginnings and invariably they are innovative in their particular field. However, most successful people have a background of privilege, as can be seen from a trawl through a list of incumbents of positions in governments, the media and major corporations worldwide. This is little different from the 19th century when a study of the origins of 303 textile, railroad and steel executives of the 1870s indicated that 90% came from middle- or upper-class families.[11] Today in the UK, we find that the great majority of government ministers were educated in private schools, the cost of which indicates wealthy parentage. Consequently, quoting a few dramatic 'success' stories does not convey a society of equal opportunity, let alone one in which discrimination and disadvantage have been eliminated.

In certain contexts of innovation, autocratic styles of leadership continue to prevail although the vogue within democratic countries is one of seeking the engagement of followers to lead through consensus rather than coercion. One way of expressing this is to appeal to followers through sporting and military metaphors. As has been argued, 'Sport offers a unique metaphor for critically examining business: the two share some common ground. Both are fast, complex and at times unpredictable'.[12]However, in drawing parallels with sport and the military, there can be a tendency for leaders to reflect and reproduce particular masculine discourses bound up with aggression, competition, conquest and control that can have counterproductive effects.[13]

Far from becoming enrolled and mobilised in team-like commitments, often employees can be left feeling bereft of any real engagement, as these discourses override any contribution that they attempt to make. There is no question that military and sporting metaphors might stimulate a competitive resilience. Still, this kind of leadership can have the effect of discounting any dissent and, thereby, displacing potential innovation. What such leadership *does* is to reinforce an individualistic narrative that, at one level, places people in competition with one another and yet, at another, in fear of a failure that is inevitable given that, for there to be winners, there have to be losers. To illustrate some of these issues, I turn now to a study that my colleague Darren McCabe and I have carried out in this field.[14]

Military Masculinity in Leadership

This research took place in a UK Building Society with a mutual status (BSM)[15] that employed 4,500 people and had a network of 250 branches, providing savings and mortgage facilities for member-consumers. The leadership was fairly bureaucratic and hierarchical, although also somewhat paternal in attempting to persuade employees of their complete job security. However, intensified competition in the late 20th century changed all this as 50% of mutual providers (including BSM) became PLCs by 2008, due mainly to mergers and acquisitions.[16] Moreover, this reduction in job security was made very real when because of the global financial crisis (GFC) in 2008, BSM became insolvent and had to be rescued by the government in a general programme of nationalising large sections of the financial services.

Our research involved documentary investigation through corporate strategy statements, training materials, staff briefs, newsletters, videos and tape-recorded strategy presentations. The research was conducted over a 12-month period and included hour-long, tape-recorded interviews with 17 senior and middle-level managers, 21 members of staff and 4 team leaders. In this chapter, however, the focus is principally on the use of corporate videos where highly masculine discourses continually referenced images of war and sport.

The research took place before the global financial crisis (GFC) at a time when there was an excessive faith in a neo-liberal, market ideology and, especially, in financial services as a form of economic growth that could eliminate the trade cycle of 'boom and bust'. Although he claims to have qualified his statement to read: no return to (Tory) boom and bust, this does not relieve the Deputy leader of the Blair government, Gordon Brown from the charge of reckless hyperbole. For, he made the claim a sufficient number of times without qualification to demonstrate his conviction that the financial sector was the panacea to break the trade cycle.[17] This encouraged a veritable 'free-for-all' of unrestrained competition to expand financial markets. Partly, as an accompaniment, new financial instruments were designed to mediate anything that was traded to secure, seemingly unending speculative gains and, by implication, economic growth. Despite many radical transformations in the sector, a number of mutual organisations continued to survive in the marketplace.[18] It was a narrative around such survival that was expressed in a dramatically masculine manner by a new leadership regime in BSM. While previous leaders had tended to be 'homegrown' through internal promotions, a new CEO was appointed whose background was as a consultant from outside the financial services sector. Immediately, this new leadership regime was heavily involved in contracting external consultants to 'modernise' BSM, and this took the form of a then fashionable practice of reengineering business processes as well as a range of other innovations.[19]

The leadership also developed a strategy to achieve radical, not just incremental, growth largely through corporate acquisitions and by entering new riskier 'mortgage to let' markets. It also introduced cost-cutting and efficiency drives, resulting in several redundancies that clearly created considerable job insecurity. The leadership sought to mitigate this by producing a series of videos shown to staff to placate their anxieties. Although no longer paternal, the new leadership mobilised an ideology of mutuality as a kind of stable continuity with the past.

Military Metaphors in Leadership

Interestingly, while deploying the language of military battles and war to sustain this stability, a defence of mutuality was seen as a way to remove staff uncertainty. Another leadership innovation was to communicate with the staff through a video presentation. Here the leadership declared a commitment to 'defend our current position [by] using mutuality as a key weapon in our armoury' (Video briefing plan document). The video has an opening brief interview with the CEO, who appears friendly, safe, and also seems to evoke a 'paternalistic' masculinity.[20] Then, it shows pictures of the Head Office accompanied by images of smiling, and apparently content, staff. Alongside, positive opinions about mutuality, the organisation and its customers were expressed by the leadership. The CEO and the Chairman of the Board are then interviewed who speak paternalistically about 'caring' for what they describe as their loyal customers and staff. The video reinforces a sense of place and belonging by concluding, with further scenic images of the local area and endorsements by local business 'men'. It finally returns to the CEO who seeks to mobilise staff in the battle to preserve mutuality by arguing passionately, 'it's down to us'. The video was accompanied by a document of model answers to the CEO's own rhetorical questions in a one-way, and aggressive masculine, mode of communication that conveyed a defensive siege mentality.

Subscribing to a mantra that 'aggression is the best form of defence', the leadership reflected a kind of Churchillian spirit of defiance in fighting the predatory designs of competitors:

> *What will we do if a potential predator makes a hostile bid by appealing directly to our members?*

> If a predator tries to do this in our case, we will launch a massive campaign to convince the customers ... that their interests are best served by refusing the offer. This really will be a *'no holds barred'*, *'all guns blazing' effort* (CEO, BSM)

Here the masculine narrative draws on the phrase 'no holds barred' in an analogy with wrestling followed by a repetition of the military metaphor. The leaders are represented as 'strong active males, collectively risking their personal safety for the greater good of the wider community'.[21] The discourse is imbued with this masculinity, which is also apparent in the preoccupation with showing strength against any opposition regardless of their size, evocative of a David and Goliath battle:

> There is little historic evidence that sheer size gives you many advantages in financial services, but quite a lot that big players tend to be unfocused. We are confident of surviving and growing by developing a very different position from these giants, which involves being stronger than them in the carefully chosen market areas where we will compete. (Video Briefing notes)

Representing the competition as 'unfocused', lumbering 'giants', BSM can apparently win by 'being stronger than them' in 'carefully chosen market areas'. With the help of staff, depicted as an agile 'army' representing a key 'weapon' in the contest with 'muscular' but unfocused predatory 'giants', the leader's guile will outwit and vanquish the 'unfocused' Goliath. Whilst intended to unite staff in this metaphorical battle with competitors, the employees were not immune to criticism. Indeed, they were targeted as failing to get more tasks 'right first time' ... and a 'lack of care in delivering services and products' (video briefing notes). These written briefing notes and documents expressed more aggressive masculinity than was often expressed by the leaders in the video. However, the use of military metaphors left no ambivalence as to the severity of a fight for survival. I turn now to a somewhat different narrative expressed by another new replacement CEO appointed only one year later, which drew more on sporting than military metaphors but still deployed videos to communicate with the staff.

Individualistic Sporting Metaphors in Leadership

Within the literature on leadership, there are numerous references to how 'actions and positions are anchored in sports references and strategies'.[22] In this vein, the new leader produced a video to introduce himself to the staff. Its opening shows him competing as an oarsman in an all-male boat race during his days at an elite University. This heroic representation is clearly intended to 'seduce audiences'.[23] However, the image of a white, aggressive, high achieving, educated, privileged, upper-class man was not necessarily so appealing to the average member of staff and was greeted with a large dose of scepticism.

In the video, this representation of the leader as a masculine 'heroic individual'[24] was combined with a concurrent emphasis on teamwork. This appeal to teamwork is an essential aspect of the language of leadership in generating a consensus that obscures any conflicts of interest between leaders and their staff.[25] Over film footage of the boat race, the CEO says that rowing is 'all about leading the team. You have to get the team to perform to the maximum of its abilities over the course'. Although one could dismiss the aggressive nature of this presentation, it is not a trivial matter for 'sports metaphors and strategies are part of the production process' of leadership. It is important since the discourse endorses 'aggressive behaviour that is deemed necessary to accomplish projects, to secure business deals or to overcome adversity'.[26]

The video then cuts to an interview of the CEO by a TV journalist. In the background are silver cups and trophies in a wooden display cabinet, which it is presumed the CEO won through his sporting prowess. Other 'symbols' of the leader's individual powers are evident including leather-bound books, which look legalistic and convey an aura of intellectual credibility. The CEO is a tall man who is powerfully built, and he appears in a casual grey polo neck shirt. The tension between 'leaders who actually lead other people toward a common vision' and the individualistic, masculine 'solitary world-maker'[27] is apparent in the video. Hence this individualistic portrayal of the CEO is juxtaposed with his comments that 'I enjoy being part of the team' and the lesson he learnt as a sportsman: 'You're always rowing with other people and you can't get there faster than the team does'. Overall, the images of individual, masculine prowess belie the textual emphasis on teamwork.

At the end of the video, the CEO is seen facing the camera whilst sitting at his desk. He is now wearing a shirt and tie, and this confirms his power, identity and status.[28] He talks directly to the camera and this creates the impression that he is talking to the staff on equal terms. On the one hand, this identity performance is meant to convey that he is 'just like us', someone who shares similar experiences to those he now commands. On the other hand, he is speaking from the CEO's office through the medium of a video that only those in authority are able to produce and distribute.[29] This medium is meant to break down hierarchical barriers, but it reproduces 'images of the 'great man', viewing leaders as dynamic agents of change and followers as passive and compliant'.[30] Moreover, videos are one-way communication devices that do not let others speak, thereby constituting 'them as objects of the activities of those'[31] in positions of authority. The imagery of the video expresses hierarchical dominance and a 'desire for control' over meaning/subjectivity and, therefore, 'mastery over the other'.[32] This suggests that teamwork is subsidiary to this imagery.

If we understand 'sport as an institutional realm in which men construct and affirm their separation from, and domination over, women',[33] others and nature, then using an elite, masculine sport to define the CEO from the vantage point of the CEO's office, can be understood as a means potentially to disengage rather than embrace others. For example, it may alienate women, working and middle-class employees, minorities and those who do not share the CEO's interest in the sport. Given this, not everyone was seduced by 'the leader's performance of mastery and power'.[34]

Nearly two years after his appointment, another video entitled 'Now and Tomorrow' was launched after 10% of the workforce had been made redundant. The CEO can be seen talking to a middle-aged, male, TV journalist who conducts the 'interview'. The images of the CEO, his dress and the context of his salubrious office, convey him as powerful, relaxed and 'in-control'. He is portrayed as an important and serious man whose words demand respect, but he is also represented as being open to questions and scrutiny even though all of it was stage-managed. The video seems designed to create an impression of 'impartiality', 'objectivity', 'honesty', and 'fairness' but the images say otherwise for they perhaps unwittingly represent the leader as an individual who is a member of a powerful, masculine elite. In the video, the CEO legitimised the redundancies in a way that deployed both a feminine, caring discourse and a masculine, ruthless one:

> The last few weeks have been pretty tough for a lot of people at BSM ..... there certainly hasn't been a time in the society's history when a large group of people in Head Office have found that their jobs have gone. That's a very difficult time not just for the people directly affected but frankly for everyone in BSM because people look for their friends and they see them going through a period of change. Whilst it isn't easy, *the reality is*, it's essential if we are going to be a successful, 21st Century Building Society. We have to have a *tight, lean* operation. (Now and Tomorrow Video; emphasis added)

In this extract, the metaphor for the organisation is like an athlete undergoing intense competitive preparations for the purpose of achieving 'success'. The leader states that this 'isn't easy' and yet the image speaks of a man who is comfortable, secure, privileged and free from the worries of work intensification or redundancy. Like athletes, the staff are urged to bite 'the bullet of pain',[35] for 'to endure pain is courageous, to survive pain is manly'[36] but they are instructed to do so by a man who appears free from such pain, although this would not be so obvious without the visual presentation of his undoubted privilege. Employees, *not leaders*, are represented as the 'fat' that needs to be discarded to render the organisation 'tight' and 'lean'. Earlier, a masculine, military discourse had been deployed as a way of enlisting employees, but then later, used to 'attack' them. In a parallel fashion, masculine, sporting metaphors were deployed as a way of enrolling and mobilising staff to raise their game, but then turned against them when treating many of them as surplus to requirements – not sufficiently 'tight' and 'lean' to win in this competitive environment.

Collective Team Metaphors in Leadership

A final video that was examined recorded an 'open' forum through which the staff could ask the leader direct questions. However, his controlling demeanour contradicted the spirit of the exercise for, rather than listening and empathising, the leader sought to 'win' the argument and, in so doing, effectively denied staff much of a voice. It indicates how 'aggression or a will to dominate', which is associated with discourses of masculinity can 'prohibit intimate personal relationships'[37]

Mike: branches have had a reduction dramatically of staff. The impact to us is we're not seeing any good news. That's the feeling and the bad news is being worsened by simple things like, the fact that we don't have diaries anymore ... when you're pulling out a competitor's diary because you haven't got one. It's one more thing that sticks in the throat (Branch Manager).

CEO: About three things. Firstly, we spend £50k a year on diaries. I bet you didn't know that. That's not what it would cost for a branch to go out and get a diary, so I don't think we need £50 K worth of centrally purchased diaries. I can get out and do some of the message for myself, but we collectively have to work together (Team Talk video)

In his response, the CEO ignored Mike's concerns regarding staff cuts and his view that 'we're not seeing any good news'. Instead, he focused narrowly on the decision not to provide diaries,[38] which was an example Mike had used only to illustrate the demoralising impact on staff of continuous cost-cutting. In a display of masculinity characterised 'as determination and resilience against all opposition',[39] the leader refused to concede that the cost-cutting drive was a problem nor to acknowledge staff feelings. He attributed the 'problem' to a lack of communication, and it is unlikely that these obfuscations will be lost on the staff who tend to 'detect discrepancies between leaders' policies, discourses [and] practices'.[40] It is also problematic to suggest that frontline employees can self-authorise the expense of paying for a diary. It could be argued that leaders are often unwilling to concede to staff for fear of appearing not to be 'in full control of others, of events or even of themselves'.[41] Yet, for us, the CEOs masculine concern to win the argument meant that he could not hear the concerns of those whose support he was concerned to mobilise through the video.

The video was at once a means to procure consent, if not commitment, and a means through which the staff could voice their dissent albeit in a highly controlled and artificial way. It was entitled 'Team Talk' and although possibly an unintended consequence of extant masculine power relations, it was plainly visible that some acted authoritatively and others were largely passive. In the video, the CEO subsequently attributed responsibility for cost-cutting to the competition. He used this to justify changes that have implications for how BSM is managed, and its impact on the lives of staff:

> We have to strip ourselves down to being focused on only spending money on those things that add value …. What's driving us to make the cost reductions is the competitive world in which we now operate. It's the Tesco's. It's the Direct Lines. It's the other competitors coming into our business who have lower cost bases than us and, therefore, can compete more aggressively. So we have to match them and beat them (Team Talk Video).

In this extract, the CEO presented the fortunes of the staff and BSM in a masculine, even gladiatorial manner. It appears that BSM is engaged in a contest with 'aggressive' competitors and so must be 'stripped' down in order to compete. However, it was visually clear that the leader, not the 'team' was directing the strategy.

Team Working in a Call Centre

From other research conducted in a call centre with the pseudonym Salesco, we concluded that in generating a promise of autonomy and egalitarianism, teamworking appeals to a human(istic) desire to be treated as a responsible 'adult' and thereby confirms individuals' sense of their own identity. This was especially welcome when the experience had been one of a strict hierarchical, command control,

> We had a culture here that said, 'You've got to check everything ....
> you mustn't try to change things' .... That's all Salesco of old and
> now we are asking them *to think for themselves* and challenge and
> take on responsibility that they never had before (Salesco Team
> Leader, emphasis added)

In the first instance, teamworking created a more relaxed atmosphere but
with this history,

> One of my hardest jobs was to give them [staff] the confidence to
> actually challenge things (Salesco Processing Section Leader)

Paul, a team leader, argues that because 'staff had previously been spoon-
fed', the hardest thing is to 'get people to start to think for themselves'.
While initially the greater responsibility and autonomy made staff feel
more valued, they soon began to detect a downside to the more enriched
work experience for, associated with it, was an expectation of total commitment to the work and the company and of 'going the extra mile', as one
of the team leaders put it. This could be seen to reflect a normalisation of
work intensification and self-discipline, as well as teamworking beginning
to intrude into the non-work lives of staff. For example, Quality Action
Teams (QAT) have been set up which bring staff together from various
areas to 'fix things'. One of these QATs is looking at ways in which to
encourage 'team building' through organising social events after work
hours, and a Team Leader (Theresa) remarked:

Theresa:	Having events outside work, I mean that was unheard of. Nobody would go out after work socially .... it's just not the done thing really. But now there are loads of events ... and a lot of people are attending
Researcher:	Why do you see that difference?
Theresa:	I suppose that's the way we've been moulded I suppose over the last six months

Theresa's explicit awareness here of how the team discourse was
aimed at transforming (moulding) everyone indicates perhaps the limitations of such a project. This was confirmed by Sandra, a processing
team leader, who argued:

> some people have changed but some people you are never going to
> change because you can't brainwash people .... you are with human
> beings who can do and say all sorts of weird and wonderful things.

In perhaps what was a Freudian slip, here, she referred to this process as
a form of brainwashing, not a term ordinarily used lightly. While many

staff went along with this without protest, some working parents and part-time staff, who had different expectations of work than their full-time or younger counterparts, resented the imposition of teamworking and especially its extra-curricular demands. They were particularly critical of the after-work social events, goal setting, and excessive communication through meetings.

The ideology behind teamworking is that of empowerment, autonomy and responsibility. Still, there is some inconsistency in thinking that these can be bestowed upon staff as if it were just like handing out confetti. Leaders tend to understand power, autonomy and responsibility as if they were a property possessed by persons whereas, as has been argued throughout these chapters, power and responsibility are relationships that are exercised in social relations. And autonomy, in the sense of acting independently of others, is a dangerous myth perpetrated by the Enlightenment, which has generated a self-seeking individualism that contradicts what it is to be human in communal and collaborative social relations. The leadership focus upon employees taking responsibility for their lives gives the *appearance* of this so-called autonomy but it is only granted on condition that staff continually contribute to the corporate agenda and objectives. It represents an attempt to secure self-regulation so as to increase the possibility of leaders being able to govern 'at a distance'.[42]

While this case has presented a clear picture of how team working was less about consent than control, I now turn to another study, typical of technological innovation in general, where business application software was steeped in discourses of masculinities and dominated by men.

Business Application Software: Masculinity and The Making of Software

In this case study, Fergus Murray and I explore the symbiotic relationship between certain masculinities and technology and the manner in which these can be manifested in the development of business application software. What we found was that leadership around systems development is suffused with and constituted through men and masculinities. Traditionally, technology has been appropriated almost exclusively as a masculine domain.[43] Consequently, gendered job segregation means that women are almost completely absent from the Information Systems arena and the vocabularies of motive employed in software (and hardware) development are tied to prevailing masculine conceptions of work and technology.

Masculinity Science and Technology

As argued in previous chapters, in their broadest sense masculinities are the ways that men, and many women and non-binary persons, may behave, think and feel about themselves. So, while more frequently observed among men, masculinities involve cultural norms that have been dominant as men have tended to be advantaged in most institutions and, as a result, they are not the exclusive prerogative of men. Far from being natural or biological categories, masculinities are socially constructed ways of seeing and being. As such, they can and do change through both time and space. For example, concepts of manhood in medieval and contemporary times have changed considerably as they also differ between cultures and ethnic groupings.[44] Furthermore, masculinity displays itself in a variety of ways within the same society depending, for example, on class or race, geographical location, form of power and sexual orientation.

If masculinities are plural and socially constructed, it follows that a masculine identity is not unambiguously conferred upon men as a function of their biological sex. It does not simply come with a penis at birth. Rather, it is the product of complex and often contradictory social processes. Moreover, while there are elements of ascription, living up to the image of what it is to be 'a man' is a continuous struggle. It is a situation where individuals feel 'driven', for no discernible reason other than as a part of what it means, and how it feels, to subscribe to an ideal of competence, and where the display of vulnerability is to threaten the image of that competence.[45] Masculinity is something that men struggle to achieve and maintain in highly competitive circumstances. Seidler says,

'Gender is not something we [as men] can be relaxed and easy about. It is something we have to constantly prove and assert'.[46]

Masculinity is a relational concept. It only makes sense; indeed, it can only be defined, in relation to femininity. Masculinity and femininity are locked in a dance where their respective positioning constrains the space within which the other can define itself. However, the dance involves more than an uneasy partnership of a single masculine and feminine identity. It's more like a crowded club where different masculinities and femininities jostle and fight amongst and between themselves. The mutual stereotyping and 'put downs' cannot be separated from the fear that each represents for the 'other' but it is masculinity that is perhaps the most vociferous in its intolerance of that which (e.g., femininity and non-conventional sexualities) threatens its precarious solidarity.

Historically, masculinities are associated with claims to rationality[47] leading readily to science and technology being a domain that men seek to dominate. As a consequence, the very idea of technology and how it comes to be understood, developed and applied is associated with masculine practices in a mutually self-defining manner. In particular, the kinds of technology associated with women is often seen by men as not 'really technology'. So, for example, work is redefined as less technical in computerised office work, and in feminised human/machine interactions such as sewing whereas men using machines in metalworking or printing are identified as engineers and technical workers.[48] In arguing that technology is a core domain of a socially constructed masculinity, it may be suggested that it is important as a boundary marker: what is perceived to be technological is frequently perceived to be masculine. In business, media, politics, science, sport, and technology, references to being manly, playing like a man, and those men not meeting these norms of manhood are told disparagingly to man-up or are accused of being feminine.

In the early 1980s, it was argued that the historical development of scientific discourse was mediated by the deployment of aggressively masculine imagery of invasion and subjugation, which involved the occupation and dissection of a passive and mysterious female 'nature'.[49] Here science developed as a distinctively masculine activity where the 'deeper the mental penetration into female nature the greater the mental virility the man of science is able to claim'.[50] This gave rise to a hierarchy of potency and status within the sciences where the most penetrative and dissecting activities such as particle physics stand above the 'softer' systemic approaches such as biology and ecology. Seen from this perspective science was articulated as a cold, dry, hard, aggressive activity that gloried in its own penetrative abilities in the pursuit of a complete 'mastery' over nature.

While there is a multiplicity of masculinities that are fluid and shifting historically,[51] what remains comparatively constant is the dominant position of men vis-à-vis women.[52] Technology appears to be one sphere in which men and masculinity are locked into one another in ways that, whether by intention or not, exclude women and femininity.

Men Making Technology, Technology Making Men

Hacker[53] set out to investigate the social formation of engineers through a comparative study of engineering students at the Massachusetts Institute of Technology (MIT). In this, she explored the relationship between the childhood experiences of the engineering students and their decision to enter the profession. She found that the engineering students, 'painfully recalled children's bodies that would not do what they should'.[54] In addition, they experienced difficulty remembering the sensual pleasures of childhood in contradistinction to the humanities students she interviewed. From these and other findings she concluded,

> The men who chose engineering had early life experiences that
> emphasised aloneness, which allowed them greater distance from
> intimacy or the pleasures and dangers of 'mixing it up' with other

people. Many became fascinated by 'things', and how they worked, and these experiences heightened the value placed on abstractions and the control of nature.[55]

Hacker's thesis suggests early life experiences predispose some individuals to become engineers. In a self-fulfilling manner, these individuals grow up and seek psychic security in the world of things almost as compensation, perhaps, for a lack of intimacy, trauma or disappointments in childhood.

In another ethnographic study of an almost exclusively male computer development team,[56] there is a link between participants' experiences of their youth and a drift into computing. In particular, a number of the development team appear to have experienced themselves as failures either in terms of their sporting or academic achievements. Others found a reassuring solidity in the world of things. For example, one of the senior team members was a small, pale, weak child who felt himself to be at the 'bottom of the pile'. When he worked out how to dismantle a telephone at an early age, he says,

> This was a fantastic high, something I could get absorbed in and forget that I had these other social problems.[57]

Masculinity and Information Systems Development

While some areas of software development are not project-based, these tend to be seen as low status and unchallenging areas of Information Systems (IS) work. High-status work is more likely to be associated with high profile new software development and it is prized for the inherent challenge it offers and the promotion prospects that follow the successful completion of major projects. Despite much debate about software quality assurance, the success of new business applications software is judged primarily in terms of meeting time and cost constraints.

Project-based work has a particular culture and tempo that sets it apart from much-routinised work. A male Project Manager defined the 'project mentality' thus,

> It is a different mentality. The mentality in admin. is very much nine to five. Here, I mean my God, I come in at eight in the morning, I leave at seven in the evening, and they're still people here. It's a different mentality. If you ask people for a little bit of extra effort you get it.

Here we see how a masculine, long-hours culture is normalised even though it is most definitely gender-exclusive in a society where domestic responsibilities are still predominantly assumed by women. Project work also appears to take on a life of its own; it is bigger than any of the individuals making it happen. You can either embrace it or take the difficult path of the conscientious objector. But to instil the project with glory and with a 'this thing is greater than us, but we have to do it' dimension, frequent recourse is made to military imagery, as in our earlier case study at BSM. A woman software developer recounted an incident which graphically illustrates this point.

A project I worked on got into difficulties and the lab manager set up a special project room with a label on the door of 'War Office'. Quite a few of us found this slightly ridiculous but nonetheless, I know others enjoyed this sort of thing and the phrase 'Blood all over the walls of the War Office' was a frequent one whenever a project manager got grilled over not meeting his dates. As a woman once active in the peace movement, I found this attitude particularly alienating and there is no way I would have been able to 'buy into' it. The fact that a fair number of my male colleagues also found the whole thing puerile was an important factor in minimising the tension at work.

From one perspective the comparison of software development with warfare is preposterous. Sitting in front of a workstation in well-appointed office accommodation around the turn of the 21st century is a world away from the 'muck and bullets' of trench warfare. But from another perspective, these evocations of another theatre of masculine practice tell us something about the psychic reality of at least some men's experience of work. In this version, work is seen as a war, as a matter of life and death struggle, of collective and individual heroism and sacrifice for an obscure and greater good.

War imagery can mobilise deep psychic energy in men. It also helps to make sense of the competitive social relations of capitalist work processes. This refers not only to the classical Marxist understanding of 'class warfare' but also to the warfare of inter-managerial and interspecialist competition. But making sense of work through warfare and mobilising energy through the evocation of war does something to the way work and masculinity are organised. Work becomes a dangerous and heroic struggle, and the imagery and practice of a dominant masculinity mediates, shapes and personalises market forces. And, as in warfare, so in work, there are many casualties.

In the practice of software development particular pressures fall on Project Managers, Project Leaders and Team Leaders. Anecdotal evidence of the results of this stress on the health of junior IS managers suggests that the pressures are not to be taken lightly. Yet it is often only by succeeding and being seen to succeed as a Project Manager or Leader that the aspiring IS staffer can gain a foothold within IS practice. This clearly creates a dilemma for those who aspire to move into senior leadership. It also leads to the worst excesses of self-destructive macho behaviour.

One of the IS staff interviewed talked surprisingly openly about his experience as a Project Leader on a highly visible project. His main re-collection of the experience was that of being 'squeezed'. He said,

Pressure definitely settles on the Project Leaders. The reason for that is you're not making the decisions ... As a Project Leader I was receiving decisions and then you're squeezed; you've got close responsibility for the team under you who are also under pressure, so you're bang in the middle where you're squeezed.

This leader has seen some of his peers move out of IS or into quiet backwaters of the department as a direct result of feeling there was too much pressure. However, despite believing that Project Leaders are made scapegoats and squeezed, he wanted to have a go, to accumulate the right stuff in his climb up the hierarchy: 'You're trying to prove yourself, to get up to the next level'. Consequently, this manager became a Project Leader and got his project in more or less on time. But as the project neared completion, as it was born, his body gave up on him. He said,

I was probably keeping myself going during [the project] and then when I'd finished my body said, 'Forget it'. Management was very sympathetic. I dragged myself back into work for a week to do the budgets. I couldn't delegate it. The last two days I was told I was slurring my words.

When the tape recorder was off this project leader recalled how he had been 'doubled up in pain' in the office during this period. Finally, he went to see a doctor and was rushed into hospital. Nevertheless, he was back at work in a week to show, as he said, 'that I was OK'. After all, he said without a trace of irony, 'I'd never been ill".

He clawed his way back into the office to demonstrate his masculine resilience only then to be forced to take two months sick leave. In this period he had time to reflect and a number of consultants suggested to him that his work life and his illness were probably connected. This led him to conclude that his illness was ninety per cent due to work stress. According to this project leader, rather than recognising how his own masculinity had been driving him, he projected his problems as a func-tion of the 'macho attitude in Data Processing' that thrived on the motto 'We will deliver'. Yet his own masculine preoccupation with climbing the 'greasy pole' of success had resulted in him playing the very game that he criticised. Only when his body gave up on him and he became ill did he begin to reflect on his situation but even then he failed to acknowledge that his own masculine identity was as much to blame as the macho workplace culture. Indeed, so much so that in speaking with him later, he said that he was determined to continue to play the game in order to progress beyond the destabilising position of Project Leader. Having moved up the hierarchy pretty quickly, he felt the danger for someone like himself was 'that if I stop at a certain level people will say I've reached my level of achievement'. Clearly, neither his body warnings nor his insights about the 'macho' culture were sufficient to enable him to reflect on his own masculinity as the driver in his concern to be seen by others as an achiever.

Summary and Conclusion

This chapter has argued that gender relations are an important condition and consequence of organisational and technological change and innovation. In particular, masculine discourses and practices have figured excessively with respect to leaders in our case studies, whether at the level of CEOs, Chairs or in the middle ranks of the hierarchy in team working. Masculinities are brought into the service of leadership in organisations where there is a question of survival in extremely competitive environments, or where innovation, technology and systems development are fundamental. Leadership in the organisations examined has drawn upon, reinforced and stimulated masculine behaviours and cultures, as has been evident from both the visual materials of corporate videos as well as from conventional interviews. The corporate videos were designed to embellish executive leadership with certain symbolic stature and, whether intended or not, to encapsulate how the leaders display an excess of masculine prowess. Such masculine grandstanding, however, is not the prerogative of those only at the top of hierarchies since it appears also to be prevalent in the lower ranks within a team working in call centres and leaders of software development.

Leadership texts and images are exercises of power that reflect and reinforce social and hierarchical inequalities, and there are occasions when these can be resisted. However, resistance is limited by individuals seeking job security and relatively stable identities. In these studies, leadership frequently sought to augment its power by deploying military and sporting metaphors to rally their staff to follow the path they were pursuing and to secure consent for their authority. Although the link is far from 'straightforward', it has been argued that 'there has long been an association between the military and images of masculinity'.[58] In many military communities, 'manliness' is 'equated with the willingness … to threaten and use force' and 'there are things professionals simply will not *say* in groups, options they simply will not argue nor write about because they know that to do so is to brand themselves as wimps'.[59] Leaders also use sporting metaphors to encourage employees into winning ways in struggles against competitors, to mobilise and consolidate their commitments in team working and, not least, to demonstrate how leaders resemble the winning mentality of celebrity sports stars. In many instances, these military and sporting metaphors display a masculine leadership and culture that eschews sensitivity and compassion since this is not viewed as 'manly' and it is perhaps understood as potentially undermining the leader's authority. While intended to generate effort, energy and enthusiasm, the absence of compassion and sensitivity did tend to diminish levels of collaborative solidarity among staff. Also, military and sporting metaphors are stretched to a breaking point for treating the competition as an enemy for purposes of 'rallying the troops' is difficult to sustain given that markets are abstract entities, lacking the somatic or corporeal visibility of armies or oppositions in a competitive game. Ultimately, however, much of this leadership effort is designed to secure a consensus by obscuring or diverting staff attention from the inequalities and inequities of the organisation.

The chapter has shown how diverse masculinities are pre-eminent in leadership discourses and practices intended to inspire employees. However, by inhibiting 'emotional sensitivity' and the expression of 'vulnerability or weakness',[60] masculine leaders may actually limit levels of employee collective engagement. This point was evident in the videoed interaction between the staff and the new leader in BSM, when he attempted to win the argument and neglected the concerns expressed by staff. It is also evident in the sphere of information technology, where for a variety of reasons from psychoanalytic to sociological and political, masculine discourses and practices prevail. In addition, where 'masculinity achieves meaning within patterns of differences' and success 'is associated with' aggression, toughness and winning at all costs, then 'femininity becomes associated with'[61] accommodation, compromise and sensitivity. Yet in a majority of organisations, these are precisely the values and embodied reasoning that help to enrol and mobilise employees to commit to the shared goals of a common enterprise. These are not exclusively feminine values and reasoning, as is so often assumed. However, under the pressure of masculine conformity, men and some women will keep their distance from what they stereotype as a feminine embodied reasoning for fear that it will be seen as weak leadership.

Notes

1 Knights and McCabe (2003a), McCabe (2020).
2 Zaleznik (1989).
3 Grint (2011).
4 Grint (2000).
5 Foucault (1982).
6 Skillicorn (2016).
7 Hammer and Champy (1993, pp. 1–3).
8 Latour (2005).
9 Knights and McCabe (2003a, p. 28).
10 Young (1994 [1958]).
11 Zinn (1980).
12 Westerbeck and Smith (2005, p. 3).
13 Kerfoot and Knights (1998).

14 McCabe and Knights (2016), Knights and McCabe (2003a), Knights and McCabe (2008).
15 BSM is a pseudonym for the organization whose mutual status meant that it was owned by its customers rather than by shareholders and, therefore, was not quoted on the stock exchange.
16 This involves demutualization where the organization transforms itself to a stock exchange listed company (PLC) to secure capital from shareholders and mutual members receive a small financial incentive to avoid their opposing it, see Galor (2008), Klimecki and Willmott (2009, p. 171).
17 http://www.channel4.com/news/articles/politics/domestic_politics/factcheck +no+more+boom+and+bust/2564157.html.
18 see He and Baruch (2010).
19 Knights and McCabe (1998, 1999, 2002).
20 Collinson and Hearn (1996).
21 Higate and Hopton (2005, p. 434).
22 Gregory (2010, p. 298), see also Coakley (2004, p. 268), Connell (2005, p. 846).
23 Sinclair (2009, p, 277).
24 Morgan (1994, p. 174).
25 Learmonth and Morrell (2019).
26 Gregory (2010, p. 302).
27 Czarniawska-Joerges and Wolf (1991, p. 535).
28 see Guthey and Jackson (2005, p. 1072).
29 see Jackson and Carter (1994).
30 Collinson (2005, p. 1424).
31 Jackson and Carter (1994, p. 156).
32 Collinson and Hearn (1996, p. 18).
33 Messner (2005, p. 314).
34 Sinclair (2009, p. 277).
35 Sabo (1995, p. 99).
36 ibid., p. 100.
37 de Garis (2000, p. 89).
38 His response focusing on diaries has been cut substantially for reasons of space.
39 Kerfoot and Knights (1998, p. 10).
40 Collinson (2005, p. 1428).
41 Collinson and Hearn (1996, p. 14).
42 Rose and Miller (1992).
43 see Cockburn (1991; 1985), Collinson et al. (1990), Henwood (1993), Wajcman (1991).
44 Bederman (1995).
45 Kerfoot and Knights (1993, p. 672).
46 Seidler (1989, p. 151).
47 Ibid.
48 Cockburn (1985).
49 Easlea (1983).
50 Ibid., p. 171.
51 Brittan (1989).
52 Kerfoot and Knights (1993, p. 663).
53 Hacker (1990).
54 Ibid., p. 115.
55 Hacker (1990, p. 124).

56 Kidder (1982).
57 Ibid., pp. 87-88.
58 Barrett (2001, pp. 77).
59 Cohn (1995, pp. 136–137, original emphasis).
60 Karner (1998, p. 200).
61 Barrett (2001, p. 82).

10 Financial Sector

Before proceeding with theoretical and empirical analyses of this sector, I need to provide some autobiographical context. First, as already outlined in Chapter 1, between leaving school at 16 and entering university as a career, I spent several years as a practitioner primarily in the financial sector, both as an employee and then in a self-employed capacity. After a few years as an academic, it was fortuitous that our school received a large financial grant from TSB, a UK bank,[1] and this enabled me to utilise my practical knowledge to pursue research in this field. Through this funding, we created the Financial Services Research Centre (FSRC) and although a director on the joint board from its inception in 1990, I became its Chief Executive in 1994. I managed several research projects in the sector with these research funds as well as securing some additional research grants from the Economic and Social Research Council (ESRC), one of which supported the research reported in Chapter 9. Once the funding from the FSRC began to be depleted, a colleague and I established a partner association—the Financial Services Research Forum, which I led for 5 years with around £1.5 m of funding, provided by 25 separate member financial institutions. Between 1994 and 1999, this was in the Manchester School of Management (later to merge with Manchester Business School) after which I moved it to Nottingham University Business School. There a professional manager was employed to lead the activity, but I remained on the executive board until 2011 when it closed down. Through these activities, I acted as the principal investigator on 38 externally funded projects, mostly from the private sector, but including 15 publicly funded Economic and Social Research Council grants. A good deal of leadership was necessary for these activities to be maintained, not in the way defined by many authors as involving followers,[2] although keeping the Forum members on board was not an easy task. The larger mission was to develop the cultural, financial, and political conditions, as well as enabling site access, to facilitate a context for several colleagues and myself to engage in research, either in producing PhDs or collaborating on projects.

Our research in the UK financial sector was conducted during a period of radical change due to governmental intervention in economically deregulating and, then, politically re-regulating the industry. The UK regulation was very different from that conducted in the rest of Europe where it took place at the point of production with tight rules about the nature and type of products that could be traded. By contrast, UK regulation was at the point of consumption, thus facilitating the development of innovations and a proliferation of different financial instruments. Regulation occurred through monitoring their distribution at the point of sale as a way of protecting consumers from the excesses of misselling products. This was later to become highly significant since it was precisely the low level of product regulation in the UK and US that allowed a proliferation of financial instruments based on re-securitisation whereby a range of debts was bundled together in packages, the toxicity of which was concealed as long as they could be profitably traded and re-traded without a final reckoning in demands for repayment. Under their casino-like construction as traded debts with an ever-receding and an ever-diminishing asset backing, these eventually brought down the financial foundations of Western economies once the US government failed to bail out Lehman Brothers leading to the global financial crisis (GFC).

The empirical research that we conducted was focused primarily on the retail end of the sector, examples of which were a part of Chapter 10[3] where BSM was heavily involved in a risky 'mortgage to let' market, with bad debts resulting in a government bailout during the GFC. While the UK had stretched credibility in participating in trading financial instruments that were eventually unsustainable, the development of sub-prime mortgages and the securitisation of debts were more pervasive in the US. Nonetheless, the economic deregulation and then light regulation of the sector in the UK, combined with a national fervour about financial services as a source of unending prosperity, certainly contributed to the crisis and the years of austerity that followed.[4] Moreover, in numerous ways, the crisis and its aftermath can be seen as of significance in creating a contemporary political climate of excessive nationalism, economic isolationism, trade wars, xenophobia, and often racism across Western democracies. Because regulatory matters were so important in the processes that led to the GFC, they will occupy substantial parts of the chapter. However, I also seek to show how excessive hubris on the part of leaders have also contributed significantly to some of the problems that have troubled the financial services.

The chapter will begin by documenting the regulatory context of the UK financial services to provide a background for some of the empirical studies that follow. I then examine questions of ethical leadership in the financial sector and how regulation failed it because, as indicated in Chapter 8, regulatory constraints leave practitioners free to exploit the loopholes. Finally, I turn briefly again to how masculine discourses and practices have dominated the industry with certain unseemly effects, especially concerning the GFC. Finally, I provide a summary and conclusion in which I reflect further on the ethics and masculinity of the sector's leadership.

Regulatory Context

The very term 'financial services', wherein a range of institutions—banking, insurance, credit and other facilities (e.g. stock market, foreign exchange, money markets)—were treated as a single sector, was only coined in the late 1980s. It is little coincidence that this occurred at a time of their increasing pre-eminence and amidst new economic freedoms and regulatory conditions. While there remain disputes about where to draw lines around different activities and divergent financial instruments, the 'packaging' of the major financial institutions within the broad category 'financial services' *cannot* be seen as merely a verbal convenience. It reflects and reproduces a discursive formation which has certain effects upon the construction and development of contemporary social relations.[5] While the focus here is on the UK, as this is where our research was primarily conducted, a radical change in the organisation of the retail financial sector took place also in Denmark, Germany, New Zealand, and the US.[6] In terms of restructuring, most countries emulated the US and UK in developing bancassurance where there was a merger of all the major functions of banking, credit, mortgages and insurance into a single corporation, instead of distinct organisational regimes. Each could see synergies in merging their services, but also in adopting each other's approaches so that insurance could benefit from linking their products to mortgages and other forms of credit, as well as securing customer payments through banker's orders or direct debits. Banking and credit could adopt similar more aggressive sales and marketing as was traditional in insurance. These transformations of the production, distribution and consumption of financial services continued as neo-liberal economic policies of deregulation reinforced the breakdown of traditional boundaries and intensified inter-industry and international competition. In Britain, as in the US, the changes in financial services were part of a broader political commitment to extend the boundaries of the so-called 'property-owning' democracy beyond mere homeownership. Government, thereby, sought to incorporate wider ownership of financial securities, stimulated either directly through offering privatised public corporation shares at discounted prices or indirectly through fiscal incentives to purchase personal equity plans (PEPs) and personal pensions.

This political preoccupation with building the population's financial stake in the national economy was paralleled in the UK by the government's concern with retaining London's importance as a centre of global finance. It was also stimulated by neo-liberal strategies of encouraging the services to fill the economic gap left by the, partly government-driven, decline of manufacturing. Believing that the financial services, like many of the professions, were bound by restrictive practices, conservative economic policy was directed toward shaking the industry out of its self-satisfied and inefficient complacency. By breaking down the artificial boundaries between specialities, the competition was intensified within a framework of regulation that *only* restrained corporations from stepping beyond the boundaries of an ethical code of some minimal protection for the consumer. Primarily, these regulations were designed to deter salespeople from exaggerating the benefits of their products. By imposing a written agreement to be signed by the client and a 'cooling off' period allowing them to cancel without charge, consumers were protected from 'high pressure' sales. I now provide a little more detail on the regulatory changes that developed in the UK.

The first major intervention concerned the removal of restrictive practices in the trading of financial securities within what is known as the 'City'.[7] Following a monopolies and mergers commission investigation that threatened legislation, the stock exchange removed the 'closed shop' practices through which new entrants had previously been prevented from obtaining a licence to trade on the floor. It also eradicated the monopolistic, exclusive power of jobbers to 'make markets' and open this up to the stockbrokers who then could trade on their account as well as trade securities to clients. The two arms of the business were kept separate through a system known as the 'Chinese Wall' where sensitive information could not be passed between producers and sellers in the market.[8]

One governmental concern behind the strategy of eliminating restrictive competition was to limit the cost of trading, which had acted as a disincentive to small investors. Of course, this was part of popular capitalism and neo-liberal politics, but the real preoccupation was to preserve London as an international financial centre, and this meant the creation, through mergers, of large investment banks that could compete in a global market.[9] These larger financial institutions were also able to negotiate much-reduced levels of broker commissions for trading large volumes of business. Financial institutions also benefited dramatically from the popular capitalism of the Thatcher regime, which was designed to incorporate large sections of the population into having a direct stakeholder interest in the economy through homeownership, share ownership, and equity invested pensions.[10] However, there was a policy disjunction here as the growth of financial services does not necessarily stimulate industry since the former makes returns on exchanges (i.e. commissions on deals) regardless of whether or not they advance the productive economy.[11] It also made the UK more dependent on financial services and thus comparatively more vulnerable to the instability created by the global financial crisis of 2008, which will be discussed later in this chapter.

The changes that transpired to reflect and reproduce the complexity constituting the financial services, clearly benefited the larger retail institutions rather than the smaller operations, because they were able to invest heavily in large sales forces, capital intensive information technology, advertising, direct mail and internet marketing. Both deregulation and regulation gave a higher profile to the sector that was highly beneficial for business even though there were considerable costs. Some of these were the extra administrative, monitoring, compliance and training costs, but there were also public relations disasters since there was a greater exposure in cases of malpractice. At this time, consequently, the financial services increased their activities, retailing larger volumes and a proliferation of products and services. The state's encouragement of individual responsibility, financial self-discipline and equity ownership served to reinforce the expanding market for financial services.

The exercise of power by producers, distributors and regulators transformed individuals into subjects that *secured* themselves and their identities through participating in the consumption of the products generated by these processes.[12] In short, this power had the effect of defining the 'truth' of what it was to be a subject in the pursuit of items of conspicuous consumption, personal security, individualised wealth, and relative independence from the state or the community.[13] These various developments reflected not only new configurations of the power of financial services and the subjectivity of its consumers but also were an outcome of the conditions that facilitated the reproduction of these social relations. Consequently, during the boom cycle of the 1980s, financial services contributed significantly to the dramatic growth of credit and indebtedness. Of course, there were setbacks and certain bankers (e.g. Pitman, chief executive of Lloyds Bank) acknowledged making bad judgements at this time and, therefore, were partly responsible 'for mounting business failures and bad debts'.[14]

Nonetheless, during the latter part of the 20th century, economic deregulation and political re-regulation have to be seen as uniting a fragmented set of institutions, at the same time as transforming the subjectivity of consumers to sustain it. Private provision for various forms of social security began to supplement and often replace state welfare and this has been a worldwide phenomenon.[15] Indeed, it may be argued that a committed consumer of financial services was created, and individuals began to be as interested in their personal investments, insurances and pensions as in their cars or other material commodities. The change encapsulated a new level of individualised material self-interest.

The Failure of Ethics in Leadership Within Finance

Insofar as the leaders of regulatory institutions within financial services draw on ethical discourse and this is not always obvious, they do so indirectly or unconsciously through adhering to a version of deontology or consequentialism. Deontology is a technical term used to describe duty and moral obligation to a set of rules generated transcendentally from a higher-order if not God. It is primarily associated with the philosopher Kant who believed in absolute right and wrong and this is readily encapsulated in the 'categorical imperative', which means behaving toward another in the way that you would wish others to behave toward you. Rationality was at the core of deontology for it is seen as enabling the discovery of universal principles of moral behaviour that treat the individual as sacrosanct and inhibits individuals using others instrumentally as a means to an end.[16] In endorsing universal principles, deontology provides an almost perfect rationale for the regulators, although, within the financial sector, there may be more difficulties in complying with the non-instrumental principle. Consequentialism, by contrast, simply refers to ethics that focuses on outcomes rather than their conditions of possibility and is best known in its utilitarian form where ethics is reduced to generating the greatest benefits in terms of maximising pleasure and minimising pain for the largest number.[17] Deontology might be seen as 'doing the right thing' whereas consequentialism would be seen as 'doing things right' so that people benefit from the outcome. In a general sense, the regulators have tended to adopt universal rules to which the financial service providers must comply regardless of context.

However, in subscribing to neoliberal free-market ideology, the regulators are also implicitly sympathetic to the kind of consequentialist ethics surrounding Adam Smith's egoistic theory. Here morality is attributed to actions that are based on the pursuit of individual self-interest because, through what is seen as the 'hidden hand' of market exchange, the aggregated consequences are deemed to have collective benefits, in the sense of increasing overall economic growth.[18] The regulators do, however, modify this through a utilitarian principle to constrain this egoism where it is thought to result in outcomes detrimental to consumers and society. They tend therefore to subscribe to a mixture of deontological universal rules, egoism and utilitarianism since the rules they create are expected to have positive, or at least *not* negative, communal or collective consequences. Accordingly, many of their rules are directed toward enforcing 'good business conduct' through transparency, information disclosure, and fair treatment for customers,[19] although the success of these rules is grounded more in faith than in solid evidence.

As argued in Chapter 7, there are many problems associated with both deontological and consequential ethics, which I now consider in turn. A major problem with the universalism of deontology is that rules and obligations cannot cover every possible contingency and so there will always be a need for continuous deliberations given the complexity of moral life. Of course, the biggest problem concerning the financial sector is that the rule makers are almost always one step behind the practitioners. Rules are often introduced as a means of preventing some action that has been identified as damaging to the industry. However, from an ethical point of view, the most serious problem with deontology is that it produces un-reflexive compliance to rules, and thereby actually removes the moral dilemma of choosing between alternative actions independently of external constraints. This can de-sensitise us all to our moral judgments. For Derrida, moral choice only exists in situations of 'undecidability', i.e., when there is no clear external guide on how we are to behave.[20] By bureaucratising morality, deontology has the effect of displacing it with rituals and routines to which we either comply or become deviants. It may also be argued that deontology separates the ethics of the act from the ethics of the agent and then focuses on the act to the neglect of the agent. Thus, acts of rewarding managers excessively, even amid the global financial crisis, were obligatory under the rules. Consequently, when there was public moral indignation, governments were prevented from overruling undeserved benefits and could only shame those who had secured huge financial rewards, despite bankrupting the organisations over which they presided.[21]

Equally, there are problems with consequentialist ethics in its focus almost exclusively on outcomes and particularly its commitment to hedonism. In terms of its focus on outcomes, it assesses whether or not an act is right or wrong wholly in terms of its consequences concerning the interests of individuals (egoism) or those of a majority in society (utilitarianism). Rarely, however, do the consequentialists speak about the conflict between egoism and utilitarianism but a simple example is in democratic elections where the majority, political rule results in minorities being disenfranchised and thus suffering for the sake of the pleasure of the larger group. Utilitarianism, therefore, displaces egoism and requires a supplementary ruling, as in the American constitution, which insists that majority rule must respect, and give a voice to, minorities.[22]

Concerning the hedonistic principle, it assumes the pursuit of pleasure and the avoidance of pain to be a universal aspect of the human condition. First, a concentration on the results that transpire from moral action is problematic insofar as, in matters of human behaviour, we do not have a strict science that can establish efficient causes in terms of a simple linear relationship between acts and their consequences. This is because, unlike natural objects, humans are meaning creating and transforming subjects so that there is a double hermeneutic of interpretation on the part of both the subject under observation and the observer who might, for purposes of social science, be recording it.[23]Furthermore, even if the interpretive dilemma did not exist, the complexity of social relations would make it difficult, if not impossible, to isolate a moral decision from all the other factors that affect the eventual consequences. Turning to the hedonistic principle, it is problematic because it is tautological since the pleasurable or painful consequences (responses) are not independent of the ethical act (stimulus) that is deemed to be their cause.[24] This is partly a function of the impossibility of developing a universal concept of pleasure. For, what can be seen as enjoyable to one person may be painful to another and vice-versa, so that the very idea of this dichotomy is contradicted, especially by the existence of sadomasochism. But more routinely, many people suffer mentally or physically from self-induced pain in their lives.

Alternative ethics of leadership that would seem to overcome the objections to deontological and consequential ethics could derive from the theories of virtue originally inspired by Aristotle.[25] There has been growing support for some form of virtue ethics within the literature on ethics and leadership.[26] Although there is not homogeneity between the various authors, generally morality is seen as internal to the subject and the key to 'good' rests not in rules or rights, but the classic notion of character (honesty, fairness, compassion, and generosity). Virtue ethics is concerned with what we become as subjects, rather than moral imperatives on how we should behave following particular rules and regulations, or in terms of specified utilitarian outcomes. It centres on the agent, the character and the dispositions of persons. Virtue-based ethics seeks to produce excellent persons who both act well (out of spontaneous goodness) and serve as examples to inspire others and, in this sense, it is closely aligned with leadership. Yet, there is considerable evidence to show that the financial sector has failed miserably to inspire ethical behaviour through leadership.

However, as has been argued throughout this book, one of the problems identified in the literature on leadership was its tendency to support individualistic notions of leaders as heroes or occasionally heroines. Unfortunately, the literature on ethical leadership does not escape this tendency for it can be equally as individualistic as the earlier leadership literature, especially when it has a strong focus on the character of leaders or is driven by *virtue* ethics. While virtue ethics does challenge the domination of deontological and utilitarian rules in discussions of ethics, it does so within leadership studies at the cost of retaining a belief in the individual, virtuous and often heroic leader. Whereas the former modes concentrate on the positive consequences of complying with deontological (duty) or utilitarian (greatest good to the greatest number) rules, virtue ethics focuses on *being* a moral subject and displaying good character and disposition. There is some irony here in that if virtue ethics is adopted in leadership studies, it is in danger of emulating the very trait approach that both mainstream and critical leadership studies have been, at some pain, to discard. Also, when morality is founded on a 'relatively arbitrary and almost in-exhaustive list of character traits', that are independent of the context in which leadership might be undertaken,[27] it is equally as problematic as the universalised rules of deontology and the consequentialist norms of utilitarianism. It might, then, be said that the failure of ethical leadership in finance, or elsewhere, resides in the inadequacy of ethics. There is another problem accompanying these ethical dilemmas within leadership, however, which is the preoccupation of many leaders with their masculine identities, as discussed in Chapters 6 and 7.

Of course, leaders within the financial sector do not exhibit universal or identical sets of behaviour. So, for example, executives in the boardroom will differ significantly from macho masculine dealers on the trading floor,[28] and clearly, masculinities differ across a wide range of other distinctive subjectivities such as ethnicity, age, culture and other socio-political contexts.[29] However, research[30] that Hugh Willmott and I conducted in an insurance company provided some dramatic evidence of aggressive masculinity, where the Chief Executive (CE) routinely humiliated one of his senior executives responsible for customer services (CS) who he did not rate as too competent. On one of the many occasions when, as observers, we attended and recorded a morning board meeting, the CS was gently questioning how the CE insisted on a 'hands-on' involvement in many of the decisions that the CS felt should be delegated whereupon the CE responded 'I want to make sure that things are done to my standard or in my way'. The CS continued his minor protest referring to the New Business function and then the Branch Automation where responsibilities do not seem clear and were 'causing some difficulties because people are getting two directions' ... and this is 'causing confusions out there, and additional work'. The CE comes back and refers to Branch Automation as an example where 'I see it as very important that I impose a set of standards inside the organisation that I wish to see adhered to'. When analysing this in the context of our presence in the company over several years, we concluded that the humiliation of the CS, who eventually was forced into resignation was about polar opposite constructions of reality where the CS felt that the CE was resistant to delegation. In contrast, the CE was convinced that his senior team and, in particular, the CS were failing to grasp the strategic significance of Branch Automation or New Business, for example, and not meeting the standards that he sought to impose.[31] Before turning to other issues, and in response to the CS's claim that 'direction is clearly your prerogative not detailed decision making', the CE says 'the idea of being in the City office and taking everything that is going on just isn't on. Not with me and my temperament. I intend to be right there, and I will stay there as long as I find, taking New Business as an example, that there have been 'hotline' cases for two and a half weeks and they still haven't left the office. That sort of thing will just drive me mad' ... 'my interests are quite calculated. They're not random. That's the end of it'.[32]

We analysed this episode as an example of the conflicting inter-pretative schema where the CE was determined to impose his reality on the organisation. We concluded that this dressing down of the CS oc-curred partly because, naively, he had not mobilised any support from his executive colleagues and was therefore isolated one to one with the CE. After this episode, the board discussed a different way of organising where a small inner cabinet would be formed to report to, and obtain sanction from, the CE for important matters of change or development. In this way, the CE demonstrated that he was not opposed to the dele-gation, but it would only be on his terms, or as the Finance Director argued, 'the CE's way of doing things'. While this brief vignette reveals a determined and authoritative masculine CE imposing his will, other examples in the period leading up to and following the financial crisis, a certain form of macho masculinity has been in evidence, that encouraged the competitive pursuit of astronomically high remuneration as a man-ifestation of their power of conquest and control.[33]

While leaders in banking will claim that they are just paid the market rate, these remuneration packages are decided by a predominantly male community of similarly wealthy executives so that they are always in-directly voting for their own pay increases. It has comparatively little to do with an efficient and free market in labour that results in salaries simply reconciling the supply of and demand for expertise. It could be argued that this is a systemic problem where corporate governance has failed to question the interlocking directorships and a self-advancing community of the 'great and the good' who support one another's ma-terial and symbolic privileges.[34]

Part of the crisis in the sector could be seen as relating to the dom-ination of masculinity. The finance industry could benefit from a broader diversity programme to prevent the cloning effect of white, elderly male managers who tend to think alike and often act in unison, and who have in recent history, followed each other like lemmings into the financial abyss. For this predominant white male, culture reflects and reinforces a masculine single-mindedness or tunnel vision that could be seen as fuelling the pursuit of short-term profits without adequate consideration for risk and the longer-term future. As with many of the arguments in this chapter, however, eroding the domination of masculine discourses and practices can only be seen as a necessary, not a sufficient, condition of diverting financial organisations away from their tendency toward self-destruction.

For, in many ways, the financial institutions have evolved to be largely self-destructive in that they are part of a system designed to create money-credit to make speculative profits through increasing the number of transactions, regardless of the stability and solidity of the underlying investments. In so far as profits are made without any fundamental material exchange, the tendency is for trade to expand exponentially since a commission or bid-offer margin is made on every transaction. By contrast with the productive economy where price rises result in a reduction of demand, the opposite is often the case with financial securities. Because they are traded not for direct consumption but only as offering the potential for a future higher return, these transactions 'inevitably generate asset price "bubbles" financed by debt'.[35] Eventually, sentiment changes as an over-extended lending results in defaults and the bubble very often bursts much more quickly than it initially expanded, leaving the assets with limited or no value since their value is dependent on people buying them. The GFC was more complex than this because many of the assets had been held 'off-balance sheet' in structured investment vehicles (SIVs) that evaded regulatory arrangements designed to ensure the adequacy of capital to back the risk of defaults.[36] However, the principle is the same and while the economy is dependent on financial exchanges to 'oil its wheels', the wheels are always in danger of coming off through the 'candy floss', surreal nature of financial booms.

Many would argue that it is *not* avarice, malice, greed, hubris, irrationality or unethical behaviour that are the cause of financial crises but simply the structure of the system whereby booms and busts are built into its very practice. It is the 'actual existence of asset markets and credit-money-creating banks' that generate the conditions for the expression and legitimacy of such behaviour.[37] However, there is a danger in this kind of analysis in either excusing bad behaviour or denying agency on the basis that the whole is greater than the sum of its parts. We do not have to reify the system any more than we should essentialise human agency for, even though financial arrangements do condition human agency, they are products of that self-same agency. So, while the system may have built-in, self-destructive tendencies, ethics and social responsibility ought to be able to make a difference.

As most people are aware, the GFC wreaked havoc on most western economies, forcing them into long periods of austerity, which were deemed necessary partly to reduce the excessive public sector debt that was created to bail out the most vulnerable financial institutions. The resulting recession has been the subject of much analytical commentary with different specialists competing with one another to provide the most definitive account of, or explanation for, the events. However, almost all of the explanations are steeped in a similar cognitive paradigm to one that could be said to have generated the crisis in the first place. Despite the impossibility of rational and mathematical risk calculations ever matching the complexities of the activities they model,[38] financial experts retain faith in them. So much so that post-crisis regulation has simply stepped up the capital adequacy requirements of the banks to limit liquidity shortfalls that usually lie behind bankruptcies.

Perhaps the severity of the GFC and its implications leaves some space, therefore, for a radical challenge to the austerity paradigm, as may already be occurring in response to the COVID pandemic.[39] Throughout this chapter, a failure of ethical leadership has been suggested as a complementary means of understanding the events for, it can be argued that the 'financial crisis was fundamentally a crisis of ethics and values'.[40] Unfortunately, the literature on ethical leadership does not provide us with a very optimistic scenario for the future in terms of transforming the financial sector. This is partly because the resort to regulation and leadership theory and practice seems dependent on the 3 traditions of consequential, deontological, or virtue ethics. Each of these arouses some misgivings, either because they rely on passive compliance with rules or norms or celebrations of the virtuous individual. Virtue ethics tends to reproduce the heroism of earlier discredited, individualistic and psychologistic theories of leadership. Consequential ethics, whether egoistic or utilitarian and deontology are universal and inflexible as to circumstances, contexts and mediating considerations. They have also been seen as incompatible with modern conceptions of ethics in so far as they displace any moral dilemma and, thereby, remove the responsibility of decisive ethical action from the subject. If this were not problematic enough, there is the additional burden within the financial sector of a dominant masculine, technical rationality and ethics that remains concentrated on constraining misbehaviour rather than transforming the sense of what it is to be ethical. In Chapter 7, this was discussed in some detail so that here I simply speculate on this embodied ethics as a way of breaking from existing overly rational paradigms.

Referring back to the previous chapter, it is clear that the masculine heroism and hubris of the leaders in BSM could be seen as an 'accident waiting to happen'. While masculine leadership cannot be seen as the principal source of the collapse of BSM during the GFC, it was an important contributory factor. It may also be seen to have contributed to the GFC itself since a gung-ho, trading machoism and excessively optimistic leadership dominated the financial sector and fuelled the false faith and hubris in the boom extending indefinitely. The kinds of masculinity conveyed by the narratives of the leaders in BSM involved battling for dominance and conquest of all that is outside of the masculine self—women, 'lesser' men, market position and territory. In this excerpt, we concentrated on providing evidence of the physical appearance and the subtleties of expression conveyed by corporate videos. This visual methodology was especially revealing of the masculine solidarity, purpose and intent, as these leaders sought to transform the subjectivity of their employees by engaging them in the images and discourses contained in the corporate videos. While visual materials cannot 'tell us the whole story',[41] they show how leaders represent themselves and their strategy[42] and provide a partial glimpse of 'the constitutive processes through which' leaders and leadership 'are created'.[43] These masculine narratives and imagery were also present in other research on teamworking and software development within the financial sector and much of the discourse, especially around sport and competition, was designed to secure the consent of employees to the 'credibility' of leaders, which 'is what first makes believers act in accord with it'.[44] As de Certeau argues, in a way that confirms the analysis above, 'every political discourse gains effects of reality from what it assumes and makes others assume, regarding the economic analysis that supports it'.[45] In our studies of the financial sector, leaders assumed and spoke with, total assurance concerning the loyalty of 'customers' and 'staff'. Their articulations were intended to leave staff with little doubt as to the survival of their respective organisations in difficult economic climates. Staff were also expected to believe in the apparent powers of the prophecy of their corporate leadership. When insolvency and a government bailout eventually contradicted the excessive optimism of their narratives, the GFC could be mobilised by leaders to deflect any responsibility for the outcome.

Summary and Conclusion

This chapter has focused primarily on seeking to understand the global financial crisis of 2008 as it has been the most dramatic economic disaster since the depression of the 1930s. Psychological attributions of greed or selfishness, on the one side, or failure of the regulatory regime on the other, are the most common accounts provided by commentators. I have offered and sought to illustrate through a few empirical vignettes, an account that focuses on the masculinity of leaders. Also, I have questioned the reliance of leaders and regulators on a restricted moral compass drawn from the traditions of deontology, consequentialism, and virtue ethics. A modern conception of ethics relies on a transformation of the self in post or neo-humanist ways, demanding responsibility to the other and a recognition that we cannot just appeal to some external guide or authority in the form of a leader or a set of rules. For, contingency, indeterminacy and uncertainty are the contexts of ethical acts, and this means that subjects cannot just follow a leader blindly or simply comply unreflectively with regulations.

While conventional thinking condemns an unconstrained pursuit of personal gain through excessive bonuses and salaries, for example, the rules have failed to constrain the financial institutions, but this cannot serve as the final explanation for the GFC. The approach offered here goes further, to explore the conditions that make it possible for the pursuit of excessive rewards to be seen as legitimate and to be able to understand why regulations fail. The reason why individual self-interest dominates leadership and society more generally is that it has been made legitimate by a range of discourses. Extending back to the enlightenment, a belief in the autonomy of individuals has served to frame modern western cultures and has elevated the importance, indeed made it an imperative, for subjects to realise their potential. This has been consolidated by faith in the 'hidden hand' of beneficial collective outcomes arising from individual economic self-interests and, more recently, the neo-liberal reinforcement of a commitment to competitive market relations. These values or some would say ideologies, legitimise individualistic behaviour in pursuit of personal, material and symbolic advantage with limited and variable constraints. On the one hand, these values support the freedom of private individuals and markets and, on the other hand, socialised concerns for fairness, a degree of equality and the overall benefits for the wider collective, community. With regulation, rules can never be sufficiently exhaustive to cover all contingencies and if they were, they would destroy the very potential for market-driven production to be innovative. An alternative is to advance a conception of leadership that might render unethical behaviour contradictory to what it is to be human. This would involve recognising how disembodied forms of cognitive rationality that inform many of the prevailing conceptions of ethics, masculinity and leadership can result in ignorance or the glossing over of responsibility to, and engagement with, the people who are often the victims of ethical failures.

Reflecting traditional moralities and masculinities, financial practices can be seen at best to restrain, rather than remove, unethical behaviour, resulting in a leadership that is often in denial regarding ethics. For, the pursuit of excessive material (economic) and symbolic (identity) advantage can be seen to be a major part of the construction and maintenance of masculine discourses and practices that lack ethical propriety. A more diverse leadership would possibly ameliorate the kind of 'gentleman's club' culture that often pervades executive remuneration committees to ensure reciprocal support for financial rewards to senior colleagues.[46] However, while an equal gender and diversity balance within the higher ranks of the financial sector may be necessary, it is not a sufficient condition for developing ethical leadership. This is because in climbing the hierarchy, women and other minorities frequently have little choice but to adopt the norms and values of masculine assertive and aggressive competition, where the control of others overrides any sense of ethical and social responsibility.[47] Consequently, there has to be a concerted effort to ensure that firstly, ethical leadership is embedded in financial organisations and secondly, that it departs from tradition to develop an ethics that involves an embodied reasoning and a sense of engagement with others in relations of common commitment. Ethical leadership has to escape from its reliance on codes of compliance and ideals of utility or virtue and, instead, bear witness to embodied engagements that embed relations in feelings, affects and responsibility to others rather than cognitive calculations of self-interest.

Although any modern economy is heavily dependent on financial services for it to function, the failure of ethics and the resort to masculine managerial forms of leadership has left the financial sector bereft of moral integrity. The global financial crisis was a clear signal that the self-interested, masculine preoccupations with control and conquest has counterproductive consequences. If, as looks likely, this has not been enough to arrest our determination to exploit others and the environment we all occupy, then perhaps the coronavirus pandemic will be metaphorically (although real for many) the 'final nail in the coffin'. I now turn to a postscript in which I discuss the coronavirus pandemic and certain leadership responses to it.

Notes

1 A bank originally established in 1810, but in 1995 a merger renamed it Lloyds TSB, and then in 2014, it was divested through an initial public offering so, once again, gaining independence as a PLC.
2 Learmonth and Morrell (2019).
3 Other, by no means exhaustive, examples were Knights and McCabe (1998, 1999, 2002, 2003a, 2003b, 2008), Knights and Odih (1995, 1999), Knights and Willmott (1995).
4 This was discussed in more detail in Chapter 10
5 Foucault (1973).
6 Knights and Tinker (1997).
7 This is the square mile in London and is the oldest and still one of the most important centres of international finance.
8 Jessop and Stones (1992).
9 Ibid., pp. 169–185.
10 Ibid., p. 185.
11 Ingham (1984), see also Ingham (2011).
12 Foucault (1982), Knights (2006).
13 Knights (1997).
14 Observer, 23.2.92.
15 Offe (1984).
16 Kant (1889).
17 Bentham (2010).
18 Smith (1793/1976).
19 see http://www.fsa.gov.uk/.
20 Derrida (1992).
21 Indeed, in one case, the Royal Bank of Scotland in the UK had to be nationalised to prevent its collapse while, on resignation, the CEO Sir Fred Goodwin received an enormous financial parachute package. Later, the shaming took the form of having his knighthood withdrawn.
22 De Tocqueville (1835/1998).
23 Giddens (1979).
24 Chomsky (1970).
25 MacIntyre (1981/2003).

26 Arjoon (2000), Whetstone (2001), Molyneaux (2003), Case et al. (2011).
27 Knights and O'Leary (2006, p. 130).
28 McDowell (1997).
29 Gilmore (1990).
30 Knights and Willmott (1992).
31 Ibid., p. 771.
32 Ibid., pp. 770–771.
33 Seidler (1989).
34 Knights and Tullberg (2012).
35 Ingham (2011).
36 Tett (2009).
37 Ingham, (2011, p. 230).
38 Ingham (2011, p. 232).
39 It is interesting that many governmental responses to an even more severe public sector debt crisis, due to the COVID pandemic, is to resist an austerity programme and seek to expand the economy through extending public debt further rather than cutting back.
40 Santoro and Strauss (2013, p. 19), see also Sternberg (2013).
41 Pink, (2004, p. 401).
42 Guthey and Jackson (2005).
43 Wood, (2005, p. 1107).
44 de Certeau (1984, p. 148).
45 de Certeau (1984, p. 188).
46 Knights and Tullberg (2012).
47 Wajcman (1991).

11 Postscript

Masculinities in a Pandemic

While occasionally in this book, I have referred to political leaders, my main focus has been leadership in non-governmental institutions. Yet in this concluding postscript, it seems appropriate to address the politics of the Coronavirus pandemic that will leave its mark on many generations to come. Just as in previous tragic periods of history, leadership during this global health crisis has been centre stage. As I argued in Chapter 1, whenever there is a crisis of any kind and the current COVID-19 pandemic perhaps is the crisis to surpass all crises, there is a turn to leadership. In the best of times, we struggle to be confident that leaders live up to the expectations that are projected onto them by the public. Consequently, during a crisis when expectations intensify and responsibilities magnify, we get numerous declarations or accusations of failing or incompetent leaders or claims of a leadership void. Rarely do commentators consider that leadership might be part of the problem rather than its solution, as I discussed in Chapter 8 concerning ethics.[1] This has occurred throughout the pandemic beginning with the Chinese government's early attempt to conceal the virus in January 2020 through to the responses of Trump to the George Floyd murder protests in June 2020. The chapter is primarily involved in providing some account of the responses of the three political leaders in Brazil, the US, and the UK in managing the COVID-19 pandemic less effectively than other nations and, in particular, those of Denmark, Germany, New Zealand, South Korea, and Taiwan, where women were the political leaders.

Leadership Masculinities during the COVID-19 Pandemic

Political leaders across the world have exploited the coronavirus pandemic as a vehicle for their masculinities but, as the pandemic has progressed, these have taken three different forms that I have labelled: Bravado, Macho and Narcissistic. While I have been able broadly to characterise these sequentially in terms of responses to the pandemic, they are neither wholly discrete nor independent but coincide, merge and overlap with one another and with other masculinities. This is especially so with the populist leaders—Bolsonaro, Johnson and Trump—whose desire for followers would seem to be a reflection of deep insecurity. Moreover, in the case of Trump, many have claimed that this insecurity is the manifestation of a mental health condition[2] that has contributed to the perpetuation of 'poison and toxicity throughout the Republican Party and amongst his supporters'.[3]

Before proceeding with this analysis, perhaps a definition of populism would be helpful. Although the term is often used loosely, populism describes a homogeneous group of citizens determined to challenge governing elites who are seen to be 'depriving (or attempting to deprive) the sovereign people of their rights, values, prosperity, identity, and voice'.[4] It can be argued that the trend of populism has predominantly mobilised those who trade on exclusion and demonisation of outsiders. Associated with a far-right politics, populists have also challenged the neo-liberal consensus for its neglect of the masses that constitute the new urban poor in technologically advanced global economies. In this sense, their attack on the liberal elite resonates with an albeit radically different politics of the left that also resists the liberal consensus for its hegemonic discipline of subjects. Often though, the populist rhetoric gives a licence to demagogues who play on the dissatisfaction of large majorities, if not the masses, with liberal elites but the danger lies in their creation of an even more repressive social order.[5] Paraphrasing Foucault, it might be suggested that populists are not necessarily either 'good' or 'bad' so much as dangerous. As he continues, 'If everything is dangerous, then we always have something to do. My position leads not to apathy but a hyper- and pessimistic activism. The ethical-political choice we have to make every day is to determine which is the main danger'.[6] Whether masculine discourses, identities and practices are the main danger in leadership is open to debate but, the three leaders discussed here have presided over the largest number of deaths of any country[7] in their handling of the coronavirus pandemic. I proceed to examine the record of Bolsonaro, Trump and Johnson in terms of the three types of masculinity.

Masculine Bravado

In the early stages, all three leaders were in denial about the virus. This masculine bravado involved downplaying its seriousness, its rate of infection that escalates exponentially without intervention, and its resilience. They also exaggerated the potential to discover and distribute a vaccine designed to stop it in its tracks. Bolsonaro likened it to the common cold and refused to countenance social distancing, resulting in the dismissal of his health minister for supporting it. He then sought continually to flout the lockdown rules that state governors and health experts demanded.[8] By Mid-May, he had relaxed the rules on access to the anti-malaria drug Hydroxychloroquine so that it could be prescribed to people even with mild symptoms despite little evidence that it was effective as a treatment for COVID-19. Indeed, the WHO had abandoned trials on the drug on safety grounds and there was some evidence that it could increase the risk of death.[9] While infections were multiplying exponentially and Brazil eventually experienced the second-highest number of deaths in the world after the US, Bolsonaro continued to breach the lockdown and to claim that more people would die because of damage to the economy than from the disease itself.

The behaviour of the UK Prime Minister Boris Johnson was equally bravado for, a few days after advice from the WHO to refrain from close physical contact with others, he boasted about shaking hands with everyone even in the hospitals. On Jan 24th, the first Cabinet Office Briefing Rooms Action (COBRA) that were co-ordinating responses to the crisis was not chaired by the PM but, by the Health Minister who concluded that there was a very low risk for the public. Johnson, then, skipped five Cobra meetings on the virus, ignored calls to order protective gear and the scientists' warnings fell on deaf ears. Failings in February may have cost thousands of lives.[10] Indeed, for 12 days from 31st January after celebrating leaving the EU and saying that some countries will panic, but the UK will be open for free trade, Johnson was holidaying at the Foreign Secretary's country home in Kent and it was clear that he was not reading long briefs on the crisis and certainly not taking it seriously. Indeed, this was the case until mid-March when a French newspaper reported on the 20th March that the French President Emmanuel Macron threatened to close France's border with Britain if Prime Minister Boris Johnson failed to take more stringent measures to contain the coronavirus outbreak.[11] His bravado led, (mis) fortunately, to him contracting COVID-19 and for it to progress to a stage where his doctors advised intensive care. He was given oxygen and after recovering, he claimed that it was 50-50 whether he would live at one critical point of his treatment, but he was never put on a ventilator. However, the tabloid press and his political colleagues were not shy in coming forward with gushing praise for his determination and resilience in fighting off the disease but, at least, he then had to take it seriously.

Turning now to the US, at the beginning of the crisis, Trump rejected the World Health Organization's (WHO) diagnostic tests, alleging them to be flawed, whereupon the US sought to produce its own but without the capacity to do so. In the same way as Bolsonaro, Trump argued that it is like flu and will kill far fewer people and on 27th Feb, he predicted: 'It's going to disappear. One day—it's like a miracle—it will disappear'.[12] Two days later, he claimed a vaccine would be available 'very quickly' and 'very rapidly' and praised his administration's actions as 'the most aggressive taken by any country', while none of this was true.[13] Despite dire warnings in early March from medical experts advocating intervention to slow the spread of the virus, Trump took no action and continued to argue, 'It's very mild'; 'I'm not concerned at all'; 'It will go away. Just stay calm'.[14] This jeopardised the health of millions of Americans and could have been partly responsible for the eventual death toll, which was higher than in any other country. Ignoring the January 2020 intelligence community warnings of a looming global pandemic, Trump's administration also allocated insufficient focus on the importance of testing.[15]

As the pandemic began to accelerate, 'the United States' ability to *lead* in a global crisis has been called into question worldwide' for 'the Trump administration had reverted to its long-held isolationist tendencies'.[16] This failure was reinforced by Trump withdrawing US funding to the WHO partly because he saw it as a puppet of the Chinese. This belief was largely the reason for the G-7 failing to issue a meaningful statement concerning the crisis, as the US insisted on calling it the 'Wuhan Virus'. Using China as a scapegoat was a tactic of Trump 'to distract attention from his administration's dangerous ineptitude in response to COVID-19'. ... 'The *void of U.S. leadership* on a global crisis will make it harder to garner the international collaboration necessary to stem the COVID-19 pandemic that has left thousands dead in its wake and will kill many more'.[17]

This bravado on the part of all three of these leaders was in sharp contrast to several women leaders in Germany, New Zealand, Denmark, Iceland, Norway, South Korea and Taiwan who were strong and decisive in intervening to prevent the transmission of the virus overwhelming their health systems and killing a very large number of people. At the same time, they were capable of expressing their feelings and sensitivity humanely, demonstrating that rationality and emotion are 'not competing and conflicting attributes, but complementary'.[18] Despite, masculine social norms whereby women leaders are expected to express their service to the community rather than be focused on achievement, Jacinda Ardern, the Prime Minister of New Zealand combined both communal and agential orientations in leading her nation through the pandemic.[19] This is not to argue that women are better leaders than men so much as to suggest that the kinds of masculinity discussed here have put populist political leaders at a disadvantage in terms of responding to the pandemic decisively and empathetically. It is also not to withdraw from the view expressed throughout this book that leadership is relational rather than a property of persons. While the authors referred to here, do not explicitly distance themselves from proprietary conceptions of leadership style or even traits, the practice of many of these women heads of government was relational, demonstrating that leadership resides beyond the person formally designated as the leader.

Macho Masculinity

While all three leaders displayed macho masculinity alongside a bravado denial of the severity of the crisis and were initially opposed to lockdown, Bolsanaro stood out in maintaining his opposition, and personally violating its restrictions, throughout the crisis. He also attempted to dismiss anyone who disagreed with him, encouraged his supporters to defy social distancing. Still, eventually, he had to concede that the virus was a reality and, like many others, declared that 'We are at war. Worse than a defeat would be the shame of not putting up a fight'. Then, without any scientific evidence and indeed, contrary to claims that it was dangerous to life, Bolsonaro argued that that 'Chloroquine is working everywhere' and was importing over 2 million doses from the US where, of course, Trump had been boasting of taking the drug himself. Later, however, when asked about the high death rate, Bolsonaro responded coldly and inhumanely that 'death is everyone's destiny' and 'what do you expect me to do?'.[20]

On realising that the virus could no longer be treated as a minor inconvenience, both the UK and the US did a U-turn, also deploying physical metaphors to describe the situation as war-like. In the absence of the Prime Minister who was hospitalised by this time, the UK's Health Minister, Matt Hancock described it as '*a war against an invisible killer*' and, after his spell in intensive care, Johnson suggested that the virus was like a 'surprise attack from a mugger'. Here the unstated implication was that he had been able to thrust it aside despite the struggle being 'touch and go' at one point. Indeed, when in hospital, his de facto deputy Dominic Raab declared: 'The cabinet will 'not flinch' in the fight against coronavirus while 'fighter' Boris Johnson is being treated in critical care'.[21]

There was no consideration as to whether a mentality of conquest and war with its insularity regarding the nation-state was appropriate. Are we enhancing compliance with health authorities by 'cultivating the image of warriors' or is it more important to appeal to 'civic duty, solidarity and respect for fellow human beings'?[22] Yet the military metaphor continues to hold sway among politicians for even as late as the 4th June, the UK Health Minister, at the daily Downing Street briefing, referred to the battle against the virus. Given our complex global interrelations, the virus cannot be seen as simply a nation-state problem, for unless the disease is eradicated everywhere, it will simply keep reoccurring in the absence of permanent lockdown and bans on international travel. What is needed is global solidarity, collaboration and cooperation to develop and distribute a treatment or vaccine protection, which is hardly encouraged by appeals to war that reside in the rhetoric of competitive, national self-interest, and a destructive vaccine nationalism.[23] Fortunately, scientists tend to seek knowledge regardless of national politics. Moreover, the virus is a pathogen—a micro-organism that generates intense disease because it has a mechanism for evading the immune system of the host. Is this use of physical rather than organic metaphors, then, simply an unconscious reflection of the binary myth of elevating the masculine (physical) over the feminine (organic)? I do not want to endorse, these binaries, but simply suggest that they are nothing other than claims to, or beliefs in, power often exercised by leaders whose insecurity directs them toward an ethics of self-aggrandisement, mythical, facile, and fake social constructions, and narcissism.

In his macho phase, Trump declared that *'I am a war-time President'*.[24] Although not connected to, but in the middle of, the pandemic, another exemplification of Trump's macho masculinity occurred when the world witnessed the murder of a black man—George Floyd in Minneapolis. Recorded on a mobile video, it showed a police officer kneeling on Lloyd's neck for nearly nine minutes, while the victim pleaded that he could not breathe, and other police just stood by watching without intervening. This served as a tipping point to unleash a massive storm of protests against police violence and racism not only in the US but also throughout the world, some of which spilt over into arson and looting. Focusing exclusively on the latter or what he called the rioting in what were predominantly peaceful protests, President Trump was accused of feeding the violence by threatening on Twitter 'when the looting starts the shooting starts' and, by implication, perhaps encouraging his white supremacist followers to confront the protesters. Some commentators proclaimed that the US was on the verge of collapse and, again, was suffering from a leadership void.[25] As the protests continued, Trump rebuked many state governors for not being tough enough with the protestors saying, 'If you don't dominate, you're wasting your time—they're going to run over you, you're going to look like a bunch of jerks'[26] and a little later threatening to call in the military. At this point, a recently resigned but long-serving, secretary of defence, Jim Mattis said he was 'angry and appalled' by the police killing of George Floyd and the subsequent week of unrest. Matis never dreamed troops 'would be ordered under any circumstance to violate the Constitutional rights of their fellow citizens—much less to provide a bizarre photo op for the elected commander-in-chief, with military leadership standing alongside'. This was an allusion to Trump's walk to St John's Church to deliver a speech after police used tear gas to forcibly clear Washington DC's Lafayette Square of mostly peaceful protesters. He went on to argue that the president was divisive and immature in his leadership:

> Donald Trump is the first President in my lifetime who does not try to unite the American people - does not even pretend to try. Instead, he tries to divide us', he continued. 'We are witnessing the consequences of three years of this deliberate effort. We are witnessing the consequences of three years without mature leadership.[27]

Later, former White House chief of staff John Kelly agreed with General Jim Mattis' stark warning saying,

I think we need to look harder at who we elect ... I think we should look at people that are running for office and put them through the filter: What is their character like? What are their ethics?[28]

In his first election rally since the pandemic on 20th June 2020, Trump gave a 2-hour speech to his faithful followers, in a less than full auditorium despite his claims that a million people had requested tickets. He made no mention of the George Floyd killing even though this had set off worldwide protests and massive global support for the Black Lives Matter movement.[29]

Narcissistic Masculinity

Concerning this form of masculinity, no leader can match Trump whose narcissism stretches most people's imagination and, as argued earlier, most likely reflects a mental health condition. Perhaps because of representing a less developed economy, Bolsanaro does not arouse the same level of publicity as Trump, but in May the British medical journal *The Lancet* concluded that the greatest threat to Brazil's ability to combat Coronavirus is its far-right president.[30] World opinion of both Trump and Johnson has been equally damning.[31] Presiding over one of the worst outbreaks in the world, Bolsonaro disregarded the lockdown and was surrounded by scandals, sackings and resignations but continued to act as if everything was fine—a sure sign of narcissism. One time during the lockdown, he rode on horseback with his supporters to protest against Congress and the Supreme Court, which is investigating his interference in police affairs. Then he was furious about the security services who raided the homes of some of his key supporters because of alleged libel and intimidation campaigns. In his anger, he delivered an expletive-filled speech outside his home wearing a tie decorated with assault rifles. Then, in June, Brazil's Supreme Court released a video of a cabinet meeting where Bolsonaro was complaining, again using numerous expletives, that he could not get intelligence from the police and 'vowing, in the clip, that he will not let his friends and family get "screwed" because he is unable to overhaul law enforcement officials'. His two sons were under investigation for potential money-laundering corruption charges. Bolsonaro argued, 'If you can't change (the official), change his boss. You can't change the boss? Change the minister. End of story. We're not kidding around'. Earlier, his Justice Minister, who had been leading a police project to clamp down on corruption, resigned when Bolsonaro sacked the director-general of the Federal Police.[32] Eventually and not surprisingly, in early July, Bolsonaro contracted the virus.

While difficult to match Trump in terms of generating fake claims and false optimism, Boris Johnson is renowned for playing to the gallery with a host of public relations stunts designed to make his mark on society from getting stuck on a zip wire venture in London's Victoria Park to driving a Digger through a polystyrene wall with the slogan GET BREXIT DONE emblazoned on the bucket in his 2019 election campaign. His false optimism is forever part of his narcissistic armoury, for example, in modifying the Brexit slogan to 'let's get this virus done' and setting targets for accomplishing different tasks that prove unattainable. The most outlandish claim was that the Health System was fully prepared and equipped to manage the crisis only to discover within a few weeks of the spread of the virus that it was in danger of being overwhelmed, as it had insufficient intensive care units, ventilators, and personal protective equipment (PPE). Almost every target to correct this failed and, despite Johnson's promises to the contrary, the attention directed at saving the health system from collapse resulted in Care Homes being neglected and consequently extremely high death rates. Finally, after several missed targets for a ground-breaking anti-body test and testing those with symptoms, Johnson announced a target of mid-May for a world-beating testing, tracking and tracing system accompanied by a mobile app. This was not in place until the second week of June (minus the App) and, even though this should *not* be treated as a vehicle for nationalist competition, it certainly was far from 'world-beating', not least because the App had failed quality tests and was now postponed without a target date. Even when expert opinion estimated that the system was only testing around 25% of infections, on 24th June, Johnson defended it as an amazing achievement and again drew on his 'getting it done' mantra. Partly, perhaps, there is an immunity to much reflexivity on these deeply masculine propensities in that the government is run like 'a "blokey" boy's club',[33] where the Prime Minister can routinely bathe in the glory of sycophancy that readily dismisses external criticisms as politically motivated.

Boris Johnson's handling of the Coronavirus pandemic, and especially his optimism and claim to success when all the evidence suggested a catastrophic failure, moved one journalist Piers Morgan to write in the UK, Daily Mail:

> I didn't think it would be possible for any world leader in this crisis to sound more delusional than Trump, whose antics at his daily briefings have become an unedifying masterclass in how not to handle a pandemic. But Boris managed to make Trump seem almost credible, and his sycophantic loyalists on social media lapped it up. 'That's our guy!' they drooled as Boris informed us in no uncertain terms that we're going to get this virus done, just as he got Brexit done. But the virus isn't like Brexit. It's not a political ideology that can be open to debate, or an argument that can be won with buffoonery, bluster and Churchillian soundbites.[34]

This criticism carries more weight, given that the journalist is known to be a Conservative party voter, and the newspaper holds to a position on the right of the political spectrum occupied generally by those in key dominant positions in the government. Interestingly, the government's response was to ostracise Piers Morgan by all Ministers refusing to appear on his TV Breakfast Show.

In his continual electioneering, Trump repeatedly argued that the virus "will go away …. It's really working out. And a lot of good things are going to happen"'.[35] We know that narcissism is a reflection of an extreme preoccupation with one's self-image and identity, stimulated partly by insecurity that can verge on, or perhaps reflect, a mental health condition.[36] In Trump's case, it is also delusional. For, at one point he suggested that because bleach killed the infection from hard surfaces, it was a good idea to take it orally like medicine and, against medical advice, he self-prescribed Hydroxychloroquine tablets for a couple of weeks.[37] Again, against all the evidence, he also subscribed to rumours that COVID-19 was manufactured in, and either purposely or accidentally leaked from, a Chinese laboratory. This delusional behaviour was equally dramatic, if less dangerous when he claimed that he knew as much as any scientist about the coronavirus:

> I like this stuff. I really get it. People are surprised that I understand it. Every one of these doctors said, "How do you know so much about this? Maybe I have a natural ability. Maybe I should have done that instead of running for president".[38]

While predictions from the scientists were more alarming, the actual infections by 8th July were over 3 million and there were 134,000 deaths. Yet up until mid-March, the President ignored scientific advice and insisted, 'It's going to be just fine'.[39] This behaviour has to be put in the context of Trump's campaign to be re-elected in Nov 2020. His masculine obsession with winning led him to resist vehemently the reporting of 'bad news' at the cost of actually helping to sustain the transmission of the virus. So, for example, when a cruise ship was docked outside of and denied entry to San Francisco, he suggested they stay on board rather than land because that would double the number of COVID cases in the national statistics. His concern was not the lives of his citizens but the statistics that might reduce his ratings in the political polls.

A previous national security adviser, John Bolton, published a book[40] in June 2020 that the administration tried to block from publication because it revealed a considerable amount of bad news for the President. It argued that Trump's only interest is his popularity and winning the next election regardless of the consequences for the US and the world. It also reveals how Trump's claim to be 'tough' on China lacks credibility.

For Trump endorsed President Xi's ethnic cleansing against Uighurs—a minority Muslim group—in what is called re-education (concentration) camps as well as asking China to help him in his forthcoming re-election campaign.[41] Of course, these claims are alleged by someone who may be bitter that his career at the White House was derailed but also whose main interest was commercial sales of his book. Earlier Bolton had refused to give this kind of evidence against his former boss at Trump's impeachment trial, which might have altered the acquittal outcome.

An equally strong example of Trump's narcissism, and escape into fantasy simply to elevate his image, was when he made fake claims about the US being the envy of the world regarding its response to the virus:

> I spoke with Angela Merkel today; I spoke with Prime Minister Abe of Japan; I spoke with many of the leaders over the last four or five days. And so many of them, almost all of them—I would say all of them, not everyone would want to admit it—but they all view us as the world leader, and they're following us, Trump told House Republicans during an on-camera meeting.[42]

Another aspect of narcissistic masculine leadership is the concern to be positive, partly because their identities are so fragile that they intensely dislike unpopularity. As discussed in Chapter 4, this is called Prozac leadership because, like the antidepressant drug, it is about making everything feel good or, at least, less bad insofar as it numbs the senses. All three of these leaders have been especially prone to this, as has been evident in this brief analysis of their responses to COVID-19. Partly this is why they construct targets regardless of whether there is any chance of meeting them because this gives them some short-term popularity. Also, they can always rely on the electorate not checking up on their claims because of comparative indifference to the detail, rather than just the soundbites, of politics. Of course, targets are also created to push others to deploy extra effort to meet them. Even in the depth of failure, however, they claim success, for 'good news' is the only dish on the menu.

Conclusion

Despite evidence to the contrary, these leaders continually claimed to have been successful in competing and winning against other countries in their management of the virus. However, as already argued, it was not a question of competition or rivalry as only through global cooperation and collaboration could the virus be eradicated. Their competitive nationalism was not only damaging to global health but highly revealing of bravado, macho and narcissistic masculinities. Problems were denied, everything was converted into a battle or a contest for leadership supremacy, and reality was sacrificed to fake accounts of success.

The countries that had experienced a much less severe impact from COVID did so partly because they introduced testing and tracing before the virus had spread beyond the level of controllability without lockdown. Brazil did not have the resources to test and trace and, not taking it seriously, Bolsonaro seemed prepared to sacrifice mass deaths. He believed that herd immunity was the only exit strategy, although the Brazilian health service eventually followed international protocol by locking down. The US initially failed to carry out tests because it rejected those of the WHO. Later it did conduct numerous tests although it possibly came out of lockdown too early to prevent spikes in Florida and Texas. The UK abandoned testing and tracing early in the crisis, claiming that it would not be effective because of the high rates of infection but more probably due to having insufficient testing equipment and resources.

The record on leadership does seem to have a gender dimension in that countries with women leaders performed on the whole much better in the crisis than the three white, masculine populists that I have examined here. Of course, some countries (e.g., China, Cuba, Greece, Japan) with men at the helm were also successful in containing the virus. However, except for Belgium, no female leaders did badly and, in perhaps expressing their femininity in a masculine manner, they showed 'strong and decisive' leadership. They were also 'capable of displaying feeling' stimulating the claim that rationality and emotion can be 'complementary', rather than 'competing and conflicting, attributes'.[43]

Clearly, it is much more complicated than this for the women's route to the highest political ranks is difficult requiring them to be, on average, particularly competent but also more capable of embodied reasoning. However, other factors were contributing to the effectiveness of their leadership in the crisis. In particular, this was the case where cultures were either broadly gender-sensitive (Denmark, Finland, New Zealand) or especially compliant (South Korea, Taiwan). I would argue that it is not a matter of displaying feelings, so much as engaging with, and demonstrating responsibility to, citizens through embodied reasoning. Such responsibility and reasoning were comparatively absent in the case of our three populist leaders. Unfortunately, narcissists are so infatuated with themselves that everyone else is merely a resource in their preoccupation with fame and fortune, and security and success.

It is perfectly understandable that the fear, anxiety, and insecurity accompanying any crisis, and especially one that threatens human life, will be met by excessive demands upon leaders. However, it seems that the knee-jerk responses of these three leaders have fallen well short of reasonable expectations. Admittedly, I have selected three of the more extreme populist heads of government for examination, so not surprisingly, the weaknesses of leadership are highly visible, especially given the extreme and unprecedented conditions of the pandemic. Nonetheless, as

I have been arguing throughout this text, such weaknesses are never far beneath the surface of leadership, partly because of the impossibility that any single individual can satisfy the ever-proliferating expectations of their populations. Rarely do leaders leave office in glory or free from condemnation.

Although democratic governments do keep controversial issues off the agenda and seek to marginalise critics in various ways, only totalitarian dictators such as Xi and Putin can block criticism completely, so that it never reaches the public domain. Nonetheless, in the early stage of the pandemic, this proved impossible even for the Chinese leader. At first, Dr Li Wenlian's disclosure of a new SARS virus was silenced through police investigations alleging that he had made 'false comments' and spread 'rumours'. His subsequent death from COVID-19, however, could not be concealed, resulting in an eruption of public anger. The protests could only be contained by government admission of 'shortcomings and deficiencies' in its response to the virus and avoidance of further concealments of knowledge.[44]

Most leaders, in dealing with the pandemic, adopted similar strategies where, guided by scientific experts, they deployed a range of interventions that, in worst-case scenarios, involved lockdown. Much of this is a variant of Ulrich Beck's[45] theory where, informed by government advice, the risk is projected onto individuals whose conduct is expected to manage the risk by disciplining the self and others to prevent chaos. Supplementing this with Foucault's analysis, it can be suggested that modern power mobilises body and soul through bio-medical and other scientific (e.g., statistical, socio-behavioural and psychological) knowledge. This is then used to generate self-disciplinary and more broad-ranging biopolitical technologies of the self in organising society. Through merging biopolitics (power over the body) and ethopolitics (power over moral existence), it is possible to lead populations in a generic, but also morally integrated manner, compatible with these mechanisms of intervention.[46] Subjectivity and behaviour were modified to ensure that risk was managed at the point where bodies and populations were most vulnerable to the spread of the virus. The pandemic could be seen as a point 'where body and population meet' and so a matter for both anatomo-political 'discipline' as well as biopolitics of regularising the population.[47] In effect, then, leadership was distributed to the population in ways that involved subjects assuming the risks and responsibilities for public health while enjoying few of the social and financial benefits that ordinarily are bestowed upon leaders.

Indeed, it can be seen that managing risk in this way can intensify prevailing social disadvantages and inequalities, for the virus affects populations differentially depending on their age, class, disability, ethnicity or race, family situation, particular occupations, physical and mental health and sexuality. It is well known that the elderly and those with health conditions were the most vulnerable to hospitalisation and death if they contracted the virus. But, other people, such as those from the black, Asian, minority ethnic (BAME) groups fared badly, and this could not be accounted for solely by their relative poverty or the kinds of occupations they held. There were also gender disadvantages, for women not only disproportionately occupied essential frontline work positions but also, when working from home, they assumed the care of children and the elderly. Also, usually, women took a larger share of educational responsibilities for children no longer at school during lockdowns.

As was well publicised, the class disadvantage was an issue particularly concerning children from deprived homes who suffered disproportionately from non-attendance at school. Potentially, repercussions from this could last long beyond the lockdown. Also, domestic abuse intensified during the lockdown because of the difficulties of cramped living space. Confinement in the home for these 'poorer' families was a considerably more devastating experience than for those that enjoyed spatial, domestic comfort not only indoors but also outdoors in private gardens. Many of the difficulties were also indirect effects of the pandemic since other social, physical and mental conditions were neglected in coping with the demands of COVID-19 and relative poverty left people particularly vulnerable. Alongside these were the economic effects of the lockdown and these would appear to have disadvantaged the young severely, as well as those workers in sectors hardest hit by the recession, such as hospitality and travel. Only the production and distribution of an effective vaccine will enable rapid recovery, and hopefully, this will have been the result by the time this book goes to press. Whatever outcome unfolds is going to put incredible stresses on leaders in all aspects of social life. The picture painted as one of white, populist masculine leaders itself constituting 'a public health problem'[48] does not inspire an excess of confidence about the outcome of this pandemic.

What is of particular concern is how white, masculine populist leaders in the democratic West and totalitarian demagogues in the East hi-jacked the political agenda. It is questionable that they were emotionally, intellectually or ethically competent to govern, let alone to lead us out of a health pandemic and the likely social unrest of its aftermath. For, populist, demagogic, and unstable leaders tend to appropriate everything and everyone in the service of the self. What is little more than an occurrence of difference (for example, black lives and inequality more generally) generates indifference or leads to in-group/out-group stereotyping that easily slides into embittered war-like relations. Part of the problem is that these leaders shared a self-obsessed focus on themselves and their image rather than caring and being responsible for their citizens.

Of course, some minimal responsibility follows from the fact that all leadership must in some way rule by consent, even if in totalitarian societies it is achieved through coercion and punishments for dissent. In democracies, consent can be manipulated by defining reality for populations, as well as through technologies of the self that give citizens a pseudo-participative involvement in their social institutions. In both kinds of regime, governmentality operates through discipline and self-disciplinary, bioethical mechanisms where subjects discipline not only themselves but one another through participating in the policing of normative behaviour. It occurs at a more generic level where scientific knowledge is brought into the service of regularising 'a population of living beings to optimise a state of life'[49] through biopolitical interventions 'at the level of their generality'.[50] As has been argued throughout this book, the fragility of identity, especially prevalent among narcissists, often renders them threatened by the mere presence of the other.[51]

Like animals that become vicious when trapped, humans readily turn to aggression when their identities are threatened. Unlike animals where instinct is more fundamental than it is for humans, we have the potential to reflect on the conditions that are the source of this threat. Insofar as one of these conditions is our attachment to identity, we can begin to weaken its hold on us, if not remove it altogether. Doing so is important for us all but has a particular significance to those in formal leadership because it is only then that they can become engaged as ethical and embodied subjects with the whole of human and non-human life. However, in reflecting on the pandemic as a potential dress rehearsal for global warming, Latour was pessimistic. He argued that the extreme levels of governmental bio-power driving leadership through the pandemic could be even 'more justified in the case of the ecological crisis than in the case of the health crisis because it affects everyone, not a few thousand people—and not for a time but forever'.[52] This is even more so as, in contrast to COVID-19, climate change is a crisis more directly 'of our own making'.[53] However, although it is questionable whether the nation-state was the most appropriate boundary setting for leading us through the health crisis, it certainly is not concerning the looming ecological crisis. Governmentality needs to be global but also to learn from a multiplicity of events, nations and peoples on how to mediate the inevitable environmental disasters of contemporary production regimes.

While the jury is out, it is questionable as to whether the COVID pandemic is so outside 'our own making', for as with climate change, it could equally be seen as an outcome of our anthropocentrism. Despite the warnings of avian influenza, BSE (mad cow disease), swine flu and now COVID-19, as well as numerous other threats from a zoonotic source, our dependence on food chains that involve questionable ethics regarding animals seem to remain a marginal concern. Even though this, and associated ecological problems, may be the greatest threat to human society, anthropocentric ideologies prevent us from radically changing our comfortable lifestyles.

Yet, might it not also be argued that the very concern to preserve the human species from extinction is itself anthropocentric, for it involves a claim to moral superiority that prioritises humans above all other species? Not only on the nuclear front, but masculine and nationalist military mentalities have also brought us close to extinction, as have zoonotic diseases. Yet, few people would willingly abandon species self-preservation and accede to self-destruction as a means of overcoming our anthropocentrism. Consequently, it may not be a question of the complete dismissal of anthropocentrism to protect us from extinction. Rather, it may simply require us to be more aware of our masculine, inclinations to treat other animals and nature as simply a resource for human-centric predilections and pursuits. For example, it might lead us to contemplate the moral contradictions of our speciesism in caring for some domestic animals while exploiting others for food, leisure and sport. Equally, leadership should reflect on the climate change implications of our continued, reliance on farm animals for food.[54] Just as white populist, leaders display their bravado, 'macho' and narcissistic masculinities so also can anthropocentrism be characterised as conveying a similar masculine ethos. For, the human species engages in masculine conquest and control of all it surveys, including the very planet upon which we are dependent. Leadership has a responsibility to demonstrate that we cannot remain morally indifferent to what, after all, is 'our only host'.[55]

Notes

1 Wray-Bliss (2013, 87); see also Learmonth and Morrell (2019).
2 Lee (2019) in which 37 psychiatrists draw this conclusion in assessing Trump's psychological health.
3 Peter Wehner a life-long supporter of the Republican Party and adviser to President George W. Bush made these claims on the UK BBC's Newsnight 18.6.20.
4 Albertazzi and McDonnell (2008).
5 Bloom (2018).
6 Foucault (1991/1984, p. 343).
7 https://www.google.co.uk/search?source=hp&ei=54gFX_SvNtiDjLsPo_OAyA4&q=world+death+rate+coronavirus&oq=world+dea&gs_lcp=CgZwc3ktYWIQARgBMgUIABCxAzIFCAAQsQMyBQgAELEDMgUIAB-CxAzIFCAAQsQMyAggAMgIIADICCAAyAggAMgUIABCxAzoICAAQ6g-IQjwE6CAgAELEDEIMBOgsILhCxAxDHARCjAjoICC4QsQMQgwE6BQ-guELEDOg4ILhCxAxDHARCjAhCDAVC7LViwQmDuXGgBcAB4AIABU-ogB_AOSAQE5mAEAoAEBqgEHZ3dzLXdperABCg&sclient=psy-ab.
8 https://www.forbes.com/sites/carlieporterfield/2020/04/10/brazils-bolsonaro-slights-social-distancing-as-coronavirus-deaths-hit-1000/ consulted 18.6.20.
9 https://www.independent.co.uk/news/world/americas/hydroxychloroquine-trump-brazil-jair-bolsonaro-coronavirus-a9542071.html consulted 20.6.20.
10 https://www.thetimes.co.uk/article/coronavirus-38-days-when-britain-sleepwalked-into-disaster-hq3b9tlgh consulted 18.6.20.

11 https://www.euractiv.com/section/uk-europe/news/macron-threatened-uk-entry-ban-without-more-stringent-measures/ Consulted 8.7.20.

12 https://www.whitehouse.gov/briefings-statements/remarks-president-trump-meeting-african-american-leaders/ Consulted 18.6.20.

13 https://www.nytimes.com/2020/03/15/opinion/trump-coronavirus.html Consulted 6.6.20.

14 https://www.whitehouse.gov/briefings-statements/remarks-president-trump-meeting-republican-senators-2/?utm_source=link&utm_medium=header Consulted 18.6.20.

15 https://thesoufancenter.org/intelbrief-the-u-s-leadership-void-limits-the-global-response-to-covid-19/ consulted 6.6.20.

16 Ibid.

17 Ibid.

18 https://thehill.com/changing-america/respect/equality/493434-countries-led-by-women-have-fared-better-against consulted 21.6.20.

19 Vroman and Danko, 2020.

20 https://video.foxnews.com/v/6025576909001#sp=show-clips Consulted 18.6.20.

21 https://www.huffingtonpost.co.uk/entry/boris-johnson-is-a-fighter-and-ministers-will-not-flinch-in-fight-against-coronavirus-says-dominic-raab_uk_5e8c728ac5b62459a92f200c?guccounter=1.

22 https://theconversation.com/war-metaphors-used-for-covid-19-are-compelling-but-also-dangerous-13540 consulted 2.6.20.

23 https://theconversation.com/as-u-s-buys-up-remdesivir-vaccine-nationalism-threatens-access-to-covid-19-treatments-141952.

24 https://www.politico.com/news/2020/03/18/trump-administration-self-swab-coronavirus-tests-135590 consulted 9.7.20.

25 https://www.nbcnews.com/think/opinion/trump-hid-bunker-george-floyd-protest-least-there-he-had-ncna1224201 consulted 17.6.20.

26 https://nypost.com/2020/06/01/trump-unloads-on-weak-governors-over-george-floyd-protest-response/ consulted 22.6.20.

27 https://www.independent.co.uk/news/world/americas/us-politics/james-mattis-resignation-farewell-letter-defence-secretary-department-trump-cabinet-a8706091.html consulted 4.6.20.

28 https://edition.cnn.com/2020/06/05/politics/john-kelly-agrees-with-jim-mattis-on-trump/index.html Consulted 6.5.20.

29 https://www.bbc.co.uk/news/world-us-canada-53129524 Consulted 24.6.20.

30 https://www.independent.co.uk/topic/coronavirus Consulted 19.6.20.

31 https://www.theguardian.com/world/2020/mar/24/confused-dangerous-flippant-worlds-media-pans-pms-handling-of-coronavirus-boris-johnson; https://www.theguardian.com/us-news/2020/may/15/donald-trump-coronavirus-response-world-leaders consulted 19.6.20.

32 https://www.independent.co.uk/topic/jair-bolsonaro Consulted 19.6.20.

33 Stewart, 2020, 17.

34 https://www.dailymail.co.uk/news/article-8275365/PIERS-MORGAN-Boris-boast-wants-death-toll-tells-real-story.html 30.4.20 consulted 3.6.20.

35 https://www.whitehouse.gov/briefings-statements/remarks-president-trump-meeting-republican-senators-2/?utm_source=link&utm_medium=header Consulted 18.6.20.

36 See Chapter 3.

37 https://www.reuters.com/article/us-health-coronavirus-usa-chloroquine-idUSKBN21A3Y2 consulted 8.7.20.

38 https://www.thetimes.co.uk/article/coronavirus-38-days-when-britain-sleepwalked-into-disaster-hq3b9tlgh Consulted 4.6.20.
39 *Susan Beachy and Ian Prasad Philbrick contributed research*.https://www.nytimes.com/2020/03/15/opinion/trump-coronavirus.html. Consulted 4.6.2.
40 Bolton, 2020.
41 https://www.theguardian.com/commentisfree/2020/jun/19/john-bolton-book-trump-china consulted 20.6.20.
42 https://www.vox.com/2020/5/8/21252319/trump-germany-japan-coronavirus-response consulted 3.6.20.
43 https://thehill.com/changing-america/respect/equality/493434-countries-led-by-women-have-fared-better-against Consulted 24.6.20.
44 https://www.bbc.co.uk/news/world-asia-china-51409801 consulted 3.6.20.
45 Beck (1992).
46 Foucault (2003/1976, pp. 239–264).
47 Ibid., pp. 251–252.
48 Ashcroft (2020).
49 Foucault (2003/1976, p. 246).
50 Ibid.
51 Ziarek, (2001, p. 74).
52 Latour, (2020, p. 2).
53 Ibid.
54 Clarke and Knights (2021).
55 I am indebted to Caroline Clarke for this phrase.

References

Acker, J. (1990). Hierarchies, jobs and bodies: A theory of gendered organizations. *Gender and Society, 4*(2), 139–158.

Acker, J. (1992). From sex-roles to gendered institutions. *Contemporary Sociology, 21*(5).

Adarves-Yorno, I. (2016). Leadership and the paradoxes of authenticity. In R. Bolden, M. Witzel, & N. Linacre (Eds.), *Leadership Paradoxes: Rethinking Leadership for an Uncertain World* (pp. 115–130). London: Routledge.

Acker, J. (1998). The future of "gender and organizations": Connections and boundaries. *Gender, Work and Organization, 5*(4), 195–206.

Ackroyd, S., & Thompson, P. (1999). *Organizational misbehaviour*. London: Sage.

Adkins, L., & Lury, C. (2009). Introduction: What is the empirical? *European Journal of Social Ideas, 12*(1), 5–20.

Albertazzi D., & McDonnell, D. (2008). *Twenty-first century populism: The spectre of western European democracy*. London: Palgrave Macmillan.

Alvesson, M., & Einola, K. (2019). Warning for excessive positivity: Authentic leadership and other traps in leadership studies. *The Leadership Quarterly, 30*, 383–395.

Alvesson, M., & Karreman, D. (2000) Varieties of discourse: On the study of organizations through discourse analysis. *Human Relations, 53*(9), 1125–1149.

Alvesson, M., & Karreman, D. (2016). Intellectual failure and ideological success in organization studies: The case of traqnsformational leadership. *Journal of Management Inquiry, 25*, 139–152.

Alvesson M., & Spicer A. (2013). Critical perspectives on leadership. In David V. Day (Eds.), *The Oxford Handbook of Leadership and Organizations*. Oxford University Press.

Alvesson, M., Ashcraft, K. L., & Thomas, R. (2008). Identity matters: Reflections on the construction of identity scholarship in organization studies. *Organization, 15*, pp.5–28.

Anhalt, E. (2017). *Ancient Greek wisdom for today's leadership crisis. The Conversation*, Oct. 16th.

Anteby, M. (2013). Why business schools need ethics. *Guardian*, 22 Oct, https://www.theguardian.com/commentisfree/2013/oct/22/business-schools-need-ethics consulted 18.2.20 Gender Work and Organization.

Apel, K.-O. (1990). *What right does ethics have?: Public philosophy in a pluralistic culture*, VU University Press.

Archer, L. (2008). The new neoliberal subjects? Young/er academics' constructions of professional identity. *Journal of Education Policy, 23*(3), 265–285.

Arjoon, S. (2000). Virtue theory as a dynamic theory of business. *Journal of Business Ethics, 28*, 159–178.

Armato M. (2013). Wolves in 'sheep's clothing: 'Men's enlightened sexism & hegemonic masculinity in academia. *Women's Studies, 42*(5), 578–598.

Ashcroft, K. (2020). *The pandemic shift: Vulnerability and viral masculinity. Gender, Work and Organization Virtual Seminar*, Gender and Work During/After COVID-19, June 23.

Ashley, L. (2010). Making a difference? The use (and abuse) of DM in the UK's elite law firms. *Work, Employment and Society, 24*(4), 711–727.

Avolio B. J., Gardner W. L., Walumbwa, F. O., Luthans F., & May D. R. (2004). Unlocking the mask: A look at the process by which authentic leaders impact follower attitudes and behaviors. *The Leadership Quarterly, 15*, 801–823.

Avolio, B. J., & Gardner, W. L. (2005). Authentic leadership development: Getting to the root of positive forms of leadership. *The Leadership Quarterly, 16*(3), 315–338.

Bagilhole, B. (2009). *Understanding equal opportunities and diversity*. Bristol: The Policy Press.

Bagilhole, B. & White, K. (Eds.). (2011). *Gender, power and management: A cross-cultural analysis of higher education*, Palgrave Macmillan.

Bagilhole, B., & White, K. (Eds.). (2013). *Battle scars: Reflections on gender and generation in academia*. Palgrave Macmillan.

Baker, S. D. (2007). Followership: The theoretical foundation of a contemporary construct. *Journal of Leadership & Organizational Studies, 14*(1), 50–60.

Bakewell, S. (2017). *At the existentialist café: Freedom, being and apricot cocktails*. London: Vintage.

Barad, K. (2003). Posthumanist performativity: Toward an understanding of how matter comes to matter. *Signs, 28*(3), 801–831.

Barad, K. (2007). *Meeting the universe halfway: quantum physics and the entanglement of matter and meaning*. Duke University Press.

Bardon, T., & Josserland, E. (2010) A Nietzschean reading of Foucauldian thinking: Constructing a project of the self with an ontology of becoming. *Organisation, 18*(4), 497–515.

Barrett, F. J. (2001). The organizational structure of hegemonic masculinity: The case of the US Navy. In S. J. Whitehead & F. J. Barrett (Eds.), *The masculinities reader* (pp. 77– 99). Oxford: Polity Press.

Bauman, Z. (1993). *Postmodern ethics*. Oxford: Blackwell.

Bauman, Z. (2008). *The art of life*. Cambridge: Polity Press.

Beck, U. (1992). *Risk society: Towards a new modernity*. London: Sage Publications.

Becker, E. (1969). *The birth and death of meaning*. New York: Free Press.

Becker, E. (1973). *The denial of death*. New York: Free Press.

Bederman, Gail (1995). *Manliness and civilization: A cultural history of gender and race in the United States 1880-1917*. Chicago and London: University of Chicago Press.

Bell, E., & Sinclair, A. (2016). Re-envisaging leadership through the feminine imaginary in film and television. In T. Beyes, M. Parker, & C. Steyaert(Eds.), *Routledge Companion to the Humanities and Social Sciences in Management Education*. London: Routledge.

Benhabib, S. (1992). *Situating the Subject*. London: Sage.

Bensman, J., & Gerver, I. (1963). Crime and punishment in the factory: The function of deviancy in maintaining the social system. *American Sociological Review, 28*, 588–598.

Bentham, J. (2010). *The works of Jeremy Bentham, 1838–1843*. In J. Bowring, (Eds.). New York: Nabu Press.

Bernauer, J. W. (1993). *Michel Foucault's force of flight: Towards an ethics for thought*. New Jersey: Humanities Press.

Biesta, G. J. J. (1998). Say you want a revolution... suggestions for the impossible future of critical pedagogy. *Educational Theory, 48*(4), 499–510.

Bishop, V. (2009). What is leadership? In V. Bishop (Eds.). *Leadership for nursing and allied health care professions* (pp. 8–31). Open University Press.

Blomberg, J. (2009). Gendering finance: Masculinities and hierarchies at the Stockholm stock exchange. *Organization, 16*, 203–225.

Bloom, P. (2018). *We live in a populist age – but who are 'the people'? The Conversation*, August 9.

Blumer, H. (1969). *Symbolic interactionism*. Englewood Cliffs, NJ: Prentice-Hall.

Bly, R. (1990). *Iron John: A book about men*. Boston: Addison-Wesley.

Bolden, R. (2016). Paradoxes of Perspectives. In R. Bolden, M. Witzel & N. Linacre (Eds.), *Leadership paradoxes: Rethinking leadership for an uncertain world* (pp. 31–52). London: Routledge.

Bolden, R., Witzel, M., & Linacre, N. (Eds.). (2016). *Leadership paradoxes: Rethinking leadership for an uncertain world* (pp. 31–52). London: Routledge.

Bolton, J. (2020). *The room where it happened*. New York: Simon & Schuster.

Bordo, S. (2004). *Unbearable weight; feminism, Western culture, and the body*. Berkeley, CA: University of California Press.

Boyatzis, R., & McKee, A. (2005). *Resonant leadership: Renewing yourself and connecting with others through mindfulness, hope and compassion*. Boston, MA: Harvard Business School Press Books.

Boyle, M.-E. (2004). Walking our talk: Business schools, legitimacy, and citizenship. *Business & Society, 43*(1), 37–68.

Braidotti, R. (2011). *Nomadic theory: The portable Rosi Braidotti*. New York: Columbia University Press.

Braidotti, R. (2013). *The Posthuman*. Malden, MA: Polity Press.

Brown, A. D. (1997). Narcissism, identity and legitimacy. *Academy of Management Review, 22*(3), 643–686.

Brier, B. (1999). *The history of ancient Egypt*, Virginia, USA: The Great Courses.

Brittan, A. (1989). *Masculinity and power*. Oxford: Blackwell.

Brod, H. (1995). Masculinity as masquerade. In Andrew Perchuk and Helaine Posner (Eds.), *The masculine masquerade: Masculinity and representation*. Cambridge MA: MIT Press.

Brown, A. D. (2001). Organization studies and identity: Towards a research agenda. *Human Relations, 54*(1), 113–121.

Brown, A. D. (2015). Identities and identity work in organizations. *International Journal of Management Reviews, 17*, 20–40.

Brown, A. D., & Coupland, C. (2015). Identity threats, identity work and elite professionals. *Organization Studies, 36*, 1315–1336.

Brown, A. D., & Lewis, M. (2011). Identities, discipline and routines. *Organization Studies, 32*, 871–896.

Burawoy, M. (1979). *Manufacturing consent*. Chicago: University of Chicago Press.

Burawoy, M. (1985). *The politics of production*. London: Verso.

Burns, J. M. (1998). Transactional and transformational leadership. In G. Robinson Hickman (Ed.), *Leading organizations*. Thousand Oaks, CA: Sage.

Burns, J. M. (1978). *Leadership*. New York: Harper-Collins.

Burns, T. (1980). *Leadership*. New York: Harper & Row.

Burrows, R. (2012). Living with the h-index? Metric assemblages in the contemporary academy. *The Sociological Review, 60*(2) 355–372.

Butler, J. (1990/1999). *Gender trouble: Feminism and the subversion of identity*. New York: Routledge.

Butler, Judith. (1993). *Bodies that matter*. London: Routledge.

Butler, J. (1997). *The psychic life of power*. Palo Alto: Stanford University Press.

Butler, J. (2004). Performative acts and genre constitution: An essay in phenomenology and feminist theory. In Henry Bial (Ed.), *The performance studies reader*. London and New York: Routledge.

Butler, J. (2011). Performance contrasted with performativity see, http://www.youtube.com/watch?v=Bo7o2LYATDc 6th July 2011 consulted 5.10.18.

Cabantous, L., Gond, J. P., Harding, N., & Learmonth, M. (2016). Critical essay: Reconsidering critical performativity. *Human Relations, 69*(2), 197–213.

Calás, M. B. & Smircich, L. (1991). Voicing seduction to silence leadership. *Organization Studies*, October, *12*(4), 567–601.

Calás, M. B., & Smircich, L. (1997). Predicando la moral en calzoncillos? Feminist inquiries into business ethics. In A. Larson, & R. E. Freeman (Eds.), *Women's studies and business ethics: Toward a new conversation* (pp. 50–80). Oxford: Oxford University Press.

Camus, A. (1956). *The Fall*. New York: Vintage Books.

Carlisle, D. (2015). Seven-day services: Setting up shop on the high street. *Health Service Journal*. 1 https://www.hsj.co.uk/leadership/delivering-change/seven-day-services-setting-up-shop-on-the-high-street/5089886.article#.Vhtnu0pfZ1A consulted 11.12.19.

Carney, M. (2014). Keynote at *Conference on Inclusive Capitalism*, London - 27 May see http://www.theguardian.com/business/2014/may/27/capitalism-critique-bank-of-england-carney consulted 25.3.15.

Carroll, J. (1993). *Humanism: The wreck of Western culture*. London: Fontana Press.

Cartledge, P. (2006). *Introduction in Xenophon, Hiero the Tyrant and other treatises*. Harmondsworth: Penguin.

Carsten, M. K., Uhl-Bien M., Bradley, J. West, B. J. Jaime L. Patera, J. L., & McGregor, R. (2010). Exploring social constructions of followership: A qualitative study. *The Leadership Quarterly, 21*(3), 543–562.

Case, P., French, R., & Simpson, P. (2011). Philosophy of leadership. In A. Bryman, D. L. Collinson, K. Grint, B. Jackson & M. Uhl Bien (Eds.), *The Sage Handbook of Leadership*. (pp. 242–254). London: Sage.

Carroll, B., Ford, J. and Taylor, S., editors (2015). *Leadership: Contemporary critical perspectives*. London: Sage.

Castells, M. (2000). *The rise of the network society* 2nd ed.. Oxford: Oxford University Press.

Caulkin S. (2005). *Business schools for scandal: What the academics teach is what created Enrons*, summarizing Goshall's thesis, e, *Observer Business Section*, March 28th.

Chalier, C. (1993). Emanuel Levinas: Responsibility and election. In *Ethics*, A. Phillips Griffiths (Eds.), *Royal Institute of Philosophy Supplement*: 35. Cambridge University Press.

Chomsky N. (1970). Recent contributions to a theory of innate ideas. In L. Hudson (Ed.), *The Ecology of Human Intelligence*. Harmondsworth: Penguin.

Cisoux, H. (1976) [1975]. *The laugh of Medusa* K. Cohen and P. Cohen (Trans.), *Signs*, 1(4) 875–893.

Cixous, H. (2010). The laugh of medusa. *The Norton Anthology of Theory and Criticism*. (2nd ed.). New York: W.W. Norton & Company Inc. 1942–1959.

Ciulla, J. (1995). Leadership ethics: mapping the territory. *Business Ethics Quarterly*, 5, 1.

Ciulla, J., Knights, D., Mabey, C., & Tomkins, L., (2018a). Guest editors, philosophical approaches to leadership ethics. *Business Ethics Quarterly*, 28, 1.

Ciulla, J., Knights, D., Mabey, C., & Tomkins, L., (2018b). Guest editors, philosophical approaches to leadership ethics. *Business Ethics Quarterly*, 28, 3.

Clarke C., & Knights, D. (2015). Careering through academia: Identity and ethical subjectivity in UK business schools. *Human Relations*, 68(12), 1865–1888.

Clarke, C., & Knights, D. (2019). Who's a good boy then? Anthropocentric masculinities in veterinary practice. *Gender, Work & Organization*, 26(3), 267–287.

Clarke, C., & Knights, D. (2020). The killing fields of identity politics. In A. Brown (Eds.), *The Oxford Handbook of Identity*. Oxford: OUP.

Clarke, C., Knights, D., & Jarvis, C. (2012). A labour of love? Academics in business schools. *Scandinavian Journal of Management*, 28(1), 5–15.

Clarke, C., & Knights, D. (2021). Milking it for all its worth? Unpalatable practices, Dairy cows and veterinary work. *Journal of Business Ethics*, Forthoming.

Clegg, H. A. (1971). *The system of industrial relations in Great Britain*. Oxford: Blackwell.

Clough, P. T. (1992). *The end(s) of ethnography: From realism to social criticism*. Newbury Park, CA: Sage.

Clough, P. T. (2007). *The affective turn: Theorizing the social*. Duke University Press.

Clough, P. T. (2009). The new empiricism: Affect and sociological method. *European Journal of Social Ideas*, 12(1), 43–61.

Coakley, J. (2004). *Sports insociety:Issuesandcontroversies* (8th ed.). London: McGraw-Hill.

Cockburn, C. (1985). *Machinery of dominance: Women, men and technical know-how*. London: Pluto.

Cockburn, C. (1991). *Men's resistance to sex equality in organisations*. Basingstoke: Macmillan.

Coetzee, J. M. (1992). Confession and double thoughts: Tolstoy, Rousseau, Dostoevsky. In D. Attwell (Ed.), *Doubling the point: Essays and interviews* (pp. 251–293). Cambridge, MA: Harvard University Press.

Cohen, D. (1990). *Being a Man*. Routledge.

Cohen, S., & Taylor, L. (1992) *Escape attempts: The theory and practice of resistance to everyday life*. London and New York: Routledge.

Collins, E. G. C., & Devanna, M. A. (Eds.). (1990). *The portable MBA*. New York: Wiley.

Collinson, D., Knights, D., & Collinson, M. (1990). *Managing to discriminate*. London: Routledge.

Collinson, D. L. (1992). *Managing the shopfloor: Subjectivity, masculinity and workplace culture*. Berlin: De Gruyter.

Collinson, D. L. (1994). Strategies of resistance: power, knowledge and subjectivity in the workplace. In John Jermier, David Knights & Walter R. Nord, (Eds.), *Resistance and power in organization* (pp. 25–68). London: Routledge.

Collinson, D. (2003). Identity and identities and insecurities: Selves at work. *Organization, 10*(3): 527–547.

Collinson, D. L. (2005). Dialectics of leadership. *Human Relations, 58*(11), 1419–1442.

Collinson, D. L. (2011). Critical leadership studies. In A. Bryman, D. Collinson, K. Grint, B Jackson, & M. Uhl-Bien (Eds.), *The sage handbook of leadership* (pp. 3–14). London: Sage.

Collinson, D. L. (2014). Dichotomies, dialectics and dilemmas: New directions for critical leadership studies? *Leadership, 10*(1), 36–55.

Collinson, D. L. & Hearn, J. (Eds.). (1996). *Men as managers. Managers as men*. London: Sage.

Collinson, D. & Tourish, D. (2015). Teaching leadership critically: New directions for leadership pedagogy. *Academy of Management Learning and Education, 14*(4), 576–594.

Connell, R. (1987). *Gender and power*. Oxford: Polity Press.

Connell, R. W. (2005). *Masculinities* (2nd ed.). Berkeley, CA: University of California Press.

Contu, A. (2020). Answering the crisis with intellectual activism: Making a difference as business schools scholars. *Human Relations, 73*(5), 737–757Stor.

Costas, J. & Taheri, A. (2012). 'The Return of the Primal Father' in postmodernity? A Lacanian analysis of authentic leadership. *Organization Studies, 33*(9), 1195–1216.

Costea, B. & Amiridis, K. (2016). Management education and the humanities. A future together? In Chris Steyaert, Timon Beyes, & Martin Parker (Eds.), *The Routledge companion to reinventing management education*. New York and London: Routledge.

Costea, B., Amiridis, K., & Crump, N. (2012). Graduate employability and the principle of potentiality: An aspect of the ethics of HRM. *Journal of Business Ethics, 111*(1), 25–36.

Craft, A., & Jeffrey, B. (2008). Creativity and performativity in teaching and learning: Tensions, dilemmas, constraints, accommodations and synthesis. *British Educational Research Journal, 34*(5), 577–584.

Crane, A., Matten, D., Glozer, S., & Spence, L. (2019). *Business ethics: Managing corporate citizenship and sustainability in the age of globalization,* (5th ed.). Oxford: Oxford University Press.

Crevani, L., & Endrissat, N. (2016). Mapping the leadership-as-practice terrain. In J. S. Raelin (Ed.). *Leadership-as-practice: Theory and application* (pp. 21–49). New York and London: Routledge.

Crossley, N. (1995). Merleau-Ponty, the elusive body and carnal sociology. *Body & Society, 1*(1), 43–63.

Cunliffe, A. L. (2009). The philosopher leader: On relationalism, ethics and reflexivity—A critical perspective to teaching leadership. *Management Learning, 40*(1), 87–101.

Cunliffe, A. L., & Erikssen, M. (2011). Relational leadership. *Human Relations, 64,* 11, 1425–1449.

Cunliffe, A. L., & Ford, J. M. (2012). Critical approaches to leadership learning and development. *Academy of Management Proceedings, 07/2012, 2012*(1), 15499.

Czarniawska-Joerges, B., & Wolf, R. (1991). Leaders, managers, entrepreneurs on and off the organizational stage. *Organization Studies, 12*(4), 529–546.

Dachler, H. P., & Hosking, D. M. (1995). The primacy of relations in socially constructing organizational realities. In D. M. Hosking, H. P. Dachler, & K. J. Gergen (Eds.), *Management and organization: Relational alternatives to individualism* (pp. 1–29). Aldershot: Avebury.

Dahl, Robert A. (1957). 'The concept of power'. *Behavioral Science;* Baltimore, Md., *2*(3), 201– 215.

Dale, K. (2001). *Anatomising embodiment and organisation theory.* Basingstoke: Palgrave.

Davies, B., & Petersen, E. (2005). Neoliberal discourse in the Academy: The forestalling of (collective) resistance. *Learning and Teaching in the Social Sciences, 2*(2), 77–97.

Davies, A., & Thomas, R. (2002). Managerialism and accountability in higher education: The gendered nature of restructuring and the costs to academic service. *Critical Perspectives in Accounting, 3*(2), 179–193.

De Certeau, M. (1984). *The practice of everyday life London.* University of California Press.

Deem, R. (1998). 'New managerialism' and higher education: The management of performances and cultures in universities in the United Kingdom. *International Studies in Sociology of Education, 8*(1), 47–70.

De Garis, L. (2000). "Be a Buddy to Your Buddy": Male identity, aggression and intimacy in a boxing gym. In J. McKay, M. A. Messner, & D. Sabo (Eds.), *Masculinities, gender relations, and sport.* London: Sage.

Deleuze, G. (1988). *Spinoza: practical philosophy.* R. Hurley (Trans.). San Francisco: City Light Books.

Deleuze, G., & Guattari, F. (1988). *A thousand plateaus: Capitalism and schizophrenia.* Brian Massumi (Trans.). London: The Athlone Press.

Demos, V., Berheide, C. W., & Segal. (Eds.). (2014). *Gender transformation in the academy: 19.* New York: Emerald.

Derrida, J. (1982). *Margins of philosophy.* A. Bass (Trans.). Chicago: University of Chicago Press.

Derrida, J. (1994). *The politics of friendship.* G. Collins (Trans.). London: Verso.

Derrida, J. (1992). *The Gift of Death.* David Wills (Trans.). Chicago: Chicago University Press.

Derrida, J. (1997/1967). *Of Grammatology.*Gayatri Chakravorty Spivak (Trans.).Baltimore: John Hopkins University Press.

Derrida, J. (1999). *Adieu to Emmanuel Levinas.* Stanford Unviersity Press.

De Tocqueville A. (1998 [1835]). *Democracy in America.* (Wordsworth ed.). Hertfordhire: Ware.

Diedrich, A., Eriksson-Zetterquist, U. & Styhre, A. (2011). Sorting people out: The uses of one-dimensional classificatory schemes in a multi-dimensional world. *Culture and Organization, 17(4),* 271–292.

Diprose, R. (1994). *The bodies of women: Ethics, embodiment and sexual difference.* London: Routledge.

Diprose, R. (2002). *Corporeal generosity: On giving with Nietzsche, Merleau-Ponty and Levinas.* Albany, NY: State University of New York Press.

Doherty, L., & Manfredi, S. (2006). Women's progression to senior positions in English universities. *Employee Relations, 28(6),* 553–572.

Du Gay, P. (2000). *In praise of bureaucracy: Weber, organization, ethics.* London: Sage.

Dunlop, J. T. (1958). *Industrial relations systems.* New York: Holt.

Dunn, R. G. (1998). *Identity crises, a social critique of postmodernity.* Minneapolis, MN: University of Minnesota Press.

Durkheim, E. (1887). La science positive de la morale en Allemagne. *Revue philosophique,* 24, 33–58; 113-42; and 275-84.

Easlea, B. (1983). *Fathering the unthinkable: Masculinity, scientists and the nuclear arms race.* London: Pluto.

Edwards, T. (2006). *Cultures of masculinity.* New York: Routledge.

Ekman, S. (2013). Work as limitless potential – How managers and employees seduce each other through dynamics of mutual recognition. *Human Relations,* 66(9), 1159–1181.

Eldridge, J. E. T. (1968). *Industrial disputes: Essays in the socoiology of industrial relations.* London: RKP.

Elias, N. (1978). *What is sociology?* Columbia University Press.

Ehrenreich, B. (2010). *Bright-sided: how positive thinking is undermining America.* New York: Picador.

Evink, E. (2009). '(In) finite responsibility How to avoid the contrary effects of Derrida's ethics. *Philosophy & Social Criticism, 35(4),* 467–481.

Fairhurst, G. T., & Grant D. (2010) 'The social construction of leadership: A sailing guide', *Management Communication Quarterly,* 24(2), 171–210.

Fairhurst, G. T., & Connaughton, S. L. (2014). Leadership: A communicative perspective. *Leadership,* 10(1), 7–35.

Falkman, L. L. (2016). Leaders are their bodies. In *The embodiment of leadership* L. R. Melina, G. J. Burgess, A. Antonio, & L. Lid-Falkman (Eds.). London: Wiley

Foucault', Capital and C/ass 9: 75–96.

Fisher, G. (2007). 'You need tits to get on round here': Gender and sexuality in the entrepreneurial university of the 21st century. *Ethnography, 8*, 503.

Flanders, A. (1971). *Management and unions*. London: Faber and Faber.

Fleming, P. (2014). *Resisting work: The corporatization of life and its discontents*. Temple University Press.

Fleming, P., & Spicer, A. (2007). *Contesting the corporation*. New York: Cambridge University Press.

Ford, J. (2006). Discourses of leadership: Gender, identity and contradiction in a UK public sector organization. *Leadership, 2*(1), 77–99.

Ford, J., & Harding, N. (2004). We went looking for an organisation and could find only the metaphysics of its presence. *Sociology, 38*(4), 815–830.

Ford, J., Harding, N., & Learmonth, M. (2008). *Leadership as identity: Constructions and deconstructions*. London: Palgrave Macmillan.

Ford, J. Harding, N., & Gilmore, S. (2017). Becoming the leader: Leadership as material presence. *Organization Studies, 38*(11), 1553–1571.

Forster N. (2001). A case study of women academics' views on equal opportunities, career prospects and work-family conflicts in a UK university. *Career Development International, 6(1), 28*–38.

Fotaki, M. (2013). No woman is like a man (in academia): The masculine symbolic order and the unwanted female body. *Organization Studies, 34*(9), 1251–1275.

Fotaki, M., Metcalfe, B. D., & Harding, N. (2014). Writing materiality into management and organization studies through and with Luce Irigaray. *Human Relations, 67*(10), 1239–1263.

Foucault, M. (1972). *The archaeology of knowledge and the discourse on language*, A. M. Sheridan Smith (Trans.). New York: Pantheon Books, Tavistock.

Foucault, M. (1973). *The order of things: An archaeology of the human sciences*. New York: Vintage Books.

Foucault, M. (1977). *The history of sexuality Vol.1: An introduction*, Harmondsworth: Penguin Books.

Foucault, M. (1979). *Discipline and punish*. Harmondsworth: Penguin.

Foucault, M. (1980a). *Power/knowledge. In* C. Gordon (Ed.). Brighton, England: Harvester Press.

Foucault, M. (1980b). *Intellectuals and power: A conversation between Michel Foucault and Gilles Deleuze in language, counter-memory and practice*. (pp. 205–217). New York: Cornell University Press.

Foucault, M. (1982). The subject and power. In H. L. Dreyfus & P. Rabinow (Eds.), *MichelFoucault: Beyond structuralism and hermeneutics* (pp. 208–228). Chicago: University of Chicago.

Foucault, M. (1985). *The history of sexuality, volume 2: The use of pleasure*. Harmondsworth: Penguin.

Foucault, M. (1986). *The care of the self*. New York: Pantheon.

Foucault, M. (1988 [1961]). *Madness and civilization: A history of insanity in the age of reason*. New York: Taylor & Francis.

Foucault, M. (1988a). Technologies of the self. In L. H. Martin, H. Gutman, & P. H. Hutton (Eds.), *Technologies of the self: A seminar with Michel Foucault* (pp. 16–49). London: Tavistock.

Foucault, M. (1988b), *The history of sexuality, volume 3: The care of the self*. Harmondsworth: Penguin.

Foucault, M. (1990) *The uses of pleasure: History of sexualities (Vol. 2)*. New York: Vintage Books.

Foucault, M. (1991 [1984]a). *The Foucault reader*. InP. Rabinow (Ed.). Harmondsworth: Penguin.

Foucault, M. (1991a) How an 'Experience Book' is born. In R. J. Goldstein, & J. Cascaito (Eds.), *Remarks on Marx*. (p. 27). New York: Semiotext(e).

Foucault, M. (1991b [1984]b). What is enlightenment?. In P. Rabinow (Ed.), *The Foucault reader* (pp. 32–50). Harmondsworth: Penguin.

Foucault, M. (1994). Biblioteque des sciences humaines, D. Defert, & F. Ewald (Eds.), *Dits et Ecrits, 1954-1988* (pp. 1–843). Paris: Gallimard.

Foucault, M. (1997). *Ethics: Essential works of Foucault 1954-1984 vol 1*, Paul Rabinow (Ed.). Harmondsworth: Penguin.

Foucault, M. (1998). Nietzsche, genealogy, history. In J. D. Faubon (Ed.), *Aesthetics essential works of Foucault 1954-1984 vol 2*. Harmondsworth: Penguin.

Foucault, M. (2005). *The hermeneutics of the subject: Lectures at the College de France, 1981-1982*. New York: Picador.

Foucault, Michel. (2003 [1976]). Lecture 11. In *Society must be defended: Lectures at the College de France* (pp. 239–264). London: Allen Lane.

Foucault, M. (2008). *The birth of biopolitics: Lectures at the College de France, 1978-9*, G. Burchell (Trans.). London: Palgrave Macmillan.

Foucault, M. (2009 [2007]). Security, territory, population. *Lectures at the College de France, 1977-8*. G. Burchell (Trans.). A. L. Davidson (Introd.). London: Palgrave Macmillan.

Foucault, M. (2009 [1961]). *History of madness*. J. Khalfa (Trans.). New York: Routledge.

Foucault, M. (2011). *The courage of truth: Lectures at the College de France 1983-4*. Basingstoke: Palgrave Macmillan.

Fowler, J. D. (1999). *Humanism: Beliefs and Practices*. Sussex Academic Press.

Fox, A., & Flanders, A. (1969). The reform of collective bargaining: From Donovan to Durkheim. *British Journal of Industrial Relations*, 7(2), 151–180.

Frank, A. W. (1990). Bringing bodies back in: A decade review. *Theory, Culture & Society*, 7(1), 131–162.

Fraser, N. (1996). Michel Foucault: A "Young Conservative"? In S. J. Hekman (Eds.), *Feminist interpretations of Michel Foucault* (pp. 15–38). PA: Pennsylvania State University Press.

Fukuyama, F. (2018). *Identity: The demand for dignity and the politics of resentment*. London: Profile Books.

Gabriel, Y. (1997). Meeting god: When organizational members come face to face with the supreme leader. *Human Relations*, 50(4), 315–342.

Gabriel, Y. (2010). Organization studies: A space for ideas, identities and agonies. *Organization Studies*. 31(6), 757–775.

Gabriel, Y. (2011). Psychoanalytic approaches to leadership in Bryman et al. In *Research methods in the study of leadership*. London: Sage.

Galor, Z. (2008). Demutualization of cooperatives: Reasons and perspectives. http://co-oppundit.org/files/demutualizationcooperatives21508.pdf consulted 30th Sept. 2019.

Game, A. (1990). *Undoing the social*. London: Routledge.

Gardner, W., Cogliser, C., Davis, K., & Dickens, M. (2011). Authentic leadership: A review of the literature and research agenda. *Leadership Quarterly*, 22(6), 1120–1145.

Gatens, M. (1997). *Imaginary bodies: Ethics, power and corporeality*. London: Routledge.

Gatens, M. (2006). *Politicizing the body: Property, contract, and rights*. na.

Gatens, M., & Lloyd, G. (1999). *Collective imaginings: Spinoza, past and present*. New York and London: Routledge.

Gatrell, C. (2008). *Embodying women's work* (pp. 19–32). McGraw-Hill Education (UK).

Geary, P. J. (2012). Ethnic identity as a situational construct in the early middle ages. In Florin Curta, & Cristina Spinei (Eds.), *Writing history: Identity, conflict, and memory in the middle ages*, Edited by Romanian Academy Institute of Archaeology of Iaşi, (pp. 19–32). Bucureşti-Brăila: Editura Academiei Române.

Gemmill, G., & Oakley, J. (1992). Leadership - an alienating social myth. *Human Relations*, 45(2), 113–129.

Gerson, L. P. (2004). Plato on identity, sameness, and difference. *The Review of Metaphysics*, 58(2), 305–332.

Gherardi, S. (1994). The gender we think, the gender we do in our everyday organizational lives. *Human Relations*, 47(6).

Giddens, A. (1971). *Capitalism and modern social theory: An analysis of the writings of Marx, Durkheim and Max Weber*. Cambridge: Cambridge University Press.

Giddens, A. (1979). *Central problems in social theory: Action, structure, and contradiction in social analysis*. London: Macmillan.

Gill, S. (Eds.). (2011). *Global crises and the crisis of global leadership*. Cambridge University Press.

Gilmore, D. C. (1990). *Manhood in the making: Cultural concepts of masculinity*. Yale: Yale University Press.

Giorgi, S., Guider, M. E., & Bartunek, J. M. (2014). Productive resistance: A study of change, emotions, and identity in the context of the apostolic visitation of US women religious, 2008–2012. *Research in the Sociology of Organizations*, 41, 259–300.

Goffman, E. (1959). *The presentation of self in everyday life*. Harmondsworth: Penguin.

Goshal, S. (2005). Bad management theories are destroying good management practices. *Academy of Management Learning and Education*, 4(1), 75–81.

Gouldner, A. W. (1954). *Wildcat strike*. New York: Antioch Press.

Gray, J. (2008). *Why mars and venus collide: Improving relationships by understanding how men and women cope differently with stress*. New York: Harper.

Gray, J. (2013). *The silence of animals: On progress and other modern myths*. Harmondsworth: Penguin, Kindle edition.

Gregory, M. R. (2010). Slam dunk: Strategic sport metaphors and the construction of masculine embodiment at work. *Advances in Gender Research*, 14, 297–318.

Grey, C. (1994). Career as a project of the self and labour process discipline. *Sociology*, 28(2), 479–497.

Grey, C. (2004). Reinventing business schools: The contribution of critical management education. *Academy of Management Learning and Education*, 3(2), 178–186.

Grint K. (2000). *The arts of leadership*. Oxford: Oxford University Press.

Grint, K. (2011). A History of Leadership. InA. Bryman, D. Collinson, K. Grint, B. Jackson, & M. Uhl-Bien (Eds.), *The sage handbook of leadership* (pp. 3–14). London: Sage.

Gros, F., Trans. Burchell, G. (2005). *The hermeneutics of the subject: Lectures at the Collège de France, 1981–1982*, New York: Springer.

Grosz, E. (1994). *Volatile bodies: Toward a corporeal feminism*. Bloomington, IN: Indiana University Press.

Grosz, E. (2005). From 'Intensities and Flows' In Tiffany Atkinson (Eds.), *The body: Readers in cultural criticism* (pp. 142–155). Basingstoke: Palgrave Macmillan.

Guthey, E., & Jackson, B. (2005). CEO portraits and the authenticity paradox. *Journal of Management Studies*, 42(5), 1057–1082.

Hacker, S. (1990). Doing it the hard way. In D. E. Smith, & S. M. Turner (Eds.). London: Unwin Hyman.

Halberstam, J. (1998). *Female masculinity*. London: Duke University Press.

Hallenbeck, S. (2012). Toward a posthuman perspective: Feminist rhetorical methodologies and everyday practices. *Advances in the History of Rhetoric*, 15(1), 9–27.

Hambrick, D. C., Davison, S. C., Snell, S. A., & Snow, C. C. (1998). When groups consist of multiple nationalities: Towards a new understanding of the implications. *Organization Studies*, 19(2), 181–205.

Hamilton, L., (2013). 'The magic of mundane objects: culture, identity and power in a country vets' practice. *The Sociological Review*, 61, 265–284.

Hammer, M., & Champy, J. (1993). *Reengineering the corporation: A manifesto for business revolution*. London: Nicholas Brealey Publishing.

Haraway, D. (1991). *Simians, cyborgs, and women: The reinvention of women*. London and New York: Routledge.

Haraway, D. (2008). *When species meet*. University of Minnesota Press

Harding, S. (2019). Films as archives of leadership theories. In Brigid Carroll, Suze Wilson, & Joshua Firth (Eds.), *After leadership*. New York: Routledge.

Harding, N., Ford, J., & Gough, B. (2010). Accounting for ourselves: Are academics exploited workers? *Critical Perspectives on Accounting*, 21, 159–168.

Hardt, M., & Negri, A. (2009). *Common wealth*. Harvard University Press.

Harley, S. (2003). Research selectivity and female academics in UK universities: From 'gentleman's club and barrack yard to smart macho? *Gender and Education*, 15(4), 377–392.

Hawkins, B. (2015). Ship-shape: Materializing leadership in the British Royal Navy. *Human Relations, 68*(6), 951–971.

Hayes, C. (2013). *Twilight of the elites*. New York: Broadway Books.

He, H. & Baruch, Y. (2010). Organizational identity and legitimacy under major environmental changes: Tales of two UK building societies. *British Journal of Management, 21*, 44–62.

Hennessy, R. (1993). *Materialist feminism and the politics of discourse*. New York: Routledge.

Hearn J., & D. J. Morgan, (Eds.). (1990). *Men, masculinities and social theory*. Unwin Hyman.

Hegel, G. W. F. (1807/1977). *The phenomenology of spirit*. A. V. Miller (Trans.). Oxford, UK: Oxford University Press.

Hekman, S. J., (Ed.). (1990). *Feminist interpretations of Michel Foucault* (pp. 39–55). The Pennsylvania State University Press.

Hekman, S. J. (1999). *The future of differences: Truth and method in feminist theory*. Oxford: Polity Press.

Henderson, J. E., & Hoy, W. K. (1983). Leader authenticity: The development and test of an operational measure. *Educational and Psychological Research, 3*(2), 63–75.

Henwood, F. (1993). Establishing gender perspectives on information technology: Problems, issues and opportunities. In E. Green, J. Owen, & D. Pain (Eds.), *Gendered by design: Information technology and office systems* (pp. 31–52). London: Taylor.

Higate, P., & Hopton, J. (2005). War, militarism, and masculinities. In M. S. Kimmel, J. Hearn, & R. W. Connell (Eds.), *Handbook of studies on men and masculinities*. London: Sage.

Hochschild, Arlie Russell (1983). *The managed heart: Commercialization of human feeling*. Berkeley, CA: University of California Press.

Hollander, J. A., & Einwohner, R. L. (2004). Conceptualizing resistance. *Sociological forum, 19*(4), 533–554.

Holliday, R. (2000). We've been framed: Visualising methodology. *The Sociological Review, 48*(4), 503–522.

Holtzhausen, D. R., & Voto, R. (2002). Resistance from the margins: The postmodern public relations practitioner as organizational activist. *Journal of Public Relations Research, 14*(1), 57–84.

Holvino, E. (2010). Intersections: The simultaneity of race, gender and class in organization studies. *Gender, Work and Organization, 17*(3), 248–277.

Hosking, D. M. (2011a). *Moving relationality: Meditations on a relational approach to leadership in Bryman*. A et al., op.cit.

Hosking, D. M. (2011b). Telling tales of relations: Appreciating relational constructionism. *Organization Studies, 32*(1), 47–65.

Hoyer, P., & Steyaert, C. (2015). Narrative identity construction in times of career change: Taking note of unconscious desires. *Human Relations, 68*(12), 1837–1863.

Huczynski, A., & Buchanan, D. (2001). *Organizational behaviour: An introductory text* (4th ed.). London: Financial Times/Prentice Hall.

Humphreys, M. (2005). Getting personal: Reflexivity and autoethnographic vignettes. *Qualitative Inquiry, 11*, 840–860.

Hyman, R. (1972). *Strikes.* London: Fontana.

Hyman, R. (1975). *Industrial relations: A marxist introduction.* London: Palgrave Macmillan.

Hyman, R. (1978). Pluralism, procedural consensus and collective bargaining. *British Journal of Industrial Relations*, XV1(2).

Hynes, M. (2013). Reconceptualizing resistance: Sociology and the affective dimension of resistance. *The British Journal of Sociology*, 64(4), 559–577.

Ibarra, H. (1999). Provisional selves: Experimenting with image and identity in professional adaptation. *Administrative Science Quarterly*, 44(4), 764–791.

Ingham, G. K. (1984). *Capitalism divided? The city and industry in British social development.* London: Macmillan.

Ingham, G. K. (2011). *Capitalism.* Oxford: Polity Press.

Irigaray, L. (1980). This sex which is not one. In E. Marks, & I. de Courtrivon (Eds.). *New French Feminisms* (pp. 99–106). Brighton: Harvester Press.

Irigaray, L. (1985). *This sex that is not one.* Ithaca, NY: Cornell University Press.

Jackson, N., & Carter, P. (1994). *Management gurus: What are we to make of them?* In J. Hassard, & R. Holliday (Eds.). Sage: Organization-Representation London.

James, A. (2014). Work–life 'balance', recession and the gendered limits to learning and innovation (or, why it pays employers to care). *Gender, Work and Organization*, 21(3), 273–294.

Jameson, F. (1991). *Postmodernism, or, the cultural logic of late capitalism.* Durham, NC: Duke University Press.

Jagger, A. M. (1983). *Feminist politics and human nature.* New York: Rowman & Littlefield.

Jessop, B., & Stones, R. (1992). Old city and new times: Economic and political aspects of deregulation. In Leslie Budd, & Sam Whimster (Eds.), *Global finance and urban living: A study of metropolitan change.* . London: Routledge.

Joecks, J., Pull, K., & Backes-Gellner, U. (2014). 'Childbearing and (female) research productivity: A personnel economics perspective on the leaky pipeline', *Journal of Business Economics*, 84(4), 517–530.

Judovitz, D. (2001). *The culture of the body.* University of Michigan Press.

Kant, I. (1879/1949). *Fundamental principles of the metaphysic of morals*, Abbott (Trans.). Liberal Arts Press.

Karner,T. X. (1998). Engendering violent men. In L. H. Bowker (ed.), *Masculinities and violence* (pp. 186–213). London: Sage.

Keenoy, T. (2003). *The discursive constructions of performing professionals.* In *Organizational relationships in the networking age*, 137–158.

Keenoy, T. (2005). Facing inwards and outwards at once: The liminal temporalities of academic performativity. *Time & Society*, 14, 303–321.

Kelly, R. (2018). Pace of UK veterinary consolidation stutters. Pets at Home hospital closures anticipated November 29, https://news.vin.com/VINNews. aspx?articleId=50965, consulted 3.12.19.

Kendall, G., & Wickham, G. (1999). *Using Foucault's methods.* London: Sage.

Kenny, K. (2010). Beyond ourselves: Passion and the dark side of identification in an ethical organization. *Human Relations*, 63(6), 857–873.

Kenny, K., & Fotaki, M. (2015). From gendered organizations to compassionate borderspaces: Reading corporeal ethics with Bracha Ettinger. *Organization*, 22(2): 183–199.

Kerfoot, D., & Knights, D. (1993). Management, manipulation and masculinity: From paternalism to corporate strategy in financial services. *Journal of Management Studies, 30*(4), 659–677.

Kerfoot, D., & Knights, D. (1996). "The Best is Yet to Come?": Searching for embodiment in management. In D. Collinson, & J. Hearn, (Eds.), *Masculinity and Management* (pp. 78–98). London: Sage.

Kerfoot, D., & Knights, D. (1998). Managing masculinity in contemporary organizational life: A 'Man'agerial Project' *Organization, 5*(1), 7–26.

Kernis, M. H., & Goldman, B. M. (2006). A multicomponent conceptualization of authenticity: Theory and research In M. P. Zanna (Ed.), *Advances in experimental social psychology* (Vol. 38, pp. 283–357). San Diego: Academic Press.

Kidder, T. (1982). *The soul of the new machine.* Harmondsworth: Penguin.

Kirton, G., & Greene A.-M. (2009). The costs and opportunities of doing diversity work in mainstream organizations. *Human Resource Management Journal, 19*(2), 159–175.

Klimecki, R., & Willmott, H. (2009). From demutualisation to meltdown: A tale of two wannabe banks. *Critical perspectives on international business, 5*(1/2), 120–140.

Knights, D. (1997). Governmentality and financial services: Welfare crises and the financially self-disciplined subject. In G. Morgan, & D. Knights (Eds.), *Deregulation and European financial services* (pp. 216–235). London: Macmillan.

Knights, D. (2000). Autonomy retentiveness: Problems and prospects for a posthumanist feminism. *Journal of Management Inquiry, 9*(2), 173–185.

Knights, D. (2002). Writing organization analysis into Foucault, organization. 9(4), November, 575–593, Reprinted in Linstead S. (Ed.). (2004). *Organizations and postmodern thought* (pp. 14–33). London: Sage.

Knights, D. (2006). Passing the time in pastimes, professionalism and politics: Reflecting on the ethics and epistemology of time studies. *Time and Society, 15*(3), 251–274.

Knights, D. (2015). Binaries need to shatter for bodies to matter: Do disembodied masculinities undermine organizational ethics? *Organization, 22*(2), 200–216.

Knights D. (2017). Leadership, masculinity and ethics in financial services. In John Storey, Jean Hartley, Jean-Louis Denis, Paul 'T Hart, & Dave Ulrich (Eds.), *The Routledge companion to leadership.* London: Routledge, 332–347.

Knights, D. (2018a). Leadership lives? Affective leaders in a neo-humanist world. In Brigid Carroll, Suze Wilson, & Joshua Firth (Eds.), *After leadership* (pp. 75–87) . London and New York: Routledge.

Knights, D. (2018b). What's more effective than affective leadership? Searching for embodiment in leadership research and practice. InC. Mabey, & D. Knights (Eds.), *"Leadership matters?": Finding voice, connection and meaning in the 21st Century.* New York: Routledge.

Knights, D. (2019a). Embodied leadership, ethics and its affects. In Brigid Carroll, Jackie Ford, Scott Taylor, & Joshua Firth (Eds.), *Leadership: Contemporary critical perspectives.* London: Sage.

Knights, D. (2019b). Gender still at work: Interrogating identity in discourses and practices of masculinity. *Gender, Work and Organization*, 26, 18–30.

Knights, D., & Clarke C. (2014). A bittersweet symphony, this life: Fragile academic selves. *Organization Studies*, 35(3), 335–357.

Knights, D., & Clarke, C. (2017). Pushing the boundaries of amnesia and myopia: A critical review of the literature on identity in management and organization studies. *International Journal of Management Reviews*, Special Issue: Exploring the Registers of Identity Research, 19(3), 337–356.

Knights, D., & D. Collinson, (1987). Disciplining the shopfloor: A comparison of the disciplinary effects of managerial psychology and financial accounting in accounting. *Organisations and Society*, 12(5), 457–477.

Knights, D., & Kerfoot, D. (2004). Between representations and subjectivity: Gender binaries and the politics of organizational transformation. *Gender, Work and Organization*, 11(4), 430–454.

Knights D., & D. McCabe, (1998). What happens when the phone goes wild? Staff, stress and spaces for escape in a BPR regime. *Journal of Management Studies*, 35(2) 163–194.

Knights, D., & McCabe, D. (1999). "There are no limits to Authority"?: TQM and organizational power relations. *Organization Studies*, 20(2), 197–224.

Knights, D., & McCabe, D. (2002). 'A road less travelled': Beyond managerialist, critical and processual approaches to total quality management. *Journal of Organizational Change Management*, 15(3), 235–254.

Knights D., & McCabe, D. (2003a). *Organization and innovation: Guru schemes and American dreams*. Milton Keynes: Open University Press.

Knights D., & McCabe D. (2003b). Governing through teamwork: Reconstituting subjectivity in a call and processing centre. *Journal of Management Studies*, 40(7), 1587–1619.

Knights, D., & D. McCabe, (2008). 'Masters of the universe': Demystifying leadership in the context of the financial crisis. *British Journal of Management*, 26, 197–210, 2015, DOI: 10.1111/1467-8551.12088

Knights, D. & D. McCabe (2015). 'Masters of the universe': Demystifying leadership in the context of the 2008 Financial Crisis', *British Journal of Management*, 26, 197–210.

Knights, D., & Morgan, G. (1991). Corporate strategy, subjectivity and organisations. *Organisation Studies*, 12(2), 1991, 251–273.

Knights D., & Morgan, G. (1992). Leadership as corporate strategy: Towards a critical analysis. *Leadership Quarterly*, 3(3), 1992, 171–190.

Knights D., & Murray F. (1994). *Managers divided: Organisational politics and information technology management*. London: Wiley.

Knights, D., Noble, F., Vurdubakis, T., & Willmott, H. (2001). Chasing shadows: Control, virtuality and the production of trust. *Organization Studies*, 22(2), 311–336.

Knights, D., Noble, F., Vurdubakis, T., & Willmott, H. (2002). Allegories of creative destruction: Technology and organisation in narratives of the e-Economy. In Woolgar, S. (Ed.), *Virtual society? Technology, cyberbole, reality* (pp. 99–114). Oxford: Oxford University Press.

Knights D., & O'Leary M. (2005). Reflecting on corporate scandals: The failure of ethical leadership. *Business Ethics: A European Review*, 14(3), 176–192.

Knights, D., & O'Leary, M., (2006). Leadership, ethics and responsibility to the other. *Journal of Business Ethics, 67*(2), 125–137.

Knights, D., & Tinker T. (Eds.). (1997). *Financial service institutions and social transformations: International studies of a sector in transition.* London: Macmillan.

Knights, D., Noble, F., Vurdubakis, T., & Willmott, H. (2002).Allegories of creative destruction: Technology and organisation in narratives of the e-economy. In S. Woolgar (Ed.), *Virtual society? Technology, cyberbole, reality* (pp. 99–114). Oxford: Oxford University Press, 2002.

Knights D., & Odih P. (1995). "It's about time": The significance of gendered time for financial services consumption. *Time & Society, 4*(2), 205–223.

Knights D., & Odih P. (1999). "It's about time!": The significance of gendered time for financial services consumption In Brownlie et al., (Eds.), *Rethinking marketing: New perspectives on the discipline and profession* (pp. 126–144). London: Sage.

Knights, D., & O' Leary, M. (2006). Leadership, ethics and responsibility to the other. *Journal of Business Ethics, 67*(2), 125–137.

Knights D., & Omanović V. (2016). (Mis)Managing diversity: Exploring the dangers of diversity management orthodoxy. *Equality Diversity and Inclusion: An International Journal, 35*(1), 5–16.

Knights D., & Tullberg, M. (2012). Managing masculinity/mismanaging the corporation. *Organization, 19*(4), 385–404.

Knights D., & Vurdubakis, T. (1994). Foucault, power, resistance and all that. In J. Jermier et al. (Eds.), *Resistance and power in organizations (pp. 167–198).* London: Routledge.

Knights D., & Willmott, H. (1985). Power and identity in theory and practice. *Sociological Review, 33*(1), 22–46.

Knights D., & Willmott, H. (1989). Power and subjectivity at work: From degradation to subjugation in social relations. *Sociology, 23*(4), 535–558, reprinted in Critical Management Studies, Edited by Mats Alvesson and Hugh Willmott, Sage 2011

Knights D., & Willmott, H. (1992). Conceptualising leadership processes: A study of senior leadership processes: A study of senior managers in a financial services company. *Journal of Management Studies, 29*(6), 761–782.

Knights D., & Willmott, H. (1995). Culture and control in an insurance company. *Culture and Symbols in Society, 1*(1), 1–25.

Knights D., & Willmott, H. (2004 [1999]). *Management lives! Power and identity in work organisations.* London: Sage.

Knights, D., & Willmott, H. (2017). *Introducing organization behaviour and management* 3rd ed. London: Cengage Thomson Learning.

Kohut, H. (1971). *The analysis of the self: A systematic approach to the psychoanalytic treatment of narcissistic personality disorders.* University of Chicago Press.

Kohut, H. (1976). Creativeness, charisma, group psychology In P. Ornstein (Ed.), *The search for the self (Vol. 2).* New York: International Universities Press.

Kolsaker, A. (2008). Academic professionalism in the managerialist era: A study of English universities. *Studies in Higher Education, 33*(5): 513–525.

Kondo, D. (1990). *Crafting selves: Power, gender and discourse of identity in a Japanese workplace*. Chicago: University of Chicago Press.

Krantz J. (1990). Lessons from the field: An essay on the crisis of leadership in contemporary organizations. *The Journal of Applied Behavioral Science*, 26(1), 49–64.

Kristeva J. (1991). *Desire in language*. New York: Columbia University Press.

Kupers W. (2013). Embodied inter-practices of leadership – Phenomenological perspectives on relational and responsive leading and following. *Leadership*, 9(3), 335–357.

Kuratko, D. F. (2007). Entrepreneurial leadership in the 21st century. *Journal of Leadership and Organizational Studies*, 13(4), 1–12.

Lacan, J. (2001 [1980]). *Ecrits*. London: Routledge.

Ladkin D. (2006). When deontology and utilitarianism aren't enough: How Heidegger's notion of "dwelling" might help organisational leaders resolve ethical issues. *Journal of Business Ethics*, 65, 87–98.

Ladkin, D. (2010). *Rethinking leadership: A new look at old leadership questions*. Cheltenham, UK: Edward Elgar.

Ladkin, D. (2013). From perception to flesh: A phenomenological account of the felt experience of leadership. *Leadership* 9(3): 320–334.

Laing, R. (1990). *Self and others*. Harmondsworth, UK: Penguin.

Lasch, C. (1979). *The culture of narcissism: American life in an age of diminishing expectations*. London: W. W. Norton.

Latour, B. (1987). *Science in action.*Cambridge, Massachuetts: *Harvard University Press*.

Latour, B. (2005). *Re-assembling the social*. Oxford: Oxford University Press.

Learmonth, M., & Humphreys, M. (2011). Autoethnography and academic identity: Glimpsing business school dopplegangers. *Organization*, 19(1), 99–117.

Learmonth, M., & Morrell, K. (2016). Is critical leadership studies 'critical'?. *Leadership*, 13(3), 257–271.

Learmonth, M., & Morrell, K. (2019). *Critical perspectives on leadership: The language of corporate power*. New York: Routledge.

Leder, D. (1990). *The absent body*. Chicago: University of Chicago Press.

Lee, B. (2019). *The dangerous case of Donald Trump: 37 psychiatrists and mental health experts assess a president*. New York: Thomas Dunne Books.

Levin, D. M. (1985). *The body's reflection of being*. Boston: Routledge & Kegan Paul.

Levine M. P., & Boaks, J. (2014). What does ethics have to do with leadership? *Journal of Business Ethics*, 124(2), 1–18.

Levinas, E. (1969). *Totality and infinity: An essay on exteriority*. Pittsburgh: Duquesne University Press.

Levinas, E. (1981 [1991]) *Otherwise than being of beyond essence*. The Hague/ Boston/ London: Martinus Niihoff Publishers.

Levinas, E. (1985). *Ethics and infinity*. R. Cohen (Trans.). Pittsburgh: Duquesne University Press.

Levinas E. (2002 [1989]). Ethics as first philosophy. In Hand S. (Ed.), *The Levinas Reader* (pp. 75–87). Oxford: Basil Blackwell.

Levinas E. (1998). *Entre-nous: On thinking of the other*. New York: Columbia University Press.

Liff S. (1999). Diversity and equal opportunities: Room for a constructive compromise?' *Human Resource Management Journal, 9*(1), 65–75.

Linstead A., & Brewis J. (2004). Special issue on beyond boundaries. *Gender, Work and Organization, 11*(4), July, 430–454.

Lorbiecki, A., & Jack, G. (2000). Critical turns in the evolution of diversity management. *British Journal of Management, 11*(Special Issue), 17–31.

Lorenz, C. (2012). If you're so smart, why are you under sSurveillance? Universities, neoliberalism, and new public management. *Critical Inquiry, 38*(3), 599–629.

Lowenstein R. (2004). *Origins of the crash: The great bubble and tts undoing.* Harmondsworth, UK: Penguin Books.

Machiavelli, N. (1961). *The Prince*. Harmondsworth, UK: Penguin.

Lukes, S. (2005 [1974]). *Power: a radical view*. London: Palgrave Macmillan.

Mabey, C., & Knights, D. (2018). "Leadership matters?": Finding voice. *Connection and meaning in the 21st Century*. New York: Routledge.

MacIntyre, A. (1991 [1981]). *After virtue: A study in moral theory*. London: Duckworth.

Macpherson, C. B. (1962). *The political theory of possessive individualism: Hobbes to Locke*. Oxford: Clarendon Press.

Maier, M. (2002). Ten years after a major malfunction…reflections on the challenger syndrome. *Journal of Management Inquiry, 11*(3).

Mars, G. (1982). *Cheats at work*. London: Unwin.

Massumi, B. (2002). *Parables for the virtual:Movement, affect, sensation*. Durham: Duke University Press.

Mayo, E. (1933). *The human problems of an industrial civilization*. New York: Macmillan.

McCabe, D. (2020). *Changing change management: Strategy, power and resistance*. London: Routledge.

McCabe, D., & Knights, D. (2016). Learning to listen? Exploring discourses and images of masculine leadership through corporate videos. *Management Learning, 47(2)*, 179–198.

McDowell, L. (1997). *Capital culture. Gender at work in the city*. Oxford: Blackwell.

McWeeny, J. (2017). Beauvoir and Merleau-Ponty. In Hengehold, L., & Bauer, N. (Eds.), *A companion to Simone de Beauvoir*, New York: Wiley.

McWhorter, L. (1999). *Bodies & pleasures: Foucault and the politics of sexual normalization*. Bloomington and Indianapolis: Indiana University Press.

Mead, G. H. (1934). *Mind, self and society*. Chicago: The University of Chicago Press.

Meindl, J. (1995). .The romance of leadership as a follower-centric theory: A social constructionist approach. *The Leadership Quarterly, 6*(3), 329–341.

Meriläinen, S., Tienari, J., Katila, S., & Benschop, Y. (2009). Diversity management versus gender equality: The Finnish case. *Canadian Journal of Administrative Science, 26*, 230–243.

Merleau-Ponty, M. (1962 [1945]) *The Phenomenology of Perception*. London: Routledge & Kegan Paul.

Merton R. K. et al. (Eds.). (1961). *Reader in bureaucracy*. New York: Free Press.

Miller, C. C (2016) As women take over a male-dominated field, the pay drops, *New York Times* March 18th, https://www.nytimes.com/2016/03/20/upshot/as-women-take-over-a-male-dominated-field-the-pay-drops.html.

Mills, C. Wright (1959). *The sociological imagination*. New York: Oxford University Press.

Mills, C. Wright (1967). In *Power, politics and people. The collective essays of C. Wright Mills*. Irving H. Horowitz (Eds.). New York: Oxford University Press.

Minkes, A., Small, M. W., & Chatterjee, S. R. (1999). Leadership and business ethics: Does it matter? Implications for management. *Journal of Business Ethics, 20*, 327–335.

Mintzberg, H. (2004). *Managers not MBAs*. London: Pearson Education.

Mintzberg, H., Simons, R., & Basu, K. (2002, Fall). *Beyond selfishness*. MIT *Sloan Management Review*, 67–74.

Misra, J., Lundquist, J., & Templer, A. (2012) Gender, work time, and care responsibilities among faculty. *Sociological Forum, 27(2)*, 300–323.

Moi T. (1985). *Sexual/textual politics: Feminist literary theory*. London: Routledge.

Moi T. (2001). *What is a woman and other essays*. Oxford: Oxford University Press.

Mol, A. (2002). *The body multiple: Ontology in medical practice*. Duke University Press Books, Kindle Version.

Molyneaux, D. (2003). Blessed are the meek, for they shall inherit the earth: An aspiration applicable to business? *Journal of Business Ethics, 48*, 347–363.

Mörck, M., & Tullberg, M. (2005). *Bolagsstämman. En homosocial ritual. Kulturella Perspektiv2*.

Morgan, D. H. J. (1994). Theatre of war: Combat, the military and masculinities. In Brod, H., & Kaufman, M. (Eds.), *Theorizing masculinities*. London: Sage.

Morrison, A. (2001). Integrity and global leadership. *Journal of Business Ethics, 31*, 65–76.

Moss Kanter, Rosabeth. 1977. *Men and women of the corporation*. New York: Basic Books.

Munro, I. (2014). Organizational ethics and 'Foucault's 'art of living': Lessons from social movement organizations. *Organization Studies, 35(8)*, 1127–1148.

Munro, I., & Thanem, T. (2018) 'The ethics of affective leadership: Organizing good encounters without leaders. In Ciulla, J., Knights, D. Mabey, C., & Tomkins, L., (Eds.), Special Issue: Philosophical Approaches to Leadership Ethics, *Business Ethics Quarterly, 28(1)*, 51–69.

Murdoch, I. (1953). *Sartre, romantic realist*. London: Collins Fontana.

Neimark, M. (1990). The king is dead, long live the king? *Critical Perspectives in Accounting 1*, 103–114.

Newton, T. (1995). *'Managing' stress: Emotion and power at work*. London: Sage.

Nietzsche, F. (1968 [1888]). *Twilight of the idols*, R. J. Hollingdale (Trans.). Penguin.

Nohria N., & Khurana, R. (Eds.). (2010). *Handbook of leadership theory and practice*. Harvard Business School Publishing Corporation.

Noon, M. (2007). The fatal flaws of diversity and the business case for ethnic minorities. *Work, Employment and Society, 2(4)*, 773–784.

Northouse, P. G. (2004). *Leadership: Theory and practice* (3rd ed.). London: Sage Publications Ltd.

Nygren, K. G., & Oloffson, A. (2020). Managing the Covid-19 pandemic through individual responsibility: The consequences of a world risk society and enhanced ethopolitics. *Journal of Risk Research*, Published on line 23.4.20 https://doi.org/10.1080/13669877.2020.1756382.

Offe, C. (1984) In J. Keane (Ed.), *Contradictions of the welfare state*. London: Routledge.

Ogbonna, E., & Harris, L. C. (2004). Work intensification and emotional labour among UK university lecturers: An exploratory study. *Organization Studies, 25(7)*, 1185–1203.

Omanović, V. (2011). Diversity in organizations: A critical examination of assumptions about diversity and organizations in twenty-first century management literature. In Jeanes, E., Knights, D., & Yancey-Martin, P. (Eds.), *Handbook of gender, work & organization* (pp. 315–332). London: Wiley.

O'Grady, H. (2004). An ethics of the self. In Taylor, D., & Vintges, K. (Eds). *Feminism and the final Foucault* (pp. 91–117). University of Illinois Press.

Özbilgin 2008 Özbilgin, M. F., & Tatli, A. (2008). *Global diversity management: An evidence based approach*, Palgrave Macmillan.

Pacholok, S. (2009). Gendered strategies of self: Navigating hierarchy and contesting masculinities. *Gender, Work and Organization, 16(4)*, 471–500.

Painter-Morland, M. (2008). Systemic leadership and the emergence of ethical responsiveness. *Journal of Business Ethics, 82(2)*, 509–524.

Painter-Morland, M., & ten Bos, R. (Eds.). (2011). *Business ethics and continental philosophy*. Cambridge University Press.

Parker, M. (2014). University, Ltd: Changing a business school. *Organization, 21(2)*, 281–292.

Parker, M. (2018).*Shut down the business school*. Chicago: University of Chicago Press.

Pfeffer, J., & Fong, C. T. (2002). The end of business schools? Less success than meets the eye. *Academy of Management Learning and Education, 1(1)*, 78–95.

Pfeffer, J., & Fong, C. T. (2004). The business school: Some lessons from the U.S. experience. *Journal of Management Studies, 41*, 1501 – 1520.

Phillips, N., & Hardy, C. (2002). *Discourse analysis investigating processes of social construction*. Thousand Oaks: Sage.

Pilgrim, D. (2017). *Key concepts in mental health*. London: Sage.

Pink, S. (2001). More visualising, more methodologies: On video, reflexivity and qualitative research. *The Sociological Review, 49(4)*, 586–599.

Pink, S. (2004) Visual Methods. In Seale, C., Gobo, G., Gubrium, J. F. and Silverman, D. (Eds.), *Qualitative Research Practice* (pp. 391–406). London: Sage.

Plato, (2007 [383BCE]). *The republic*. Harmondsworth: Penguin.

Pullen, A. (2007). Introduction: You, me, us and identify introducing exploring identity. In Pullen Beech, N., & Sims, D. (Eds.), *Exploring identity: Concepts and methods* (pp. 1–25). London: Palgrave Macmillan.

Pullen, A., & Rhodes, C. (2008). 'It's all about me!': Gendered narcissism and leaders' identity work. *Leadership, 4*(1), 5–25.

Pullen, A., & Rhodes, C. (2010). Gender, ethics and the eace. In P. Lewis. & R. Simpson (Eds.), *Concealing and revealing gender* (pp. 233–248). Basingstoke: Palgrave.

Pullen, A., & Rhodes, C. (2014). Corporeal ethics and the politics of resistance in organizations. *Organization, 21*(6), 782–796.

Pullen, A., & Rhodes, C. (2015). Ethics, embodiment and organizations. *Organization, 22*(2), 159–165.

Pullen, A., Rhodes, C., & ten Bos, R. (Guest Editors). (2015). Special issue on ethics, embodiment and organizations. *Organization, 22(2).*

Pullen, A., & Simpson, R. (2009). Managing difference in feminized work: Men, otherness and social practice. *Human Relations, 62*(4), 561–587.

Pullen A., & Vachhani, S. (2013). The materiality of leadership. *Leadership, 9*(3), 315–319.

Raelin J. A. (2007). *Toward an epistemology of practice. Academy of Management Learning & Education.* 6(4) 495–519.

Raelin, J. A. (2010). *The leaderful fieldbook: Strategies and activities for developing leadership in everyone.* Boston: Nicholas Brealey.

Raelin J. A. (2011). From leadership-as-practice to leaderful practice. *Leadership, 7*(2) 195–211.

Raelin J. A. (2014). The ethical essence of leaderful practice. *Journal of Leadership, Accountability and Ethics, 11*(1), 64–72.

Raelin J. A. (Ed.). (2016). *Leadership as practice: Theory and application.* New York: Routledge.

Rhodes, C. (2012). Ethics, alterity and the rationality of leadership justice. *Human Relations, 65*, 1311–1331.

Rhodes, C. (2020). *Disturbing business ethics: Emmanuelle Levinas and the politics of organization.* New York and London: Routledge.

Rhodes C., & Badham, R. (2018). Ethical irony and the relational leader: Grappling with the infinity of ethics and the finitude of practice. *Business Ethics Quarterly, 28*(1), 71–98.

Rhodes, C., & Wray-Bliss, E. (2013). The ethical difference of organization. *Organization, 20*(1), 39–50.

Roberson, Q. M., & Park, H. J. (2007). Examining the link between diversity and firm performance: The effects of diversity reputation and leader racial diversity. *Group & Organization Management, 32*(5), 548–568.

Robinson, G., & Dechant, K. (1997). Building the business case. *Academy of Management Executive, 11*(3), 21–31.

Roethlisberger F. J., & Dickson, W. J. (1939). *Management and the worker,* Cambridge, MA: Harvard University Press.

Roper, M. (1996). Seduction and succession: Circuits of homosocial desire in management. In D. L. Collinson, & J. Hearn (Eds). *Men as managers. Managers as men* (pp. 210–227). London: Sage.

Ropo, A., Sauer, E., & Salovaara, P. (2019) Spacing leadership as an embodied and performative process. *Leadership, 15*(4), 461–479.

Rose, N., & Miller, P. (1992). Political power beyond the state: Problematics of government. *British Journal of Sociology, 43*(2), 173–205.

Rosenwald, M. S. (2020). History's deadliest pandemics, from ancient Rome to modern America Washington Post. https://www.washingtonpost.com/gdpr-consent/?next_url=https%3a%2f%2fError! Hyperlink reference not valid.f Consulted 20.5.20.

Roth, K. (2017). The dangerous rise of populism. https://www.hrw.org/world-report/2017/country-chapters/dangerous-rise-of-populism.

Roy, D. (1952). Quota restriction and gold-bricking in a machine shop. *American Journal of Sociology, 57*, 427–442.

Russell, A. (2019). *Philosophy collection*, Amazon Kindle Edition.

Rutherford, J. (1992). *Men's silences*. London: Routledge.

Sabo, D. (1995). Pigskin, Patriarchy and Pain In M. S. Kimmel, & M. A. Messner (Eds.), *Men's lives* (3rd ed.). London: Allyn and Bacon.

Santoro, M. A., & Strauss R. J. (2013). *Wall street values: Business ethics and the global financial crisis*. New York: Cambridge University Press.

Sartre, J. P. (1938/1949). *Nausea*. Harmondsworth, UK: Penguin.

Sartre, J.-P. (1943/1996). *Being and nothingness*. Barnes, H. (Trans.). London: Routledge.

Sartre, J. P. (1949). *The reprieve*. Harmondsworth, UK: Penguin.

Sartre, J. P. (1949). *Iron in the soul*. Harmondsworth, UK: Penguin.

Sartre, J. P. (1991). *Critique of dialectical reason vol. 2*, unfinished. The intelligibility of history. A. Elkaim-Sartre (Eds.). Q. Hoare (Trans.). London: Verso 1991.

Savigny, H. (2014). Women, know your limits: Cultural sexism in academia. *Gender and Education, 26*(7), 794–809.

Sawday, J. (1995). *The body emblazoned: Dissection and the human body in renaissance culture*. London and New York: Routledge.

Scialabba, G. (2009). *What are intellectuals good for?* Canada: Pressed Wafer.

Schechner, R. (2002). *Performance studies*. London: Routledge.

Schedlitzki, D., & Edwards, G. (2014). *Studying leadership: Traditional and critical approaches*. London: Sage.

Schwarz, B. (1987). *The battle for human nature*. New York: W. W Norton & Co.

Sen, A. (2009). *Capitalism beyond the crisis*. The New York Review of Books, 56(5) March 26th.

Sennett, R., & J. Cobb. (1977). *The hidden injuries of class*. New York: Vintage Books.

Seymour-Jones, C. (2008). *A dangerous liaison: Simone de Beauvoir and Jean-Paul Sartre*, London: Century.

Seidler, V. J. (1989) *Rediscovering masculinity*. London: Routledge.

Sennett, R., & Cobb, J. (1977). *The hidden injuries of class*. New York: Vintage Books.

Shilling, C. (1993). *The body in sociology*. London, Newbury Park, California: Sage Publications, Ltd.

Shirazi, F. (2009). *Velvet jihad: Muslim women's quiet resistance to islamic fundamentalism*. Gainesville: University Press of Florida.

Silva, A. (2016). What is leadership? *Journal of Business Studies Quarterly, 8*(1), 1–5.

Sims, R., & J. Brinkmann (2002). Leaders as role models: The case of John Gutfreund at Solomon Brothers. *Journal of Business Ethics, 35*, 327–339.

Sinclair, A. (2005 [1998]). *Doing leadership differently: Gender, power and sexuality in changing business culture*, Carlton South, VIC: University of Melbourne Press.

Sinclair, A. (2007). *Leadership for the disillusioned*, Crows Nest, Australia: Allen & Unwin.

Sinclair, A. (2009). Seducing leadership: Stories of leadership development. *Gender, Work and Organization 16(2)*, 266–284.

Sinclair, A. (2011). Being leaders: Identities and identity work in leadership. In A. Bryman, D. Collinson, K. Grint, B. Jackson, & M. Uhl-Bien (Eds.), *The Sage Handbook of Leadership*. London: Sage.

Skillicorn, N. (2016). What is innovation? https://www.ideatovalue.com/inno/nickskillicorn/2016/03/innovation-15-experts-share-innovation-definition/ March 18th, 2016, Consulted 12.9.19.

Skinner, B. F. (1953). *Science and human behavior*. New York: Simon and Schuster.

Skinner, B. F. (1971). *Beyond freedom and dignity*. New York: Random House.

Smith, A. (1793/1976). In R. H. Campbell, & A. S. Skinner (Eds.), *An inquiry into the nature and causes of the wealth of nations*. London: Clarendon Press.

Smith, P., & Peters, J. (1997). The corporate leadership crisis: break out this way. *The Learning Organization, 4(2)*, 61–69.

Snow, D. A., & Anderson, L. (1987). Identity work among the homeless: The verbal construction and avowal of personal identities. *American Journal of Sociology, 92(6)* 1336–1371.

Sotirin, P. (2011). Becoming-woman. In C. Stivale (Ed.), *Gilles Deleuze: Key concepts* (pp. 116–130). Durham, UK: Acumen Publishing.

Sparkes, A. (2007). Embodiment, academics, and the audit culture: A story seeking consideration. *Qualitative Research, 7*, 521—550.

Sparkes, A. (2013). *Qualitative research methods in sport, exercise and health: From process to product*. London and New York: Routledge.

Sparrow, T. (2013). *Levinas unhinged*. Zero Books, Kindle Edition.

Spinoza, B. (1677/1883). *The ethics*, R. H. M. Elwes (Trans.). A Public Domain Book, Kindle.

Standish, P. (2001). .Ethics before equality: Moral education after Levinas. *Journal of Moral Education, 30(4)*, 339–347.

Stanford Encyclopedia of Philosophy, https://plato.stanford.edu/entries/ancient-political/#CicRomRep, consulted 24.5.20.

Starkey, K., & Tiratsoo, N. (2007). *The business school and the bottom line*. Cambridge: Cambridge University Press.

Starr, Bradley E. (1999).The structure of max weber's ethic of responsibility. *The Journal of Religious Ethics, 27(3)*, 407–434.

Stavro-Pearce, E., Barrett M. & Cunningham F. (1994). Towards a post-humanist feminism. *Economy and Society, 23(2)*, 217–246.

Stead, V. (2013). Learning to deploy (in)visibility: An examination of women leaders' lived experiences. *Management Learning, 44(1)*: 63–79.

Stephens, L. (1882). *The science of ethics*. New York: G.P. 'Putnam's and Son's.

Sternberg, E. (2013). Ethical misconduct and the global financial crisis. *Economic Affairs, 33(1)*, 18–33.

Stogdill, R. (1974). *Handbook of leadership: A survey of theory and research.* New York: The Free Press.

Storey, J., Hartley, J., Jean-Louis Denis, J.-L., Paul 'T Hart, P., & Ulrich, D. (Eds.) (2017). *The Routledge Companion to Leadership.* London: Routledge.

Storr, W. (2018). *Selfie: How the west became self-obsessed.* London: Picador.

Styhre, A., & Eriksson-Zetterquist, U. (2008). Thinking the multiple in gender and diversity studies: Examining the concept of intersectionality. *Gender in Management: An International Journal, 23(8),* 567–582.

Sverke, M., Hellgren, J., & Näswall, K. (2006). *Job insecurity: A literature review,* Stockholm: National Institute for Working Life and authors.

Takala, T. (1998). Plato on Leadership. *Journal of Business Ethics, 17,* 785–798.

Tanner, J., Davies, S., & O'Grady, B., (1992). Immanence changes everything: A Ccitical comment on the labour process and class consciousness. *Sociology, 26(3),* 439–454.

Taylor, F. W. (1911). *Principles of scientific management.* New York: Harper Bros.

Taylor, L., & Walton, P. (1971). Industrial sabotage. In L. Taylor, & P. Walton, (Eds.), *Images of Deviance,* Harmondsworth: Penguin.

Tett, G. (2009). *Fool's gold: How unrestrained greed corrupted a dream, shattered global markets and unleashed a catastrophe.* London: Abacus.

Thanem, T. (2011). *The monstrous organization.* Cheltenham, UK: Edward Elgar.

Thanem, T., & Knights, D. (2012). Feeling and speaking through our gendered bodies: Embodied self-reflection and research practice in organization studies. *International Journal of Work Organizations and Emotion. 5(1),* 91–108.

Thanem, T. (2013). More passion than the job requires? Monstrously transgressive leadership in the promotion of health at work. *Leadership, 9(3),* 396–415.

Thanem, T., & Knights, D. (2019). *Embodied research methods.* London: Sage.

Thanem, T., & Wallenberg, L. (2015). What can bodies do? Reading Spinoza for an affective ethics of organizational life. *Organization, 22(2),* 235–250.

Thiran, R. (2019), Leadership lessons from the roman empire, May 29th, https://leaderonomics.com/leadership/leadership-lessons-from-the-roman-empire.

Thomas, R., & Davies, A. (2002). Gender and new public management: Reconstituting academic subjectivities. *Gender, Work and Organization, 9(4),* 372–396.

Thomas, R., & Davies, A. (2005). What have the feminists done for us? Feminist theory and organizational resistance. *Organization, 12(5),* 711–740.

Thomas, R., & Davies, A. (2005a). Theorising the micro-politics of resistance: Discourses of change and professional identities in the UK public services. *Organization Studies, 25(5),* 683–706.

Thomas, R., & Linstead, A. (2002). Losing the plot? Middle managers and identity. *Organization, 9(1),* 71–93.

Thompson, P. (1990). 'Crawling from the wreckage': The labour process and the politics of production. In D. Knights and H. Willmott (Eds.), *Labour Process Theory.* London: Macmillan.

Thompson, P. (1991). *The fatal distraction: Postmodernism and organizational analysis.* paper delivered at the Conference on New Theories of Organisation, Keele University, 3–5 April.

Thucydides, (2000 [411BCE]). *The history of the Peloponenesian war.* Harmondsworth: Penguin.

Tiratsoo, N. (2004a). Mintzberg, shareholder value, and the business schools: Who has a case to answer? *Unpublished paper*, University of Nottingham Business School.

Tiratsoo, N. (2004b). Doing the MBA: Motivations, opinions, and evaluations. *Unpublished paper*, University of Nottingham Business School.

Tolson, A. (1977). *The limits of masculinity.* London: Tavistock.

Tomkins, L., & Simpson, P. (2015). Caring leadership: A Heideggerian perspective. *Organization Studies, 36*(8), 1013–1031.

Tosh, J. (1999). The old adam and the new man: Emerging themes in the history of English masculinities 1750-1850. In Tim, Hitchcock, & Michelle, Cohen (Eds.), *English Masculinities 1660-1800* (pp. 217–238). London and New York: Longman.

Tourish, D. (2013). *The dark side of transformational leadership: A critical perspective.* London and New York: Routledge.

Trethewey, A. (1999). Disciplined bodies: Women's embodied identities at work. *Organization Studies, 20*(3), 423–450.

Treviño, L. K., Klebe, L., Brown, M., & Hartman, L. P. (2003). A qualitative investigation of perceived executive ethical leadership: Perceptions from inside and outside the executive suite. *Human Relations, 56*(1), 5–37.

Trungpa, C. (1973). *Cutting through spiritual materialism.* New York: Shambala Publications.

Turner, B. S. (1992). *Regulating bodies: Essays in medical sociology.* London: Routledge.

Turner, M. E., & Pratkanis, A. R. (1998). Twenty-five years of groupthink theory and research: Lessons from the evaluation of a theory. *Organizational Behavior and Human Decision Processes, 73*(2/3), 105–115.

Uhl-Bien, M. (2006). Relational leadership theory: Exploring the social processes of leadership and organizing. *The Leadership Quarterly 17*, 654–676.

Van den Brink, M., & Benschop, Y. (2012). Slaying the seven-headed dragon: The quest for gender change in academia. *Gender, Work and Organization, 19*(1), 71–92.

Van den Brink, M. & Benschop Y. (2014). Practicing gender in academic networking: The role of gatekeepers in professorial recruitment. *Journal of Management Studies, 51*(3), 460–492.

Wacjman, J. (1991). *Feminism confronts technology.* Oxford: Polity Press.

Waghid, Y., & Davids, N. (2017). Muslim education and ethics: On autonomy, community, and (dis)agreement. In M. Peters (Eds.), *Encyclopedia of educational philosophy and theory.* Singapore: Springer.

Walsh, F. (2010). *Male trouble: Masculinity and the performance of crisis.* New York: Palgrave Macmillan.

Watson, T. J. (1994). *In search of management.* Boston: International Thomson Business Press.

Watson, W. E., Kumar, K., & Michaelsen, L. K. (1993). Cultural diversity's impact on interaction process and performance: comparing homogeneous and diverse task groups. *Academy of Management Journal 36*(3) 590–602.

Watson, T. J. (1995). Shaping the story: Rhetoric, persuasion and creative writing in organisational ethnography. *Studies in Cultures, Organizations and Societies, 1*(2), 301–311.

Watts, A. (1951). *The wisdom of insecurity.* Pantheon Books.

Watts, A. (1973). *Psychotherapy east and west.* Harmondsworth: Penguin.

Watts, A. (1989). *On the taboo of knowing who you are.* USA: Vintage Books Edition.

Weber, M. (1949). *The methodology of the social sciences.* Glencoe, IL: Free Press.

Weber, M. (1968/1925). *Economy and society, 3 vols.* New York: Bedminster.

Weber, M. (1930/2001). *The protestant ethic and the spirit of capitalism.* New York: Taylor.

West, C., & Zimmerman, D. H. (1987). Doing gender. *Gender & Society. 1*(2).

Westerbeck H., & Smith A. (2005). *Business and leadership and the lessons from sport.* London: Palgrave Macmillan.

Wetherell, M. (2015). Trends in the turn to affect A social psychological critique. *Body & Society, 21*(2), 139–166.

Whetstone, J. (2001). How virtue ethics fits within business ethics. *Journal of Business Ethics, 33*, 101–114.

Willer, D. E. (1967). *Scientific sociology theory and method.* NJ: Prentice-Hall.

Williams, R. R. (2000). *Hegel's ethics of recognition.* LA: University of California Press.

Williams, S. J., & Bendelow, G. A. (1999). *The lived body: Sociological themes, embodied issues.* London: Routledge.

Willmott, H., & D. Knights (1982). The problem of freedom: Fromm's contribution to a critical theory of work organisation. *Praxis International, 2*(2), 204–225.

Willmott, H., & Mingers, J. (2012). Taylorizing business school research: On the "One Best Way" performative effects of journal ranking lists. *Human Relations, 66*(8), 1051–1073.

Wilson, N. G. (2006). *Encyclopedia of ancient Greece* (p. 511). New York: Routledge.

Wilson, S. E. (2013). *Thinking differently about leadership: A critical history of leadership studies,* PhD, Victoria University of Wellington.

Wilson, S. E. (2016). *Thinking differently about leadership: A critical history of leadership studies.* Cheltenham: Edward Elgar.

Wilson, S. E., Cummings, S., Jackson, B., & Proctor-Thomson, S. (2018). *Revitalising leadership: Putting theory and practice into context.* London and New York: Routledge.

Winter, R. (2009). Academic manager or managed academic? Academic identity schisms in higher education. *Journal of Higher Education Policy and Management. 31*(2), 1–13.

Witz, A., Warhurst, C., & Nickson, D. (2003). The labour of aesthetics and the aesthetics of organization. *Organization, 10*(1), 33–54.

Wood,M. (2005). 'The fallacy of misplaced leadership. *Journal of Management Studies, 42*(6): 1101–1121.

Wood, M. (2008). Process philosophy. In R. Thorpe, & R..Holt (Eds.), *Dictionary of qualitative management research* (pp. 171–173). London: Sage.

Wood M., & Ladkin, D. (2008). The event's the thing: Brief encounters with the leaderful moment. In K. Turnbull James, & J. Collins (Eds.), *Leadership perspectives: Knowledge into action.* Houndmills: Palgrave Macmillan.

Wolfe, C. (2010). *What is posthumanism?* Minneapolis: UMP.

Worthington, F., & Hodgson, J. (2005). Academic labour and the politics of quality in higher education: A critical evaluation of the conditions of possibility of resistance. *Critical Quarterly, 47*(1/2), 96–110.

Wray-Bliss, E. (2002). Abstract ethics, embodied ethics: The strange marriage of Foucault and positivism in labour process theory. *Organization, 9*(1), 5–39.

Wray-Bliss, E. (2003). Research subjects/research subjections: Exploring the ethics and politics of critical research. *Organization, 10*(2), 307–325.

Wray-Bliss, E. (2013). A crisis of leadership: Towards an anti-sovereign ethics of organisation, business. *Ethics: A European Review, 22*(1), 86–101.

Wray-Bliss, E. (2019). *Neoliberalism, management and religion: Re-examining the spirits of capitalism.* London and New York: Routledge.

Ybema, S., & Kamsteeg, F. (2009). Making the familiar strange: A case for disengaged organizational ethnography. In S. Ybema, D. Yanow, H. Wels, & F. Kamsteeg (Eds.), *Organizational ethnography* (pp. 101–119). London: Sage.

Ybema, S., Keenoy, T., Oswick, C., Beverungen, A., Ellis, N., & Sabelis, I. (2009). Articulating identities, *Human Relations, 62,* 299.

Young, I. M. (2005). *On female body experience: Throwing like a girl and other essays.* Oxford: Oxford University Press.

Young, M. (1994 [1958]). The rise of the meritocracy. *Penguin. Qualitative Research in Education, 1*(2).

Yukl, G. A. (1989/2006). *Leadership in organizations.* New Jersey: Prentice-Hall.

Zaccaro, S., Kemp, C., & Bader, P. (2004). Leader traits and attributes. In J. Antonakis, A. Cianciolo, & R. Sternberg (Eds.), *The Nature of Leadership.* Thousand Oaks, CA: Sage Publications.

Zaleznik, A. (1989). Managers and leaders: Are they different? In A. Levinson, (Ed.), *Designing and managing your career* (pp. 64–77). Harvard Business Review Publishing.

Ziarek, E. P. (2001). *An ethics of dissensus: Postmodernity, feminism and the politics of radical democracy.* Stanford University Press.

Zinn, H. (1980). *A people's history of the United States.* New York: Harper Collins.

Zizek, S. (1989) *Sublime object of ideology.* London: Verso.

Index

Printed in the United States
by Baker & Taylor Publisher Services

Printed in the United States
by Baker & Taylor Publisher Services